The Annotated Ramona

by Antoinette May

WIDE WORLD PUBLSIHING/TETRA

Acknowledgements

This book owes its existence most directly to a special friend and mentor, Charles Beardsley, who provided the spark; and to Clara Trusel who first introduced me to the Ramona legend.

Another debt is to Mr. & Mrs. William S. Jackson Jr. whose trust and generosity made this project possible.

Helen Hunt Jackson's writings — her books, articles and, most importantly, her letters — comprise the primary source for the annotation for this book. But the work could not have been done without the assistance of Bruce LaLanne, Mary Ward, Peggy McQuown and the Ramona Pageant Association, Inc., the San Diego Historical Society, The Huntington Library, the California State Library and Barbara Neilon and her staff at the Colorado College Library, Special Collections.

cover — San Juan Capistrano Mission by Henry Sandham. Circa 1913.
title page—San Juan Bautista Mission by Henry Sandham. Circa 1913.

Wide World Publishing/Tetra
P.O. Box 476
San Carlos, CA 94070

1st printing 1989
Printed in the United States of America.

ISBN 0-933174-52-7

Library of Congress Cataloging-in-Publication Data

May, Antoinette
The Annotated Ramona.

Includes the text of Helen Hunt Jackson's Ramona.
1. Jackson, Helen Hunt, 1830-1885. Ramona.
I. Jackson, Helen Hunt, 1830-1885. Ramona. II. Title.
PS2107 .R42M3 1989 813' .4 88-27696
ISBN 0-933174-52-7

Table of Contents

Helen of California

Those closest to Helen Hunt Jackson could agree on one thing and one thing only: she was the "most brilliant, impetuous and thoroughly independent woman of her time."

Passionate, daring, defiant, an individualist who lived by her own rules, moving as freely in an age of stagecoaches and steamships as jet setters do today, Helen lived a life that few women of her day had the courage to live. In any era she would qualify as an original.

Though descended from a long and distinguished line of missionaries and clergyman, she must have missed her father's sermon on turning the other cheek. Helen was a fighter as well as a lover, at odds almost from birth with the rigid Calvinism of her father.

Her parents, Nathan and Deborah Fiske, were New Englanders who took their Puritan heritage to heart. When their firstborn died in infancy, they bore up bravely. "The Lord hath given and the Lord hath taken away," Nathan, a Congregational clergyman and professor of philosophy and language at Amherst College, intoned. "We feel it to be the fatherly chastisement we need," Deborah dutifuly agreed.

—Courtesy of Special Collections, the Colorado College Library, Colorado Springs SUN.

The Fiskes had hoped for another son, but it was Helen Maria who was born a few minutes before midnight on October 14, 1830. Unlike the two children who followed—Herman Humphrey, who died in infancy, and Ann —she was a problem. "I cannot play so well with Helen as with Ann," their mother admitted. "Helen is so wild—jumping rope, dressing up in odd things, jumping out behind doors. Ann does not require the vigilance that Helen does. She is honest, artless, affectionate—telling the whole of everything *right out*, and everybody how well she loves them, whereas Miss Helen has no idea of 'liking all those folks.' They are as unlike, Papa, often says, as if they belonged to two separate nations." Impulsive, selective, private—Helen as she was then and as she would remain.

It couldn't have been easy for Nathan with his stern, Calvinist ways to understand Helen's high spirits, and his attitudes were an even greater enigma to her. "I inherited nothing from either of my parents except my mother's gift for cheer," Helen admitted. She was a strange fledgling for such a nest. A born radical, eager for experience, unwilling to accept anything that she herself had not tested, Helen was as disturbing and provocative as a tropical bird among wrens.

Fortunately there was a special friend to whom she could tell her troubles. Just down the street lived Emily Dickinson, only two months younger than Helen and destined to be a lifelong friend. Tiny, frail Emily with her soft voice and shy, diffident manner, was outwardly as different from the chubby, bubbly Helen as two girls could be; but beneath the surface, she was much like her: bright, impish, fanciful.

Helen needed a happy respite from the sadness that was beginning to pervade the Fiske household. Deborah was seriously ill. Each day she slipped a little further into the shadows. Helen tried desperately to please. She adored her mother, but chafed at any restraint. Lessons were particularly arduous. While Ann learned slowly, puzzling over each word, Helen leaped ahead, sometimes skipping words she didn't know or replacing them with substitutes that *seemed* right. "Deborah often despaired of teaching her. "Helen learns very well," she wrote, "but I do not drive her very much to make her literary—she is quite inclined to question the authority of everything; the Bible she says does not feel as if it were true...."

Poor mother, perhaps realizing that her own soul wasn't long for this world, worried all the more for Helen's. When Deborah grew too weak to see to her daughter's education, the recalcitrant nine-year-old joined her friend Emily at Amherst Academy, a public school, even though both parents feared it wasn't strict enough for her.

Helen was only a few months past her twelfth birthday when Deborah died of tuberculosis. Ann was sent to live with relatives, Helen to a series of seminaries. From that time they would see one another only on holidays and later on occasional visits as married women.

Nathan, also suffering from tuberculosis, had but one wish—to visit the Holy Land. After collecting all of Deborah's letters and other mementoes and entrusting them to Helen and Ann, he resigned his position at Amherst College and set off. A few months later he was buried on Mount Zion.

Helen as a baby — Courtesy of Special Collections, the Colorado College Library.

Moving from school to school, her vacations divided among a variety of relatives, Helen was already a bird of passage. The wanderings that would characterize her entire life had begun.

Though popular and very much a party girl, she was also highly intellectual. Helen was pleased and flattered when, upon graduation from the Abbott Institute—a select New York boarding school—she was invited to join the staff as a teacher. "New York is my Arcadia," she confided to a friend. "Teaching I enjoy most highly—so much that I can truly say, I was never so happy in my life as at this time."

It appeared that Helen had found her niche. She was impatient with the summer delay, eager to assume her new duties. Then a chance invitation sumoned her to visit family friends in Albany. It wasn't where Helen wanted to be, but at least it was some place where she hadn't been. As always, her spirits brightened at the prospect of an adventure. Albany was the state capital and just might be interesting.

At twenty Helen Fiske was more than beautiful. An elegant ash blond, her voluptuous figure was set off to perfection by the fashions of the day—bodices that looked as though they'd been pasted on and skirts that flared just enough to emphasize a tiny waistline without being too full for graceful movement. The appreciation of elegance that had surfaced early despite her parents bleak conservatism had matured into an original sense of style that would always distinguish her.

A natural flirt, she created a stir in Albany. Then one evening Helen attended a grand ball hosted by the state governor and met his brother. Lieutenant Edward Bissel Hunt was in town to deliver a paper at the American Association for the Advancement of Science. Bright—he'd graduated second in his West Point class— and ambitious, Hunt had progressed to his present high ranking position in the Treasury Department by determining exactly what he wanted, then proceeding unwaveringly in that direction. During the intermission he moved without hesitation to a place beside Helen. From then on they danced every dance together.

Fall came and went and with it the teaching position at the Abbott Institute. Helen remained in Albany. Edward was transferred to Washington and within a few months she followed him as his wife. They were a dashing couple. He tall, ruggedly handsome, she brilliant, vivacious and volatile; an upwardly mobile couple in a city of politics and fashion.

Helen at age 20. — Courtesy of Special Collections, the Colorado College Library.

Helen Fiske
—Courtesy of the Pioneers' Museum, Colorado Springs, Colorado

A son was born to them but died only a few months later. A year later there was a second boy. Helen's pregnancy was marred by inexplicable doubts, of which she wrote a friend: "I could talk with you a long time about the strange mixture of longing and fear with which I *wait*:—how I almost dread to find again my whole soul bound up with in one frail little life!—You know me well enough to know that I can't love after any *half way* fashion—but you can probably a little idea of the painful intensity of how my love for a child — in spite of the exquisite delight, *saddens* every moment of my consciousness." But holding, Rennie, as she called her child, she forgot for a time the fears that plagued her.

"They were intimate friends when he was little more than a baby," a companion would later recall, describing the closeness between mother and child as "the best and happiest" she had ever seen.

Helen's friend continued, "She was gay, pleasure-loving, impulsive to the point of rashness of speech and action, never able to comprehend that a word or act of hers could cause unkind comment or misconstruction but she was so fresh, so warmhearted, so entertaining, that no one who knew her well could help loving her."

Then the Civil War began. There were many separations and finally happy news. Edward was being sent back north to develop his latest invention, a submarine gun. If successful, his creation—a prototype of the modern torpedo—would revolutionalize modern warfare.

He didn't live to see it. Edward died during a test run just a few days short of their eleventh wedding anniversary. And then a further blow: eighteen months later, nine-year-old Rennie contracted diphtheria. Within a few days, he too, was buried at West Point beside his father and brother.

For months after Rennie's death, Helen shut herself away from friends and family; and when she appeared among them at last, she was smiling vivacious, outwardly unchanged.

* * *

At thirty-five Helen Fiske Hunt was at the height of her physical appeal. The heavy mourning she'd adopted merely added an air of piquancy to her voluptuous figure and vivid coloring.

She was starting over, beginning a new life, and had chosen her strategy carefully. She would write. Not merely letters: all women in her circle were adept at that, cultivating early the skill of penning stylish little notes just as they'd learned to paint china or play the piano—not well necessarily, but pleasingly. In the months following Rennie's death she began to write poetry.

Out of the depths of her grief had come "The Key to the Casket," written just six weeks after her loss. On an impulse she signed the poem Marah—a play on "Ma of Rennie Hunt"—and sent it off to the *New York Evening Post.*

Its appearance on June 9, 1865, was a beginning. There were other Marah poems, the best known, "Lifted Over," bringing encouragement and recognition as other bereaved mothers responded with warm notes. She liked the thought that words of hers had brought comfort to others. Then as variations of her work began to appear, Helen realized that she was actually being imitated.

Rennie Hunt —Courtesy of the Pioneers' Museum, Colorado Springs, Colorado

The flattery raised her spirits immeasurably. She was inspired to travel once again, and her New England rambles were recorded in a prose piece that was also published. It was her first actual sale and the first money she'd ever earned. Helen decided to forsake the pseudonym Marah — its connotatons were too sorrowful. Well aware that readers were frequently hostile to women writers, calling them "ink-stained women" and refusing to take them seriously, she chose the initials H.H.

She was very serious about her writing and ready to do something about it. The place from which to launch herself was indisputably Newport, Rhode Island, a select seaport city where writing had become a lifestyle. Reputed to have more authors than any other city in the country, its king was Thomas Wentworth Higginson.

For years Helen had admired his articles in *Atlantic Monthly;* then one in particular, "A Letter to a Young Contributor," caught her eye. It discussed everything from the art of writing to methods of getting an editor's attention. An essayist, a reformer, a friend of everyone who was anyone—surely Higginson was the very one to advise her.

Hannah Dame's boardinghouse was *the* place to stay in Newport. Colonel Higginson himself presided in the dining room, carving for as many as forty people on special occasions. He was a handsome, vigorous man, quick yet tactful, a mocking gentleness about the eyes and mouth. Helen detected a look of hidden sadness as well, a sense of quiet resignation that touched her. Soon she learned the cause. Higginson's wife, Mary, found her passion in dependency. Mary's affection was for her illness, a mysterious affliction that kept her confined to a wheelcair.

Small wonder the quality that first impressed Higginson about Helen was her cheerfulness. Whatever private devils may have plagued her, she appeared high spirited and vital in the presence of others. Invited to small gatherings in the two rooms assigned her, he found them transformed by Japanese prints, cherished family silver, flowers and oriental hangings. Like Helen herself, the place was warm and inviting, an oasis promising excitement as well as peace.

Newport, the self-styled literary capital of America, considered itself avant-garde, but even there Helen was thought "modern," a sophisticated woman of the the world whose presence livened any gathering. Higginson saw to it that she met everybody worth knowing, including Ralph Waldo Emerson and Julia Ward Howe, whose "Battle Hynn of the Republic" had made her a Newport star; but he managed time alone with her as well. There were evenings at the theater—once he took her all the way to Boston to hear Charles Dickens read from his own works—and days of horseback riding and sailing.

Within a month Helen had shown him a few of her verses and asked for advice. She saw in Higginson's style a model for her own. Using his work as a guide, she set out to take his pieces apart word by word, sentence by sentence, experimenting to see if she could take out a word or transpose a clause without destroying their perfection.

He was surprised by the rapidity with which she wrote, covering large sheets of paper with a pencil—pen and ink were too slow for her. But for all her quickness, she was a patient and ruthless editor of her own work and a good critic of others.

"H.H." — Courtesy of Special Collections, the Colorado Colege Library.

Before long the hard bargains that H.H. drove were a legend among editors. "Cash is a vile article," she admitted to one. Then added, "But there is one thing viler; and that is a purse without any cash in it." More than once she stated her sentiments succinctly: "I don't write for money, I write for love—I *print* for money." She was also quick to plant her sentiments in the mouths of her fictional heroines. ("If selling is an honorable business for men, it ought to be for women and girls," one protagonist argued.")

The pattern of Helen's relationship with Higginson was established early. That it was a passionate friendship kept from complete fulfillment only by his sense of obligation to Mary seems obvious. In May of 1866, only three months after Helen's move to Newport, *Nation* published another of her poems. Though the title was "The Burial Service," the subject was not death but renucniation. It began:

To this burying
We come alone—you and I—not with our dead,
But with our dearest living; O, could mortal tread
Be unfaltering!

There was no signature, not even H. H., after the conclusion:

In Christ's protection
Now let us leave it—the tomb and the key! He
Will remember us if there may ever be
Resurrection!

Not long afterward Helen made a sentimental visit to Brattleboro, Vermont, the village where Higginson's siblings lived, and in the fall returned to the boarding house. The two were much together, but by the following summer Helen was off again. It was a pattern that continued for five years, broken only in November 1868 when she left rather suddenly for Europe and remained away until February of 1870.

During this period Helen published the first of a number of popular novels written under the pseudonym Saxe Holm and never publicly acknowledged. Most share a recurrent theme—unhappy marriages with true love stifled by obligation. The heroine, often a writer, sometimes removes herself from temptation by going to Europe.

Higginson seems to have understood her very well—an incredibly resilient woman, still something of a flirt who sometimes got more than she bargained for. Twenty years later he would write with rueful tenderness, "She had great virtues, marked inconsistencies, and plenty of fascinating faults that came near to virtues."

If he could be nothing more, he was secure in his position as her closest confidant, Helen trusted him implicitly, pledging him to burn all her letters in the event of her death. It was a wise course, he wrote later, "not without reason, for she lived in the moment and was a most hazardous correspondent."

Under Thomas Higginson's tutelage, Helen had become a prolific writer turning out streams of poems, articles and finally novels. She wrote with elegance and emotion, her independence giving zest to her opinions. Helen's heroines were much like she was, strong individualists often in conflict with the conventions of the time.

Her life had taken on many of the qualities of a novel. If Helen didn't care for a plot or a character, if a situation became too confining, she could aways change it. And that's exactly what she did.

First there was a summer's jaunt to Northern California that enthralled her, then a trip back to Amherst where she became seriously ill with a respiratory ailment. She would not have survived, Helen later insisted, without the aid of Dr. Hamilton J. Cate, who "saved" her life.

Perhaps Cate saved her life, perhaps not; he most certainly changed its course by emphatically urging her to try the Colorado climate. Friends were shocked. Colorado was considered a wild, barbarous place with its Indian massacres and train robberies. Helen debated, well aware that she was forty-two—older now by four years than her mother had been when she died. She feared that her own persistent ailments presaged the beginning of a similar illness. The salubrious effects of the Colorado climate on respiratory ailments was currently being touted. Once again her spirits rose at the prospect of some place new.

William Jackson —Courtesy ofthe Pioneers' Museum, Colorado Springs, Colorado

Within a week Helen checked into the Colorado Springs Hotel which was actually a large boarding house. Seated among six "agreeable talkers," she was happily reminded of her Newport companions—with one notable difference. Here the most attractive male guest was unmarried.

The seventh tablemate, William Sharpless Jackson, wasn't an agreeable talker at all. He was of the strong silent variety, benignly oblivious to all the chatter going on around him. During conversational lulls, Helen studied Jackson—a big man with deep-set blue eyes and a touch of gray in his heavy beard and whiskers. She was curious about him, wondering what his story might be.

The quiet man was equally drawn to the worldly stranger, with her dramatic sense of style and warm, vivacious manner. Very soon after their initial meeting, he invited her to ride with him into the countryside.

It was an experience that Helen would remember always. Some of it she recorded later in the article, "A Winter Morning at Colorado Springs." Though it was December 14, 1873, she wrote of a season "that woos and warms" like June. Wrapped in furs, she leaned back in William's open carriage and admired his magnificent white horses prancing "like frolicsome kittens." They rode through the Ute Pass, admiring the beauty of the creek that flowed alongside. There was an otherworldly quality about it all. "Ice bridges, ice arches," she later wrote, "ice veils over little falls," and in the center reaching almost to the rushing stream, hung "one pendant globule, pear-shaped, flashing like a diamond."

William reined in and they dismounted. Taking his hand, Helen stepped to the edge of a sharp rock where they could sit in the warm, noonday sun. Looking down "into the huge crystal bowl—solid white snow at the bottom and frost-work on the sides," she listened as Jackson told her the story of his life. He was a little more than five years younger than she, born to a Pennsylvania Quaker family on January 16, 1836. Apprenticed as a boy to an agricultural machinist, there'd been no opportunity to acquire a formal education; but Jackson had a quick mind and knew what he wanted. Once his period of indenture had been completed, he'd gone to work for a railway car building company, finally working his way up to treasurer of the Superior and Mississippi Railroad. Then three years ago he'd shocked everyone by giving it all up to come west.

Helen nooded sympathetically. She understood his wanderlust well and wasn't surprised to learn that the move had worked out well for him. The modest, mild mannered man beside her was not only vice president of the Denver and Rio Grande Railroad, but founder and president of a bank in Colorado Springs as well. Later she wrote that they had galloped home "seven miles to the hour." The sun was bright, the snow dazzling. It was a day she would never forget.

There were many outings. By April Helen had sent east for her trunks. A simple, uncomplicated man, Jackson made his intentions clear. He wanted to marry her. Helen was flattered but hesitant. Will was very possibly the best catch in the territory. There was no question that he could offer her peace and security, but there was the difference in their ages and backgrounds to consider and the possibility that he might one day regret not having children. Besides, Helen had been a widow for ten years and was used to coming and going as she pleased. "I have commitments to my publishers," she evaded.

"I'll wait," he assured her and did—for nearly two years. At last in the fall of 1875, the couple was married. Will bought a showplace for his bride and encouraged her to decorate it to suit her taste. Visitors from the East found vines and leaves framing pictures and windows, pinon logs blazing in stone fireplaces. Tables were festooned with fresh flowers, and individual bouquets marked each place. One guest remembered a luncheon with twenty-three different varieties of wildflowers decorating the house.

Unfortunately those treasured eastern companions weren't able to make the long trip often, and Helen—try as she might—could not find their like in Colorado Springs. The stimulation she craved was lacking. In addition, the nouveau society of the town thought her something of a snob—all those effete eastern magazines lying about and so *many* books.

Perhaps the differences between Will and Helen first became apparent when he decided to run for senator from Colorado. Sickened by a decade of political corruption—impeachments, shocking scandals, blatant miscarriages of private justice and public funds—Helen was horrified.

When a friend wrote wishing Will success in his venture, she replied with her usual candor: "Every election year is a bad one, human nature being what it is. I believe that our institutions will always bring to the surface of political power the scum of the land. Now I know these are unpopular views so I rarely air them but you have forced me to declare myself. To see my husband in that crew of liars and psychopaths will almost kill me." Her consolation, she said, was that "votes are bought and sold in Colorado and he will not buy a vote. So I think he will be defeated."

Though Will's motives were impeccable and his objectives honest, he was a practical man who lived in the available world. He neither sought nor expected miracles of reform, but Helen's stance was a keen disappointment. He had expected his stylish, socially adept bride to be at his side during the campaign. She demurred whenever possible. Not only was his cause anathema to her, but her nerves shrank from the "tangled vibrations" of crowds. She was frustrated by the pull between his needs and desires and her own. To Helen, political socializing was senseless, if not dishonest; and, even worse, it cut into her writing time.

Hour after hour she sat at her desk scribbling, occasionally looking up from her yellow notepad to admire the bold outline of Cheyenne Mountain. Often it seemed the massive bastion of Pike's Peak was a kind of beacon. The novel that evolved that difficult winter was *Mercy Philbrick's Choice*, the story of a woman very like herself—pragmatic, energetic, resilient, an individualist who "did things, said things and felt things with the instantaneous intensity of the poetic temperament," and sometimes regretted them. Helen was most certainly speaking for herself when her heroine philosophized. "The loneliness of intense individuality is the loneliest loneliness in the world—a loneliness which crowds only aggravate."

But Helen couldn't and didn't write all the time. In her journal there were often notations: "Went riding with Will, a perfect day." And in one of her nature sketches she referred to him obliquely: "There is a part of Cheyenne Mountain which I and one other have come to call 'our garden.' When we drive down from 'our garden,' there is seldom room for another flower in our carriage. The top thrown back is filled, the space in front of the driver is filled, and our laps are filled with the more delicate blooms. We look as if we were on our way to the ceremonies of Decoration Day. So we are but it is the joy of life we decorate—not the sacred sadness of death."

Such days were especially precious to Helen, for the differences between herself and Will that she'd sensed before their marriage were becoming more and more apparent. Both meant well, each taking pride in the achievents of the other; but more and more frequently the demands of their careers took them in different directions. Helen was vastly relieved when Will lost the election; but if she had thought the void in his life would bring them closer, she was mistaken. Jackson had been a bachelor for thirty-nine years; like herself, he was independent, accustomed to coming and going as he pleased. Often he was away on railroad or banking business, but even when he was at home, it was sometimes as if a chasm divided them.

Then an invitation. Helen was asked to join in a celebraton honoring Oliver Wendell Holmes's seventieth birthday. Included in the festivities would be the reading of one of her poems. Again there was the hope that her problems would be solved by a change of scene. A trip east, old friends, new faces—she rationalized the possible advantages without an inkling of the real change that awaited her.

* * *

Helen was born, twice married, and once widowed in October; the month held a special signficance for her. Once again she was destined for a rite of passage—one so startling, so profound, that it would change the course of her life. It occurred curiously enough at a reception honoring some crusading Indians.

Helen Hunt Jackson — Courtesy of Cspecial Collections, the Colorado College Library.

The two Indians who addressed the assembled group on October 29, 1879, told a tragic story. Bright Eyes translated for her uncle, Standing Bear, who appealed to the Father in Washington, the Great Spirit and his White Brothers. They hoped to acquaint the public with the government's systematic extermination of Nebraska's Ponca Indians.

Helen listened intently as Bright Eyes explained how on three ocassions the Poncas had been deprived of their rightful lands. Speaking for Standing Bear, she told of his most recent ordeal: "The soldiers collected all the chiefs together in counsel; and then they took wagons and went round and broke open the houses. When we came back from the council we found the women and children surrounded by a guard of soliders.

"They took our reapers, mowers, hay-rakes, spades, ploughs, bedsteads, stoves, cupboards, everything we had on our farms and put them in one large building. Then they put into the wagons such things as they could carry. We told them that we would rather die than leave our lands; but we could not help ourselves. Many died on the road. Two of my children died. The water was very bad. All our cattle died; not one was left."

Standing Bear and a few survivors had run away and taken refuge with the Omahas on their reservation but were forced back at gunpoint to the barren Nebraska sand hills, a totally arid region where nothing could grow and where the last of their horses had quickly died of starvation. Finally the Poncas had taken their case to court, but while the suit dragged on, many died of malnutrion. The case was one of civil rights and individual land reforms, but the immmediate need was for money and food.

As always with Helen it had come down to a matter of individuals. Never one to involve herself in organized charities, she was invariably warmhearted and generous to anyone who approached her directly. Again and again preconceived beliefs had been tempered or swept aside entirely by the charm or need of an individual. Bright, attractive, needy, Standing Bear and Bright Eyes appealed to Helen, and she immediately determined to help them.

But this time it was different—much more than a kindly whim. For once the urge to do something, to actually make a differnce, went beyond the individual. For the first time Helen Hunt Jackson was a woman with a cause. She would never be the same.

Helen's sudden enthusiasm for her "hobby" had the fervor and obsessive quality of a religious conversion. She had become quite literally a holy terror, bombarding editors with letters and articles, circulating petitions and tracts, raising money for the Ponca's forthcoming lawsuit against the government and finally declaring open war on Secretary of the Interior Carl Schurz.

When Schurz condescendlingly pointed out to her that the lawsuit fund was a waste since the Indians had no legal right to sue either the state or national governments, she attempted to empower these nonpersons by forming the Boston Indian Citizenship Association. It wasn't enough. A broader audience was needed, and Helen decided to marshal all her forces in a book. She would make it "simple and *curtly* a record of our broken treaties— and call it *"A Century of Dishonor*."

She settled down in the Aster Library, where she read and catalogued every document, every bit of testimony, compiling a grim record of fraud, pillage, oppression, and the worst kind of cruelty. Her first chapter was a kind of lawyer's brief, which she read to two critical attorneys who assured her that it was "strong" and "without a waste word in it."

In conclusion she reminded her readers, "The testimony of the highest military officers of the United States is on record to the effect that, in our Indian wars, almost without exception, the first aggressions have been made by the white man; and the assertion is supported by every civilian of reputation who has studied the subject. In addition to the class of robbers and outlaws who find impunity in their nefarious pursuits on the frontiers, there is a large class of professedly reputable men who use every means in their power to bring on Indian wars for the sake of the profit to be realized from the presence of troops and the expenditures of Government funds in their midst."

Later—many years later—*A Century of Dishonor* would be referred to as a "watershed book," after it, everything flowing in favor of the Indians. But in Janury 1881 the immediate outcry of righteous indignation that Helen had hoped to provoke was not forthcoming. Both the public and private sector remained silent; Congress was unmoved.

Helen's next move was to secure an assignment from *Century Magazine* to do a series on California. It was an opportunity for her to study firsthand the condition of the Mission Indians, the most fascinating to her of all she'd researched.

Armed with letters of introduction, she arrived in Los Angeles and was fortunate in her contacts. First there was Don Antonio Coronel who shared Helen's concern for the Indians who'd saved his life more than once during the early violence of the American takeover. Coronel outlined a travel plan that enabled Helen to visit the last of the land grant ranchos as well as see first- hand what had become of the Mission Indians.

Following Coronel's leads, she went on to San Diego and met another valuable ally, Father Anthony Ubach. Together they toured the remnants of missions, attended trials of Indian offenders, visited pitiful hovels where the dispossessed just managed to survive. Traveling into the back country, they saw San Pasqual Valley, once a thriving community of some three hundred Indians, before greedy settlers—"robber whites," to Helen — forced them off the land. Only one old man remained, now working for the very people who'd dispossessed him. Sadly, Temecula was even worse. All that remained of the Indians there was their graveyard.

Helen listened eagerly as Father Ubach talked to the Indians and then translated for her. In this way she learned of an Indian school in Saboba, the first in the state. She was excited by its possibilities and prevailed on Ubach to make the seventy-five mile trip with her. They found a village of one hundred and fifty Indians from the Serrano tribe living in a fertile section of the San Jacinto Valley watered by a natural spring. Their chief explained that his people had settled on the land more than one hundred years earlier. Looking about the attractive, well cared for village, Helen suspected that it was too good to last and she was right.

"The Serranos are in danger of losing their lands, Mary Sheriff, the teacher, confided as they toured the village. "If the Government says we must go, we must," the chief had told Sheriff, "but we would rather die right here than move." She in turn confided her own fears, "The Indians may give in without a struggle." Helen determined that this not happen.

***

By the first of April, she was back in Los Angeles where she met Abbot Kinney, a globe-trotting visionary with a warm heart and a lively curiosity. The thirty-two-year-old wunderkind who'd already made, lost and re-made a fortune and would one day found the city of Venice, was a kindred spirit with a sympathy for the Indians that came close to matching her own. With little effort, Helen persuaded him to join her rambles.

The following month the Eastern artist, Henry Sandham arrived to illustrate her articles. Together they retraced the journey to San Diego, to the missions San Luis Rey and San Juan Capistrano, and to numerous Indian villages. At Helen's suggestion—he later complained she was always at his elbow—Sandham made sketches of crumbling chapels and Indian huts, cracked mission bells and colorful Indian baskets.

Next, the trio sailed north to Santa Barbara. After a few days of additional fact finding for Helen and sketching for Sandham, they continued on to San Luis Obispo, Paso Robes, Mission San Antonio de Padua , Jolon and San Juan Bautista. A telegram from Will awaited her in Monterey. He was en route to Caliornia and wanted her to meet him at the Palace Hotel in San Francisco. From there they would sail to Oregon, Puget Sound, and Vancouver. She was waiting for him at the Palace.

The holiday was the happiest kind, a physical and emotional renewal. Will urged her to return with him by rail to Colorado. "There's no reason why you can't write your stories back home with me instead of alone in Los Angeles," he pointed out. She agreed. There really wasn't—just as long as he realized that she had no intension of giving up her crusade.

Ralph Waldo Emerson had called Helen "America's greatest poet"; but with *A Century of Dishonor,* she'd forsaken the muse along with her precious anonymity. The tract had been a savage attack, her pencil a crusader's lance tearing relentlessly at the vulnerability of a flaccid, frequently corrupt government.

Back in Colorado Springs, she readied herself for another assault. Awaiting her return was a letter from Mary Sheriff. The validity of the Saboba Indian land grant had been contested. The Sabobas were threatened with eviction. At first distraught by the news, Helen strengthened her resolve. If the Indians were to be saved, it was she who would have to do it. She determined to return again to Calfiornia; but this time with the authority to effect changes.

Helen immediately fired off a letter to Secretary of the Interior Henry Teller, warning : "There is grave danger of continued Indian massacres. If the United States Government does not take steps to avert this danger, the chapter of the Mission Indians will be the blackest one in the record of your dealings with the Indian race."

She appealed to Teller because they'd met once in Denver when the politican had been briefly associated with Will. Writing back to Mary, Helen offered what little encouragement she could. Doubt and frustration were apparent in her closing. "I hope something will come of the letter." When nothing did, she wrote Teller again on June 11, 1882. This time she enclosed a pleading note from the Saboba chief. Teller promised to take the matter under advisement.

Skeptical of promises, Helen then applied to Commissioner of Indian Affairs Hiram Price. She was seeking a government appointment to serve as a one-woman fact finding committee. Her proposal was clear. She would report directly to the Interior Department concerning: (l) the present number of Indians living in Southern California and their living conditions, (2) the amount of government land available to them, (3) the possibility of other areas that might be purchased for the Indians in the absence of government land, and (4) the Indians' own feelings about being moved to reservations.

Teller and Price were impressed by the plan, sufficiently impressed for the latter to recommend that she be designated Special Commission of Indian Affairs—the first woman to hold that position. President Chester Arthur approved the measure on July 7, 1882.

When the elation of winning her first round with the governmment subsided a bit, the enormity of it all became apparent. She needed an associate, someone to interface with the Indians. Abbot Kinney came immediately to mind. He not only had a working knowledge of their language, but understood and sympathized with their culture. Equally important, he was conversant with California land laws.

Her proposal to have Kinney appointed co-agent was rejected. Helen was adamant. She would wait as long as necessary and used the time to complete her *Century* series. The editor wanted "a popular treatment." Helen had a message to impart. Reconciling the two was a challenge. She was relieved by his enthusiastic response, but would have been flabbergasted could she have known the ultimate success of the articles, that they would be assembed in book form twenty years later as *Glimpses of California and the Missions,* the definitive early-twentieth-century travel guide to Southern California.

Then on January 12, 1883, the Interior Department announced Abbot Kinney's confirmation as her co-agent. Seven days later Helen stepped off the train in Los Angeles where Kinney found her enthusiasm contagious. Jokingly, he referred to Helen as "the general," for she was definitely in charge. She called him Comrade, quickly shortened to Co. The talented illustrator, Henry Sandham, who reluctantly accompanied them—grumbling all the way—was always Harry.

The party bounced along the byways of Southern California in a carriage. Following old stagecoach routes, they visited reservation after reservation, Kinney digging for details, Sandham sketching, and Helen tirelessly writing, recording for her passionate indictment names, facts, figures. On two occasions they arrived just in time to intercede for San Ysidro Indians at the very moment when white squatters were attempting to seize their land.

Concurrent with Helen's field trips was the running battle over the rights of the Saboba Indians. Upon her initial return to California, she and Co had gone directly to Saboba where they found the situation every bit as grim as Mary Sherriff had indicated in her letter. The Indians were threatened by eviction at any moment. When Helen attempted to pursue the matter with the local Indian agent, she got nowhere. He made it clear that he had no intention of locking horns with local dignitaries and resented her interference.

Once the fact finding mission was at last completed, it remained for Helen to assemble her recommendations for the Bureau of Indian Affairs; in the meantime, however, something had to be done for the Sabobas. It appeared the only avenue open to them was one suggested by Co. Helen decided to pursue it. Before departing for Colorado Springs, she engaged at her own expense, a Los Angeles legal firm to defend the Sabobas.

On June 1, Will's newest enterprise, the Antlers Hotel, opened. The "noble structure," fronting on Pike's Peak Avenue, was reported to have cost one hundred thousand dollars. Helen may well have been the only one in town who didn't attend the gala opening. She was home alone working on her report.

Toward the end of the month, Co joined her. He went over the completed manuscript and offered only minor suggestions. Fifty-six pages long, the report dealt primarily with the three southernmost California counties and included some mention of the fugitive tribes on the outskirts of Riverside County, San Bernardino, and the San Gabriel Valley. Following a short history of each band, she made her recommendatons. Helen gave Commissioner Price a long list of influential persons, which included every member of Congress, and asked him to send them copies. Then, once again, she sat back and waited.

The response took a curious and disappointing form. Shortly after publication, Helen received a letter from Mary Sheriff. The teacher's salary was being cut to a pittance. Both women believed it was an act of open retaliation. Determined that the Indian children not be deserted, Helen made up the difference herself.

Despondent, Helen wondered if it was naive to imagine that she could influence the American people by cold hard facts. The summer was dragging on with no congressional response. What was needed was a novel, something that would do for the Indian what *Uncle Tom's Cabin* had done for the Blacks. Could she, Helen Hunt Jackson, move a nation and right a wrong with just a story?

She had the material for such a novel, but its form eluded her. For once the prolific author's mind was blank. Then, late in October, Helen awoke one morning with a start. "Before I was wide awake, the whole plot flashed before my mind," she later wrote Higginson. "In less than five minutes, as if someone spoke it, I sprang up, went to my husband's room and told him. I was half frightened."

* * *

Helen arrived in New York on November 20, 1883, and settled into her favorite hotel, The Berkeley, on the corner of Fifth Avenue and Ninth Street. If for whatever obscure reason she thought it better not to do her writing in Calforonia, she at least contrived to bring Calfornia to New York. In trunks and boxes all around the room were her "traps"—as Will called them—baskets, weavings, embroideries, in the rich warm colors of the golden state.

On the desk before her—beside the portrait of her son Rennie , which accompanied Helen on all her travels—she placed a photograph of a young couple set against a halo of clouds. They were her inspiration, the hero and heroine she would bring to life: he, an Indian sheep shearer named Alessandro—after a bright young chief she'd met on her travels—the woman, the beautiful Ramona.

Helen wrote every day and usually long into the night scribbling on at what she would later describe to Higginson as "lightning speed," turning out one and two thousand words in a single session. "I have never done half that amount of work in the same time," she marveled.

But the cost was dear. It was a dreadful winter; Helen working as fast and frantically as she did, had rarely felt worse. Alternating between marathon writing stints and periods of total exhaustion, she scarcely knew whether to blame the frantic pace or the awful weather for her recurrent illnesses. She was certain only of the urgent need to continue, to complete her work. Compulsively, she plunged on, plagued as always by a nagging sense that time was running out.

"As soon as I began it was impossible to write fast enough," she admitted to Higginson. "It racks me like an outside power. I cannot help being superstitous about it. Twice, since beginning it, I have broken down utterly for a week. What I have to endure holding myself away from it, no words can tell. It is like keeping from a lover whose hand I can reach."

In another letter she complained of the snow, so thick that she couldn't leave the hotel and had to send a boy out to obtain copies of the *Independent* at Brentano's so she could read her Mission Indian articles. Referring again to her new work, Helen confided her strategy. She hoped to sugar her pill, masking her message in the romantic aura of old California. In an effort to create atmsophere, Helen ignored the wind and snow outside and tried to evoke memories of brilliant sunshine and the sharp outlines of amber hills. A sense of warmth and color was essential, and Helen searched her memory for scenes to weave into her narrative.

Transcending time and space, Helen reached across the miles, recalling the clear, hot noondays and quickly falling nights, the golden fields of ripening grain and the dull, autumn hints of the California landscape before the winter rains. It was essential to the success of her story to capture the mystique of bygone days to beguile her readers with images of an idealized past reachable only through imagination.

Higginson had urged Helen—possibly fearing for her health—to calm down and write more slowly. Interpreting his caution as concern for the quality of her work, she reassured him, "You will ask what sort of English I write at this lightning speed. So far as I can tell, the best I ever wrote!" But despite her passion, Helen remained a pragmatist. Bills had to be paid, and it was necessary to take time off from her novel to write poems and essays. These went out at regular intervals, often followed by bitter complaints after publication regarding errors in the text. (Probably the editors and printers were unable to interpret her deplorable handwriting.) Always, however, she returned to the all-consuming novel.

At 11 p.m. March 8, 1884, *Ramona* was completed. Helen Hunt Jackson had written 150,000 words in four months. The *Christian Union* announced that it would be serializing a new novel in weekly installments.

The departure from the twice a month format was Helen's idea. She wanted to get her message across in a hurry. On May 15, the first installment appeared beneath the byline Helen Hunt Jackson. The editors added in parentheses H.H. to at last identify the author to her vast reading public.

Two weeks later she returned to Colorado Springs. With the publicaton of *Ramona*, a great burden had been lifted. Helen believed that she had done her best, given the fullest measure of talent and energy. Now she could begin to relax and enjoy life as she not done in years. In a quick note to Co, she spoke of her sense of well being: never had she had "such a sense of delight in the prospect of the summer."

Then on June 28, 1884, Helen—hurrying as usual—caught the heel of her slipper and fell headlong the entire length of her stairway. The fall resulted in a compound fracture that would cripple her for life. Her left leg smashed, Helen was unable to move for weeks.

The housemaid proved a cheerful and efficient nurse. Helen had need of solace from someone. Will was "never home except for a Sunday or overnight, but in Denver most of the time." For once, Helen was glad of his absence. "I dread having people know I am an invalid," she admitted to Effie, "and most of all Mr. Jackson."

Helen had her bed brought downstairs where she could feel more a part of things while enjoying an unobstructed view of her beloved Cheyenne Mountain. Before long she was writing again. This too was a message novel about the California Indians, but one for children.

By August Helen was allowed out of bed twice a day to sit; then finally the cast was removed, and she could take her first step on crutches. But the privacy she'd hoped for was not to be hers. Without realizing it and against her will, Helen had become a celebrity. Everything she did was considered news. Soon an account of the accident appeared in newspapers throughout the country. One of the first to respond was Emily Dickinson whose concern was deep and genuine. "I shall watch your passage from Crutch to Cane with jealous affection," she promised. "From there to your Wings is but a stride—"

Helen was, indeed, ready to fly. The idea of being "cooped up in Colorado" for the winter depressed her. Within a month, she was off to California. Helen had no qualms about setting out a cripple on such a far journey. As always, looking ahead to new possibilities, she felt a fresh wave of optimism.

She compromised with the Coronels, who wanted her to stay with them by making daily visits, but spent nights at a boardinghouse. Once again their hospitality was lavish. Don Antonio sang for her and told his old-California stories. Doña Mariana, too, was warm and generous, with the clear olive skin, soft brown eyes and gentle smiling mouth of a Spanish madonna—a mature Ramona born into happier circumstances.

They were the best kind of friends, understanding and accepting as well as affectionate. Recognizing that what Helen needed most during her long and difficult convalescence was the sense of continuity and independence that only writing could give her, they provided not only comfort and solace, but time and space.

Since she could write only in a reclining position, Don Antonio designed a special table for her—small and light, with two lower shelves for notes. Using this and lying on a couch, Helen wrote a number of poems and at least one article, "From Icicles to Oranges,"—another paean to Southern California.

Whenever Helen had a manuscript ready to mail east, she and Doña Mariana made an outing of driving to the post office. One afternoon late in November they found a package there addressed to Helen. When she read Roberts Brothers above the return address, the author guessed the contents immediately:

an advance copy of *Ramona.* After serialization in the *Christian Union*, the manuscript had been rushed into print with Christmas sales in mind. She had seen it listed in the November issue of *Publishers Weekly*, but this was her first glimpse of the book itself. Impulsively, Helen reached into her reticule. Pulling out a pencil, she wrote quickly, "With the compliments of the author" and handed the first copy of *Ramona* to Mariana.

As the weeks passed, more than Helen's leg troubled her. She had a persistent fever and nausea so insistent that she was unable to eat. The weight "poured" off—forty pounds in a little over a month—leaving her wan, sallow, and badly frightened.

Once again a new locale promised the answer. Someone had heard of a marvelous physician in San Francisco. He would cure her, she was certain. Leave-takings were cruel. The Coronels came with her to the railroad station. Miller, Helen's former driver, helped carry her belongings on board, then stood before her speechless, his eyes filling with tears. Don Antonio put his arms around her. Unable to control his emotion, he sobbed. Only Helen refused to cry. Knowing that none of them expected to see her again alive, it remained for her to cheer them. She forced a smile.

The whistle hooted, and Helen waved from the window. This time the smile was real. Once more she was on her way.

The San Francisco doctor advised her to abandon all reading and writing if she was to prolong her life. It was an impossible dictum. Helen could temporarily forsake reading, but never writing. "I must write, she told him, "I can't just lie here and have my friends and Mr. Jackson think I have forgotten them."

Her letters to the Coronels were full of lively enthusiasm. She'd interviewed a new appointee of the Indian Rights Association and was encouraged and impressed by his interest. Helen reminded them of some baskets she'd ordered from an Indian woman. She sent them money— fearing the woman would think her "a lying white" if they weren't picked up soon. "I have no doubt that I shall have to lie here for many weeks yet, and I shall enjoy having them," she explained. "Send with them the flat one I gave you to keep. I'd like to keep work in it on my bed." Helen was digging in for a long siege.

A friend came to call. The two had met years before in Colorado Springs prior to Helen's marriage. Their paths separated only to converge again in Los Angeles, where Helen had gone to research her *Century* articles on the Mission Indians. Then she'd found the author much changed. The gaiety she recalled had dissipated; Helen seemed all "high purpose and commanding decision." Now on entering the bedroom, she found to her surprise that "the gentle blue-eyed woman with her merry laugh was back. She seemed not only at peace but happy."

The cancer that was destroying Helen wasn't discussed. She refused to speak of her symptoms, "completely ignoring her weak bodily condition and entering into conversation with spirit and zest that made one forget she was an invalid and be conscious only of the clear analytical mind with its flashes of humor and of the great and generous heart."

Helen's greatest concern was with Will, and at last she felt free to say everything that was in her heart. "I am sure I am not going to get well and I want to bid you goodbye while my mind is clear," she explained to him in a letter. "I realize now how I have failed to be to you what I longed and hoped to be, but it is not too late, my beloved, for you to have a wife and children and live the life that will satisfy your longings . . .let me implore you darling to marry someone else *very soon*—do not live the life of a homeless, tie-less man any longer than you must—but be *sure* this time, dearest, to marry some one whose standards in all matters of living are like your own. Don't make the same mistake, love,—you will wonder I can write so calmly as this. I am writing as if I spoke to you from another world. . . ."

Sometimes it pleased Helen to fancy herself a ghost, but her practical side remained. Most of her estate would go to a niece, but there were bequests to Will's family; and Dr. Cate who'd "saved" her life years before by ordering her to Colorado would receive $1000. Publishers were instructed to make payments to various persons. Boxes of personal possessions were sent to friends—some dating back more than thirty years to the Abbott Institute days.

Finally, Helen wasn't about to leave the world without a last appeal to Washington. Just four days before her death, she wrote to President Grover Cleveland: "From my death-bed I send you a message of heart-felt thanks for what you have already done for the Indians. I ask you to read my *Century of Dishonor.* I am dying happier for the belief that it is your hand that is destined to strike the first blow toward lifting this burden of infamy from our country, and righting the wrongs of the Indian race."

Her editor at Roberts Brothers had written of his pleasure in his new office and his regret that she couldn't see it. Helen gathered up the nearly completed manuscript of her last novel, *Zeph*, and sent it off to him with final instructions.

She had no fear of death, she assured him. "It is only passing from one country to another. My only regret is that I have not accomplished more work; especially that it was so late in the day when I began to work in real earnest. But I do not doubt that we shall keep on working. There isn't so much difference, I fancy, between this life, and the next as we think, not so much barrier. I shall look in upon you in the next rooms some day; but you will not see me. Good-bye."

The time came when Will had to be summoned, something she'd resisted until the last. On the evening of August 8, Helen placed her hand in his, passing into a painless sleep from which she never awakened. Four days later, on August 12, 1885, she died.

Helen Hunt Jackson —Courtesy of the Califomia State Library, Caifomia Section

Chapter I

IT was sheep-shearing time in Southern California; but sheep-shearing was late at the Señora Moreno's. The Fates had seemed to combine to put it off. In the first place, Felipe Moreno had been ill. He was the Señora's eldest son, and since his father's death had been at the head of his mother's house. Without him, nothing could be done on the ranch, the Señora thought. It had been always, "Ask Señor Felipe," "Go to Señor Felipe," "Señor Felipe will attend to it," ever since Felipe had had the dawning of a beard on his handsome face.

In truth, it was not Felipe, but the Señora, who 1
really decided all questions from greatest to least, and managed everything on the place, from the sheep-pastures to the artichoke-patch; but nobody except the Señora herself knew this. An exceedingly clever woman for her day and generation was Señora Gonzaga Moreno, — as for that matter, exceedingly clever for any day and generation; but exceptionally clever for the day and generation to which she belonged. Her life, the mere surface of it, if it had been written, would have made a romance, to grow hot and cold over: sixty years of the best of old Spain and the wildest of New Spain, Bay of Biscay, Gulf of Mexico, Pacific Ocean, — the waves of them all had tossed destinies for the Señora. The Holy Catholic Church had had its arms round her from first to last; and that was what had brought her safe through, she would have said, if she had ever said anything about herself, which she never did, — one of her many wisdoms. So quiet, so reserved, so gentle an exterior never was known to veil such an imperious and passionate nature, brimful of storm, always passing through stress; never thwarted, except at peril of those who did it; adored and hated by turns, and each at the hottest. A tremendous force, wherever she appeared, was Señora Moreno; but no stranger would suspect it, to see her gliding about, in her scanty black gown, with her rosary hanging at her side, her soft dark eyes cast down, and an expression of mingled melancholy and devotion on her

Painting by Henry Sandham

1 Following the introduction to the waltz in 1834 by officers of the S.S. Natalia, San Diego—said to be the liveliest town in California— danced on for a week at the Bandini House. Today the historic home is a restaurant.

the Bandini House — Photograph by author

While investigating the conditions of the California Indians for the government in 1882, Helen Hunt Jackson made the acquaintance of Señora Ysidora Bandini Couts and heard her romantic story. Doña Ysidora was one of three daughters born to Don Juan Bandini and his wife, Dolores Estudillo. (Readers of *Two Years Before the Mast* are familiar with Don Juan.) While living at home the Bandini girls made the first American flag in California.

The oldest daughter, Josefa, became the wife of Pedro Carillo and settled down on a rancho that comprised all of present day Coronado and North Island. Their grandson would be the screen actor Leo Carrillo, a romantic personification of the Californio. The second sister, Arcadia Bandini, was married at fourteen to Abel Stearns, a soldier-of-fortune who introduced a Yankee work ethic into the aristocratic strain.

The youngest daughter, Ysidora, said to have been "the most beautiful woman in all Southern California—if not the West Coast" and described by one admirer as the most perfect coquette he'd ever seen, created a lasting impression on Lt. Cave Couts when she literally fell for him.

Couts, named for his uncle, Cave Johnson, secretary of the treasury under President James Polk, was a West Point graduate who'd served in the Mexican-American War. He was twenty-seven in 1849 on the day he rode into the sleepy village of San Diego as commanding officer of a company of dragoons. The dragoons were a lively bunch with a reputation for being well able to ride all day despite having danced all the previous night.

The town was divided. Some—Don Juan Bandini among them— welcomed the Americans, believing that they would bring stability and prosperity to the area. Others—quite rightly—distrusted the promises of the new government and lamented the passing of a gentler era. But everyone was intrigued and excited by these attractive young men with their dashing blue uniforms, clanking swords and shiny medals.

Ysidora went with a group of friends to watch the dragoons parade before the old mission. To get a better view they climbed up onto the roof. Ysidora leaned forward, slipped on a tile and fell. She might easily have been killed had not Lt. Couts galloped forward and caught her in his arms.

The town had barely recovered from the furor when a new development occurred. Couts challenged a fellow officer to a duel for speaking lightly of Ysidora. It was soon obvious to all that, though Cave spoke no Spanish and Ysidora no English, they had found their own means of communication. Gallons of champagne were consumed at their wedding which began on April 5, 1851 and lasted for an entire week.

A 2220 acre parcel of land was a wedding gift to the young couple from brother-in-law, Abel Stearns, who was by then known as "El Rico." It was a lovely windfall for a young officer just starting out, but scarcely to be missed by Stearns, whose lands were the most extensive in the state. Present-day Long Beach is but a small part of his Los Almitos Ranch which comprised thousands of acres extending from San Pedro to San Bernadino.

face. She looked simply like a sad, spiritual-minded old lady, amiable and indolent, like her race, but sweeter and more thoughtful than their wont. Her voice heightened this mistaken impression. She was never heard to speak either loud or fast. There was at times even a curious hesitancy in her speech, which came near being a stammer, or suggested the measured care with which people speak who have been cured of stammering. It made her often appear as if she did not know her own mind: at which people sometimes took heart; when, if they had only known the truth, they would have known that the speech hesitated solely because the Señora knew her mind so exactly that she was finding it hard to make the words convey it as she desired, or in a way to best attain her ends.

About this very sheep-shearing there had been, between her and the head shepherd, Juan Canito, called Juan Can for short, and to distinguish him from Juan Jose, the upper herdsman of the cattle, some discussions which would have been hot and angry ones in any other hands than the Señora's.

Juan Canito wanted the shearing to begin, even though Señor Felipe were ill in bed, and though that lazy shepherd Luigo had not yet got back with the flock that had been driven up the coast for pasture. "There were plenty of sheep on the place to begin with," he said one morning,—"at least a thousand;" and by the time they were done, Luigo would surely be back with the rest; and as for Señor Felipe's being in bed, had not he, Juan Canito, stood at the packing-bag, and handled the wool, when Señor Felipe was a boy? Why could he not do it again? The Señora did not realize how time was going; there would be no shearers to be hired presently, since the Señora was determined to have none but Indians. Of course, if she would employ Mexicans, as all the other ranches in the valley did, it would be different; but she was resolved upon having Indians,—"God knows why," he interpolated surlily, under his breath.

"I do not quite understand you, Juan," interrupted Señora Moreno at the precise instant the last syllable of this disrespectful ejaculation had escaped Juan's lips; "speak a little louder. I fear I am growing deaf in my old age."

What gentle, suave, courteous tones! and the calm dark eyes rested on Juan Canito with a look to the fathoming of which he was as unequal as one of his own sheep would have been. He could not have told why he instantly and involuntarily said, "Beg your pardon, Señora."

"Oh, you need not ask my pardon, Juan," the Señora replied with exquisite gentleness; "it is not you who are to blame, if I am deaf. I have fancied for a year I did not hear quite as well as I once did. But about the Indians, Juan; did not Señor Felipe tell you that he had positively engaged the same band of shearers we had last autumn, Alessandro's band from Temecula? They will wait until we are ready for them. Señor Felipe will send a messenger for them. He thinks them the best shearers in the country. He will be well enough in a week or two, he thinks, and the poor sheep must bear their loads a few days longer. Are they looking well, do you think, Juan? Will the crop be a good one? General Moreno used to say that you could reckon up the wool-crop to a pound, while it was on the sheep's backs."

"Yes, Señora," answered the mollified Juan; "the poor beasts look wonderfully well considering the 2
scant feed they have had all winter. We'll not come many pounds short of our last year's crop, if any. Though, to be sure, there is no telling in what case that — Luigo will bring his flock back."

The Señora smiled, in spite of herself, at the pause and gulp with which Juan had filled in the hiatus where he had longed to set a contemptuous epithet before Luigo's name.

This was another of the instances where the Señora's will and Juan Canito's had clashed and he did not dream of it, having set it all down as usual to the score of young Señor Felipe.

Encouraged by the Señora's smile, Juan proceeded: "Señor Felipe can see no fault in Luigo, because they were boys together; but I can tell him, he will rue it, one of these mornings, when he finds a flock of sheep worse than dead on his hands, and no thanks to anybody but Luigo. While I can have him under my eye, here in the valley, it is all very well; but he is no more fit to take responsibility of a flock, than one of the very lambs themselves. He'll drive them off their feet one day, and starve them the next; and I've known him to forget to give them water. When he's in his dreams, the Virgin only knows what he won't do."

During this brief and almost unprecedented outburst of Juan's the Señora's countenance had been slowly growing stern. Juan had not seen it. His eyes had been turned away from her, looking down into the upturned eager face of his favorite colley, who was leaping and gambolling and barking at his feet.

"Down, Capitan, down!" he said in a fond tone, gently repulsing him; "thou makest such a noise the Señora can hear nothing but thy voice."

"I heard only too distinctly, Juan Canito," said 3
the Señora, in a sweet but icy tone. "It is not well for one servant to backbite another. It gives me great grief to hear such words; and I hope when Father Salvierderra comes, next month, you will not forget to confess this sin of which you have been guilty in thus seeking to injure a fellow-being. If Señor Felipe listens to you, the poor boy Luigo will be cast out homeless on the world some day; and what sort of a deed would that be, Juan Canito, for one Christian to do to another? I fear the Father will give you penance, when he hears what you have said."

"Señora, it is not to harm the lad," Juan began,

2 A scene from the 20th Century-Fox film, *Ramona*, produced in 1936 starring Don Ameche as the Indian, Alessandro.

3 Illustration by Henry Sandham.

Couts became wealthy almost overnight in a cattle venture with stock raised on his new property. Huge profits from the sale of beef to forty-niners made it possible for the the young rancher to build a grand estate. Soon Rancho Guajomewas the focal point of the Anglo-Hispanic barony. The house designed by Couts for his bride in 1852 has been called the Taj Majal of adobes. Three hundred Indians were employed in its construction.

Rancho Guajome — Photograph by author

Guajome (gwah-hoe-may) got its name from an Indian word, meaning frog, for it was believed by the Indians who once lived there that the ancients took on the appearance of frogs in order to cast spells. 4

San Luis Rey — Illustration by Henry Sandham

Four miles away, the abandoned Mission San Luis Rey provided an assortment of building materials. Couts transferred huge hand-hewn sycamore beams as well as roof tiles which the Mission Indians had made some fifty years before by shaping them about their legs.

Today the Guajome Ranch house, protected through public ownership by the County of San Diego and designation as a national monument, is one of the finest examples of cultural, scientific and technical change in the United States.

—Photograpph by author.

every fibre of his faithful frame thrilling with a sense of the injustice of her reproach.

But the Señora had turned her back. Evidently she would hear no more from him then. He stood watching her as she walked away, at her usual slow pace, her head slightly bent forward, her rosary lifted in her left hand, and the fingers of the right hand mechanically slipping the beads.

"Prayers, always prayers!" thought Juan to himself, as his eyes followed her. "If they'll take one to heaven, the Señora'll go by the straight road, that's sure! I'm sorry I vexed her. But what's a man to do, if he's the interest of the place at heart, I'd like to know. Is he to stand by, and see a lot of idle mooning louts run away with every-
4 thing? Ah, but it was an ill day for the estate when the General died, — an ill day! an ill day! And they may scold me as much as they please, and set me to confessing my sins to the Father; it's very well for them, they've got me to look after matters. Señor Felipe will do well enough when he's a man, maybe; but a boy like him! Bah!" And the old man stamped his foot with a not wholly unreasonable irritation, at the false position in which he felt himself put.

"Confess to Father Salvierderra, indeed!" he muttered aloud. "Ay, that will I. He's a man of sense, if he is a priest," — at which slip of the tongue the pious Juan hastily crossed himself, — "and I'll ask him to give me some good advice as to how I'm to manage between this young boy at the head of everything, and a doting mother who thinks he has the wisdom of a dozen grown men. The Father knew the place in the olden time. He knows it's no child's play to look after the estate even now, much smaller as it is! An ill day when the old General died, an ill day indeed, the saints rest his soul!" Saying this, Juan shrugged his shoulders, and whistling to Capitan, walked towards the sunny veranda of the south side of the kitchen wing of the house, where it had been for twenty odd years his habit to sit on the long bench and smoke his pipe of a morning. Before he had got half-way across the court-yard, however, a thought struck him. He halted so suddenly that Capitan, with the quick sensitiveness of his breed, thought so sudden a change of purpose could only come from something in connection with sheep; and, true to his instinct of duty, pricked up his ears, poised himself for a full run, and looked up in his master's face waiting for explanation and signal. But Juan did not observe him.

"Ha!" he said, "Father Salvierderra comes next month, does he? Let's see. To-day is the 25th. That's it. The sheep-shearing is not to come off till the Father gets here. Then each morning it will be mass in the chapel, and each night vespers; and the crowd will be here at least two days longer to feed, for the time they will lose by that and by the confessions. That's what Señor Felipe is up to.

He's a pious lad. I recollect now, it was the same way two years ago. Well, well, it is a good thing for those poor Indian devils to get a bit of religion now and then; and it's like old times to see the chapel full of them kneeling, and more than can get in at the door; I doubt not it warms the Señora's heart to see them all there, as if they belonged to the house, as they used to: and now I know when it's to be, I have only to make my arrangements accordingly. It is always in the first week of the month the Father gets here. Yes; she said, 'Señor Felipe will be well enough in a week or two, he thinks.' Ha! ha! It will be nearer two; ten days or thereabouts. I'll begin the booths next week. A plague on that Luigo for not being back here. He's the best hand I have to cut the willow boughs for the roofs. He knows the difference between one year's growth and another's; I'll say that much for him, spite of the silly dreaming head he's got on his shoulders."

Juan was so pleased with this clearing up in his mind as to Señor Felipe's purpose about the time of the sheep-shearing, that it put him in good humor for the day, — good humor with everybody, and himself most of all. As he sat on the low bench, his head leaning back against the whitewashed wall, his long legs stretched out nearly across the whole width of the veranda, his pipe firm wedged in the extreme left corner of his mouth, his hands in his pockets, he was the picture of placid content. The troop of youngsters which still swarmed around the kitchen quarters of Señora Moreno's house, almost as numerous and inexplicable as in the grand old days of
the General's time, ran back and forth across Juan's 5
legs, fell down between them, and picked themselves up by help of clutches at his leather trousers, all unreproved by Juan, though loudly scolded and warned by their respective mothers from the kitchen.

"What's come to Juan Can to be so good-natured to-day?" saucily asked Margarita, the youngest and prettiest of the maids, popping her head out of a
window, and twitching Juan's hair. He was so gray 6
and wrinkled that the maids all felt at ease with him. He seemed to them as old as Methuselah; but he was not really so old as they thought, nor they so safe in their tricks. The old man had hot blood in his veins yet, as the under-shepherds could testify.

"The sight of your pretty face, Señorita Margarita," answered Juan, quickly, cocking his eye at her, rising to his feet, and making a mock bow towards the window.

"He! he! Señorita, indeed!" chuckled Margarita's mother, old Marda the cook. "Señor Juan Canito is pleased to be merry at the doors of his betters;" and she flung a copper saucepan full of not over-clean water so deftly past Juan's head, that not a drop touched him, and yet he had the appearance of having been ducked. At which bit of sleight-of-hand the whole court-yard, young and old, babies, cocks, hens, and turkeys, all set up a shout and a cackle, and

5

Cave Couts — Courtesy of the San Diego Historical Society - Ticor Collection

Cave Couts was a hot tempered man— the defense of Ysidora's honor not his only call to arms. Three times he was indicted for murder, but was released on a technicality. On his own property he was both judge and jury. Once he beat an Indian servant to death with his leather reata; many others were incarcerated in a jail adjoining the house.

When he died in 1873, he left everything to Doña Ysidora. Described as a woman "possessed of an iron and indomitable spirit," she had no difficulty running the estate.

Though Couts resisted conversion until the last days of his life, he respected Ysidora's beliefs and built a chapel for her only a few feet from the house. The first of its kind built in California, the tiny church required special permission from the Pope. It was dedicated by Bishop Amat, First Bishop of California in 1868. The place of worship, filled with treasures that had been brought to Doña Ysidora for safekeeping from Mission San Luis Rey, was a showplace in her day.

Guajome Chapel —Photo by author

6

—Illustration by Henry Sandham

Doña Ysidora —Illustration by Henry Sandham

Both a belle and a beauty during the days of her youth, Dona Ysidora loved parties all her life. Soon one of the wealthiest men in Southern California, Couts—quick to adapt to the old Californio traditions—was 7
happy to indulge her. Their fiestas and fandangos were legendary. *Sal si podres* ("Get away if you can," reflected the openhanded attitude of Don Cuevas, as Cave Couts came to be called. Rancho Guajome, the favorite oasis of visitors traveling to and from San Diego from the north, was known throughout the state for its hospitality as well as its architecture.

Cave and Ysidora had ten children. Two of 8
them—including their firstborn, named for his Uncle Abel—died in infancy. Cave Couts Jr., born in 1856, was living at home with his widowed mother and convalescing from an accident at the time of Jackson's visit.

dispersed to the four corners of the yard as if scattered by a volley of bird-shot. Hearing the racket, the rest of the maids came running, — Anita and Maria, the twins, women forty years old, born on the place the year after General Moreno brought home his handsome young bride; their two daughters, Rosa and Anita the Little, as she was still called, though she outweighed her mother; old Juanita, the oldest woman in the household, of whom even the Señora was said not to know the exact age or history; and she, poor thing, could tell nothing, having been silly for ten years or more, good for nothing except to shell beans: that she did as fast and well as ever, and was never happy except she was at it. Luckily for her, beans are the one crop never omitted or stinted on a Mexican estate; and for sake of old Juanita they stored every year in the Moreno house, rooms full of beans in the pod (tons of them, one would think), enough to feed an army. But then, it was like a little army even now, the Señora's household; nobody ever knew exactly how many women were in the kitchen, or how many men in the fields. There were always women cousins, or brothers' wives or widows or daughters, who had come to stay, or men cousins, or sisters' husbands or sons, who were stopping on their way up or down the valley. When it came to the pay-roll, Señor Felipe knew to whom he paid wages; but who were fed and lodged under his roof, that was quite another thing. It could not enter into the head of a Mexican gentleman to make either count or account of that. It would be a disgraceful niggardly thought.

7 To the Señora it seemed as if there were no longer any people about the place. A beggarly handful, they would have said, hardly enough to do the work of the house, or of the estate, sadly as the latter had dwindled. In the General's day, it had been a free-handed boast of his that never less than fifty persons, men, women, and children, were fed within his gates each day; how many more, he did not care, nor know. But that time had indeed gone, gone forever; and though a stranger, seeing the sudden rush and muster at door and window, which followed on old Marda's letting fly the water at Juan's head, would have thought, "Good heavens, do all those women, children, and babies belong in that one house!" the Señora's sole thought, as she at that moment went past the gate, was, "Poor things! how few there are left of them! I am afraid old Marda has to work too hard. I must spare Margarita more from the house to help her." And she sighed deeply, and unconsciously held her rosary
8 nearer to her heart, as she went into the house and entered her son's bedroom. The picture she saw there was one to thrill any mother's heart; and as it met her eye, she paused on the threshold for a second, — only a second, however; and nothing could have astonished Felipe Moreno so much as to have been told that at the very moment when his mother's calm voice was saying to him, "Good morning, my

son, I hope you have slept well, and are better," there was welling up in her heart a passionate ejaculation, "O my glorious son! The saints have sent me in him the face of his father! He is fit for a kingdom!"

The truth is, Felipe Moreno was not fit for a kingdom at all. If he had been, he would not have been so ruled by his mother without ever finding it out. But so far as mere physical beauty goes, there never was a king born, whose face, stature, and bearing would set off a crown or a throne, or any of the things of which the outside of royalty is made up, better than would Felipe Moreno's. And it was true, as the Señora said, whether the saints had anything to do with it or not, that he had the face of his father. So strong a likeness is seldom seen. When Felipe once, on the occasion of a grand celebration and procession, put on the gold-wrought velvet mantle, gayly embroidered short breeches fastened at the knee with red ribbons, and gold-and-silver-trimmed sombrero,
which his father had worn twenty-five years before 9
the Señora fainted at her first look at him,—fainted and fell; and when she opened her eyes, and saw the same splendid, gayly arrayed, dark-bearded man, bending over her in distress, with words of endearment and alarm, she fainted again.

"Mother, mother mia," cried Felipe, "I will not wear them if it makes you feel like this! Let me take them off. I will not go to their cursed parade;" and he sprang to his feet, and began with trembling fingers to unbuckle the sword-belt.

"No, no, Felipe," faintly cried the Señora, from the ground. "It is my wish that you wear them;" and staggering to her feet, with a burst of tears, she rebuckled the old sword-belt, which her fingers had so many times—never unkissed—buckled, in the days when her husband had bade her farewell and gone forth to the uncertain fates of war. "Wear them!" she cried, with gathering fire in her tones, and her eyes dry of tears,—"wear them, and let the American hounds see what a Mexican officer and gentleman
looked like before they had set their base, usurping 10
feet on our necks!" And she followed him to the gate, and stood erect, bravely waving her handkerchief as he galloped off, till he was out of sight. Then with a changed face and a bent head she crept slowly to her room, locked herself in, fell on her knees before the Madonna at the head of her bed, and spent the greater part of the day praying that she might be forgiven, and that all heretics might be discomfited. From which part of these supplications she derived most comfort is easy to imagine.

Juan Canito had been right in his sudden surmise that it was for Father Salvierderra's coming that the sheep-shearing was being delayed, and not in consequence of Señor Felipe's illness, or by the nonappearance of Luigo and his flock of sheep. Juan would have chuckled to himself still more at his perspicacity, had he overheard the conversation going on between the Señora and her son, at the very time when he, half asleep on the veranda, was, as he would

Photograph by George Wharton James. Circa 1911

Ramona's "Godparents" — Jackson's pro-Indian stance obviously did not come from the Couts family. If anyone deserves credit for inspiring Ramona it is Don Antonio Coronel and his young wife, Mariana. Coronel had served as a captain in the Mexican army, mayor of Los Angeles and state treasurer.

In 1881 the aristocratic Coronels sur-
9 prised everyone by befriending
an Anglo newcomer, Helen Hunt Jackson. She was enchanted by their hospitality. The sixty-four-year-old don was, Jackson found, "of an intense and poetic nature" and the "best waltzer in Los Angeles." She spent many days at Coronel's home, listening as Don Antonio played the guitar and —with Doña Mariana acting as interpreter — told stories of the missions and ranchos. "His memory," she wrote, "is like a burning-glass, bringing into sharp focus a half century as if it were yesterday." But Jackson, too, had a sharp memory and the Don's anecdotes soon provided the romantic view of old California that pervades *Ramona.*

Camulos Ranch —Photograph by George Wharton James. Circa 1911

El Recreo, the Coronel's adobe hacienda surrounded by orchards, orange groves and vineyards at what is now the northwest corner of Seventh and Alameda streets.

While visiting here on Christmas Day 1881, Jackson was present when five desperate Indians rode in. Coronel explained to her that they were tribal chiefs who had come to complain that the water rights to their land had been sold to a syndicate of white men. Jackson followed every word with her eyes.

Deeply sympathetic to the Indians' cause, she arranged to visit their village. On the way she stopped at the Camulos Ranch in Ventura County. Once a spread of
10 45,000 acres, Camulos had dwindled to less than 2,000,
but was still representative of the old pastoral ranch life of early Caliornia. Although she did not meet the mistress of Camulos, Señora del Valle, Jackson heard stories of her adoption of homeless orphans.

have called it, putting two and two together and convincing himself that old Juan was as smart as they were, and not to be kept in the dark by all their reticence and equivocation.

"Juan Can is growing very impatient about the sheep-shearing," said the Señora. "I suppose you are still of the same mind about it, Felipe, — that it is better to wait till Father Salvierderra comes? As the only chance those Indians have of seeing him is here, it would seem a Christian duty to so arrange it, if it be possible; but Juan is very restive. He is getting old, and chafes a little, I fancy, under your control. He cannot forget that you were a boy on his knee. Now I, for my part, am like to forget that you were ever anything but a man for me to lean on."

Felipe turned his handsome face toward his mother with a beaming smile of filial affection and gratified manly vanity. "Indeed, my mother, if I can be sufficient for you to lean on, I will ask nothing more of the saints;" and he took his mother's thin and wasted little hands, both at once, in his own strong right hand, and carried them to his lips as a lover might have done. "You will spoil me, mother," he said, "you make me so proud."

"No, Felipe, it is I who am proud," promptly replied the mother; "and I do not call it being proud, only grateful to God for having given me a son wise enough to take his father's place, and guide and protect me through the few remaining years I have to live. I shall die content, seeing you at the head of the estate, and living as a Mexican gentleman should; that is, so far as now remains possible in this unfortunate country. But about the sheep-shearing, Felipe. Do you wish to have it begun before the Father is here? Of course, Alessandro is all ready with his band. It is but two days' journey for a messenger to bring him. Father Salvierderra cannot be here before the 10th of the month. He leaves Santa Barbara on the 1st, and he will walk all the way, — a good six days' journey, for he is old now and feeble; then he must stop in Ventura for a Sunday, and a day at the Ortega's ranch, and at the Lopez's, — there, there is a christening. Yes, the 10th is the very earliest that he can be here, — near two weeks from now. So far as your getting up is concerned, it might perhaps be next week. You will be nearly well by that time."

"Yes, indeed," laughed Felipe, stretching himself out in the bed and giving a kick to the bedclothes that made the high bedposts and the fringed canopy roof shake and creak; "I am well now, if it were not for this cursed weakness when I stand on my feet. I believe it would do me good to get out of doors."

In truth, Felipe had been hankering for the sheep-shearing himself. It was a brisk, busy, holiday sort of time to him, hard as he worked in it; and two weeks looked long to wait.

"It is always thus after a fever," said his mother. "The weakness lasts many weeks. I am not sure that you will be strong enough even in two weeks to do the packing; but, as Juan Can said this morning, he stood at the packing-bag when you were a boy, and there was no need of waiting for you for that!"

"He said that, did he!" exclaimed Felipe, wrathfully. "The old man is getting insolent. I'll tell him that nobody will pack the sacks but myself, while I am master here; and I will have the sheep-shearing when I please, and not before."

"I suppose it would not be wise to say that it is not to take place till the Father comes, would it?" asked the Señora, hesitatingly, as if the thing were evenly balanced in her mind. "The Father has not that hold on the younger men he used to have, and I have thought that even in Juan himself I have detected a remissness. The spirit of unbelief is spreading in the country since the Americans are running up and down everywhere seeking money, like dogs with their noses to the ground! It might vex Juan if he knew that you were waiting only for the Father. What do you think?"

"I think it is enough for him to know that the sheep-shearing waits for my pleasure," answered Felipe, still wrathful, "and that is the end of it." And so it was; and, moreover, precisely the end which Señora Moreno had had in her own mind from the beginning; but not even Juan Canito himself suspected its being solely her purpose, and not her son's. As for Felipe, if any person had suggested to him that it was his mother, and not he, who had decided that the sheep-shearing would better be deferred until the arrival of Father Salvierderra from Santa Barbara, and that nothing should be said on the ranch about this being the real reason of the postponing, Felipe would have stared in astonishment, and have thought that person either crazy or a fool.

To attain one's ends in this way is the consummate triumph of art. Never to appear as a factor in the situation; to be able to wield other men, as instruments, with the same direct and implicit response to will that one gets from a hand or a foot, — this is to triumph, indeed: to be as nearly controller and conqueror of Fates as fate permits. There have been men prominent in the world's affairs at one time and another, who have sought and studied such a power and have acquired it to a great degree. By it they have manipulated legislators, ambassadors, sovereigns; and have grasped, held, and played with the destinies of empires. But it is to be questioned whether even in these notable instances there has ever been so marvellous completeness of success as is sometimes seen in the case of a woman in whom the power is an instinct and not an attainment; a passion rather than a purpose. Between the two results, between the two processes, there is just that difference which is always to be seen between the stroke of talent and the stroke of genius.

Señora Moreno's was the stroke of genius.

Chapter II

THE Señora Moreno's house was one of the best specimens to be found in California of the representative house of the half barbaric, half elegant, 1
wholly generous and free-handed life led there by Mexican men and women of degree in the early part of this century, under the rule of the Spanish and Mexican viceroys, when the laws of the Indies were still the law of the land, and its old name, "New Spain," was an ever-present link and stimulus to the warmest memories and deepest patriotisms of its people.

It was a picturesque life, with more of sentiment and gayety in it, more also that was truly dramatic, more romance, than will ever be seen again on those sunny shores. The aroma of it all lingers there still; industries and inventions have not yet slain it; it will last out its century, — in fact, it can never be quite lost, so long as there is left standing one such house as the Señora Moreno's.

When the house was built, General Moreno owned all the land within a radius of forty miles, — forty 2
miles westward, down the valley to the sea; forty miles eastward, into the San Fernando Mountains; and good forty miles more or less along the coast. The boundaries were not very strictly defined; there was no occasion, in those happy days, to reckon land by inches. It might be asked, perhaps, just how General Moreno owned all this land, and the question might not be easy to answer. It was not and could not be answered to the satisfaction of the United 3
States Land Commission, which, after the surrender of California, undertook to sift and adjust Mexican land-titles; and that was the way it had come about that the Señora Moreno now called herself a poor woman. Tract after tract, her lands had been taken away from her; it looked for a time as if nothing would be left. Every one of the claims based on deeds of gift from Governor Pio Pico, her husband's most intimate friend, was disallowed. They all went by the board in one batch, and took away from the Señora in a day the greater part of her best pasture-lands. They were lands which had belonged to the Bonaventura Mission, and lay along the coast at the

Ever mindful of libel, Helen Hunt Jackson needed a setting for Ramona that could not be confused with Rancho Guajome, yet would be its equal. Rancho Camulos, with its still splendid hacienda surrounded by
1 flowering orange groves, silver-leaved olive trees and sunburnt hills, was tailormade. Jackson had stopped at the Ventura county showplace for only two hours two years prior to the writing of her novel, yet the impression held. The owner, Señora Susanna del Valle, had been absent. Jackson was only able to see the exterior but that had sufficed.

* * *

Rancho Camulo, located in Ventura County not far from Santa Barbara, was visited by Helen Hunt Jackson on January 23, 1882. It was one of the largest of California's Spanish ranchos and, in Jackson's time, was owned by descendants of its founders. Today the estate is a county landmark.

2

Rancho Camulos — Photograph by A. C. Vroman. Circa 1913.

* * * *

Following the Mexican American War, the conquering Americans immediately challenged the Californios—the pioneer Latino citizens of California—to establish
3 ownership of their land. It did them no good to point out that an old forgotten piece of paper was unnecessary to prove title to land that everyone knew had been in the family for decades. Ancient families were ruined in a day. The del Valles were among the more fortunate, but land grant disputes whittled Rancho Camulos from 45,000 acres to less than 2000.

The fictional Californio General Moreno—unlike the American Cave Couts—was the personification of the California don. The title of "don," derived from the Latin *dominus* or "lord," was applied in Mexican California to almost any man of more or less substantial means. The dons were first ordered by the King of Spain to establish military posts at San Diego and Monterey to protect the coast from foreign invasion and to provide safe harbors from buccaneers for the Manila galleons. Some of the dons were scions of noble families; others were soldiers of fortune, later elevated in rank for their bravery. For seventy-five years from 1769 to 1845, they controlled California.

* * *

An anything but impartial study of Californio land titles ordered by the new American governor in 1849 cast doubt on the original grants, many of which dated back to Spanish days. It had the effect of encouraging the claims of those who were known to themselves as "settlers" and less favorably described by the dons as "squatters." It's not surprising that in the twentieth century the services of title insurance companies have been more widely required and used in California than any other state.

4

The back of Rancho Camulos — Photograph by A. C. Vroman. Circa 1913.

mouth of the valley down which the little stream which ran past her house went to the sea; and it had been a great pride and delight to the Señora, when she was young, to ride that forty miles by her husband's side, all the way on their own lands, straight from their house to their own strip of shore. No wonder she believed the Americans thieves, and spoke of them always as hounds. The people of the United States have never in the least realized that the taking possession of California was not only a conquering of Mexico, but a conquering of California as well; that the real bitterness of the surrender was not so much to the empire which gave up the country, as to the country itself which was given up. Provinces passed back and forth in that way, helpless in the hands of great powers, have all the ignominy and humiliation of defeat, with none of the dignities or compensations of the transaction.

Mexico saved much by her treaty, spite of having to acknowledge herself beaten; but California lost all. Words cannot tell the sting of such a transfer. It is a marvel that a Mexican remained in the country; probably none did, except those who were absolutely forced to it.

Luckily for the Señora Moreno, her title to the lands midway in the valley was better than to those lying to the east and the west, which had once belonged to the Missions of San Fernando and Bonaventura; and after all the claims, counter-claims, petitions, appeals, and adjudications were ended, she still was left in undisputed possession of what would have been thought by any new-comer into the country to be a handsome estate, but which seemed to the despoiled and indignant Señora a pitiful fragment of one. Moreover, she declared that she should never feel secure of a foot of even this. Any day, she said, the United States Government might send out a new Land Commission to examine the decrees of the first, and revoke such as they saw fit. Once a thief, always a thief. Nobody need feel himself safe under American rule. There was no knowing what might happen any day; and year by year the lines of sadness, resentment, anxiety, and antagonism deepened on the Señora's fast aging face.

4 It gave her unspeakable satisfaction, when the Commissioners, laying out a road down the valley, ran it at the back of her house instead of past the front. "It is well," she said. "Let their travel be where it belongs, behind our kitchens; and no one have sight of the front doors of our houses, except friends who have come to visit us." Her enjoyment of this never flagged. Whenever she saw, passing the place, wagons or carriages belonging to the hated Americans, it gave her a distinct thrill of pleasure to think that the house turned its back on them. She would like always to be able to do the same herself; but whatever she, by policy or in business, might be forced to do, the old house, at any rate, would always keep the attitude of contempt,—its face turned away.

One other pleasure she provided herself with, soon after this road was opened, — a pleasure in which religious devotion and race antagonism were so closely blended that it would have puzzled the subtlest of priests to decide whether her act were a sin or a virtue. She caused to be set up, upon every one of the soft rounded hills which made the beautiful rolling sides of that part of the valley, a large wooden 5
cross; not a hill in sight of her house left without the sacred emblem of her faith. "That the heretics may know, when they go by, that they are on the estate of a good Catholic," she said, "and that the faithful may be reminded to pray. There have been miracles of conversion wrought on the most hardened by a sudden sight of the Blessed Cross."

There they stood, summer and winter, rain and shine, the silent, solemn, outstretched arms, and became landmarks to many a guideless traveller who had been told that his way would be by the first turn to the left or the right, after passing the last one of the Señora Moreno's crosses, which he could n't miss seeing. And who shall say that it did not often happen that the crosses bore a sudden message to some idle heart journeying by, and thus justified the pious half of the Señora's impulse? Certain it is, that many a good Catholic halted and crossed himself when he first beheld them, in the lonely places, standing out in sudden relief against the blue sky; and if he said a swift short prayer at the sight, was he not so much the better?

The house was of adobe, low, with a wide veranda 6
on the three sides of the inner court, and a still broader one across the entire front, which looked to the south. These verandas, especially those on the inner court, were supplementary rooms to the house. The greater part of the family life went on in them. Nobody stayed inside the walls, except when it was necessary. All the kitchen work, except the actual cooking, was done here, in front of the kitchen doors and windows. Babies slept, were washed, sat in the dirt, and played, on the veranda. The women said their prayers, took their naps, and wove their lace there. Old Juanita shelled her beans there, and threw the pods down on the tile floor, till towards night they were sometimes piled up high around her, like corn-husks at a husking. The herdsmen and shepherds smoked there, lounged there, trained their dogs there; there the young made love, and the old dozed; the benches, which ran the entire length of the walls, were worn into hollows, and shone like satin; the tiled floors also were broken and sunk in places, making little wells, which filled up in times of hard rains, and were then an invaluable addition to the children's resources for amusement, and also to the comfort of the dogs, cats, and fowls, who picked about among them, taking sips from each.

The arched veranda along the front was a delightsome place. It must have been eighty feet long, at least, for the doors of five large rooms opened

5

wooden cross — Photograph by A. C. Vroman. Circa 1913.

6

the inner court — Photograph by A. C. Vroman. Circa 1913.

the veranda — Photograph by A. C. Vroman 7

Adelaide Clark portrayed the Señora in the Hemet pagent from 1923-35.
—Courtesy of the Ramona Pageant Assoc., Inc. 8

Adelaide Clarke portrayed Señora Moreno in the first Hemet Pageant in 1923 and continued in that role through 1935. Her dedication was and is typical of the hundreds who've made the annual spectacle possible. Beginning in 1923 with a budget of $2500 and an attendance of 3,023 the residents of the Hemet-San Jacinto Valley have built one of the greatest outdoor historical pageants in the country requiring $200,000 to produce and attended by more than 40,000 annually.

on it. The two westernmost rooms had been added
7 on, and made four steps higher than the others;
which gave to that end of the veranda the look of a balcony, or loggia. Here the Señora kept her flowers; great red water-jars, hand-made by the Indians of San Luis Obispo Mission, stood in close rows against the walls, and in them were always growing fine geraniums, carnations, and yellow-flowered musk. The Señora's passion for musk she had inherited from her mother. It was so strong that she sometimes wondered at it; and one day, as she sat with Father Salvierderra in the veranda, she picked a handful of the blossoms, and giving them to him, said, "I do not know why it is, but it seems to me if I were dead I could be brought to life by the smell of musk."

"It is in your blood, Señora," the old monk replied. "When I was last in your father's house in Seville, your mother sent for me to her room, and under her window was a stone balcony full of growing musk, which so filled the room with its odor that I was like to faint. But she said it cured her of diseases, and without it she fell ill.
8 You were a baby then."

"Yes," cried the Señora, "but I recollect that balcony. I recollect being lifted up to a window, and looking down into a bed of blooming yellow flowers; but I did not know what they were. How strange!"

"No. Not strange, daughter," replied Father Salvierderra. "It would have been stranger if you had not acquired the taste, thus drawing it in with the mother's milk. It would behoove mothers to remember this far more than they do."

Besides the geraniums and carnations and musk in the red jars, there were many sorts of climbing vines —some coming from the ground, and twining around the pillars of the veranda; some growing in great bowls, swung by cords from the roof of the veranda, or set on shelves against the walls. These bowls were of gray stone, hollowed and polished, shining smooth inside and out. They also had been made by the Indians, nobody knew how many ages ago, scooped and polished by the patient creatures, with only stones for tools.

Among these vines, singing from morning till night, hung the Señora's canaries and finches, half a dozen of each, all of different generations, raised by the Señora. She was never without a young bird-family on hand; and all the way from Bonaventura to Monterey, it was thought a piece of good luck to come into possession of a canary or finch of Señora Moreno's raising.

Between the veranda and the river meadows, out on which it looked, all was garden, orange grove, and almond orchard; the orange grove always green, never without snowy bloom or golden fruit; the garden never without flowers, summer or winter; and the almond orchard, in early spring, a fluttering canopy of pink and white petals, which, seen from

the hills on the opposite side of the river, looked as if rosy sunrise clouds had fallen, and become tangled in the tree-tops. On either hand stretched away other orchards, — peach, apricot, pear, apple, pomegranate; and beyond these, vineyards. Nothing was to be seen but verdure or bloom or fruit, at whatever 9
time of year you sat on the Señora's south veranda.

A wide straight walk shaded by a trellis so knotted and twisted with grapevines that little was to be seen of the trellis wood-work, led straight down from the veranda steps, through the middle of the garden, to a little brook at the foot of it. Across this brook, in the shade of a dozen gnarled old willow-trees, were set the broad flat stone washboards on which was done all the family washing. No long dawdling, and no running away from work on the part of the maids, thus close to the eye of the Señora at the upper end of the garden; and if they had known how picturesque they looked there, kneeling on the grass, lifting the dripping linen out of the water, rubbing it back and forth on the stones, sousing it, wringing it, splashing the clear water in each other's faces, they would have been content to stay at the washing day in and day out, for there was always somebody to look on from above. Hardly a day passed that the Señora had not visitors. She was still a person of note; her house the natural resting-place for all who journeyed through the valley; and whoever came, spent all of his time, when not eating, sleeping, or walking over the place, sitting with the Señora on the sunny veranda. Few days in winter were cold enough, and in summer the day must be hot indeed to drive the Señora and her friends indoors. 10
There stood on the veranda three carved oaken chairs, and a carved bench, also of oak, which had been brought to the Señora for safe keeping by the faithful old sacristan of San Luis Rey, at the time of the occupation of that Mission by the United States troops, soon after the conquest of California. Aghast at the sacrilegious acts of the soldiers, who were quartered in the very church itself, and amused themselves by making targets of the eyes and noses of the saints' statues, the sacristan, stealthily, day by day and night after night, bore out of the church all that he dared to remove, burying some articles in cottonwood copses, hiding others in his own poor little hovel, until he had wagon-loads of sacred treasures. Then, still more stealthily, he carried them, a few at a time, concealed in the bottom of a cart, under a load of hay or of brush, to the house of the Señora, who felt herself deeply honored by his confidence, and received everything as a sacred trust, to be given back into the hands of the Church again, whenever the Missions should be restored, of which at that time all Catholics had good hope. And so it had come about that no bedroom in the Señora's house was without a picture or a statue of a saint or of the Madonna; and some had two; and in the little chapel in the garden the altar was surrounded by a really imposing row of holy and apostolic fig-

9 California's agricultural abundance seemed almost immoral to the daughter of rigid Calvanists. A bit of Jackson's Puritan background crept unrealized into an earlier account appearing in a *Century* article: "No winter to be prepared for, no fixed time at which anything must be done or not done at all; the air sunny, palmy, dreamy, seductive, making the mere being alive in it a pleasure; all sorts of fruits and grains growing a-riot, and taking care of themselves—it is easy to understand the character; or more accurately, the lack of character, of the old Mexican and Spanish Californians."

* * *

10

Photograph by George Wharton James. Circa 1911.

In 1847, the Mormon Battalion, a branch of Kearny's Army of the West, occupied San Luis Rey Mission. During this time many relics such as this mission chair were saved by discreet removal.

It was the Franciscans who established Alta California's 11
first mission in 1769. The system that evolved over the years was highly successful thanks largely to the enforced assistance of the Indians. Its death knell sounded on January 6, 1831, when, under pressure from the Mexican government, Governor Escheandia made a public proclamation that freed the native Californians by breaking the land monopoly that kept them in virtual slavery. Known as Secularization, the process was designed to turn the feudal missions into pueblos where each Indian family was to receive land and livestock. Many of the priests, outraged by the loss of their empires, were unwilling to remain as mere chapel curates. Their posts were filled for the most part by missionaries from Mexico.

ures, which had looked down on the splendid ceremonies of the San Luis Rey Mission, in Father Peyri's time, no more benignly than they now did on the humbler worship of the Señora's family in its diminished estate. That one had lost an eye, another an arm, that the once brilliant colors of the drapery were now faded and shabby, only enhanced the tender reverence with which the Señora knelt before them, her eyes filling with indignant tears at thought of the heretic hands which had wrought such defilement. Even the crumbling wreaths which had been placed on some of these statues' heads at the time of the last ceremonial at which they had figured in the Mission, had been brought away with them by the devout sacristan, and the Señora had replaced each one, holding it only a degree less sacred than the statue itself.

This chapel was dearer to the Señora than her house. It had been built by the General in the second year of their married life. In it her four children had been christened, and from it all but one, her handsome Felipe, had been buried while they were yet infants. In the General's time, while the estate was at its best, and hundreds of Indians living within its borders, there was many a Sunday when the scene to be witnessed there was like the scenes at the Missions, — the chapel full of kneeling men and women; those who could not find room inside kneeling on the garden walks outside; Father Salvierderra, in gorgeous vestments, coming, at close of the services, slowly down the aisle, the close-packed rows of worshippers parting to right and left to let him through, all looking up eagerly for his blessing, women giving him offerings of fruit or flowers, and holding up their babies that he might lay his hands on their heads. No one but Father Salvierderra had ever officiated in the Moreno chapel, or heard the confession of a Moreno. He was a
11 Franciscan, one of the few now left in the country; so revered and beloved by all who had come under his influence, that they would wait long months without the offices of the Church, rather than confess their sins or confide their perplexities to any one else. From this deep-seated attachment on the part of the Indians and the older Mexican families in the country to the Franciscan Order, there had grown up, not unnaturally, some jealousy of them in the minds of the later-come secular priests, and the position of the few monks left was not wholly a pleasant one. It had even been rumored that they were to be forbidden to continue longer their practice of going up and down the country, ministering everywhere; were to be compelled to restrict their labors to their own colleges at Santa Barbara and Santa Inez. When something to this effect was one day said in the Señora Moreno's presence, two scarlet spots sprang on her cheeks, and before she bethought herself, she exclaimed, "That day, I burn down my chapel!"

Luckily, nobody but Felipe heard the rash threat,

and his exclamation of unbounded astonishment recalled the Señora to herself.
"I spoke rashly, my son," she said. "The Church
is to be obeyed always; but the Franciscan Fathers
are responsible to no one but the Superior of their
own order; and there is no one in this land who has
the authority to forbid their journeying and ministering to whoever desires their offices. As for these
Catalan priests who are coming in here, I cannot
abide them. No Catalan but has bad blood in his
veins!"
There was every reason in the world why the
Señora should be thus warmly attached to the Franciscan Order. From her earliest recollections the
gray gown and cowl had been familiar to her eyes,
and had represented the things which she was taught
to hold most sacred and dear. Father Salvierderra
himself had come from Mexico to Monterey in the
same ship which had brought her father to be the
commandante of the Santa Barbara Presidio; and her 12
best-beloved uncle, her father's eldest brother, was at
that time the Superior of the Santa Barbara Mission.
The sentiment and romance of her youth were almost
equally divided between the gayeties, excitements,
adornments of the life at the Presidio, and the ceremonies and devotions of the life at the Mission. She
was famed as the most beautiful girl in the country. 13
Men of the army, men of the navy, and men of the
Church, alike adored her. Her name was a toast
from Monterey to San Diego. When at last she was
wooed and won by Felipe Moreno, one of the most
distinguished of the Mexican generals, her wedding
ceremonies were the most splendid ever seen in the
country. The right tower of the Mission church at
Santa Barbara had been just completed, and it was
arranged that the consecration of this tower should
take place at the time of her wedding, and that her
wedding feast should be spread in the long outside
corridor of the Mission building. The whole country, far and near, was bid. The feast lasted three 14
days; open tables to everybody; singing, dancing, eating, drinking, and making merry. At that time there
were long streets of Indian houses stretching eastward from the Mission; before each of these houses
was built a booth of green boughs. The Indians, as
well as the Fathers from all the other Missions, were
invited to come. The Indians came in bands, singing songs and bringing gifts. As they appeared, the
Santa Barbara Indians went out to meet them, also
singing, bearing gifts, and strewing seeds on the
ground, in token of welcome. The young Señora
and her bridegroom, splendidly clothed, were seen of
all, and greeted, whenever they appeared, by showers
of seeds and grains and blossoms. On the third day,
still in their wedding attire, and bearing lighted candles in their hands, they walked with the monks in
a procession, round and round the new tower, the
monks chanting, and sprinkling incense and holy
water on its walls, the ceremony seeming to all devout beholders to give a blessed consecration to the

12 

Santa Barbara Mission —Photograph by A.C. Vroman. Circa 1913.

13 

Though possibly not "the most beautiful girl in the country," the former Helen Fiske (Helen Hunt Jackson) had still been the toast of Albany. An elegant ash blond with a voluptuous figure set off to perfection by the fashions of her day, she was brilliant, vivacious and something of a flirt.
—Courtesy of Special Collections. The Colorado College Library

14 Helen Hunt Jackson, at the time of her visit in 1881, met the beauty of some fifty years back who inspired this sequence by recounting details of her lavish wedding, an affair to which the entire town had been invited. Elderly residents of Santa Barbara still nostaligically recalled the event.

15

—Courtesy of Pioneer Museum. Colorado Springs, Colorado.

Like Señora Moreno, the young Helen also had a penchant for officers. Her choice was the ruggedly handsome Lt. Edward Hunt, brother of the governor of New York.

union of the young pair as well as to the newly completed tower. After this they journeyed in state, accompanied by several of the General's aids and officers, and by two Franciscan Fathers, up to Monterey, stopping on their way at all the Missions, and being warmly welcomed and entertained at each.

General Moreno was much beloved by both army and Church. In many of the frequent clashings between the military and the ecclesiastical powers he, being as devout and enthusiastic a Catholic as he was zealous and enthusiastic a soldier, had had the good fortune to be of material assistance to each party. The Indians also knew his name well, having heard it many times mentioned with public thanksgivings in the Mission churches, after some signal service he had rendered to the Fathers either in Mexico or Monterey. And now, by taking as his bride the daughter of a distinguished officer, and the niece of the Santa Barbara Superior, he had linked himself anew to the two dominant powers and interests of the country.

When they reached San Luis Obispo, the whole Indian population turned out to meet them, the Padre walking at the head. As they approached the Mission doors the Indians swarmed closer and closer and
15 still closer, took the General's horse by the head, and finally almost by actual force compelled him to allow himself to be lifted into a blanket, held high up by twenty strong men; and thus he was borne up the steps, across the corridor, and into the Padre's room. It was a position ludicrously undignified in itself, but the General submitted to it good-naturedly.

"Oh, let them do it, if they like," he cried, laughingly, to Padre Martinez, who was endeavoring to quiet the Indians and hold them back; "let them do it. It pleases the poor creatures."

On the morning of their departure, the good Padre, having exhausted all his resources for entertaining his distinguished guests, caused to be driven past the corridors, for their inspection, all the poultry belonging to the Mission. The procession took an hour to pass. For music, there was the squeaking, cackling, hissing, gobbling, crowing, quacking of the fowls, combined with the screaming, scolding, and whip-cracking of the excited Indian marshals of the lines. First came the turkeys, then the roosters, then the white hens, then the black, and then the yellow, next the ducks, and at the tail of the spectacle long files of geese, some strutting, some half flying and hissing in resentment and terror at the unwonted coercions to which they were subjected. The Indians had been hard at work all night capturing, sorting, assorting, and guarding the rank and file of their novel pageant. It would be safe to say that a droller sight never was seen, and never will be, on the Pacific coast or any other. Before it was done with, the General and his bride had nearly died with laughter; and the General could never allude to it without laughing almost as heartily again.

At Monterey they were more magnificently fêted;

at the Presidio, at the Mission, on board Spanish, Mexican, and Russian ships lying in harbor, balls, dances, bull-fights, dinners, all that the country knew of festivity, was lavished on the beautiful and winning young bride. The belles of the coast, from San Diego up, had all gathered at Monterey for these gayeties; but not one of them could be for a moment compared to her. This was the beginning of the Señora's life as a married woman. She was then just twenty. A close observer would have seen even then, underneath the joyous smile, the laughing eye, the merry voice, a look thoughtful, tender, earnest, at times enthusiastic. This look was the reflection of those qualities in her, then hardly aroused, which made her, as years developed her character and stormy fates thickened around her life, the unflinching comrade of her soldier husband, the passionate adherent of the Church. Through wars, insurrections, revolutions, downfalls, Spanish, Mexican, civil, ecclesiastical, her standpoint, her poise, remained the same. She simply grew more and more proudly, passionately, a Spaniard and a Moreno; more and more stanchly and fierily a Catholic, and a lover of the Franciscans.

During the height of the despoiling and plunder- 16
ing of the Missions, under the Secularization Act, she was for a few years almost beside herself. More than once she journeyed alone, when the journey was by no means without danger, to Monterey, to stir up the Prefect of the Missions to more energetic action, to implore the governmental authorities to interfere, and protect the Church's property. It was largely in consequence of her eloquent entreaties that Governor Micheltorena issued his bootless order, restoring to the Church all
the Missions south of San Luis Obispo. But this 17
order cost Micheltorena his political head, and General Moreno was severely wounded in one of the skirmishes of the insurrection which drove Micheltorena out of the country.

In silence and bitter humiliation the Señora nursed her husband back to health again, and resolved to meddle no more in the affairs of her unhappy country and still more unhappy Church. As year by year she saw the ruin of the Missions steadily going on, their vast properties melting away, like dew before the sun, in the hands of dishonest administrators and politicians, the Church powerless to contend with the unprincipled greed in high places, her beloved Franciscan Fathers driven from the country or dying of starvation at their posts, she submitted herself to what, she was forced to admit, seemed to be the inscrutable will of God for the discipline and humiliation of the Church. In a sort of bewildered resignation she waited to see what farther sufferings were to come, to fill up the measure of the punishment which, for some mysterious purpose, the faithful must endure. But when close upon all this discomfiture and humiliation of
her Church followed the discomfiture and humilia- 18
tion of her country in war, and the near and evident

16 Señora Moreno's views were probably inspired by those of Don Antonio Coronel, ex-mayor of Los Angeles, who, with his wife, Mariana, befriended Jackson upon her arrival. Devout Catholics, the Coronels viewed the Secularization Act as a travesty. Others considered it long overdue.

By the end of the decade, the Indians had been freed from slavery. Some continued to live unmolested on the land they'd once been forced to till. Others—as the mission property was sold—were dispersed but given substitute land by the new private owners.

* *

17 Governor Manuel Micheltorena was unpopular from the start. His downfall became inevitable when he recruited some 300 soldiers comprised for the most part of ex-convicts, who appropriated whatever took their fancy: food, clothing or women. After three stormy years, a popular uprising in 1845 succeeded in ousting Micheltorea and his army.

18 In 1836 Mexicans living in the state of Coahuila declared their independence from the Republic of Mexico and formed the Republic of Texas, comprised mostly of American Mexicans but containing some Spanish surnamed Mexicans as well. Fanned by the American expansionist fervor known as "manifest destiny," the conflict accelerated into the Mexican-American War. The battle raged for some time in California after the surrender of Mexico.

The war in California ended January 13, 1847 with the signing of a treaty between John C. Fremont and Andres Pico. This treaty pardoning the Californios for past hostilities and guaranteeing them protection with all privileges as citizens, was followed a year later by the Treaty of Guadalupe-Hildalgo which ceded California and New Mexico to the United States and acknowledged the Rio Grande as the boundary of Texas. Extremists on both sides of the political spectrum wanted to take all of Mexico. As it was, the United States had swallowed up forty percent of its neighbor's territory. 19

Signing the treaty at Cahuega.
—© Automobile Club of Southern California. Reproduction by Permission.

Like Señora Moreno, the author of *Ramona* was widowed as a young woman. Edward Hunt was a casualty of the Civil War. The officer's wife once described as "gay, pleasure-loving, impulsive to the point of rashness" evolved into quite a different person, a woman of power and passion. 20

danger of an English-speaking people's possessing the land, all the smothered fire of the Señora's nature broke out afresh. With unfaltering hands she buckled on her husband's sword, and with dry eyes saw him go forth to fight. She had but one regret, that she was not the mother of sons to fight also.

"Would thou wert a man, Felipe!" she exclaimed again and again in tones the child never forgot. "Would thou wert a man, that thou might go also to fight these foreigners!"

Any race under the sun would have been to the Señora less hateful than the American. She had scorned them in her girlhood, when they came trading to post after post. She scorned them still. The idea of being forced to wage a war with pedlers was to her too monstrous to be believed. In the outset she had no doubt that the Mexicans would win in the contest.

19 "What!" she cried, "shall we who won independence from Spain, be beaten by these traders? It is impossible!"

When her husband was brought home to her dead, killed in the last fight the Mexican forces made, she said icily, "He would have chosen to die rather than to have been forced to see his country in the hands of the enemy." And she was almost frightened at herself to see how this thought, as it dwelt in her mind, slew the grief in her heart. She had believed she could not live if her husband were to be taken away from her; but she found herself often glad that he was dead, — glad that he was spared the sight and the knowledge of the things which happened; and even the yearning tenderness with which her imagination pictured him among the saints, was often turned into a fierce wondering whether indignation did not fill his soul, even in heaven, at the way things were going in the land for whose sake he had died.

Out of such throes as these had been born the second nature which made Señora Moreno the silent, reserved, stern, implacable woman they knew,
20 who knew her first when she was sixty. Of the gay, tender, sentimental girl, who danced and laughed with the officers, and prayed and confessed with the Fathers, forty years before, there was small trace left now, in the low-voiced, white-haired, aged woman, silent, unsmiling, placid-faced, who manœuvred with her son and her head shepherd alike, to bring it about that a handful of Indians might once more confess their sins to a Franciscan monk in the Moreno chapel.

Chapter III

JUAN CANITO and Señor Felipe were not the only members of the Señora's family who were impatient for the sheep-shearing. There was also Ramona. Ramona was, to the world at large, a far more important person than the Señora herself. The Señora was of the past; Ramona was of the present. For one eye that could see the significant, at times solemn, beauty of the Señora's pale and shadowed countenance, there were a hundred that flashed with eager pleasure at the barest glimpse of Ramona's face; the shepherds, the herdsmen, the maids, the babies, the dogs, the poultry, all loved 1
the sight of Ramona; all loved her, except the Señora. The Señora loved her not; never had loved her, never could love her; and yet she had stood in the place of mother to the girl ever since her childhood, and never once during the whole sixteen years of her life had shown her any unkindness in act. She had promised to be a mother to her; and with all the inalienable stanchness of her nature she fulfilled the letter of her promise. More than the bond lay in the bond; but that was not the Señora's fault.

The story of Ramona the Señora never told. To most of the Señora's acquaintances now, Ramona was a mystery. They did not know — and no one ever asked a prying question of the Señora Moreno — who Ramona's parents were, whether they were living or dead, or why Ramona, her name not being Moreno, lived always in the Señora's house as a daughter, tended and attended equally with the adored Felipe. A few gray-haired men and women here and there in the country could have told the strange story of Ramona; but its beginning was more than a half-century back, and much had happened since then. They seldom thought of the child. They knew she was in the Señora Moreno's keeping, and that was enough. The affairs of the generation just going out were not the business of the young people coming in. They would have tragedies enough of their own presently; what was the use of passing down the old ones? Yet the story was not one to be forgotten; and now and

1 

Courtesy of the San Diego Historical Society – Ticor Collection

The Ramona mystique was felt almost immediately; soon it had captured the imagination of the entire country. Streets, schools, a popular song, a town and even a convent were named for the romantic heroine. This unknown artist's concept was one of thousands of renditions.

2

© Automobile Club of Southern California. Reproduction by Permission.

In 1822, a pair of canny English traders, Hugh McCulloch and William Hartnell, first realized the potential of California's burgeoning cattle industry. While most of the meat itself remained at home, tallow and hides were shipped to the Orient to be bartered for silks, spices, ivory and jewels. McCulloch took his fortune and retired to Lima. Hartnell became a Catholic convert and married Teresa de la Guerra, the aristocratic daughter of a prominent Californio family. Together they developed a rancho near Monterey—a very large one to accommodate their twenty sons and five daughters.

Many trade ships—floating shopping malls—followed. Rancheros and their wives and daughters could scarcely wait to board. Often they dined there, lavish meals prepared from recipes used in kitchens in Boston, New York and Philadelphia, and then danced to music provided by an improvised ship's orchestra. Later they were escorted to the ships' stores where they could leisurely examine items of jade and lacquer, pearls, amber, rosewood and crystal. Ships officers in turn were invited back to the ranchos where they dined and danced once again with the beautiful and lively women of California.

Before long the crude benches along the walls of the adobe haciendas acquired exqusite silken pillows, then couches, chairs and sofas appeared. Into the homes

then it was told in the twilight of a summer evening, or in the shadows of vines on a lingering afternoon, and all young men and maidens thrilled who heard it.

It was an elder sister of the Señora's, — a sister old enough to be wooed and won while the Señora was yet at play, — who had been promised in marriage to a young Scotchman named Angus Phail. She was a beautiful woman; and Angus Phail, from the day that he first saw her standing in the Presidio gate, became so madly her lover, that he was like a man bereft of his senses. This was the only excuse ever to be made for Ramona Gonzaga's deed. It could never be denied, by her bitterest accusers, that, at the first, and indeed for many months, she told Angus she did not love him, and could not marry him; and that it was only after his stormy and ceaseless entreaties, that she did finally promise to become his wife. Then, almost immediately, she went away to Monterey, and Angus set sail for San
2 Blas. He was the owner of the richest line of ships which traded along the coast at that time; the richest stuffs, carvings, woods, pearls, and jewels, which came into the country, came in his ships. The arrival of one of them was always an event; and Angus himself, having been well-born in Scotland, and being wonderfully well-mannered for a seafaring man, was made welcome in all the best houses, wherever his ships went into harbor, from Monterey to San Diego.

The Señorita Ramona Gonzaga sailed for Monterey the same day and hour her lover sailed for San Blas. They stood on the decks waving signals to each other as one sailed away to the south, the other to the north. It was remembered afterward by those who were in the ship with the Señorita, that she ceased to wave her signals, and had turned her face away, long before her lover's ship was out of sight. But the men of the "San Jose" said that Angus Phail stood immovable, gazing northward, till nightfall shut from his sight even the horizon line at which the Monterey ship had long before disappeared from view.

This was to be his last voyage. He went on this only because his honor was pledged to do so. Also, he comforted himself by thinking that he would bring back for his bride, and for the home he meant to give her, treasures of all sorts, which none could select so well as he. Through the long weeks of the voyage he sat on deck, gazing dreamily at the waves, and letting his imagination feed on pictures of jewels, satins, velvets, laces, which would best deck his wife's form and face. When he could no longer bear the vivid fancies' heat in his blood, he would pace the deck, swifter and swifter, till his steps were like those of one flying in fear; at such times the men heard him muttering and whispering to himself, "Ramona! Ramona!" Mad with love from the first to the last was Angus Phail; and there were many who believed that if he had ever seen the hour when he called Ramona Gonzaga his own, his reason would have fled forever at that moment, and he would have killed either her or himself, as men thus mad have been known to do. But that hour never came. When, eight months later, the "San Jose" sailed into the Santa Barbara harbor, and Angus Phail leaped breathless on shore, the second man he met, no friend of his, looking him maliciously in the face, said: "So, ho! You're just too late for the wedding! Your sweetheart, the handsome Gonzaga girl, was married here, yesterday, to a fine young officer of the Monterey Presidio!"

Angus reeled, struck the man a blow full in the face, and fell on the ground, foaming at the mouth. He was lifted and carried into a house, and, speedily recovering, burst with the strength of a giant from the hands of those who were holding him, sprang out of the door, and ran bareheaded up the road towards the Presidio. At the gate he was stopped by the guard, who knew him.

"Is it true?" gasped Angus.

"Yes, Señor," replied the man, who said afterward that his knees shook under him with terror at the look on the Scotchman's face. He feared he would strike him dead for his reply. But, instead, Angus burst into a maudlin laugh, and, turning away, went staggering down the street, singing and laughing.

The next that was known of him was in a low drinking-place, where he was seen lying on the floor, dead drunk; and from that day he sank lower and lower, till one of the commonest sights to be seen in Santa Barbara was Angus Phail reeling about, tipsy, coarse, loud, profane, dangerous.

"See what the Señorita escaped!" said the thoughtless. "She was quite right not to have married such a drunken wretch."

In the rare intervals when he was partially sober, he sold all he possessed, — ship after ship sold for a song, and the proceeds squandered in drinking or worse. He never had a sight of his lost bride. He did not seek it; and she, terrified, took every precaution to avoid it, and soon returned with her husband to Monterey.

Finally Angus disappeared, and after a time the 3
news came up from Los Angeles that he was there, had gone out to the San Gabriel Mission, and was living with the Indians. Some years later came the still more surprising news that he had married a squaw, — a squaw with several Indian children, — had been legally married by the priest in the San Gabriel Mission Church. And that was the last that the faithless Ramona Gonzaga ever heard of her lover, until twenty-five years after her marriage, when one day he suddenly appeared in her presence. How he had gained admittance to the house was never known; but there he stood before her, bearing in his arms a beautiful babe, asleep. Drawing himself up to the utmost of his six feet of height, and looking at her sternly, with eyes blue like steel, he said: "Señora Ortegna, you once did me a great

came fine mahogany, walnut and rosewood tables, beds, sideboards, card tables, buffets, fine china, gleaming silver.

—Photograph by author

In the initial McCulloch and Hartnell contract, hides went for one dollar a piece. In 1830, they'd doubled in value. It's been estimated that between 1831 and 1836, thirteen ships exported 300,000 hides. By the 1840s, the price had jumped to three dollars per hide, eventually climbing to four and even higher.

In China, many of these were made into chests, ornately decorated with handpaintings and brass fittings. These were sometimes traded back—often filled with tea and other hard to come by treasures— eventually making the return voyage to California where they were coveted for their exotic designs.

* * * *

3

The character of Angus Phail may have been loosely patterned after Hugo Reid, a prominent Scotsman who became a ranchero, ultimately marrying a spirited Indian woman who had grown up in Mission San Gabriel. Reid, aware of the treatment received by his wife, and, after further investigation of the mission's conditions, observed that Father José Maria Zlvidea, "must have considered whipping as meat and drink to the Indians, for they had it morning, noon and night."

Angus Phail's wife might well have looked like this Indian woman—at least to Ramona Gonzaga.
—Courtesy of the San Diego Historical Society
– Title Insurance & Trust Collection

wrong. You sinned, and the Lord has punished you. He has denied you children. I also have done a wrong; I have sinned, and the Lord has punished me. He has given me a child. I ask once more at your hands a boon. Will you take this child of mine, and bring it up as a child of yours, or of mine, ought to be brought up?"

The tears were rolling down the Señora Ortegna's cheeks. The Lord had indeed punished her in more ways than Angus Phail knew. Her childlessness, bitter as that had been, was the least of them. Speechless, she rose, and stretched out her arms for the child. He placed it in them. Still the child slept on, undisturbed.

"I do not know if I will be permitted," she said falteringly; "my husband —"

"Father Salvierderra will command it. I have seen him," replied Angus.

The Señora's face brightened. "If that be so, I hope it can be as you wish," she said. Then a strange embarrassment came upon her, and looking down upon the infant, she said inquiringly, "But the child's mother?"

Angus's face turned swarthy red. Perhaps, face to face with this gentle and still lovely woman he had once so loved, he first realized to the full how wickedly he had thrown away his life. With a quick wave of his hand, which spoke volumes, he said: "That is nothing. She has other children, of her own blood. This is mine, my only one, my daughter. I wish her to be yours; otherwise, she will be taken by the Church."

With each second that she felt the little warm body's tender weight in her arms, Ramona Ortegna's heart had more and more yearned towards the infant. At these words she bent her face down and kissed its cheek. "Oh no! not to the Church! I will love it as my own," she said.

Angus Phail's face quivered. Feelings long dead within him stirred in their graves. He gazed at the sad and altered face, once so beautiful, so dear. "I should hardly have known you, Señora!" burst from him involuntarily.

She smiled piteously, with no resentment. "That is not strange. I hardly know myself," she whispered. "Life has dealt very hardly with me. I should not have known you either — Angus." She pronounced his name hesitatingly, half appealingly. At the sound of the familiar syllables, so long unheard, the man's heart broke down. He buried his face in his hands, and sobbed out: "O Ramona, forgive me! I brought the child here, not wholly in love: partly in vengeance. But I am melted now. Are you sure you wish to keep her? I will take her away if you are not."

"Never, so long as I live, Angus," replied Señora Ortegna. "Already I feel that she is a mercy from the Lord. If my husband sees no offence in her presence, she will be a joy in my life. Has she been christened?"

Angus cast his eyes down. A sudden fear smote him. "Before I had thought of bringing her to you," he stammered, "at first I had only the thought of giving her to the Church. I had had her christened by" — the words refused to leave his lips — "the name — Can you not guess, Señora, what name she bears?"

The Señora knew. "My own?" she said.

Angus bowed his head. "The only woman's name that my lips ever spoke with love," he said, reassured, "was the name my daughter should bear."

"It is well," replied the Señora. Then a great silence fell between them. Each studied the other's face, tenderly, bewilderedly. Then by a simultaneous impulse they drew nearer. Angus stretched out both his arms with a gesture of infinite love and despair, bent down and kissed the hands which lovingly held his sleeping child.

"God bless you, Ramona! Farewell! You will never see me more," he cried, and was gone.

In a moment more he reappeared on the threshold of the door, but only to say in a low tone, "There is no need to be alarmed if the child does not wake for some hours yet. She has had a safe sleeping-potion given her. It will not harm her."

One more long lingering look into each other's faces, and the two lovers, so strangely parted, still more strangely met, had parted again, forever. The quarter of a century which had lain between them had been bridged in both their hearts as if it were but a day. In the heart of the man it was the old passionate adoring love reawakening; a resurrection of the buried dead, to full life, with lineaments unchanged. In the woman it was not that; there was no buried love to come to such resurrection in her heart, for she had never loved Angus Phail. But, long unloved, ill-treated, heart-broken, she woke at that moment to the realization of what manner of love it had been which she had thrown away in her youth; her whole being yearned for it now, and Angus was avenged.

When Francis Ortegna, late that night, reeled, half-tipsy, into his wife's room, he was suddenly sobered by the sight which met his eyes, — his wife kneeling by the side of a cradle, in which lay, smiling in its sleep, a beautiful infant.

"What in the devil's name," he began; then recollecting, he muttered: "Oh, the Indian brat! I see! I wish you joy, Señora Ortegna, of your first child!" and with a mock bow, and cruel sneer, he staggered by, giving the cradle an angry thrust with his foot as he passed.

The brutal taunt did not much wound the Señora. The time had long since passed when unkind words from her husband could give her keen pain. But it was a warning not lost upon her new-born mother instinct, and from that day the little Ramona was carefully kept and tended in apartments where there was no danger of her being seen by the man to whom the sight of her baby face was only a signal for anger and indecency.

Hitherto Ramona Ortegna had, so far as was possible, carefully concealed from her family the unhappiness of her married life. Ortegna's character was indeed well known; his neglect of his wife, his shameful dissipations of all sorts, were notorious in every port in the country. But from the wife herself no one had even heard so much as a syllable of complaint. She was a Gonzaga, and she knew how to suffer in silence. But now she saw a reason for taking her sister into her confidence. It was plain to her that she had not many years to live; and what then would become of the child? Left to the tender mercies of Ortegna, it was only too certain what would become of her. Long sad hours of perplexity the lonely woman passed, with the little laughing babe in her arms, vainly endeavoring to forecast her future. The near chance of her own 4
death had not occurred to her mind when she accepted the trust.

Before the little Ramona was a year old, Angus Phail died. An Indian messenger from San Gabriel brought the news to Señora Ortegna. He brought her also a box and a letter, given to him by Angus 5
the day before his death. The box contained jewels of value, of fashions a quarter of a century old. They were the jewels which Angus had bought for his bride. These alone remained of all his fortune. Even in the lowest depths of his degradation, a certain sentiment had restrained him from parting with them. The letter contained only these words: "I send you all I have to leave my daughter. I meant to bring them myself this year. I wished to kiss your hands and hers once more. But I am dying. Farewell."

After these jewels were in her possession, Señora Ortegna rested not till she had persuaded Señora Moreno to journey to Monterey, and had put the box into her keeping as a sacred trust. She also 6
won from her a solemn promise that at her own death she would adopt the little Ramona. This promise came hard from Señora Moreno. Except for Father Salvierderra's influence, she had not given it. She did not wish any dealings with such alien and mongrel blood. "If the child were pure Indian, I would like it better," she said. "I like not these crosses. It is the worst, and not the best of each, that remains."

But the promise once given, Señora Ortegna was content. Well she knew that her sister would not lie, nor evade a trust. The little Ramona's future was assured. During the last years of the unhappy woman's life the child was her only comfort. Ortegna's conduct had become so openly and defiantly infamous, that he even flaunted his illegitimate relations in his wife's presence; subjecting her to gross insults, spite of her helpless invalidism. This last outrage was too much for the Gonzaga blood to endure; the Señora never afterward left her apart-

4 The baby and this portion of the *Ramona* narrative is a blending of two youngsters who grew up in the del Valle household.

The first of these was the ward of Señora del Valle, the aristocratic Blanca Yndart, whose parents were of Castilian Spanish lineage. A few days before her death the widowed Señora Yndart entrusted her only child to her dearest friend. The infant, Blanca, arrived at the del Valle ranch with a chest of jewels, the legacy of her grandfather, an immensely wealthy sea captain.

* * * *

5 Blanca Yndart's legacy was said to consist of a large cross of pearls "of unusual purity and size," a rosary of pearls, and a single pearl, pear-shaped, of extraordinary dimensions and valued at several hundred thousand dollars; an East Indian shawl of a texture so delicate that it can be drawn through an ordinary finger ring; "a number of dainty kerchiefs and other rich and costly fabrics from the Orient—shawls and rebosos of damask, laces, gowns of satin of velvet."

Señora Yndart's instructions were clear: everything was to be held in trust for Blanca until her marriage. Like the fictional Ramona, the girl knew nothing of her wealth until the Señora deemed it appropriate.

6 For thirteen years—until the time of Blanca's marriage to James Maguire of Los Angeles—the treasure remained in a stout chest beneath Señora del Valle's bed.

ment, or spoke to her husband. Once more she sent for her sister to come; this time, to see her die. Every valuable she possessed, jewels, laces, brocades, and damasks, she gave into her sister's charge, to save them from falling into the hands of the base creature that she knew only too well would stand in her place as soon as the funeral services had been said over her dead body.

Stealthily, as if she had been a thief, the sorrowing Señora Moreno conveyed her sister's wardrobe, article by article, out of the house, to be sent to her own home. It was the wardrobe of a princess. The Ortegnas lavished money always on the women whose hearts they broke; and never ceased to demand of them that they should sit superbly arrayed in their lonely wretchedness.

One hour after the funeral, with a scant and icy ceremony of farewell to her dead sister's husband, Señora Moreno, leading the little four-year-old Ramona by the hand, left the house, and early the next morning set sail for home.

When Ortegna discovered that his wife's jewels and valuables of all kinds were gone, he fell into a great rage, and sent a messenger off, post-haste, with an insulting letter to the Señora Moreno, demanding their return. For answer, he got a copy of his wife's memoranda of instructions to her sister, giving all the said valuables to her in trust for Ramona; also a letter from Father Salvierderra, upon reading which he sank into a fit of despondency that lasted a day or two, and gave his infamous associates considerable alarm, lest they had lost their comrade. But he soon shook off the influence, whatever it was, and settled back into his old gait on the same old high-road to the devil. Father Salvierderra could alarm him, but not save him.

And this was the mystery of Ramona. No wonder the Señora Moreno never told the story. No wonder, perhaps, that she never loved the child. It was a sad legacy, indissolubly linked with memories which had in them nothing but bitterness, shame, and sorrow from first to last.

How much of all this the young Ramona knew or suspected, was locked in her own breast. Her Indian blood had as much proud reserve in it as was ever infused into the haughtiest Gonzaga's veins. While she was yet a little child, she had one day said to the Señora Moreno, "Señora, why did my mother give me to the Señora Ortegna?"

Taken unawares, the Señora replied hastily: "Your mother had nothing whatever to do with it. It was your father."

"Was my mother dead?" continued the child.

Too late the Señora saw her mistake. "I do not know," she replied; which was literally true, but had the spirit of a lie in it. "I never saw your mother."

"Did the Señora Ortegna ever see her?" persisted Ramona.

"No, never," answered the Señora, coldly, the old wounds burning at the innocent child's unconscious touch.

Ramona felt the chill, and was silent for a time, her face sad, and her eyes tearful. At last she said, "I wish I knew if my mother was dead."

"Why?" asked the Señora.

"Because if she is not dead I would ask her why she did not want me to stay with her."

The gentle piteousness of this reply smote the Señora's conscience. Taking the child in her arms, she said, "Who has been talking to you of these things, Ramona?"

"Juan Can," she replied.

"What did he say?" asked the Señora, with a look in her eye which boded no good to Juan Canito.

"It was not to me he said it, it was to Luigo; but I heard him," answered Ramona, speaking slowly, as if collecting her various reminiscences on the subject. "Twice I heard him. He said that my mother was no good, and that my father was bad too." And the tears rolled down the child's cheeks.

The Señora's sense of justice stood her well in place of tenderness, now. Caressing the little orphan as she had never before done, she said, with an earnestness which sank deep into the child's mind, "Ramona must not believe any such thing as that. Juan Can is a bad man to say it. He never saw either your father or your mother, and so he could know nothing about them. I knew your father very well. He was not a bad man. He was my friend, and the friend of the Señora Ortegna; and that was the reason he gave you to the Señora Ortegna, because she had no child of her own. And I think your mother had a good many."

"Oh!" said Ramona, relieved, for the moment, at this new view of the situation, — that the gift had been not as a charity to her, but to the Señora Ortegna. "Did the Señora Ortegna want a little daughter very much?"

"Yes, very much indeed," said the Señora, heartily and with fervor. "She had grieved many years because she had no child."

Silence again for a brief space, during which the little lonely heart, grappling with its vague instinct of loss and wrong, made wide thrusts into the perplexities hedging it about, and presently electrified the Señora by saying in a half-whisper, "Why did not my father bring me to you first? Did he know you did not want any daughter?"

The Señora was dumb for a second; then recovering herself, she said: "Your father was the Señora Ortegna's friend more than he was mine. I was only a child, then."

"Of course you did not need any daughter when you had Felipe," continued Ramona, pursuing her original line of inquiry and reflection without noticing the Señora's reply. "A son is more than a daughter; but most people have both," eying the Señora keenly, to see what response this would bring.

But the Señora was weary and uncomfortable with the talk. At the very mention of Felipe, a swift flash of consciousness of her inability to love Ramona had swept through her mind. "Ramona," she said firmly, "while you are a little girl, you cannot understand any of these things. When you are a woman, I will tell you all that I know myself about your father and your mother. It is very little. Your father died when you were only two years old. All that you have to do is to be a good child, and say your prayers, and when Father Salvierderra comes he will be pleased with you. And he will not be pleased if you ask troublesome questions. Don't ever speak to me again about this. When the proper time comes I will tell you myself."

This was when Ramona was ten. She was now nineteen. She had never again asked the Señora a question bearing on the forbidden subject. She had been a good child and said her prayers, and Father Salvierderra had been always pleased with her, growing more and more deeply attached to her year by year. But the proper time had not yet come for the Señora to tell her anything more about her father and mother. There were few mornings on which the girl did not think, "Perhaps it may be to-day that she will tell me." But she would not ask. Every word of that conversation was as vivid in her mind as it had been the day it occurred; and it would hardly be an exaggeration to say that during every day of the whole nine years had deepened in her heart the conviction which had prompted the child's question, "Did he know that you did not want any daughter?"

A nature less gentle than Ramona's would have been embittered, or at least hardened, by this consciousness. But Ramona's was not. She never put it in words to herself. She accepted it, as those born deformed seem sometimes to accept the pain and isolation caused by their deformity, with an unquestioning acceptance, which is as far above resignation, as resignation is above rebellious repining.

No one would have known, from Ramona's face, manner, or habitual conduct, that she had ever experienced a sorrow or had a care. Her face was sunny, she had a joyous voice, and never was seen to pass a human being without a cheerful greeting, to highest and lowest the same. Her industry was tireless. She had had two years at school, in the Convent of the Sacred Heart at Los Angeles, where the Señora had placed her at much personal sacrifice, during one of the hardest times the Moreno estate had ever seen. Here she had won the affection of all the Sisters, who spoke of her habitually as the "blessed child." They had taught her all the dainty arts of lace-weaving, embroidery, and simple fashions of painting and drawing, which they knew; not overmuch learning out of books, but enough to make her a passionate lover of verse and romance. For serious study or for deep thought she had no vocation. She was a simple, joyous, gentle, clinging, faithful nature,

Mission windows illustrated by Henry Sandham. Circa 1883.

like a clear brook rippling along in the sun,—a nature as unlike as possible to the Señora's, with its mysterious depths and stormy, hidden currents.

Of these Ramona was dimly conscious, and at times had a tender, sorrowful pity for the Señora, which she dared not show, and could only express by renewed industry, and tireless endeavor to fulfil every duty possible in the house. This gentle faithfulness was not wholly lost on Señora Moreno, though its source she never suspected; and it won no new recognition from her for Ramona, no increase of love.

7 But there was one on whom not an act, not a look, not a smile of all this graciousness was thrown away. That one was Felipe. Daily more and more he wondered at his mother's lack of affection of Ramona. Nobody knew so well as he how far short she stopped of loving her. Felipe knew what it meant, how it felt, to be loved by the Señora Moreno. But Felipe had learned while he was a boy that one sure way to displease his mother was to appear to be aware that she did not treat Ramona as she treated him. And long before he had become a man he had acquired the habit of keeping to himself most of the things he thought and felt about his little playmate sister,—a dangerous habit, out of which were slowly ripening bitter fruits for the Señora's gathering in later years.

7

—Illustration by Henry Sandham. Circa 1900.

Chapter IV

IT was longer even than the Señora had thought it would be, before Father Salvierderra arrived. The old man had grown feeble during the year that she had not seen him, and it was a very short day's journey that he could make now without too great fatigue. It was not only his body that had failed. He had lost heart; and the miles which would have been nothing to him, had he walked in the companionship of hopeful and happy thoughts, stretched out wearily as he brooded over sad memories and still sadder anticipations, — the downfall of the Missions, 1
the loss of their vast estates, and the growing power of the ungodly in the land. The final decision of the United States Government in regard to the Mission-lands had been a terrible blow to him. He had devoutly believed that ultimate restoration of these great estates to the Church was inevitable. In the long vigils which he always kept when at home at the Franciscan Monastery in Santa Barbara, kneeling on the stone pavement in the church, and praying ceaselessly from midnight till dawn, he had often had visions vouchsafed him of a new dispensation, in which the Mission establishments should be reinstated in all their old splendor and prosperity, and their Indian converts again numbered by tens of thousands.

Long after every one knew that this was impossible, he would narrate these visions with the faith of an old Bible seer, and declare that they must come true, and that it was a sin to despond. But as year after year he journeyed up and down the country, seeing, at Mission after Mission, the buildings crumbling into ruin, the lands all taken, sold, resold, and settled by greedy speculators; the Indian converts disappearing, driven back to their original wildernesses, the last traces of the noble work of his order being rapidly swept away, his courage faltered, his faith died out. Changes in the manners and customs of his order itself, also, were giving him deep pain. He was a Franciscan of the same type as Francis of Assisi. To wear a shoe in place of a sandal, to take money in a purse for a journey, above all to lay aside the gray gown and cowl for any sort of secular gar-

1 Theoretically the missions were to have been only a temporary measure. The plan of the Spanish government was to secularize each mission within ten years of its founding. At this time, property was to be parceled out among the Indians, who were supposed to be trained in self government. The mission church would then be turned over to parish priests, known as "secular' clergy. In reality, the missions continued for decades with the Indians serving as serfs to the padres who made no effort to encourage their independence. When secularization was finally forced upon the priests by the Mexican government, they argued quite rightly that the Indians weren't ready. The fact that their system had failed to make them ready—after more than half a century—and showed no signs of *ever* making them ready was ignored.

Church and fountain, Santa Barbara Mission. —by Henry Sandham

Illustrations by Henry Sandham. Circa 1883.

Father Salvierderra. —by Henry Sandham.

2

An orchard protected by a breakfront of eucalyptus trees. —Illustration by Henry Sandham.

St. Francis of Assisi had founded the Order of Friars Minor, 3
oldest and largest of his orders, in the thirteenth century. The Franciscans were the first missionaries in the new world, where their work began with Columbus's second voyage. In manfestations of zeal, none surpassed Father Junipero Serra, the first and most famous of the California padres, who had migrated from Mexico where he'd been a part of the Inquisition. While delivering missionary sermons he would sometimes scourge himself with a chain, or, holding a cross in one hand, beat his breast with a stone held in the other, or burn his bared chest with lighted candles. He also kept a thong of sharp-pointed iron links hanging on the wall beside the bed for scourging himself when thoughts that he regarded as sinful came in the night. Anything but saintlike when his authortiy was challenged, Serra's attempts to rule California were challenged repeatedly by every governor of the province.

ment, seemed to him wicked. To own comfortable clothes while there were others suffering for want of them — and there were always such — seemed to him a sin for which one might not undeservedly be smitten with sudden and terrible punishment. In vain the Brothers again and again supplied him with a warm cloak; he gave it away to the first beggar he met: and as for food, the refectory would have been left bare, and the whole brotherhood starving, if the supplies had not been carefully hidden and locked, so that Father Salvierderra could not give them all away. He was fast becoming that most tragic yet often sublime sight, a man who has survived, not only his own time, but the ideas and ideals of it. Earth holds no sharper loneliness: the bitterness of exile, the anguish of friendlessness at their utmost, are in it; and yet it is so much greater than they, that even they seem small part of it.

It was with thoughts such as these that Father Salvierderra drew near the home of the Señora Moreno late in the afternoon of one of those mid-summer days of which Southern California has so
2 many in spring.
The almonds had bloomed and the blossoms fallen; the apricots also, and the peaches and pears; on all the orchards of these fruits had come a filmy tint of green, so light it was hardly more than a shadow on the gray. The willows were vivid light green, and the orange groves dark and glossy like laurel. The billowy hills on either side the valley were covered with verdure and bloom, — myriads of low blossoming plants, so close to the earth that their tints lapped and overlapped on each other, and on the green of the grass, as feathers in fine plumage overlap each other and blend into a changeful color.

The countless curves, hollows, and crests of the coast-hills in Southern California heighten these chameleon effects of the spring verdure; they are like nothing in nature except the glitter of a brilliant lizard in the sun or the iridescent sheen of a peacock's neck.

Father Salvierderra paused many times to gaze at the beautiful picture. Flowers were always dear to the Franciscans. Saint Francis himself permitted all decorations which could be made of flowers. He classed them with his brothers and sisters, the sun, moon, and stars, — all members of the sacred choir praising God.

It was melancholy to see how, after each one of these pauses, each fresh drinking in of the beauty of the landscape and the balmy air, the old man resumed his slow pace, with a long sigh and his eyes
3 cast down.
The fairer this beautiful land, the sadder to know it lost to the Church, — alien hands reaping its fulness, establishing new customs, new laws. All the way down the coast from Santa Barbara he had seen, at every stopping-place, new tokens of the settling up of the country, — farms opening, towns growing; the Americans pouring in, at all points, to reap the advantages of their new possessions. It was this

which had made his journey heavy-hearted, and made him feel, in approaching the Señora Moreno's, as if he were coming to one of the last sure strongholds of the Catholic faith left in the country.

When he was within two miles of the house, he struck off from the highway into a narrow path that he recollected led by a short-cut through the hills, and saved nearly a third of the distance. It was more than a year since he had trod this path, and as he found it growing fainter and fainter, and more and more overgrown with the wild mustard, he said to himself, "I think no one can have passed through here this year."

As he proceeded he found the mustard thicker and 4
thicker. The wild mustard in Southern California is like that spoken of in the New Testament, in the branches of which the birds of the air may rest. Coming up out of the earth, so slender a stem that dozens can find starting-point in an inch, it darts up, a slender straight shoot, five, ten, twenty feet, with hundreds of fine feathery branches locking and interlocking with all the other hundreds around it, till it is an inextricable network like lace. Then it bursts into yellow bloom still finer, more feathery and lace-like. The stems are so infinitesimally small, and of so dark a green, that at a short distance they do not show, and the cloud of blossom seems floating in the air; at times it looks like golden dust. With a clear blue sky behind it, as it is often seen, it looks like a golden snow-storm. The plant is a tyrant and a nuisance,—the terror of the farmer; it takes riotous possession of a whole field in a season; once in, never out; for one plant this year, a million the next; but it is impossible to wish that the land were freed from it. Its gold is as distinct a value to the eye as the nugget gold is in the pocket.

Father Salvierderra soon found himself in a veritable thicket of these delicate branches, high above his head, and so interlaced that he could make headway only by slowly and patiently disentangling them, as one would disentangle a skein of silk. It was a fantastic sort of dilemma, and not unpleasing. Except that the Father was in haste to reach his journey's end, he would have enjoyed threading his way through the golden meshes. Suddenly he heard faint notes of singing. He paused,—listened. It was the voice of a woman. It was slowly drawing nearer, apparently from the direction in which he was going. At intervals it ceased abruptly, then began again; as if by a sudden but brief interruption, like that made by question and answer. Then, peering ahead through the mustard blossoms, he saw them waving and bending, and heard sounds as if they were being broken. Evidently some one entering on the path from the opposite end had been caught in the fragrant thicket as he was. The notes grew clearer, though still low and sweet as the twilight notes of the thrush; the mustard branches waved more and more violently; light steps were now to be heard. Father Salvierderra stood still

4 Helen Hunt Jackson found the wild mustard native to California stunning. "It's as though California's hidden gold had grown impatient of darkness and burst into flower," she wrote on her first visit to the state.

Once while riding with a woman friend in the back of a spring wagon pulled by two half-wild broncos, she startled the young Chinese house servant at the reins by crying, "Stop! Stop! Let me out!" He'd barely pulled in the spirited pair when—without another word--the plump, 50-year-old author jumped from the wagon. The object of her excitement was a huge clump of wild mustard.

Running toward the thicket, she called over her shoulder, "Don't speak to me, don't say a word." Both friend and driver watched in amazement as Jackson whipped out a pencil and notebook and began writing furiously. Her impressions would eventually provide a dramatic frame for her most famous romantic heroine.

Rancheros found the great masses of waving blooms far less charming. Flaming shoots of gold proliferated to such an extent that they choked out the range grass. Periodically the *vaqueros* or cowboys were ordered to cut it back, a process known then as a "run through the mustard."

Dolores Del Rio appeared as Ramona in a film which opened March 28, 1928 at United Artists Theater in Los Angeles. This advertisement from the *Los Angeles Times* shows her with her co-star, Warner Baxter.

as one in a dream, his eyes straining forward into the golden mist of blossoms. In a moment more came, distinct and clear to his ear, the beautiful words of the second stanza of Saint Francis's inimitable lyric, "The Canticle of the Sun:"

"Praise be to thee, O Lord, for all thy creatures, and especially for our brother the Sun, — who illuminates the day, and by his beauty and splendor shadows forth unto us thine."

"Ramona!" exclaimed the Father, his thin cheeks flushing with pleasure. "The blessed child!" And as he spoke, her face came into sight, set in a swaying frame of the blossoms, as she parted them lightly to right and left with her hands, and half crept, half danced through the loop-hole openings thus made. Father Salvierderra was past eighty, but his blood was not too old to move quicker at the sight of this picture. A man must be dead not to thrill at it. Ramona's beauty was of the sort to be best enhanced by the waving gold which now framed her face. She had just enough of olive tint in her complexion to underlie and enrich her skin without making it swarthy. Her hair was like her Indian mother's, heavy and black, but her eyes were like her father's, steel-blue. Only those who came very near to Ramona knew, however, that her eyes were blue, for the heavy black eyebrows and long black lashes so shaded and shadowed them that they looked black as night. At the same instant that Father Salvierderra first caught sight of her face, Ramona also saw him, and crying out joyfully, "Ah, Father, I knew you would come by this path, and something told me you were near!" she sprang forward, and sank on her knees before him, bowing her head for his blessing. In silence he laid his hands on her brow. It would not have been easy for him to speak to her at that first moment. She had looked to the devout old monk, as she sprang through the cloud of golden flowers, the sun falling on her bared head, her cheeks flushed, her eyes shining, more like an apparition of an angel or saint, than like the flesh-and-blood maiden whom he had carried in his arms when she was a babe.

"We have been waiting, waiting, oh, so long for you, Father!" she said, rising. "We began to fear that you might be ill. The shearers have been sent for, and will be here to-night, and that was the reason I felt so sure you would come. I knew the Virgin would bring you in time for mass in the chapel on the first morning."

The monk smiled half sadly. "Would there were more with such faith as yours, daughter," he said. "Are all well on the place?"

"Yes, Father, all well," she answered. "Felipe has been ill with a fever; but he is out now, these ten days, and fretting for — for your coming."

Ramona had like to have said the literal truth, — "fretting for the sheep-shearing," but recollected herself in time.

"And the Señora?" said the Father.

"She is well," answered Ramona, gently, but with a slight change of tone, — so slight as to be almost imperceptible; but an acute observer would have always detected it in the girl's tone whenever she spoke of the Señora Moreno. "And you, — are you well yourself, Father?" she asked affectionately, noting with her quick, loving eye how feebly the old man walked, and that he carried what she had never before seen in his hand, — a stout staff to steady his steps. "You must be very tired with the long journey on foot."

"Ay, Ramona, I am tired," he replied. "Old age is conquering me. It will not be many times more that I shall see this place."

"Oh, do not say that, Father," cried Ramona; "you can ride, when it tires you too much to walk. The Señora said, only the other day, that she wished you would let her give you a horse; that it was not right for you to take these long journeys on foot. You know we have hundreds of horses. It is nothing, one horse," she added, seeing the Father slowly shake his head.

"No," he said; "it is not that. I could not refuse anything at the hands of the Señora. But it was the rule of our order to go on foot. We must deny the flesh. Look at our beloved master in this land, Father Junipero, when he was past eighty, walking from San Diego to Monterey, and all the while a running ulcer in one of his legs, for which most men would have taken to a bed, to be healed. It is a sinful fashion that is coming in, for monks to take their ease doing God's work. I can no longer walk swiftly, but I must walk all the more diligently." 6

While they were talking, they had been slowly moving forward, Ramona slightly in advance, gracefully bending the mustard branches, and holding them down till the Father had followed in her steps. As they came out from the thicket, she exclaimed, laughing, "There is Felipe, in the willows. I told him I was coming to meet you, and he laughed at me. Now he will see I was right."

Astonished enough, Felipe, hearing voices, looked up, and saw Ramona and the Father approaching. Throwing down the knife with which he had been cutting the willows, he hastened to meet them, and dropped on his knees, as Ramona had done, for the monk's blessing. As he knelt there, the wind blowing his hair loosely off his brow, his large brown eyes lifted in gentle reverence to the Father's face, and his face full of affectionate welcome, Ramona thought to herself, as she had thought hundreds of times since she became a woman, "How beautiful Felipe is! No wonder the Señora loves him so much! If I had been beautiful like that she would have liked me better." Never was a little child more unconscious of her own beauty than Ramona still was. All the admiration which was expressed to her in word and look she took for simple kindness and good-will. Her face, as she herself saw it in her glass, did not please

6 Father Serra's ailments perhaps contributed to his surly disposition. Even contemporaries were critical of the padre's not so benevolent dictatorship. In 1783 Pedro Fages, military commander of Alta California, condemned Serra's excessive flogging of the Indians for relatively minor indiscretions. "Chastisement by putting in chains was very frequent in all the missions," he reported, "but principally in Carmel (Serra's primary headquarters)."

Jackson knew that the Indian population had dropped significanty since the seizing of California by the Americans, but ignored the larger picture: Under the original mission system the statewide Indian population fell from 135,000 in 1770 to 100,000 in 1823 to 73,000 in 1851.

Arriving in 1881, Jackson found only fragile fragments of the past walled in crumbling adobe. The system was gone, the missions themselves in almost total collapse — each to her a treasure trove of the history she sought to recapture. The result of the author's enthusiasm was the deification of their founder, Father Junipero Serra, as a kind of saint as pioneer. For Jackson — and later largely as a result of her--the mission system shimmered in a golden haze, half memory, half myth.

Bertram Grassby played the part of Felipe in the 1930 Hemet production of *Ramona*. —Courtesy of the Ramona Pageant Assoc., Inc.

7

8 The character of Margarita is loosely based upon the other child left in the care of Susana del Valle. Guadalupe, an Indian girl, was brought to Rancho Camulos by a Saboba chief following the disbursement of the Indians from Temecula—an event to be later described in *Ramona* . She was raised as a kind of servant-companion to the Señora's ward, Blanca Yndart.

Guadalupe's true story was as romantic as a Jackson novel. One day an army captain stopped at Camulos and happened to see her. " That girl is the exact image of my sister!" he exclaimed. "Who is she?" Señora del Valle knew little of Guadalupe's background. "The girl's mother disappeared a few years ago when the Saboba tribe was driven out of Temecula," she explained, adding, "the father appears to have been an American."

"May I talk with her?" he asked. The following day the captain left the rancho with the young girl riding beside him. Guadalupe was a daughter he'd not known about.

her. She compared her straight, massive black eyebrows with Felipe's, arched and delicately pencilled, and found her own ugly. The expression of gentle repose which her countenance wore, seemed to her an expression of stupidity. "Felipe looks so bright!" she thought, as she noted his mobile changing face, never for two successive seconds the same. "There
7 is nobody like Felipe." And when his brown eyes were fixed on her, as they so often were, in a long lingering gaze, she looked steadily back into their velvet depths with an abstracted sort of intensity which profoundly puzzled Felipe. It was this look, more than any other one thing, which had for two years held Felipe's tongue in leash, as it were, and made it impossible for him to say to Ramona any of the loving things of which his heart had been full ever since he could remember. The boy had spoken them unhesitatingly, unconsciously; but the man found himself suddenly afraid. "What is it she thinks when she looks into my eyes so?" he wondered. If he had known that the thing she was usually thinking was simply, "How much handsomer brown eyes are than blue! I wish my eyes were the color of Felipe's!" he would have perceived, perhaps, what would have saved him sorrow, if he had known it, that a girl who looked at a man thus, would be hard to win to look at him as a lover. But being a lover, he could not see this. He saw only enough to perplex and deter him.

8 As they drew near the house, Ramona saw Margarita standing at the gate of the garden. She was holding something white in her hands, looking down at it, and crying piteously. As she perceived Ramona, she made an eager leap forward, and then shrank back again, making dumb signals of distress to her. Her whole attitude was one of misery and entreaty. Margarita was, of all the maids, most beloved by Ramona. Though they were nearly of the same age, it had been Margarita who first had charge of Ramona; the nurse and her charge had played together, grown up together, become women together, and were now, although Margarita never presumed on the relation, or forgot to address Ramona as Señorita, more like friends than like mistress and maid.

"Pardon me, Father," said Ramona. "I see that Margarita there is in trouble. I will leave Felipe to go with you to the house. I will be with you again in a few moments." And kissing his hand, she flew rather than ran across the field to the foot of the garden.

Before she reached the spot, Margarita had dropped on the ground and buried her face in her hands. A mass of crumpled and stained linen lay at her feet.

"What is it? What has happened, Margarita mia?" cried Ramona, in the affectionate Spanish phrase. For answer, Margarita removed one wet hand from her eyes, and pointed with a gesture of despair to the crumpled linen. Sobs choked her voice, and she buried her face again in her hands.

Ramona stooped, and lifted one corner of the linen

An involuntary cry of dismay broke from her, at which Margarita's sobs redoubled, and she gasped out, "Yes, Señorita, it is totally ruined! It can never be mended, and it will be needed for the mass to-morrow morning. When I saw the Father coming by your side, I prayed to the Virgin to let me die. The Señora will never forgive me." 9

It was indeed a sorry sight. The white linen altar-cloth, the cloth which the Señora Moreno had with her own hands made into one solid front of beautiful lace of the Mexican fashion, by drawing out part of the threads and sewing the remainder into intricate patterns, the cloth which had always been on the altar, when mass was said, since Margarita's and Ramona's earliest recollections, — there it lay, torn, stained, as if it had been dragged through muddy brambles. In silence, aghast, Ramona opened it out and held it up. "How did it happen, Margarita?" she whispered, glancing in terror up towards the house.

"Oh, that is the worst of it, Señorita!" sobbed the girl. "That is the worst of it! If it were not for that, I would not be so afraid. If it had happened any other way, the Señora might have forgiven me; but she never will. I would rather die than tell her;" and she shook from head to foot.

"Stop crying, Margarita!" said Ramona, firmly, "and tell me all about it. It is n't so bad as it looks. I think I can mend it."

"Oh, the saints bless you!" cried Margarita, looking up for the first time. "Do you really think you can mend it, Señorita? If you will mend that lace, I'll go on my knees for you all the rest of my life!"

Ramona laughed in spite of herself. "You 'll serve me better by keeping on your feet," she said merrily; at which Margarita laughed too, through her tears. They were both young.

"Oh, but Señorita," Margarita began again in a tone of anguish, her tears flowing afresh, "there is not time! It must be washed and ironed to-night, for the mass to-morrow morning, and I have to help at the supper. Anita and Rosa are both ill in bed, you know, and Maria has gone away for a week. The Señora said if the Father came to-night I must help mother, and must wait on table. It cannot be done. I was just going to iron it now, and I found it — so — It was in the artichoke-patch, and Capitan, the beast, had been tossing it among the sharp pricks of the old last year's seeds."

"In the artichoke-patch!" ejaculated Ramona. "How under heavens did it get there?"

"Oh, that was what I meant, Señorita, when I said she never would forgive me. She has forbidden me many times to hang anything to dry on the fence there; and if I had only washed it when she first told me, two days ago, all would have been well. But I forgot it till this afternoon, and there was no sun in the court to dry it, and you know how the sun lies on the artichoke-patch, and I put a strong cloth over the fence, so that the wood should not pierce the lace,

—Photograph by George Wharton James. Circa 1911.

9 During her short visit to Camulos, Helen Hunt Jackson visited the small chapel and observed the torn altar cloth. A few years later the small detail observed and cataloged in her novelist's brain resurfaced in the writing of *Ramona*.

and I did not leave it more than half an hour, just while I said a few words to Luigo, and there was no wind; and I believe the saints must have fetched it down to the ground to punish me for my disobedience."

Ramona had been all this time carefully smoothing out the torn places. "It is not so bad as it looks," she said; "if it were not for the hurry, there would be no trouble in mending it. But I will do it the best I can, so that it will not show, for to-morrow, and then, after the Father is gone, I can repair it at leisure, and make it just as good as new. I think I can mend it and wash it before dark," and she glanced at the sun. "Oh, yes, there are good three hours of daylight yet. I can do it. You put irons on the fire, to have them hot, to iron it as soon as it is partly dried. You will see it will not show that anything has happened to it."

"Will the Señora know?" asked poor Margarita, calmed and reassured, but still in mortal terror.

Ramona turned her steady glance full on Margarita's face. "You would not be any happier if she were deceived, do you think?" she said gravely.

"O Señorita, after it is mended? If it really does not show?" pleaded the girl.

"I will tell her myself, and not till after it is mended," said Ramona; but she did not smile.

"Ah, Señorita," said Margarita, deprecatingly, "you do not know what it is to have the Señora displeased with one."

"Nothing can be so bad as to be displeased with one's self," retorted Ramona, as she walked swiftly away to her room with the linen rolled up under her arm. Luckily for Margarita's cause, she met no one on the way. The Señora had welcomed Father Salvierderra at the foot of the veranda steps, and had immediately closeted herself with him. She had much to say to him, — much about which she wished his help and counsel, and much which she wished to learn from him as to affairs in the Church and in the country generally.

Felipe had gone off at once to find Juan Canito to see if everything were ready for the sheep-shearing to begin on the next day, if the shearers arrived in time; and there was very good chance of their coming in by sundown this day, Felipe thought, for he had privately instructed his messenger to make all possible haste, and to impress on the Indians the urgent need of their losing no time on the road.

It had been a great concession on the Señora's part to allow the messenger to be sent off before she had positive intelligence as to the Father's movements. But as day after day passed and no news came, even she perceived that it would not do to put off the sheep-shearing much longer, or, as Juan Canito said, "forever." The Father might have fallen ill; and if that were so, it might very easily be weeks before they heard of it, so scanty were the means of communication between the remote places on his route of visitation. The messenger had therefore been sent to summon the Temecula shearers, and the Señora had resigned herself to the inevitable; piously praying, however, morning and night, and at odd moments in the day, that the Father might arrive before the Indians did. When she saw him coming up the garden-walk, leaning on the arm of her Felipe, on the afternoon of the very day which was the earliest possible day for the Indians to arrive, it was not strange that she felt, mingled with the joy of her greeting to her long-loved friend and confessor, a triumphant exultation that the saints had heard her prayers.

In the kitchen all was bustle and stir. The coming of any guest into the house was a signal for unwonted activities there, — even the coming of Father Salvierderra, who never knew whether the soup had forcemeat balls in it or not, old Marda said; and that was to her the last extreme of indifference to good things of the flesh. "But if he will not eat, he can see," she said; and her pride for herself and for the house was enlisted in setting forth as goodly an array of viands as her larder afforded. She grew suddenly fastidious over the size and color of the cabbages to go into the beef-pot, and threw away one whole saucepan full of rice, because Margarita had put only one onion in instead of two.

"Have I not told you again and again that for the Father it is always two onions?" she exclaimed. "It is the dish he most favors of all; and it is a pity too, old as he is. It makes him no blood. It is good beef he should take now."

The dining-room was on the opposite side of the court-yard from the kitchen, and there was a perpetual procession of small messengers going back and forth between the rooms. It was the highest ambition of each child to be allowed to fetch and carry dishes in the preparation of the meals at all times; but when by so doing they could perchance get a glimpse through the dining-room door, open on the veranda, of strangers and guests, their restless rivalry became unmanageable. Poor Margarita, between her own private anxieties and her multiplied duties of helping in the kitchen, and setting the table, restraining and overseeing her army of infant volunteers, was nearly distraught; not so distraught, however, but that she remembered and found time to seize a lighted candle in the kitchen, run and set it before the statue of Saint Francis of Paula in her bedroom, hurriedly whispering a prayer that the lace might be made whole like new. Several times before the afternoon had waned she snatched a moment to fling herself down at the statue's feet and pray her foolish little prayer over again. We think we are quite sure that it is a foolish little prayer, when people pray to have torn lace made whole. But it would be hard to show the odds between asking that, and asking that it may rain, or that the sick may get well. As the grand old Russian says, what men usually ask for, when they pray to God, is, that two and two may not make four. All the same he is to be pitied who prays not. It was only the thought of that candle at Saint Francis's feet, which enabled Margarita to struggle through this anxious and unhappy afternoon and evening.

At last supper was ready, — a great dish of spiced 10
beef and cabbage in the centre of the table; a tureen of thick soup, with forcemeat balls and red peppers in it; two red earthen platters heaped, one with the boiled rice and onions, the other with the delicious *frijoles* (beans) so dear to all Mexican hearts; cut-glass dishes filled with hot stewed pears, or preserved quinces, or grape jelly; plates of frosted cakes of various sorts; and a steaming silver teakettle, from which went up an aroma of tea such as had never been bought or sold in all California, the Señora's one extravagance and passion.

"Where is Ramona?" asked the Señora, surprised and displeased, as she entered the dining-room. "Margarita, go tell the Señorita that we are waiting for her."

Margarita started tremblingly, with flushed face, towards the door. What would happen now! "O Saint Francis," she inwardly prayed, "help us this once!"

"Stay," said Felipe. "Do not call Señorita Ramona." Then, turning to his mother, "Ramona cannot come. She is not in the house. She has a duty to perform for to-morrow," he said; and he looked meaningly at his mother, adding, "we will not wait for her."

Much bewildered, the Señora took her seat at the head of the table in a mechanical way, and began, "But —" Felipe, seeing that questions were to follow, interrupted her: "I have just spoken with her. It is impossible for her to come;" and turning to Father Salvierderra, he at once engaged him in conversation, and left the baffled Señora to bear her unsatisfied curiosity as best she could.

Margarita looked at Felipe with an expression of profound gratitude, which he did not observe, and would not in the least have understood; for Ramona had not confided to him any details of the disaster. Seeing him under her window, she had called cautiously to him, and said: "Dear Felipe, do you think you can save me from having to come to supper? A dreadful accident has happened to the altar-cloth, and I must mend it and wash it, and there is barely time before dark. Don't let them call me; I shall be down at the brook, and they will not find me, and your mother will be displeased."

This wise precaution of Ramona's was the salva- 11
tion of everything, so far as the altar-cloth was concerned. The rents had proved far less serious than she had feared; the daylight held out till the last of them was skilfully mended; and just as the red beams of the sinking sun came streaming through the willow-trees at the foot of the garden, Ramona, darting down the garden, had reached the brook, and

10 Rich as California was in beef, meat rotting in the sun was a frequent sight. Lacking refrigeration, there was little that could be done with it other than eat it immediately— large, lavish barbecues inevitably followed — or dry it.

The latter was the mainstay of the Californio's diet. When a steer was killed, the hide was spread out, hair side down, and used as a receptacle for the meat. The best cuts of beef were sliced into strips about an inch thick and several inches wide and about a foot in length. These were dipped in salt brine, hung out to dry in the sun, and turned every day. In a few days the meat was hard, dry and black.

Each steer netted about 50 pounds of dried beef or *carne seca*, which, combined with onion, chile, tomato and potato, found its way into an infinite variety of dishes.

11 

Illustration by Henry Sandham. Circa 1913.

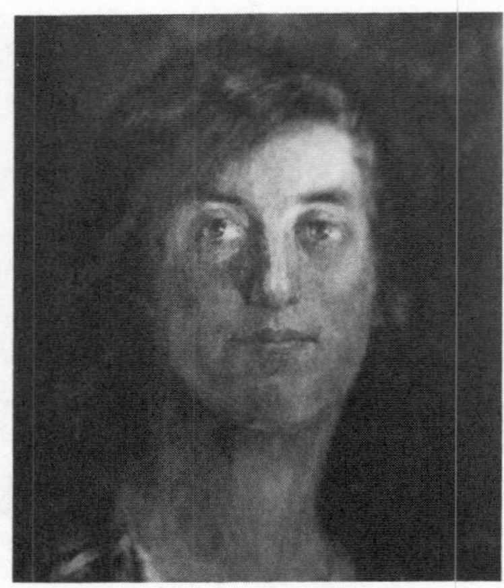

Alessandro. — by Henry Sandham.

12 It's been suggested that Jackson's unfamiliarity with Spanish led her to use an Italian form of the name instead of the Spanish, which is Alejandro. More likely, she simply wanted a word that would be easily pronouncable by her Anglo readers.

Incidents in the narrative parallel the life of Juan Diego, whose fate partially inspired the Jackson novel, but the character of Alessandro remains a writer's creation. Though clearly a social protest novel decrying the treatment of the California Mission Indian, there is only one Indian character of any importance in *Ramona* — Alessandro. He is Jackson's cleverly designed pill, Ramona remains the sugar coating.

—Illustration by Henry Sandham. Circa 1883.

13

kneeling on the grass, had dipped the linen into the water.

Her hurried working over the lace, and her anxiety, had made her cheeks scarlet. As she ran down the garden, her comb had loosened and her hair fallen to her waist. Stopping only to pick up the comb and thrust it in her pocket, she had sped on, as it would soon be too dark for her to see the stains on the linen, and it was going to be no small trouble to get them out without fraying the lace.

Her hair in disorder, her sleeves pinned loosely on her shoulders, her whole face aglow with the earnestness of her task, she bent low over the stones, rinsing the altar-cloth up and down in the water, anxiously scanning it, then plunging it in again.

The sunset beams played around her hair like a halo; the whole place was aglow with red light, and her face was kindled into transcendent beauty. A sound arrested her attention. She looked up. Forms, dusky black against the fiery western sky, were coming down the valley. It was the band of Indian shearers. They turned to the left, and went towards the sheep sheds and booths. But there was one of them that Ramona did not see. He had been standing for some minutes concealed behind a large willow-tree a few rods from the place where Ramona
12 was kneeling. It was Alessandro, son of Pablo Assis, captain of the shearing band. Walking slowly along in advance of his men, he had felt a light, as from a mirror held in the sun, smite his eyes. It was the red sunbeam on the glittering water where Ramona knelt. In the same second he saw Ramona.

He halted, as wild creatures of the forest halt at a sound; gazed; walked abruptly away from his men, who kept on, not noticing his disappearance. Cautiously he moved a few steps nearer, into the shelter of a gnarled old willow, from behind which he could gaze unperceived on the beautiful vision,— for so it seemed to him.

13 As he gazed, his senses seemed leaving him, and unconsciously he spoke aloud: "Christ! What shall I do!"

Chapter V

The sunrise hymn. —by Henry Sandham. Circa 1883.

THE room in which Father Salvierderra always slept when at the Señora Moreno's house was the southeast corner room. It had a window to the south and one to the east. When the first glow of dawn came in the sky, this eastern window was lit up as by a fire. The Father was always on watch for it, having usually been at prayer for hours. As the first ray reached the window, he would throw the casement wide open, and standing there with bared head, strike up the melody of the sunrise hymn sung in all devout Mexican families. 1
It was a beautiful custom, not yet wholly abandoned. At the first dawn of light, the oldest member of the family arose, and began singing some hymn familiar to the 1
household. It was the duty of each person hearing it to immediately rise, or at least sit up in bed, and join in the singing. In a few moments the whole family would be singing, and the joyous sounds pouring out from the house like the music of the birds in the fields at dawn. The hymns were usually invocations to the Virgin, or to the saint of the day, and the melodies were sweet and simple.

On this morning there was another watcher for the dawn besides Father Salvierderra. It was Alessandro, who had been restlessly wandering about since midnight, and had finally seated himself under the willow-trees by the brook, at the spot where he had seen Ramona the evening before. He recollected this custom of the sunrise hymn when he and his band were at the Señora's the last year, and he had chanced then to learn that the Father slept in the southeast room. From the spot where he sat, he could see the south window of this room. He could also see the low eastern horizon, at which a faint luminous line already showed. The sky was like amber; a few stars still shone faintly in the zenith. There was not a sound. It was one of those rare moments in which one can without difficulty realize the noiseless spinning of the earth through space. Alessandro knew nothing of this; he could not have been made to believe that the earth was moving. He thought the sun was coming up apace, and the

2

Music score from old choir book printed by Mission Indians.

earth was standing still, — a belief just as grand, just as thrilling, so far as all that goes, as the other: men worshipped the sun long before they found out that it stood still. Not the most reverent astronomer, with the mathematics of the heavens at his tongue's end, could have had more delight in the wondrous phenomenon of the dawn, than did this simple-minded, unlearned man.

His eyes wandered from the horizon line of slowly increasing light, to the windows of the house, yet dark and still. "Which window is hers? Will she open it when the song begins?" he thought. "Is it on this side of the house? Who can she be? She was not here last year. Saw the saints ever so beautiful a creature!"

At last came the full red ray across the meadow. Alessandro sprang to his feet. In the next second Father Salvierderra flung up his south window, and leaning out, his cowl thrown off, his thin gray locks streaming back, began in a feeble but not unmelodious voice to sing, —

> "O beautiful Queen,
> Princess of Heaven."

Before he had finished the second line, a half-dozen voices had joined in, — the Señora, from her room at the west end of the veranda, beyond the flowers; Felipe, from the adjoining room; Ramona, from hers, the next; and Margarita and other of the maids already astir in the wings of the house.

As the volume of melody swelled, the canaries waked, and the finches and the linnets in the veranda roof. The tiles of this roof were laid on bundles of tule reeds, in which the linnets delighted to build their nests. The roof was alive with them, — scores and scores, nay hundreds, tame as chickens; their tiny shrill twitter was like the tuning of myriads of violins.

> "Singers at dawn
> From the heavens above
> People all regions;
> Gladly we too sing,"

continued the hymn, the birds corroborating the stanza. Then men's voices joined in, — Juan and Luigo, and a dozen more, walking slowly up from the sheepfolds. The hymn was a favorite one, known to all.

> "Come, O sinners,
> Come, and we will sing
> Tender hymns
> To our refuge,"

was the chorus, repeated after each of the five verses of the hymn.

Alessandro also knew the hymn well. His father,
2 Chief Pablo, had been the leader of the choir at the San Luis Rey Mission in the last years of its splendor, and had brought away with him much of the old choir music. Some of the books had been written by his own hand, on parchment. He not only sang well, but was a good player on the violin.

There was not at any of the Missions so fine a band 3
of performers on stringed instruments as at San Luis Rey. Father Peyri was passionately fond of music, and spared no pains in training all of the neophytes under his charge who showed any special talent in that direction. Chief Pablo, after the breaking up of the Mission, had settled at Temecula, with a small band of his Indians, and endeavored, so far as was in his power, to keep up the old religious services. The music in the little chapel of the Temecula Indians was a surprise to all who heard it.

Alessandro had inherited his father's love and talent for music, and knew all the old Mission music by heart. This hymn to the

"Beautiful Queen,
Princess of Heaven,"

was one of his special favorites; and as he heard verse after verse rising, he could not forbear striking in.

At the first notes of this rich new voice, Ramona's voice ceased in surprise; and, throwing up her window, she leaned out, eagerly looking in all directions to see who it could be. Alessandro saw her, and sang no more.

"What could it have been? Did I dream it?" thought Ramona, drew in her head, and began to sing again.

With the next stanza of the chorus, the same rich barytone notes. They seemed to float in under all the rest, and bear them along, as a great wave bears a boat. Ramona had never heard such a voice. Felipe had a good tenor, and she liked to sing with him, or to hear him; but this — this was from another world, this sound. Ramona felt every note of it penetrating her consciousness with a subtle thrill almost like pain. When the hymn ended, she listened eagerly, hoping Father Salvierderra would strike up a second hymn, as he often did; but he did not this morning; there was too much to be done; everybody was in a hurry to be at work: windows shut, doors opened; the sounds of voices from all directions, ordering, questioning, answering, began to be heard. The sun rose and let a flood of work-a-day light on the whole place.

Margarita ran and unlocked the chapel door, putting up a heartfelt thanksgiving to Saint Francis and the Señorita, as she saw the snowy altar-cloth in its place, looking, from that distance at least, as good as new.

The Indians and the shepherds, and laborers of all
sorts, were coming towards the chapel. The Señora, 4
with her best black silk handkerchief bound tight around her forehead, the ends hanging down each side of her face, making her look like an Assyrian priestess, was descending the veranda steps, Felipe at her side; and Father Salvierderra had already entered the chapel before Ramona appeared, or Alessandro stirred from his vantage-post of observation at the willows.

3

Vestiges of the San Luis Rey Mission —by Henry Sandham

4

The Señora, an orginal illustration of the painting by Henry Sandham.

It was not at all uncommon for the ranchos—vast feudal estates that they were—to have their own chapels. —drawing by Henry Sandham.

Old padre's chair at San Luis Rey Mission. Father Antonio Peyri actually existed. He was a kindly padre so beloved by the Indians that when he left the country many tried to detain him, mounting their ponies and galloping the forty-five miles to San Diego where they flung themselves into the bay and swam alongside his ship. Four reached it, and clinging to the side, begged the priest to take them with him. Fearing the men would drown, Peyri consented; they accompanied him to Rome, where one became a priest. —drawing by Henry Sandham

Since any ranchero could acquire virtual slaves at the city jail by helping himself to Indians who'd been picked up for drinking, it's small wonder that occasional rebellions occurred. The surprising part is that there were so few and that when conditions became really bad, they ceased entirely.

One of the most dramatic was among the earliest. It occured at Rancho Jamul east of San Diego. The estate was owned by Pio Pico who'd received the 8,926-acre grant from the governor of California in 1829. It was considered a splended windfall even for those open-handed times.
An imposing hacienda was built, cattle stocked, and before long the rancho was a showplace. Then in 1837, while Pico was away and his mother and three unmarried sisters were staying at the rancho, a servant warned the family that neighboring Indians were massing for attack. The Pico family fled; but their majordomo, Juan Leiva, remained with his family.

It was a tragic mistake. Leiva's son, Jose, and the other *vaqueros* were killed almost immediately by Indians. Juan Leiva, though wounded, was able to stagger to the gun room just in time to see an Indian servant lock the door and run away. He was finally reduced to

7 When Ramona came out from the door she bore in her hands a high silver urn filled with ferns. She had been for many days gathering and hoarding these. They were hard to find, growing only in one place in a rocky cañon, several miles away.

As she stepped from the veranda to the ground, Alessandro walked slowly up the garden-walk, facing her. She met his eyes, and, without knowing why, thought, "That must be the Indian who sang." As
5 she turned to the right and entered the chapel, Alessandro followed her hurriedly, and knelt on the stones close to the chapel door. He would be near when she came out. As he looked in at the door, he saw her glide up the aisle, place the ferns on the reading-desk, and then kneel down by Felipe in front of the altar. Felipe turned towards her, smiling slightly, with a look as of secret intelligence.

"Ah, Señor Felipe has married. She is his wife," thought Alessandro, and a strange pain seized him. He did not analyze it; hardly knew what it meant. He was only twenty-one. He had not thought much about women. He was a distant, cold boy, his own people of the Temecula village said. It had come, they believed, of learning to read, which was always bad. Chief Pablo had not done his son any good by trying to make him like white men. If the Fathers could have stayed, and the life at the Mission have gone on, why, Alessandro could have had work to do for the Fathers, as his father had before him. Pablo
6 had been Father Peyri's right-hand man at the Mission; had kept all the accounts about the cattle; paid the wages; handled thousands of dollars of gold every month. But that was "in the time of the king;" it was very different now. The Americans would not let an Indian do anything but plough and sow and herd cattle. A man need not read and write, to do that.

Even Pablo sometimes doubted whether he had done wisely in teaching Alessandro all he knew himself. Pablo was, for one of his race, wise and far-seeing. He perceived the danger threatening his people on all sides. Father Peyri, before he left the country, had said to him: "Pablo, your people will be driven like sheep to the slaughter, unless you keep them together. Knit firm bonds between them; band them into pueblos; make them work; and above all, keep peace with the whites. It is your only chance."

Most strenuously Pablo had striven to obey Father Peyri's directions. He had set his people the example of constant industry, working steadily in his fields and caring well for his herds. He had built a chapel in his little village, and kept up forms of
7 religious service there. Whenever there were troubles with the whites, or rumors of them, he went from house to house, urging, persuading, commanding his people to keep the peace. At one time when there was an insurrection of some of the Indian tribes farther south, and for a few days it looked as if there would be a general Indian war, he removed

the greater part of his band, men, women, and children driving their flocks and herds with them, to Los Angeles, and camped there for several days, that they might be identified with the whites in case hostilities became serious.

But his labors did not receive the reward that they deserved. With every day that the intercourse between his people and the whites increased, he saw the whites gaining, his people surely losing ground, and his anxieties deepened. The Mexican owner of the Temecula valley, a friend of Father Peyri's, and a good friend also of Pablo's, had returned to
Mexico in disgust with the state of affairs in Califor- 8
nia, and was reported to be lying at the point of death. This man's promise to Pablo, that he and his people should always live in the valley undisturbed, was all the title Pablo had to the village lands. In the days when the promise was given, it was all that was necessary. The lines marking off the Indians' lands were surveyed, and put on the map of the estate. No Mexican proprietor ever broke faith with an Indian family or village thus placed on his lands.

But Pablo had heard rumors, which greatly disquieted him, that such pledges and surveyed lines as these were coming to be held as of no value, not binding on purchasers of grants. He was intelligent enough to see that if this were so, he and his people were ruined. All these perplexities and fears he confided to Alessandro; long anxious hours the father and son spent together, walking back and forth in the village, or sitting in front of their little adobe house, discussing what could be done. There was always the same ending to the discussion, — a long sigh, and, "We must wait, we can do nothing."

No wonder Alessandro seemed, to the more ignorant and thoughtless young men and women of his village, a cold and distant lad. He was made old before his time. He was carrying in his heart burdens of which they knew nothing. So long as the wheat-fields came up well, and there was no drought, and the horses and sheep had good pasture, in plenty, on the hills, the Temecula people could be merry, go day by day to their easy work, play games at sunset, and sleep sound all night. But Alessandro and his father looked beyond. And this was the one great reason why Alessandro had not yet thought about women, in way of love; this, and also the fact that even the little education he had received was sufficient to raise a slight barrier, of which he was unconsciously aware, between him and the maidens of the village. If a quick, warm fancy for any one of them ever stirred in his veins, he found himself soon, he knew not how, cured of it. For a dance, or a game, or a friendly chat, for the trips into the mountains after acorns, or to the marshes for grasses and reeds, he was their good comrade, and they were his; but never had the desire to take one of them for his wife, entered into Alessandro's mind. The vista of the future, for him, was filled full by thoughts which left no room for love's dreaming;

defending his family by flinging coals from the fireplace at the advancing Indians.

The courageous stand was useless. Leiva was slaughtered; his wife, Doña Maria, and their young son were stripped and then abandoned in the wilderness. The proud Pico estate was set afire, the house totally destroyed. Doña Maria watched helplessly as her two teenage daughters were carrried away by the Indians. She and her small son then walked the twenty-one miles to San Diego barefoot and naked.

For three months a small, but determined expedition searched for the girls. Once they could be seen in the distance, bodies smeared with white paint, hair cut Indian fashion. Many were killed in the battle that followed, but the surviving Indians dragged the screaming girls back into the hills.

When the contingent finally reluctantly returned to San Diego, Doña Maria was dead. The violent tragedy had proved too much for her. Though a large reward was offered for the recovery of the hostages, they were never seen again.

8 Small wonder the Californios were disgusted; everything was stacked against them. Spanish and Mexican land grants that had been in the family for years were arbitrarily held in doubt until proved valid. Establishing claims took time—seventeen years to clear title an average. In the past, ready cash had never been important to the Californios; wealth was measured in cattle, land, and ranching experience. Now vast tracts of land were sacrificed to pay legal fees, but these were the lucky rancheros. Many of the 800 holders of pre-1846 land grants were ruined entirely.

Illustration by Henry Sandham. Circa 1900.

An Indian woman like many of Alessandro's acquaintance.
—illustraion by Hnery Sandham.

one purpose and one fear filled it, — the purpose to be his father's worthy successor, for Pablo was old now, and very feeble; the fear, that exile and ruin were in store for them all.

It was of these things he had been thinking as he walked alone, in advance of his men, on the previous night, when he first saw Ramona kneeling at the brook. Between that moment and the present, it seemed to Alessandro that some strange miracle must have happened to him. The purposes and the fears had alike gone. A face replaced them; a vague wonder, pain, joy, he knew not what, filled him so to overflowing that he was bewildered. If he had been what the world calls a civilized man, he would have known instantly, and would have been capable of weighing, analyzing, and reflecting on his sensations at leisure. But he was not a civilized man; he had to bring to bear on his present situation only simple, primitive, uneducated instincts and impulses. If Ramona had been a maiden of his own people or
9 race, he would have drawn near to her as quickly as iron to the magnet. But now, if he had gone so far as to even think of her in such a way, she would
9 have been, to his view, as far removed from him as was the morning star beneath whose radiance he had that morning watched, hoping for sight of her at her window. He did not, however, go so far as to thus think of her. Even that would have been impossible. He only knelt on the stones outside the chapel door, mechanically repeating the prayers with the rest, waiting for her to reappear. He had no doubt, now, that she was Señor Felipe's wife; all the same he wished to kneel there till she came out, that he might see her face again. His vista of purpose, fear, hope, had narrowed now down to that, — just one more sight of her. Ever so civilized, he could hardly have worshipped a woman better. The mass seemed to him endlessly long. Until near the last, he forgot to sing; then, in the closing of the final hymn, he suddenly remembered, and the clear deep-toned voice pealed out, as before, like the undertone of a great sea-wave, sweeping along.

Ramona heard the first note, and felt again the same thrill. She was as much a musician born as Alessandro himself. As she rose from her knees, she whispered to Felipe: "Felipe, do find out which one of the Indians it is has that superb voice. I never heard anything like it."

"Oh, that is Alessandro," replied Felipe, "old Pablo's son. He is a splendid fellow. Don't you recollect his singing two years ago?"

"I was not here," replied Ramona; "you forget."

"Ah, yes, so you were away; I had forgotten," said Felipe. "Well, he was here. They made him captain of the shearing-band, though he was only twenty, and he managed the men splendidly. They saved nearly all their money to carry home, and I never knew them do such a thing before. Father Salvierderra was here, which might have had something to do with it; but I think it was quite as much

Alessandro. He plays the violin beautifully. I hope he has brought it along. He plays the old San Luis Rey music. His father was band-master there."

Ramona's eyes kindled with pleasure. "Does your mother like it, to have him play?" she asked.

Felipe nodded. "We'll have him up on the veranda to-night," he said.

While this whispered colloquy was going on, the chapel had emptied, the Indians and Mexicans all hurrying out to set about the day's work. Alessandro lingered at the doorway as long as he dared, till he was sharply called by Juan Canito, looking back: "What are you gaping at there, you Alessandro? Hurry, now, and get your men to work. After waiting till near midsummer for this shearing, we'll make as quick work of it as we can. Have you got your best shearers here?"

"Ay, that I have," answered Alessandro; "not a man of them but can shear his hundred in a day. There is not such a band as ours in all San Diego County; and we don't turn out the sheep all bleeding, either; you'll see scarce a scratch on their sides."

"Humph!" retorted Juan Can. "'T is a poor shearer, indeed, that draws blood to speak of. I've sheared many a thousand sheep in my day, and never a red stain on the shears. But the Mexicans have always been famed for good shearers."

Juan's invidious emphasis on the word "Mexicans" did not escape Alessandro. "And we Indians also," he answered good-naturedly, betraying no annoyance; "but as for these Americans, I saw one at work the other day, that man Lomax, who has settled near Temecula, and upon my faith, Juan Can, I thought it was a slaughter-pen, and not a shearing. The poor beasts limped off with the blood running."

Juan did not see his way clear at the moment to any fitting rejoinder to this easy assumption, on Alessandro's part, of the equal superiority of Indians and Mexicans in the sheep-shearing art; so, much vexed, with another "Humph!" he walked away; walked away so fast, that he lost the sight of a smile on Alessandro's face, which would have vexed him still farther.

At the sheep-shearing sheds and pens all was stir 10
and bustle. The shearing shed was a huge caricature of a summer-house, — a long, narrow structure, sixty feet long by twenty or thirty wide, all roof and pillars; no walls; the supports, slender rough posts, as far apart as was safe, for the upholding the roof, which was of rough planks loosely laid from beam to beam. On three sides of this were the sheep-pens filled with sheep and lambs.

A few rods away stood the booths in which the shearers' food was to be cooked and the shearers fed. These were mere temporary affairs, roofed only by willow boughs with the leaves left on. Near these, the Indians had already arranged their camp; a hut or two of green boughs had been built, but for the most part they would sleep rolled up in their

10

Illustration by Henry Sandham.

Helen Hunt Jackson, upon visiting a shearing at a California sheep ranch, described it as "a grand thing." Three thousand sheep had been sheared the day before and another twenty-five hundred waited to be shorn. The Indians were famous for skill at shearing; and, organized into shearing bands with captains, went from ranch to ranch in the shearing season. Reporting in an article for *Century*, Jackson recalled, "There were a half dozen Indians lying on the ground outside the shearing shed looking on wistfully. The Mexicans had crowded them out that day, and they would have no chance to work."

She found the workers an agreeable lot. "As soon as the shearers perceived their pictures were being drawn by the artist in our party, they were all agog; by twos and threes they left their work and crowded around the carriage, peering, commenting, asking to have their portraits taken. One tattered fellow, whose shoeless feet were tied up in bits of gunny-bags, was distressed because his trousers were too short. 'Would the gentleman kindly make them in the drawing a little farther down his legs. It was an accident that they were too short.' All were ready to pose and stand, even in the most difficult attitudes, as long as was required. Those who had done so asked, like children, if their names could be put in the book, so I wrote them down: 'Juan Canero, Juan Rivera, Felipe Ybara, Jose Jesus Lopez, and Domingo Garcia.' "

Jackson noted that the space they filled "was a little thing to give, and there is satisfaction in the good faith of printing them, though the shearers will most assuredly never know it."

—Illustration by Henry Sandham.

11 Bagging wool for transportation. Jackson went on to research the California sheep industry for her article, reporting that the wool crop in 1881 was 21,500 tons. The cost of keeping a sheep averaged $1.25 a year while its wool sold for $1.50. Additionally, for each hundred sheep there would be forty-five lambs each worth 75 cents.

She was struck by the "pitious" faces of the sheep being shorn. "Not a struggle, not a bleat, the whole of their unwillingness and terror being written in their up turned eyes. 'As a sheep before her shearers is dumb,' will always have a new significance." It's obvious by the colorful treatment the sheep shearing scene receives in *Ramona* that the day's activities had a profound effect upon the author. 12

blankets, on the ground. There was a brisk wind, and the gay-colored wings of the windmill blew furiously round and round, pumping out into the tank below a stream of water so swift and strong, that as the men crowded around, wetting and sharpening their knives, they got well spattered, and had much merriment, pushing and elbowing each other into the spray.

A high four-posted frame stood close to the shed; in this, swung from the four corners, hung one of the great sacking bags in which the fleeces were to be packed. A big pile of these bags lay on the ground at foot of the posts. Juan Can eyed them with a chuckle. "We 'll fill more than those before night, Señor Felipe," he said. He was in his element, Juan Can, at shearing times. Then came his reward for the somewhat monotonous and stupid year's work.
11 The world held no better feast for his eyes than the sight of a long row of big bales of fleece, tied, stamped with the Moreno brand, ready to be drawn away to the mills. "Now, there is something substantial," he thought; "no chance of wool going amiss in market!"

If a year's crop were good, Juan's happiness was assured for the next six months. If it proved poor, he turned devout immediately, and spent the next six months calling on the saints for better luck, and redoubling his exertions with the sheep.

On one of the posts of the shed short projecting slats were nailed, like half-rounds of a ladder. Lightly as a rope-walker Felipe ran up these, to the roof, and took his stand there, ready to take the fleeces and pack them in the bag as fast as they should be tossed up from below. Luigo, with a big leathern wallet fastened in front of him, filled with five-cent pieces, took his stand in the centre of the shed. The thirty shearers, running into the nearest pen, dragged each his sheep into the shed, in a
12 twinkling of an eye had the creature between his knees, helpless, immovable, and the sharp sound of the shears set in. The sheep-shearing had begun. No rest now. Not a second's silence from the bleating, baa-ing, opening and shutting, clicking, sharpening of shears, flying of fleeces through the air to the roof, pressing and stamping them down in the bales; not a second's intermission, except the hour of rest at noon, from sunrise till sunset, till the whole eight thousand of the Señora Moreno's sheep were shorn. It was a dramatic spectacle. As soon as a sheep was shorn, the shearer ran with the fleece in his hand to Luigo, threw it down on a table, received his five-cent piece, dropped it in his pocket, ran to the pen, dragged out another sheep, and in less than five minutes was back again with a second fleece. The shorn sheep, released, bounded off into another pen, where, light in the head no doubt from being three to five pounds lighter on their legs, they trotted round bewilderedly for a moment, then flung up their heels and capered for joy.

It was warm work. The dust from the fleeces and

the trampling feet filled the air. As the sun rose higher in the sky the sweat poured off the men's faces; and Felipe, standing without shelter on the roof, found out very soon that he had by no means yet got back his full strength since the fever. Long before noon, except for sheer pride, and for the recollection of Juan Canito's speech, he would have come down and yielded his place to the old man. But he was resolved not to give up, and he worked on, though his face was purple and his head throbbing. After the bag of fleeces is half full, the packer stands in it, jumping with his full weight on the wool, as he throws in the fleeces, to compress them as much as possible. When Felipe began to do this, he found that he had indeed overrated his strength. As the first cloud of the sickening dust came up, enveloping his head, choking his breath, he turned suddenly dizzy, and calling faintly, "Juan, I am ill," sank helpless down in the wool. He had fainted. At Juan Canito's scream of dismay, a great hubbub and outcry arose; all saw instantly what had happened. Felipe's head was hanging limp over the edge of the bag, Juan in vain endeavoring to get sufficient foothold by his side to lift him. One after another the men rushed up the ladder, until they were all standing, a helpless, excited crowd, on the roof, one proposing one thing, one another. Only Luigo had had the presence of mind to run to the house for help. The Señora was away from home. She had gone with Father Salvierderra to a friend's house, a half-day's journey off. But Ramona was there. Snatching all she could think of in way of restoratives, she came flying back with Luigo, followed by every servant of the establishment, all talking, groaning, gesticulating, suggesting, wringing their hands, — as disheartening a Babel as ever made bad matters worse.

Reaching the shed, Ramona looked up to the roof bewildered. "Where is he?" she cried. The next instant she saw his head, held in Juan Canito's arms, just above the edge of the wool-bag. She groaned, "Oh, how will he ever be lifted out!"

"I will lift him, Señora," cried Alessandro, coming to the front. "I am very strong. Do not be afraid; I will bring him safe down." And swinging himself down the ladder, he ran swiftly to the camp, and returned, bringing in his hands blankets. Springing quickly to the roof again, he knotted the blankets firmly together, and tying them at the middle around his waist, threw the ends to his men, telling them to hold him firm. He spoke in the Indian tongue as he was hurriedly doing this, and Ramona did not at first understand his plan. But when she saw the Indians move a little back from the edge of the roof, holding the blankets firm grasped, while Alessandro stepped out on one of the narrow cross-beams from which the bag swung, she saw what he meant to do. She held her breath. Felipe was a slender man; Alessandro was much heavier, and many inches taller. Still, could any man carry such a burden safely on that narrow beam! Ramona looked away, and shut her eyes, through the silence which followed. It was only a few moments; but it seemed an eternity before a glad murmur of voices told her that it was done, and looking up, she saw Felipe lying on the roof, unconscious, his face white, his eyes shut. At this sight, all the servants broke out afresh, weeping and wailing, "He is dead! He is dead!"

Ramona stood motionless, her eyes fixed on Felipe's face. She, too, believed him dead; but her thought was of the Señora.

"He is not dead," cried Juan Canito, who had thrust his hand under Felipe's shirt. "He is not dead. It is only a faint."

At this the first tears rolled down Ramona's face. She looked piteously at the ladder up and down which she had seen Alessandro run as if it were an easy indoors staircase. "If I could only get up there!" she said, looking from one to another. "I think I can;" and she put one foot on the lower round.

"Holy Virgin!" cried Juan Can, seeing her movement. "Señorita! Señorita! do not attempt it. It is not too easy for a man. You will break your neck. He is fast coming to his senses."

Alessandro caught the words. Spite of all the confusion and terror of the scene, his heart heard the word, "Señorita." Ramona was not the wife of Felipe, or of any man. Yet Alessandro recollected that he had addressed her as Señora, and she did not seem surprised. Coming to the front of the group he said, bending forward, "Señorita!" There must have been something in the tone which made Ramona start. The simple word could not have done it. "Señorita," said Alessandro, "it will be nothing to bring Señor Felipe down the ladder. He is, in my arms, no more than one of the lambs yonder. I will bring him down as soon as he is recovered. He is better here till then. He will very soon be himself again. It was only the heat." Seeing that the expression of anxious distress did not grow less on Ramona's face, he continued, in a tone still more earnest, "Will not the Señorita trust me to bring him safe down?"

Ramona smiled faintly through her tears. "Yes," she said, "I will trust you. You are Alessandro, are you not?"

"Yes, Señorita," he answered, greatly surprised, "I am Alessandro."

Chapter VI

A BAD beginning did not make a good ending of the Señora Moreno's sheep-shearing this year. One as superstitiously prejudiced against Roman Catholic rule as she was in favor of it, would have found, in the way things fell out, ample reason for a belief that the Señora was being punished for having let all the affairs of her place come to a stand-still, to await the coming of an old monk. But the pious Señora, looking at the other side of the shield, was filled with gratitude that, since all this ill luck was to befall her, she had the good Father Salvierderra at her side to give her comfort and counsel.

It was not yet quite noon of the first day, when 1
Felipe fainted and fell in the wool; and it was only a little past noon of the third, when Juan Canito, who, not without some secret exultation, had taken Señor Felipe's place at the packing, fell from the cross-beam to the ground, and broke his right leg, — a bad break near the knee; and Juan Canito's bones were much too old for fresh knitting. He would never again be able to do more than hobble about on crutches, dragging along the useless leg. It was a cruel blow to the old man. He could not be resigned to it. He lost faith in his saints, and privately indulged in blasphemous beratings and reproaches of them, which would have filled the Señora with terror, had she known that such blasphemies were being committed under her roof.

"As many times as I have crossed that plank, in my day!" cried Juan; "only the fiends themselves could have made me trip; and there was that whole box of candles I paid for with my own money last month, and burned to Saint Francis in the chapel for this very sheep-shearing! He may sit in the dark, for all me, to the end of time! He is no saint at all! What are they for, if not to keep us from harm when we pray to them? I'll pray no more. I believe the Americans are right, who laugh at us." From morning till night, and nearly from night till morning, for the leg ached so he slept little, poor Juan groaned and grumbled and swore, and swore and grumbled and groaned. Taking care of him was enough, Margarita said, to wear out the patience of the Madonna herself. There was no pleasing him, whatever you did, and his tongue was never still a minute. For her part, she believed that it must be as he said, that the fiends had pushed him off the plank, and that the saints had had their reasons for leaving him to his fate. A coldness and suspicion gradually grew up in the minds of all the servants towards him. His own reckless language, combined with Margarita's reports, gave the superstitious fair ground for believing that something had gone mysteriously wrong, and that the Devil was in a fair way to get his soul, which was very hard for the old man, in addition to all the rest he had to bear. The only alleviation he had for his torments, was in having his fellow-servants, men and women, drop in, sit by his pallet, and chat with him, telling him all that was going on; and when by degrees they dropped off, coming more and more seldom, and one by one leaving off coming altogether, it was the one drop that overflowed his cup of misery; and he turned his face to the wall, left off grumbling, and spoke only when he must.

This phase frightened Margarita even more than the first. Now, she thought, surely the dumb terror and remorse of one who belongs to the Devil had seized him, and her hands trembled as she went through the needful ministrations for him each day. Three months, at least, the doctor, who had come from Ventura to set the leg, had said he must lie still in bed and be thus tended. "Three months!" sighed Margarita. "If I be not dead or gone crazy myself before the end of that be come!"

The Señora was too busy with Felipe to pay attention or to give thought to Juan. Felipe's fainting had been the symptom and beginning of a fierce relapse of the fever, and he was lying in his bed, tossing and raving in delirium, always about the wool.

"Throw them faster, faster! That's a good fleece; five pounds more; a round ton in those bales. Juan! Alessandro! Capitan! — Jesus, how this sun burns my head!"

Several times he had called "Alessandro" so earnestly, that Father Salvierderra advised bringing Alessandro into the room, to see if by any chance there might have been something in his mind that he wished to say to him. But when Alessandro stood by the bedside, Felipe gazed at him vacantly, as he did at all the others, still repeating, however, "Alessandro! Alessandro!"

"I think perhaps he wants Alessandro to play on his violin," sobbed out Ramona. "He was telling me how beautifully Alessandro played, and said he would have him up on the veranda in the evening to play to us."

"We might try it," said Father Salvierderra. "Have you your violin here, Alessandro?"

"Alas, no, Father," replied Alessandro, "I did not bring it."

"Perhaps it would do him good if you were to sing, then," said Ramona. "He was speaking of your voice also."

"Oh, try, try!" said the Señora, turning to Alessandro. "Sing something low and soft."

Alessandro walked from the bed to the open window, and after thinking for a moment, began a slow strain from one of the masses.

At the first note, Felipe became suddenly quiet, evidently listening. An expression of pleasure spread over his feverish face. He turned his head to one side, put his hand under his cheek and closed his eyes. The three watching him looked at each other in astonishment.

"It is a miracle," said Father Salvierderra. "He will sleep."

"It was what he wanted!" whispered Ramona.

The Señora spoke not, but buried her face in the bedclothes for a second; then lifting it, she gazed at Alessandro as if she were praying to a saint. He, too, saw the change in Felipe, and sang lower and lower, till the notes sounded as if they came from afar; lower and lower, slower; finally they ceased, as if they died away lost in distance. As they ceased, Felipe opened his eyes.

"Oh, go on, go on!" the Señora implored in a whisper shrill with anxiety. "Do not stop!"

Alessandro repeated the strain, slow, solemn; his voice trembled; the air in the room seemed stifling, spite of the open windows; he felt something like terror, as he saw Felipe evidently sinking to sleep by reason of the notes of his voice. There had been nothing in Alessandro's healthy outdoor experience to enable him to understand such a phenomenon. Felipe breathed more and more slowly, softly, regularly; soon he was in a deep sleep. The singing stopped; Felipe did not stir.

"Can I go?" whispered Alessandro.

"No, no!" replied the Señora, impatiently. "He may wake any minute."

Alessandro looked troubled, but bowed his head submissively, and remained standing by the window. Father Salvierderra was kneeling on one side of the bed, the Señora at the other, Ramona at the foot,—all praying; the silence was so great that the slight sounds of the rosary beads slipping against each other seemed loud. In a niche in the wall, at the head of the bed, stood a statue of the Madonna, on the other side a picture of Santa Barbara. Candles were burning before each. The long wicks smouldered and died down, sputtering, then flared up again as the ends fell into the melted wax. The Señora's eyes were fixed on the Madonna. The Father's were closed. Ramona gazed at Felipe with tears streaming down her face as she mechanically told her beads.

"She is his betrothed, no doubt," thought Alessandro. "The saints will not let him die;" and Alessandro also prayed. But the oppression of the scene was too much for him. Laying his hand on

1

Juan Canito (Watson Gilmore) and Pablo (Robert Martinez) from *The Ramona Pageant* at Hemet 1986.
—Courtesy of the Ramona Pageant Assoc., Inc.

The authors clever plot twist presaged a tragedy of her own. Two months after the completion of *Ramona,* Jackson caught the heel of her slipper in the carpet and fell headlong the length of her stairway. The fall resulted in a compound fracture. Her left leg smashed, she was unable to move for weeks. Emily Dickinson, Jackson's lifelong friend, responded to a cherry note: "He who is slain and smiles, steals something from the Sword, but you have stolen the Sword itself, which is far better ... I shall watch your passage from Crutch to Cane with Jealous affection. From there to wings is but a stride ..."

the low window-sill, he vaulted over it, saying to Ramona, who turned her head at the sound, "I will not go away, Señorita. I will be close under the window, if he awakes."

Once in the open air, he drew a long breath, and gazed bewilderedly about him, like one just recovering consciousness after a faint. Then he threw himself on the ground under the window, and lay looking up into the sky. Capitan came up, and with a low whine stretched himself out at full length by his side. The dog knew as well as any other one of the house that danger and anguish were there.

One hour passed, two, three; still no sound from Felipe's room. Alessandro rose, and looked in at the window. The Father and the Señora had not changed their attitudes; their lips were yet moving in prayer. But Ramona had yielded to her fatigue; slipped from her knees into a sitting posture, with her head leaning against the post of the bedstead, and fallen asleep. Her face was swollen and discolored by weeping, and heavy circles under her eyes told how tired she was. For three days and nights she had scarcely rested, so constant were the demands on her. Between Felipe's illness and Juan Can's, there was not a moment without something to be done, or some perplexing question to be settled, and above all, and through all, the terrible sorrow. Ramona was broken down with grief at the thought of Felipe's death. She had never known till she saw him lying there delirious, and as she in her inexperience thought, dying, how her whole life was entwined with his. But now, at the very thought of what it would be to live without him, her heart sickened. "When he is buried, I will ask Father Salvierderra to take me away. I never can live here alone," she said to herself, never for a moment perceiving that the word "alone" was a strange one to have come into her mind in the connection. The thought of the Señora did not enter into her imaginations of the future which so smote her with terror. In the Señora's presence, Ramona always felt herself alone.

Alessandro stood at the window, his arms folded, leaning on the sill, his eyes fixed on Ramona's face and form. To any other than a lover's eyes she had not looked beautiful now; but to Alessandro she looked more beautiful than the picture of Santa Barbara on the wall beyond. With a lover's instinct he knew the thoughts which had written such lines on her face in the last three days. "It will kill her if he dies," he thought, "if these three days have made her look like that." And Alessandro threw himself on the ground again, his face down. He did not know whether it were an hour or a day that he had lain there, when he heard Father Salvierderra's voice speaking his name. He sprang up, to see the old monk standing in the window, tears running down his cheeks. "God be praised," he said, "the Señor Felipe will get well. A sweat has broken out on his skin; he still sleeps, but when he wakes he will be in his right mind. The strength of the fever is broken. But, Alessandro, we know not how to spare you. Can you not let the men go without you, and remain here? The Señora would like to have you remain in Juan Can's place till he is about. She will give you the same wages he had. Would it not be a good thing for you, Alessandro? You cannot be sure of earning so much as that for the next three months, can you?"

While the Father was speaking, a tumult had been going on in Alessandro's breast. He did not know by name any of the impulses which were warring there, tearing him in twain, as it were, by their pulling in opposite directions; one saying "Stay!" and the other saying "Go!" He would not have known what any one meant, who had said to him, "It is danger to stay; it is safety to fly." All the same, he felt as if he could do neither.

"There is another shearing yet, Father," he began, "at the Ortega's ranch. I had promised to go to them as soon as I had finished here, and they have been wroth enough with us for the delay already. It will not do to break the promise, Father."

Father Salvierderra's face fell. "No, my son, certainly not," he said; "but could no one else take your place with the band?"

Hearing these words, Ramona came to the window, and leaning out, whispered, "Are you talking about Alessandro's staying? Let me come and talk to him. He must not go." And running swiftly through the hall, across the veranda, and down the steps, she stood by Alessandro's side in a moment. Looking up in his face pleadingly, she said: "We can't let you go, Alessandro. The Señora will pay wages to some other to go in your place with the shearers. We want you to stay here in Juan Can's place till he is well. Don't say you can't stay! Felipe may need you to sing again, and what would we do then? Can't you stay?"

"Yes, I can stay, Señorita," answered Alessandro, gravely. "I will stay so long as you need me."

"Oh, thank you, Alessandro!" Ramona cried. "You are good, to stay. The Señora will see that it is no loss to you;" and she flew back to the house.

"It is not for the wages, Señorita," Alessandro began; but Ramona was gone. She did not hear him, and he turned away with a sense of humiliation. "I don't want the Señorita to think that it was the money kept me," he said, turning to Father Salvierderra. "I would not leave the band for money; it is to help, because they are in trouble, Father."

"Yes, yes, son. I understand that," replied the monk, who had known Alessandro since he was a little fellow playing in the corridors of San Luis Rey, the pet of all the Brothers there. "That is quite right of you, and the Señora will not be insensible of it. It is not for such things that money can pay. They are indeed in great trouble now, and only the two women in the house; and I must soon be going on my way North again."

"Is it sure that Señor Felipe will get well?" asked Alessandro.

"I think so," replied Father Salvierderra. "These relapses are always worse than the first attack; but I have never known one to die, after he had the natural sweat to break from the skin, and got good sleep. I doubt not he will be in his bed, though, for many days, and there will be much to be seen to. It was an ill luck to have Juan Can laid up, too, just at this time. I must go and see him; I hear he is in most rebellious frame of mind, and blasphemes impiously."

"That does he!" said Alessandro. "He swears the saints gave him over to the fiends to push him off the plank, and he 'll have none of them from this out! I told him to beware, or they might bring him to worse things yet if he did not mend his speech of them."

Sighing deeply as they walked along, the monk said: "It is but a sign of the times. Blasphemers are on the highway. The people are being corrupted. Keeps your father the worship in the chapel still, and does a priest come often to the village?"

"Only twice a year," replied Alessandro; "and sometimes for a funeral, if there is money enough to pay for the mass. But my father has the chapel open, and each Sunday we sing what we know of the mass; and the people are often there praying."

"Ay, ay! Ever for money!" groaned Father Salvierderra, not heeding the latter part of the sentence. "Ever for money! It is a shame. But that it were sure to be held as a trespass, I would go myself to Temecula once in three months; but I may not. The priests do not love our order."

"Oh, if you could, Father," exclaimed Alessandro, "it would make my father very glad! He speaks often to me of the difference he sees between the words of the Church now and in the days of the Mission. He is very sad, Father, and in great fear about our village. They say the Americans, when they buy the Mexicans' lands, drive the Indians away as if they were dogs; they say we have no right to our lands. Do you think that can be so, Father, when we have always lived on them, and the owners promised them to us forever?"

Father Salvierderra was silent a long time before replying, and Alessandro watched his face anxiously. He seemed to be hesitating for words to convey his meaning. At last he said: "Got your father any notice, at any time since the Americans took the country,—notice to appear before a court, or anything about a title to the land?"

"No, Father," replied Alessandro.

"There has to be some such paper, as I understand their laws," continued the monk; "some notice, before any steps can be taken to remove Indians from an estate. It must be done according to the law, in

Dorise Schukow appeared as Ramona in the first Hemet production in 1923 and returned to perform the lead for the next seven years.
—Courtesy of the Ramona Pageant Assoc., Inc.

The Indian village of Temecula was located on 2
ancestral land belonging to what had once been the San Luis Rey Mission in the north east corner of San Diego County. The claim was a clear one based on a protective clause in an early Mexican land grant deeding the area back to the Indians. In 1852 the United States government conceded the grant in its Treaty of Peace and Freedom. The land should have been inviolate.

 3

San Luis Rey. —Illustration by Henry Sandham.

the courts. If you have had no such notice, you are not in danger."

"But, Father," persisted Alessandro, "how could there be a law to take away from us the land which the Señor Valdez gave us forever?"

"Gave he to you any paper, any writing to show it?"

"No, no paper; but it is marked in red lines on the map. It was marked off by José Ramirez, of Los Angeles, when they marked all the boundaries of Señor Valdez's estate. They had many instruments of brass and wood to measure with, and a long chain, very heavy, which I helped them carry. I myself saw it marked on the map. They all slept in
my father's house, — Señor Valdez, and Ramirez, and
2 the man who made the measures. He hired one of
our men to carry his instruments, and I went to help, for I wished to see how it was done; but I could understand nothing, and José told me a man must study many years to learn the way of it. It seemed to me our way, by the stones, was much better. But I know it is all marked on the map, for it was with a red line; and my father understood it and José Ramirez and Señor Valdez both pointed to it with their finger, and they said, 'All this here is your land, Pablo, always.' I do not think my father need fear, do you?"

"I hope not," replied Father Salvierderra, cautiously; "but since the way that all the lands of the Missions have been taken away, I have small faith in the honesty of the Americans. I think they will take all that they can. The Church has suffered terrible loss at their hands."

"That is what my father says," replied Alessandro.
3 "He says, 'Look at San Luis Rey! Nothing but the
garden and orchard left, of all their vast lands where they used to pasture thirty thousand sheep. If the Church and the Fathers could not keep their lands, what can we Indians do?' That is what my father says."

"True, true!" said the monk, as he turned into the door of the room where Juan Can lay on his narrow bed, longing yet fearing to see Father Salvierderra's face coming in. "We are all alike helpless in their hands, Alessandro. They possess the country, and can make what laws they please. We can only say, 'God's will be done;'" and he crossed himself devoutly, repeating the words twice.

Alessandro did the same, and with a truly devout spirit, for he was full of veneration for the Fathers and their teachings; but as he walked on towards the shearing-shed he thought: "Then, again, how can it be God's will that wrong be done? It cannot be God's will that one man should steal from another all he has. That would make God no better than a thief, it looks to me. But how can it happen, if it is
not God's will?"

4 It does not need that one be educated, to see the
logic in this formula. Generations of the oppressed and despoiled, before Alessandro, had grappled with the problem in one shape or another.

At the shearing-shed, Alessandro found his men in confusion and ill-humor. The shearing had been over and done by ten in the morning, and why were they not on their way to the Ortega's? Waiting all day, — it was now near sunset, — with nothing to do, and still worse with not much of anything to eat, had made them all cross; and no wonder. The economical Juan Can, finding that the work would be done by ten, and supposing they would be off before noon, had ordered only two sheep killed for them the day before, and the mutton was all gone, and old Marda, getting her cue from Juan, had cooked no more *frijoles* than the family needed themselves; so the poor shearers had indeed had a sorry day of it, in no wise alleviated either by the reports brought from time to time that their captain was lying on the ground, face down, under Señor Felipe's window, and must not be spoken to.

It was not a propitious moment for Alessandro to make the announcement of his purpose to leave the band; but he made a clean breast of it in few words, and diplomatically diverted all resentment from himself by setting them immediately to voting for a new captain to take his place for the remainder of the season.

"Very well!" they said hotly; "captain for this year, captain for next, too!" It was n't so easy to step out and in again of the captaincy of the shearers!

"All right," said Alessandro; "please yourselves! It is all the same to me. But here I am going to stay for the present. Father Salvierderra wishes it."

"Oh, if the Father wishes it, that is different!" "Ah, that alters the case!" "Alessandro is right!" came up in confused murmur from the appeased crowd. They were all good Catholics, every one of the Temecula men, and would never think of going against the Father's orders. But when they understood that Alessandro's intention was to remain until Juan Canito's leg should be well enough for him to go about again, fresh grumblings began. That would not do. It would be all summer. Alessandro must be at home for the Saint Juan's Day fête, in midsummer, — no doing anything without Alessandro then. What was he thinking of? Not of the midsummer fête, that was certain, when he promised to stay as long as the Señorita Ramona should need him. Alessandro had remembered nothing except the Señorita's voice, while she was speaking to him. If he had had a hundred engagements for the summer, he would have forgotten them all. Now that he was reminded of the midsummer fête, it must be confessed he was for a moment dismayed at the recollection; for that was a time when, as he well knew, his father could not do without his help. There were sometimes a thousand Indians at this fête, and disorderly whites took advantage of the occasion to sell whiskey and encourage all sorts of license and disturbance. Yes, Alessandro's clear path of duty lay at Temecula when that fête came off. That was certain.

Church and graveyard of San Luis Rey.
—Illustration by Henry Snadham. Circa 1900.

4 This was a true account provided by an actual participant in the incident, Don Antonio Franco Coronel. Early in 1884, Jackson wrote her friend: "I am going to write a novel, in which will be set forth some Indian experiences in a way to move people's hearts. People will read a novel when they will not read serious books. The scenes of the novel will be in Southern California, and I shall introduce enough of Mexicans and Americans to give it variety. The thing I want most, in the way of help, from you, is this: I would like an account, written in as much detail as you remember of the time when you, dear Mr. Coronel, went to Temecula and marked off the boundaries of the Indians' land there. How many Indians were living there then? What crops had they? Had they a chapel? etc.. Was Pablos Assis, their chief, alive? I would like to know his whole history, life, death, and all, minutely. The Temecula ejectment will be one of the episodes in my story, and any and every detail in connection with it will be of value to me."

"I will manage to be at home then," he said. "If I am not through here by that time, I will at least come for the fête. That you may depend on."

The voting for the new captain did not take long. There was, in fact, but one man in the band fit for the office. That was Fernando, the only old man in the band; all the rest were young men under thirty, or boys. Fernando had been captain for several years, but had himself begged, two years ago, that the band would elect Alessandro in his place. He was getting old, and he did not like to have to sit up and walk about the first half of every night, to see that the shearers were not gambling away all their money at cards; he preferred to roll himself up in his blanket at sunset and sleep till dawn the next morning. But just for these few remaining weeks he had no objection to taking the office again. And Alessandro was right, entirely right, in remaining; they ought all to see that, Fernando said; and his word had great weight with the men.

The Señora Moreno, he reminded them, had always been a good friend of theirs, and had said that so long as she had sheep to shear, the Temecula shearers should do it; and it would be very ungrateful now if they did not do all they could to help her in her need.

The blankets were rolled up, the saddles collected, the ponies caught and driven up to the shed, when Ramona and Margarita were seen coming at full speed from the house.

"Alessandro! Alessandro!" cried Ramona, out of breath, "I have only just now heard that the men have had no dinner to-day. I am ashamed; but you know it would not have happened except for the sickness in the house. Everybody thought they were going away this morning. Now they must have a good supper before they go. It is already cooking. Tell them to wait."

Those of the men who understood the Spanish language, in which Ramona spoke, translated it to those who did not, and there was a cordial outburst of thanks to the Señorita from all lips. All were only too ready to wait for the supper. Their haste to begin on the Ortega sheep-shearing had suddenly faded from their minds. Only Alessandro hesitated.

"It is a good six hours' ride to Ortega's," he said to the men. "You 'll be late in, if you do not start now."

"Supper will be ready in an hour," said Ramona. "Please let them stay; one hour can't make any difference."

Alessandro smiled. "It will take nearer two, Señorita, before they are off," he said; "but it shall be as you wish, and many thanks to you, Señorita, for thinking of it."

"Oh, I did not think of it myself," said Ramona. "It was Margarita, here, who came and told me. She knew we would be ashamed to have the shearers go away hungry. I am afraid they are very hungry indeed," she added ruefully. "It must be dreadful to go a whole day without anything to eat; they had their breakfast soon after sunrise, did they not?"

"Yes, Señorita," answered Alessandro, "but that is not long; one can do without food very well for one day. I often do."

"Often!" exclaimed Ramona; "but why should you do that?" Then suddenly bethinking herself, she said in her heart, "Oh, what a thoughtless question! Can it be they are so poor as that?" And to save Alessandro from replying, she set off on a run for the house, saying, "Come, come, Margarita, we must go and help at the supper."

"Will the Señorita let me help, too," asked Alessandro, wondering at his own boldness, — "if there is anything I can do?"

"Oh, no," she cried, "there is not. Yes, there is, too. You can help carry the things down to the booth; for we are short of hands now, with Juan Can in bed, and Luigo gone to Ventura for the doctor. You and some of your men might carry all the supper over. I 'll call you when we are ready."

The men sat down in a group and waited contentedly, smoking, chatting, and laughing. Alessandro walked up and down between the kitchen and the shed. He could hear the sounds of rattling dishes, jingling spoons, frying, pouring water. Savory smells began to be wafted out. Evidently old Marda meant to atone for the shortcoming of the noon. Juan Can, in his bed, also heard and smelled what was going on. "May the fiends get me," he growled, "if that wasteful old hussy is n't getting up a feast for those beast of Indians! There's mutton and onions, and peppers stewing, and potatoes, I 'll be bound, and God knows what else, for beggars that are only too thankful to get a handful of roasted wheat or a bowl of acorn porridge at home. Well, they 'll have to say they were well feasted at the Moreno's, — that 's one comfort. I wonder if Margarita 'll think I am worthy of tasting that stew! San José! but it smells well! Margarita! Margarita!" he called at top of his lungs; but Margarita did not hear. She was absorbed in her duties in the kitchen; and having already taken Juan at sundown a bowl of the good broth which the doctor had said was the only sort of food he must eat for two weeks, she had dismissed him from her mind for the night. Moreover, Margarita was absent-minded to-night. She was more than half in love with the handsome Alessandro, who, when he had been on the ranch the year before, had danced with her, and said many a light pleasant word to her, evenings, as a young man may; and what ailed him now, that he seemed, when he saw her, as if she were no more than a transparent shade, through which he stared at the sky behind her, she did not know. Señor Felipe's illness, she thought, and the general misery and confusion, had perhaps put everything else out of his head; but now he was going to stay, and it would be good fun having him there, if only Señor Felipe got well, which he seemed like to do. And as Margarita flew about, here, there, and everywhere, she cast frequent glances at the tall straight figure pacing up and down in the dusk outside.

Alessandro did not see her. He did not see anything. He was looking off at the sunset, and listening. Ramona had said, "I will call you when we are ready." But she did not do as she said. She told Margarita to call.

"Run, Margarita," she said. "All is ready now; see if Alessandro is in sight. Call him to come and take the things."

So it was Margarita's voice, and not Ramona's that called, "Alessandro! Alessandro! the supper is ready."

But it was Ramona who, when Alessandro reached 5
the doorway, stood there holding in her arms a huge smoking platter of the stew which had so roused poor Juan Can's longings; and it was Ramona who said, as she gave it into Alessandro's hands, "Take care, Alessandro, it is very full. The gravy will run over if you are not careful. You are not used to waiting on table;" and as she said it, she smiled full into Alessandro's eyes, — a little flitting, gentle, friendly smile, which went near to making him drop the platter, mutton, gravy, and all, then and there, at her feet.

The men ate fast and greedily, and it was not, after all, much more than an hour, when, full fed and happy, they were mounting their horses to set off. At the last moment Alessandro drew one of them aside. "José," he said, "whose horse is the faster, yours or Antonio's?"

"Mine," promptly replied José. "Mine, by a great deal. I will run Antonio any day he likes."

Alessandro knew this as well before asking as after. But Alessandro was learning a great many things in these days, among other things a little diplomacy. He wanted a man to ride at the swiftest to Temecula and back. He knew that José's pony could go like the wind. He also knew that there was a perpetual feud of rivalry between him and Antonio, in matter of the fleetness of their respective ponies. So, having chosen José for his messenger, he went thus to work to make sure that he would urge his horse to its utmost speed.

Whispering in José's ear a few words, he said, "Will you go? I will pay you for the time, all you could earn at the shearing."

"I will go," said José, elated. "You will see me back to-morrow by sundown."

"Not earlier?" asked Alessandro. "I thought by noon."

"Well, by noon be it, then," said José. "The horse can do it."

"Have great care!" said Alessandro.

"That will I," replied José; and giving his horse's
sides a sharp punch with his knees, set off at full 6
gallop westward.

"I have sent José with a message to Temecula," said Alessandro, walking up to Fernando. "He

5 The Cook's (Old Marda's) Window. — Photograph by V.C. Vroman. Circa 1913.

6 Illustration by Henry Sandham. Circa 1883.

will be back here to-morrow noon, and join you at the Ortega's the next morning."

"Back here by noon to-morrow!" exclaimed Fernando. "Not unless he kills his horse!"

"That was what he said," replied Alessandro, nonchalantly.

"Easy enough, too!" cried Antonio, riding up on his little dun mare. "I'd go in less time than that, on this mare. José's is no match for her, and never was. Why did you not send me, Alessandro?"

"Is your horse really faster than José's?" said Alessandro. "Then I wish I had sent you. I'll send you next time."

Chapter VII

Don Ameche portrayed the Indian, Alessandro, in the 1937 20th Century-Fox production of *Ramona*.

IT was strange to see how quickly and naturally Alessandro fitted into his place in the household. How tangles straightened out, and rough places became smooth, as he quietly took matters in hand. Luckily, old Juan Can had always liked him, and felt a great sense of relief at the news of his staying on. Not a wholly unselfish relief, perhaps, for since his accident Juan had not been without fears that he might lose his place altogether; there was a Mexican he knew, who had long been scheming to get the situation, and had once openly boasted at a fandango, where he was dancing with Anita, that as soon as that superannuated old fool, Juan Canito, was out of the way, he meant to be the Señora Moreno's head shepherd himself. To have seen this man in authority on the place, would have driven Juan out of his mind. 1

But the gentle Alessandro, only an Indian, — and of course the Señora would never think of putting an Indian permanently in so responsible a position on the estate, — it was exactly as Juan would have wished; and he fraternized with Alessandro heartily from the outset; kept him in his room by the hour, giving him hundreds of long-winded directions and explanations about things which, if only he had known it, Alessandro understood far better than he did.

Alessandro's father had managed the Mission flocks and herds at San Luis Rey for twenty years; few were as skilful as he; he himself owned nearly as many sheep as the Señora Moreno; but this Juan did not know. Neither did he realize that Alessandro, as Chief Pablo's son, had a position of his own not without dignity and authority. To Juan, an Indian was an Indian, and that was the end of it. The gentle courteousness of Alessandro's manner, his quiet behavior, were all set down in Juan's mind to the score of the boy's native amiability and sweetness. If Juan had been told that the Señor Felipe himself had not been more carefully trained in all precepts of kindliness, honorable dealing, and polite usage, by the Señora, his mother, than had Alessandro by his father, he would have opened his

1 The term "Digger" as applied to the California Indians is a misnomer based on the mistaken idea that these Native Americans lived largely on roots. Settlers soon learned better but found that continuing to perceive the Indians as miserable, subhuman creatures made it much easier to deprive them of their lands and lives. The survival of a stone age culture in California up until the Spanish conquest was the result of geographic and cultural isolation, not any hereditary biological limitions on the part of the Indians. Actually there is much to be said for their culture just as it was. California supported a far greater number of Indians than did any other region of comparable size in North America, yet its original inhabitants had made a successful adaptation to their environment and they had done so without destroying each other.

Kent Taylor appeared as Felipe in the 20th Century-Fox production of *Ramona* which starred Loretta Young in the title role.

eyes wide. The standards of the two parents were different, to be sure; but the advantage could not be shown to be entirely on the Señora's side. There were many things that Felipe knew, of which Alessandro was profoundly ignorant; but there were others in which Alessandro could have taught Felipe; and when it came to the things of the soul, and of honor, Alessandro's plane was the higher of the two. Felipe was a fair-minded, honorable man, as men go; but circumstance and opportunity would have a hold on him they could never get on Alessandro. Alessandro would not lie; Felipe might. Alessandro was by nature full of veneration and the religious instinct; Felipe had been trained into being a good Catholic. But they were both singularly pure-minded, open-hearted, generous-souled young men, and destined, by the strange chance which had thus brought them into familiar relations, to become strongly attached to each other. After the day on which the madness of Felipe's fever had been so miraculously soothed and controlled by Alessandro's singing, he was never again wildly delirious. When he waked in the night from that first long sleep, he was, as Father Salvierderra had predicted, in his right mind; knew every one, and asked rational questions. But the overheated and excited brain did not for some time wholly resume normal action. At intervals he wandered, especially when just arousing from sleep; and, strangely enough, it was always for Alessandro that he called at these times, and it seemed always to be music that he craved. He recollected Alessandro's having sung to him that first night. "I was not so crazy as you all thought," he said. "I knew a great many of the things I said, but I could n't help saying them; and I heard Ramona ask Alessandro to sing; and when he began, I remember I thought the Virgin had reached down and put her hand on my head and cooled it."

On the second evening, the first after the shearers had left, Alessandro, seeing Ramona in the veranda, went to the foot of the steps, and said, "Señorita, would Señor Felipe like to have me play on the violin to him to-night?"

"Why, whose violin have you got?" exclaimed Ramona, astonished.

"My own, Señorita."

"Your own! I thought you said you did not bring it."

"Yes, Señorita, that is true; but I sent for it last night, and it is here."

"Sent to Temecula and back already!" cried Ramona.

"Yes, Señorita. Our ponies are swift and strong. They can go a hundred miles in a day, and not suffer. It was José brought it, and he is at the Ortega's by this time."

Ramona's eyes glistened. "I wish I could have thanked him," she said. "You should have let me know. He ought to have been paid for going."

"I paid him, Señorita; he went for me;" said Alessandro, with a shade of wounded pride in the tone, which Ramona should have perceived, but did not, and went on hurting the lover's heart still more.

"But it was for us that you sent for it, Alessandro; the Señora would rather pay the messenger herself."

"It is paid, Señorita. It is nothing. If the Señor Felipe wishes to hear the violin, I will play;" and Alessandro walked slowly away.

Ramona gazed after him. For the first time, she looked at him with no thought of his being an Indian, — a thought there had surely been no need of her having, since his skin was not a shade darker than Felipe's; but so strong was the race feeling, that never till that moment had she forgotten it.

"What a superb head, and what a walk!" she thought. Then, looking more observantly, she said: "He walks as if he were offended. He did not like my offering to pay for the messenger. He wanted to do it for dear Felipe. I will tell Felipe, and we will give him some present when he goes away."

"Is n't he splendid, Señorita?" came in a light laughing tone from Margarita's lips close to her ear, in the fond freedom of their relation. "Is n't he splendid? And oh, Señorita, you can't think how he dances! Last year I danced with him every night; he has wings on his feet, for all he is so tall and big."

There was a coquettish consciousness in the girl's tone, that was suddenly, for some unexplained reason, exceedingly displeasing to Ramona. Drawing herself away, she spoke to Margarita in a tone she had never before in her life used. "It is not fitting to speak like that about young men. The Señora would be displeased if she heard you," she said, and walked swiftly away, leaving poor Margarita as astounded as if she had got a box on the ear.

She looked after Ramona's retreating figure, then after Alessandro's. She had heard them talking together just before she came up. Thoroughly bewildered and puzzled, she stood motionless for several seconds, reflecting; then, shaking her head, she ran away, trying to dismiss the harsh speech from her mind. "Alessandro must have vexed the Señorita," she thought, "to make her speak like that to me." But the incident was not so easily dismissed from Margarita's thoughts. Many times in the day it recurred to her, still a bewilderment and a puzzle, as far from solution as ever. It was a tiny seed, whose name she did not dream of; but it was dropped in soil where it would grow some day, — forcing-house soil, and a bitter seed; and when it blossomed, Ramona would have an enemy.

All unconscious, equally of Margarita's heart and her own, Ramona proceeded to Felipe's room. Felipe was sleeping, the Señora sitting by his side, as she had sat for days and nights, — her dark face looking thinner and more drawn each day; her hair

Scene from the 20th Century-Fox production of *Ramona* starring Loretta Young.

—Painting by Henry Sandham.

—Painting by Henry Sandham.

looking even whiter, if that could be; and her voice growing hollow from faintness and sorrow.

"Dear Señora," whispered Ramona, "do go out for a few moments while he sleeps, and let me watch, — just on the walk in front of the veranda. The sun is still lying there, bright and warm. You will be ill if you do not have air."

The Señora shook her head. "My place is here," she answered, speaking in a dry, hard tone. Sympathy was hateful to the Señora Moreno; she wished neither to give it nor take it. "I shall not leave him. I do not need the air."

Ramona had a cloth-of-gold rose in her hand. The veranda eaves were now shaded with them, hanging down like a thick fringe of golden tassels. It was the rose Felipe loved best. Stooping, she laid it on the bed, near Felipe's head. "He will like to see it when he wakes," she said.

The Señora seized it, and flung it far out in the room. "Take it away! Flowers are poison when one is ill," she said coldly. "Have I never told you that?"

"No, Señora," replied Ramona, meekly; and she glanced involuntarily at the saucer of musk which the Señora kept on the table close to Felipe's pillow.

"The musk is different," said the Señora, seeing the glance. "Musk is a medicine; it revives."

Ramona knew, but she would have never dared to say, that Felipe hated musk. Many times he had said to her how he hated the odor; but his mother was so fond of it, that it must always be that the veranda and the house would be full of it. Ramona hated it too. At times it made her faint, with a deadly faintness. But neither she nor Felipe would have confessed as much to the Señora; and if they had, she would have thought it all a fancy.

"Shall I stay?" asked Ramona, gently.

"As you please," replied the Señora. The simple presence of Ramona irked her now with a feeling she did not pretend to analyze, and would have been terrified at if she had. She would not have dared to say to herself, in plain words: "Why is that girl well and strong, and my Felipe lying here like to die! If Felipe dies, I cannot bear the sight of her. What is she, to be preserved of the saints!"

2 It was the Indians who showed the Anglo settlers how to make mud mortar and to use asphalt on roofs. They also understood irrigation and were excellent herders and reapers. Nevertheless, Indians received half the wages paid Anglos.

But that, or something like it, was what she felt whenever Ramona entered the room; still more, whenever she assisted in ministering to Felipe. If it had been possible, the Señora would have had no hands but her own to do aught for her boy. Even tears from Ramona sometimes irritated her. "What does she know about loving Felipe! He is nothing to her!" thought the Señora, strangely mistaken, strangely blind, strangely forgetting how feeble is the tie of blood in the veins by the side of love in the heart.

If into this fiery soul of the Señora's could have been dropped one second's knowledge of the relative positions she and Ramona already occupied in

Felipe's heart, she would, on the spot, have either died herself, or have slain Ramona, one or the other. But no such knowledge was possible; no such idea could have found entrance into the Señora's mind. A revelation from Heaven of it could hardly have reached even her ears. So impenetrable are the veils which, fortunately for us all, are forever held by viewless hands between us and the nearest and closest of our daily companions.

At twilight of this day Felipe was restless and feverish again. He had dozed at intervals all day long, but had had no refreshing sleep.

"Send for Alessandro," he said. "Let him come and sing to me."

"He has his violin now; he can play, if you would like that better," said Ramona; and she related what Alessandro had told her of the messenger's having ridden to Temecula and back in a night and half a day, to bring it.

"I wanted to pay the man," she said; "I knew of course your mother would wish to reward him. But I fancy Alessandro was offended. He answered me shortly that it was paid, and it was nothing."

"You could n't have offended him more," said Felipe. "What a pity! He is as proud as Lucifer himself, that Alessandro. You know his father has always been the head of their band; in fact, he has authority over several bands; General, they call it now, since they got the title from the Americans; they used to call it Chief, and until Father Peyri left San Luis Rey, Pablo was in charge of all the sheep, and general steward and paymaster. Father Peyri trusted him with everything; I've heard he would leave boxes full of uncounted gold in Pablo's charge to pay off the Indians. Pablo reads and writes, and 2
is very well off; he has as many sheep as we have, I fancy!"

"What!" exclaimed Ramona, astonished. "They all look as if they were poor."

"Oh, well, so they are," replied Felipe, "compared with us; but one reason is, they share everything with each other. Old Pablo feeds and supports half his village, they say. So long as he has anything, he will never see one of his Indians hungry."

"How generous!" warmly exclaimed Ramona; "I think they are better than we are, Felipe!"

"I think so, too," said Felipe. "That 's what I have always said. The Indians are the most generous people in the world. Of course they have learned it partly from us; but they were very much so when the Fathers first came here. You ask Father Salvierderra some day. He has read all Father Junipero's and Father Crespi's diaries, and he says it is wonderful how the wild savages gave food to every one who came."

"Felipe! you are talking too much," said the Señora's voice, in the doorway; and as she spoke she looked reproachfully at Ramona. If she had said in words, "See how unfit you are to be trusted with Felipe. No wonder I do not leave the room except when I must!" her meaning could not have been plainer. Ramona felt it keenly, and not without some misgiving that it was deserved.

"Oh, dear Felipe, has it hurt you?" she said timidly; and to the Señora, "Indeed, Señora, he has been speaking but a very few moments, very low."

"Go call Alessandro, Ramona, will you?" said Felipe. "Tell him to bring his violin. I think I will go to sleep if he plays."

A long search Ramona had for Alessandro. Everybody had seen him a few minutes ago, but nobody knew where he was now. Kitchens, sheepfolds, vineyards, orchards, Juan Can's bedchamber,— Ramona searched them all in vain. At last, standing at the foot of the veranda steps, and looking down the garden, she thought she saw figures moving under the willows by the washing-stones.

"Can he be there?" she said. "What can he be doing there? Who is it with him?" And she walked down the path, calling, "Alessandro! Alessandro!"

At the first sound, Alessandro sprang from the side of his companion, and almost before the second syllables had been said, was standing face to face with Ramona.

"Here I am, Señorita. Does Señor Felipe want me? I have my violin here. I thought perhaps he would like to have me play to him in the twilight."

"Yes," replied Ramona, "he wishes to hear you I have been looking everywhere for you." As she spoke, she was half unconsciously peering beyond into the dusk, to see whose figure it was, slowly moving by the brook.

Nothing escaped Alessandro's notice where Ramona was concerned. "It is Margarita," he said instantly. "Does the Señorita want her? Shall I run and call her?"

"No," said Ramona, again displeased, she knew not why, nor in fact knew she was displeased; "no, I was not looking for her. What is she doing there?"

"She is washing," replied Alessandro, innocently.

"Washing at this time of day!" thought Ramona, severely. "A mere pretext. I shall watch Margarita. The Señora would never allow this sort of thing." And as she walked back to the house by Alessandro's side, she meditated whether or no she would herself speak to Margarita on the subject in the morning.

Margarita, in the mean time, was also having her season of reflections not the pleasantest. As she soused her aprons up and down in the water, she said to herself, "I may as well finish them now I am here. How provoking! I 've no more than got a word with him, than she must come, calling him away. And he flies as if he was shot on an arrow, at the first word. I'd like to know what's come over the man, to be so different. If I could ever get a good half-hour with him alone, I'd soon find out. Oh, but his eyes go through me, through and through me! I know he's an Indian, but what do I care for

Katherine De Mille played the part of Margarita in the 1937 20th Century-Fox production of *Ramona*.

The washing place at Guajome. — Photograph by A.C. Vroman. Circa 1913.

that. He's a million times handsomer than Señor Felipe. And Juan José said the other day he'd make enough better head shepherd than old Juan Can, if Señor Felipe'd only see it; and why shouldn't he get to see it, if Alessandro's here all summer?" And before the aprons were done, Margarita had a fine air-castle up: herself and Alessandro married, a nice little house, children playing in the sunshine below the artichoke-patch, she herself still working for the Señora. "And the Señorita will perhaps marry Señor Felipe," she added, her thoughts moving more hesitatingly. "He worships the ground she walks on. Anybody with quarter of a blind eye can see that; but maybe the Señora would not let him. Anyhow, Señor Felipe is sure to have a wife, and so and so." It was an innocent, girlish castle, built of sweet and natural longings, for which no maiden, high or low, need blush; but its foundations were laid in sand, on which would presently beat such winds and floods as poor little Margarita never dreamed of.

The next day Margarita and Ramona both went about their day's business with a secret purpose in their hearts. Margarita had made up her mind that before night she would, by fair means or foul, have a good long talk with Alessandro. "He was fond enough of me last year, I know," she said to herself, recalling some of the dances and the good-night leave-takings at that time. "It's because he is so put upon by everybody now. What with Juan Can in one bed sending for him to prate to him about the sheep, and Señor Felipe in another sending for him to fiddle him to sleep, and all the care of the sheep, it's a wonder he's not out of his mind altogether. But I'll find a chance, or make one, before this day's sun sets. If I can once get a half-hour with him, I'm not afraid after that; I know the way it is with men!" said the confident Margarita, who, truth being told, it must be admitted, did indeed know a great deal about the way it is with men, and could be safely backed, in a fair field, with a fair start, against any girl of her age and station in the country. So much for Margarita's purpose, at the outset of a day destined to be an eventful one in her life.

Ramona's purpose was no less clear. She had decided, after some reflection, that she would not speak to the Señora about Margarita's having been under the willows with Alessandro in the previous evening, but would watch her carefully and see whether there were any farther signs of her attempting to have clandestine interviews with him.

This course she adopted, she thought, chiefly because of her affection for Margarita, and her unwillingness to expose her to the Señora's displeasure, which would be great, and terrible to bear. She was also aware of an unwillingness to bring anything to light which would reflect ever so lightly upon Alessandro in the Señora's estimation. "And he is not really to blame," thought Ramona, "if a girl follows him about and makes free with him. She must have seen him at the willows, and gone down there on purpose to meet him, making a pretext of the washing. For she never in this world would have gone to wash in the dark, as he must have known, if he were not a fool. He is not the sort of person, it seems to me, to be fooling with maids. He seems as full of grave thought as Father Salvierderra. If I see anything amiss in Margarita to-day, I shall speak to her myself, kindly but firmly, and tell her to conduct herself more discreetly."

Then, as the other maiden's had done, Ramona's thoughts, being concentrated on Alessandro, altered a little from their first key, and grew softer and more imaginative; strangely enough, taking some of the phrases, as it were, out of the other maiden's mouth.

"I never saw such eyes as Alessandro has," she said. "I wonder any girl should make free with him. Even I myself, when he fixes his eyes on me, feel a constraint. There is something in them like the eyes of a saint, so solemn, yet so mild. I am sure he is very good."

And so the day opened; and if there were abroad in the valley that day a demon of mischief, let loose to tangle the skeins of human affairs, things could not have fallen out better for his purpose than they did; for it was not yet ten o'clock of the morning, when Ramona, sitting at her embroidery in the veranda, half hid behind the vines, saw Alessandro going with his pruning-knife in his hand towards the artichoke-patch at the east of the garden, and joining the almond orchard. "I wonder what he is going to do there," she thought. "He can't be going to cut willows;" and her eyes followed him till he disappeared among the trees.

Ramona was not the only one who saw this. Margarita, looking from the east window of Father Salvierderra's room, saw the same thing. "Now 's my chance!" she said; and throwing a white reboso coquettishly over her head, she slipped around the corner of the house. She ran swiftly in the direction in which Alessandro had gone. The sound of her steps reached Ramona, who, lifting her eyes, took in the whole situation at a glance. There was no possible duty, no possible message, which would take Margarita there. Ramona's cheeks blazed with a disproportionate indignation. But she bethought herself, "Ah, the Señora may have sent her to call Alessandro!" She rose, went to the door of Felipe's room, and looked in. The Señora was sitting in the chair by Felipe's bed, with her eyes closed. Felipe was dozing. The Señora opened her eyes, and looked inquiringly at Ramona.

"Do you know where Margarita is?" said Ramona.

"In Father Salvierderra's room, or else in the kitchen helping Marda," replied the Señora, in a whisper. "I told her to help Marda with the peppers this morning."

Ramona nodded, returned to the veranda, and sat down to decide on her course of action. Then she rose again, and going to Father Salvierderra's room, looked in. The room was still in disorder. Margarita had left her work there unfinished. The color deepened on Ramona's cheeks. It was strange how accurately she divined each process of the incident. "She saw him from this window," said Ramona, "and has run after him. It is shameful. I will go and call her back, and let her see that I saw it all. It is high time that this was stopped."

But once back in the veranda, Ramona halted, and seated herself in her chair again. The idea of seeming to spy was revolting to her.

"I will wait here till she comes back," she said, and took up her embroidery. But she could not work. As the minutes went slowly by, she sat with her eyes fixed on the almond orchard, where first Alessandro and then Margarita had disappeared. At last she could bear it no longer. It seemed to her already a very long time. It was not in reality very long, — a half hour or so, perhaps; but it was long enough for Margarita to have made great headway, as she thought, in her talk with Alessandro, and for things to have reached just the worst possible crisis at which they could have been surprised, when Ramona suddenly appeared at the orchard gate, saying in a stern tone, "Margarita, you are wanted in the house!" At a bad crisis, indeed, for everybody concerned. The picture which Ramona had seen, as she reached the gate, was this: Alessandro, standing with his back against the fence, his right hand hanging listlessly down, with the pruning-knife in it, his left hand in the hand of Margarita, who stood close to him, looking up in his face, with a half-saucy, half-loving expression. What made bad matters worse, was, that at the first sight of Ramona, Alessandro snatched his hand from Margarita's, and tried to draw farther off from her, looking at her with an expression which, even in her anger, Ramona could not help seeing was one of disgust and repulsion. And if Ramona saw it, how much more did Margarita! Saw it, felt it, as only a woman repulsed in presence of another woman can see and feel. The whole thing was over in the twinkling of an eye; the telling it takes double, treble the time of the happening. Before Alessandro was fairly aware what had befallen, Ramona and Margarita were disappearing from view under the garden trellis, — Ramona walking in advance, stately, silent, and Margarita following, sulky, abject in her gait, but with a raging whirlwind in her heart.

It had taken only the twinkling of an eye, but it had told Margarita the truth. Alessandro too.

"My God!" he said, "the Señorita thought me making love to that girl. May the fiends get her! The Señorita looked at me as if I were a dog. How could she think a man would look at a woman after he had once seen her! And I can never, never speak to her to tell her! Oh, this cannot be borne!" And in his rage Alessandro threw his pruning-knife whirling through the air so fiercely, it sank to the hilt in one of the old olive-trees. He wished he were dead. He was minded to flee the place. How could he ever look the Señorita in the face again!

"Perdition take that girl!" he said over and over in his helpless despair. An ill outlook for Margarita after this; and the girl had not deserved it.

In Margarita's heart the pain was more clearly defined. She had seen Ramona a half-second before Alessandro had; and dreaming no special harm, except a little confusion at being seen thus standing with him, — for she would tell the Señorita all about it when matters had gone a little farther, — had not let go of Alessandro's hand. But the next second she had seen in his face a look; oh, she would never forget it, never! That she should live to have had any man look at her like that! At the first glimpse of the Señorita, all the blood in his body seemed rushing into his face, and he had snatched his hand away, — for it was Margarita herself that had taken his hand, not he hers, — had snatched his hand away, and pushed her from him, till she had nearly fallen. All this might have been borne, if it had been only a fear of the Señorita's seeing them, which had made him do it. But Margarita knew a great deal better than that. That one swift, anguished, shame-smitten, appealing, worshipping look on Alessandro's face, as his eyes rested on Ramona, was like a flash of light into Margarita's consciousness. Far better than Alessandro himself, she now knew his secret. In her first rage she did not realize either the gulf between herself and Ramona, or that between Ramona and Alessandro. Her jealous rage was as entire as if they had all been equals together. She lost her head altogether, and there was embodied insolence in the tone in which she said presently, "Did the Señorita want me?"

Turning swiftly on her, and looking her full in the eye, Ramona said: "I saw you go to the orchard, Margarita, and I knew what you went for. I knew that you were at the brook last night with Alessandro. All I wanted of you was to tell you that if I see anything more of this sort, I shall speak to the Señora."

"There is no harm," muttered Margarita, sullenly "I don't know what the Señorita means."

"You know very well, Margarita," retorted Ramona. "You know that the Señora permits nothing of the kind. Be careful, now, what you do." And with that the two separated, Ramona returning to the veranda and her embroidery, and Margarita to her neglected duty of making the good Father's bed. But each girl's heart was hot and unhappy; and Margarita's would have been still hotter and unhappier, had she heard the words which were being spoken on the veranda a little later.

After a few minutes of his blind rage at Margarita, himself, and fate generally, Alessandro, recovering his senses, had ingeniously persuaded himself that, as the Señora's and also the Señorita's servant, for the time being, he owed it to them to explain the situation in which he had just been found. Just what he was to say he did not know; but no sooner had the thought struck him, than he set off at full speed for the house, hoping to find Ramona on the veranda, where he knew she spent all her time when not with Señor Felipe.

When Ramona saw him coming, she lowered her eyes, and was absorbed in her embroidery. She did not wish to look at him.

The footsteps stopped. She knew he was standing at the steps. She would not look up. She thought if she did not, he would go away. She did not know either the Indian or the lover nature. After a time, finding the consciousness of the soundless presence intolerable, she looked up, and surprised on Alessandro's face a gaze which had, in its long interval of freedom from observation, been slowly gathering up into it all the passion of a man's soul, as a burning-glass draws the fire of the sun's rays. Involuntarily a low cry burst from Ramona's lips, and she sprang to her feet.

"Ah! did I frighten the Señorita? Forgive. I have been waiting here a long time to speak to her. I wished to say — "

Suddenly Alessandro discovered that he did not know what he wished to say.

As suddenly, Ramona discovered that she knew all he wished to say. But she spoke not, only looked at him searchingly.

"Señorita," he began again, "I would never be unfaithful to my duty to the Señora, and to you."

"I believe you, Alessandro," said Ramona. "It is not necessary to say more."

At these words a radiant joy spread over Alessandro's face. He had not hoped for this. He felt, rather than heard, that Ramona understood him. He felt, for the first time, a personal relation between himself and her.

"It is well," he said, in the brief phrase so frequent with his people. "It is well." And with a reverent inclination of his head, he walked away. Margarita, still dawdling surlily over her work in Father Salvierderra's room, heard Alessandro's voice, and running to discover to whom he was speaking, caught these last words. Peering from behind a curtain, she saw the look with which he said them; saw also the expression on Ramona's face as she listened.

Margarita clenched her hands. The seed had blossomed. Ramona had an enemy.

"Oh, but I am glad Father Salvierderra has gone!" said the girl, bitterly. "He'd have had this out of me, spite of everything. I haven't got to confess for a year, maybe; and much can happen in that time."

Much, indeed!

Chapter VIII

FELIPE gained but slowly. The relapse was indeed, as Father Salvierderra had said, worse 1
than the original attack. Day after day he lay with
little apparent change; no pain, but a weakness so
great that it was almost harder to bear than sharp
suffering would have been. Nearly every day Alessandro was sent for to play or sing to him. It seemed
to be the only thing that roused him from his half
lethargic state. Sometimes he would talk with Ales- 1
sandro on matters relative to the estate, and show for
a few moments something like his old animation; but
he was soon tired, and would close his eyes, saying:

"I will speak with you again about this, Alessandro; I am going to sleep now. Sing."

The Señora, seeing Felipe's enjoyment of Alessandro's presence, soon came to have a warm feeling towards him herself; moreover, she greatly liked his quiet reticence. There was hardly a surer road to the Señora's favor, for man or woman, than to be chary of speech and reserved in demeanor. She had an instinct of kinship to all that was silent, self-contained, mysterious, in human nature. The more she observed Alessandro, the more she trusted and approved him. Luckily for Juan Can, he did not know how matters were working in his mistress's mind. If he had, he would have been in a fever of apprehension, and would have got at swords' points with Alessandro immediately. On the contrary, all unaware of the real situation of affairs, and never quite sure that the Mexican he dreaded might not any day hear of his misfortune, and appear, asking for the place, he took every opportunity to praise Alessandro to the Señora. She never visited his bedside that he had not something to say in favor of the lad, as he called him.

"Truly, Señora," he said again and again, "I do marvel where the lad got so much knowledge, at his age. He is like an old hand at the sheep business. He knows more than any shepherd I have, — a deal more; and it is not only of sheep. He has had experience, too, in the handling of cattle. Juan José has been beholden to him more than once, already, for a remedy of which he knew not. And such modesty.

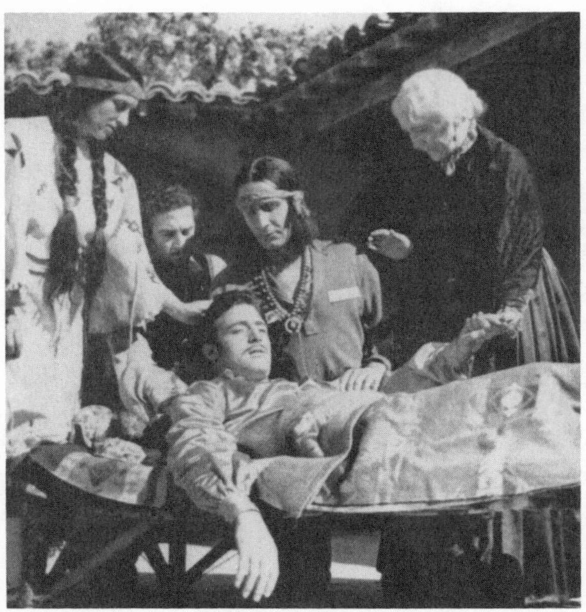

Photograph from the 1940 Hemet Pageant program.
—Courtesy of the Ramona Pageant Assoc., Inc.

—Illustration by Henry Sandham. Circa 1913.

withal. I knew not that there were such Indians; surely there cannot be many such."

"No, I fancy not," the Señora would reply, absently. "His father is a man of intelligence, and has trained his son well."

"There is nothing he is not ready to do," continued Alessandro's eulogist. "He is as handy with tools as if he had been 'prenticed to a carpenter. He has made me a new splint for my leg, which was a relief like salve to a wound, so much easier was it than before. He is a good lad, — a good lad."

None of these sayings of Juan's were thrown away on the Señora. More and more closely she watched Alessandro; and the very thing which Juan had feared, and which he had thought to avert by having Alessandro his temporary substitute, was slowly coming to pass. The idea was working in the Señora's mind, that she might do a worse thing than engage this young, strong, active, willing man to remain permanently in her employ. The possibility of an Indian's being so born and placed that he would hesitate about becoming permanently a servant even of the Señora Moreno, did not occur to her. However, she would do nothing hastily. There would be plenty of time before Juan Can's leg was well. She would study the young man more. In the mean time, she would cause Felipe to think of the idea, and propose it.

So one day she said to Felipe: "What a voice that Alessandro has, Felipe. We shall miss his music sorely when he goes, shall we not?"

"He's not going!" exclaimed Felipe, startled.

"Oh, no, no; not at present. He agreed to stay till Juan Can was about again; but that will be not more than six weeks now, or eight, I suppose. You forget how time has flown while you have been lying here ill, my son."

"True, true!" said Felipe. "Is it really a month already?" and he sighed.

"Juan Can tells me that the lad has a marvellous knowledge for one of his years," continued the Señora. "He says he is as skilled with cattle as with sheep; knows more than any shepherd we have on the place. He seems wonderfully quiet and well-mannered. I never saw an Indian who had such behavior."

"Old Pablo is just like him," said Felipe. "It was natural enough, living so long with Father Peyri. And I've seen other Indians, too, with a good deal the same manner as Alessandro. It's born in them."

"I can't bear the idea of Alessandro's going away. But by that time you will be well and strong," said the Señora; "you would not miss him then, would you?"

"Yes, I would, too!" said Felipe, pettishly. He was still weak enough to be childish. "I like him about me. He's worth a dozen times as much as any man we've got. But I don't suppose money could hire him to stay on any ranch."

"Were you thinking of hiring him permanently?" asked the Señora, in a surprised tone. "I don't doubt you could do so if you wished. They are all

2 The padres considered it their duty to teach the Indians what sin was. If they transgressed, they were flogged and in this way they "learned." Every detail of work, play, clothing, and even the choice of a mate was rigidly controlled. It's doubtful that any group of adults could be happy within a system that treated them like hopelessly retarded children.

Señora Moreno's attitude, like that of the founding padres, differed substantially from the prevalent Anglo view that the only good Indian was a dead one. Far from being the nonpersons seen by the United States Interior Department as nothing more than troublesome animals to be exterminated, the padres perceived Indians as valuable commodities with souls to be saved and bodies to be worked. If their grand designs frequently resulted in death, it was still for the Indians' own good.

poor, I suppose; he would not work with the shearers if he were not poor."

"Oh, it is n't that," said Felipe, impatiently. "You can't understand, because you 've never been among them. But they are just as proud as we are. Some of them, I mean; such men as old Pablo. They shear sheep for money just as I sell wool for money. There is n't so much difference. Alessandro's men in the band obey him, and all the men in the village obey Pablo, just as implicitly as my men here obey me. Faith, much more so!" added Felipe, laughing. "You can't understand it, mother, but it 's so. I am not at all sure I could offer Alessandro Assis money enough to tempt him to stay here as my servant."

The Señora's nostrils dilated in scorn. "No, I do 2
not understand it," she said. "Most certainly I do not understand it. Of what is it that these noble lords of villages are so proud? their ancestors,— naked savages less than a hundred years ago? Naked savages they themselves too, to-day, if we had not come here to teach and civilize them. The race was never meant for anything but servants. That was all the Fathers ever expected to make of them,— good, faithful Catholics, and contented laborers in the fields. Of course there are always exceptional instances, and I think, myself, Alessandro is one. I don't believe, however, he is so exceptional, but that if you were to offer him, for instance, the same wages you pay Juan Can, he would jump at the chance of staying on the place."

"Well, I shall think about it," said Felipe. "I 'd like nothing better than to have him here always. He 's a fellow I heartily like. I 'll think about it."

Which was all the Señora wanted done at present.

Ramona had chanced to come in as this conversation was going on. Hearing Alessandro's name, she seated herself at the window, looking out, but listening intently. The month had done much for Alessandro with Ramona, though neither Alessandro nor Ramona knew it. It had done this much,— that Ramona knew always when Alessandro was near, that she trusted him, and that she had ceased to think of him as an Indian any more than when she thought of Felipe, she thought of him as a Mexican. Moreover, seeing the two men frequently together, she had admitted to herself, as Margarita had done before her, that Alessandro was far the handsomer man of the two. This Ramona did not like to admit, but she could not help it.

"I wish Felipe were as tall and strong as Alessandro," she said to herself many a time. "I do not see why he could not have been. I wonder if the Señora sees how much handsomer Alessandro is."

When Felipe said that he did not believe he could offer Alessandro Assis money enough to tempt him to stay on the place, Ramona opened her lips suddenly, as if to speak, then changed her mind, and remained silent. She had sometimes displeased the Señora by taking part in conversations between her and her son.

Felipe saw the motion, but he also thought it wiser to wait till after his mother had left the room, before he asked Ramona what she was on the point of saying. As soon as the Señora went out, he said, "What was it, Ramona, you were going to say just now?"

Ramona colored. She had decided not to say it.

"Tell me, Ramona," persisted Felipe. "You were going to say something about Alessandro's staying; I know you were."

Ramona did not answer. For the first time in her life she found herself embarrassed before Felipe.

"Don't you like Alessandro?" said Felipe.

"Oh, yes!" replied Ramona, with instant eagerness. "It was not that at all. I like him very much." But then she stopped.

"Well, what is it, then? Have you heard anything on the place about his staying?"

"Oh, no, no; not a word!" said Ramona. "Everybody understands that he is here only till Juan Can gets well. But you said you did not believe you could offer him money enough to tempt him to stay."

"Well," said Felipe, inquiringly, "I do not. Do you?"

"I think he would like to stay," said Ramona, hesitatingly. "That was what I was going to say."

"What makes you think so?" asked Felipe.

"I don't know," Ramona said, still more hesitatingly. Now that she had said it, she was sorry. Felipe looked curiously at her. Hesitancy like this, doubts, uncertainty as to her impressions, were not characteristic of Ramona. A flitting something which was far from being suspicion or jealousy, and yet was of kin to them both, went through Felipe's mind,— went through so swiftly that he was scarce conscious of it; if he had been, he would have scorned himself. Jealous of an Indian sheep-shearer? Impossible! Nevertheless, the flitting something left a trace, and prevented Felipe from forgetting the trivial incident; and after this, it was certain that Felipe would observe Ramona more closely than he had done; would weigh her words and actions; and if she should seem by a shade altered in either, would watch still more closely. Meshes were closing around Ramona. Three watchers of her every look and act,— Alessandro in pure love, Margarita in jealous hate, Felipe in love and perplexity. Only the Señora observed her not. If she had, matters might have turned out very differently; for the Señora was clear-sighted, rarely mistaken in her reading of people's motives, never long deceived; but her observing and discriminating powers were not in focus, so far as Ramona was concerned. The girl was curiously outside of the Señora's real life. Shelter, food, clothes, all external needs, in so far as her means allowed, the Señora would, without fail, provide for the child her sister had left in her hands as a trust; but a personal relation with her, a mother's affection, or even interest and acquaintance, no. The Señora had not that to give. And if she had it not, was she to blame? What could she do? Years ago Father Salvierderra had left off remonstrating with her on this point. "Is there more I should do for the child? Do you see aught lacking, aught amiss?" the Señora would ask, conscientiously, but with pride. And the Father, thus inquired of, could not point out a duty which had been neglected.

"You do not love her, my daughter," he said.

"No." Señora Moreno's truthfulness was of the adamantine order. "No, I do not. I cannot. One cannot love by act of will."

"That is true," the Father would say sadly; "but affection may be cultivated."

"Yes, if it exists," was the Señora's constant answer. "But in this case it does not exist. I shall never love Ramona. Only at your command, and to save my sister a sorrow, I took her. I will never fail in my duty to her."

It was of no use. As well say to the mountain, "Be cast into the sea," as try to turn the Señora's heart in any direction whither it did not of itself tend. All that Father Salvierderra could do, was to love Ramona the more himself, which he did heartily, and more and more each year, and small marvel at it; for a gentler, sweeter maiden never drew breath than this same Ramona, who had been all these years, save for Felipe, lonely in the Señora Moreno's house.

Three watchers of Ramona now. If there had been a fourth, and that fourth herself, matters might have turned out differently. But how should Ramona watch? How should Ramona know? Except for her one year at school with the nuns, she had never been away from the Señora's house. Felipe was the only young man she had known, — Felipe, her brother since she was five years old.

There were no gayeties in the Señora Moreno's home. Felipe, when he needed them, went one day's journey, or two, or three, to get them; went as often as he liked. Ramona never went. How many times she had longed to go to Santa Barbara, or to Monterey, or Los Angeles; but to have asked the Señora's permission to accompany her on some of her now infrequent journeys to these places would have required more courage than Ramona possessed. It was now three years since she left the convent school, but she was still as fresh from the hands of the nuns as on the day when, with loving tears, they had kissed her in farewell. The few romances and tales and bits of verse she had read were of the most innocent and old-fashioned kind, and left her hardly less childlike than before. This childlikeness, combined with her happy temperament, had kept her singularly contented in her monotonous life. She had fed the birds, taken care of the flowers, kept the chapel in order, helped in light household work, embroidered, sung, and, as the Señora eight years before had bade her do, said her prayers and pleased Father Salvierderra.

By processes strangely unlike, she and Alessandro had both been kept strangely free from thoughts of love and of marriage, — he by living in the shadow, and she by living in the sun; his heart and thoughts filled with perplexities and fears, hers filled by a placid routine of light and easy tasks, and the outdoor pleasures of a child.

As the days went on, and Felipe still remained feeble, Alessandro meditated a bold stroke. Each time that he went to Felipe's room to sing or to play, he felt himself oppressed by the air. An hour of it made him uncomfortable. The room was large, and had two windows, and the door was never shut; yet the air seemed to Alessandro stifling.

"I should be as ill as the Señor Felipe, if I had to stay in that room, and a bed is a weakening thing, enough to pull the strongest man down," said Alessandro to Juan Can one day. "Do you think I should anger them if I asked them to let me bring Señor Felipe out to the veranda and put him on a bed of my making? I'd wager my head I'd put him on his feet in a week."

"And if you did that, you might ask the Señora for the half of the estate, and get it, lad," replied Juan. Seeing the hot blood darkening in Alessandro's face at his words, he hastened to add, "Do not be so hot-blooded. I meant not that you would ask any reward for doing it; I was only thinking what joy it would be to the Señora to see Señor Felipe on his feet again. It has often crossed my thoughts that if he did not get up from this sickness the Señora would not be long behind him. It is but for him that she lives. And who would have the estate in that case, I have never been able to find out."

"Would it not be the Señorita?" asked Alessandro.

Juan Can laughed an ugly laugh. "Ha, ha! Let the Señora hear you say that!" he said. "Faith, it will be little the Señorita gets more than enough for her bread, maybe, out of the Moreno estate. Hark ye, Alessandro; if you will not tell, I will tell you the story of the Señorita. You know she is not of the Moreno blood; is no relation of theirs."

"Yes," said Alessandro; "Margarita has said to me that the Señorita Ramona was only the foster-child of the Señora Moreno."

"Foster-child!" repeated Juan Can, contemptuously, "there is something to the tale I know not, nor ever could find out; for when I was in Monterey the Ortegna house was shut, and I could not get speech of any of their people. But this much I know, that it was the Señora Ortegna that had the girl first in keeping; and there was a scandalous tale about her birth."

If Juan Can's eyes had not been purblind with old age, he would have seen that in Alessandro's face which would have made him choose his words more carefully. But he went on: "It was after the Señora Ortegna was buried, that our Señora returned, bringing this child with her; and I do assure you, lad, I have seen the Señora look at her many a time as if she wished her dead. And it is a shame, for she was always as fair and good a child as the saints ever saw. But a stain on the blood, a stain on the blood, lad, is a bitter thing in a house. This much I know, her mother was an Indian. Once when I was in the chapel, behind the big Saint Joseph there, I overheard the Señora say as much. She was talking to Father Salvierderra, and she said, ' If the child had only the one blood in her veins, it would be different. I like not these crosses with Indians.' "

If Alessandro had been civilized, he would at this word " Indian " have bounded to his feet. Being Alessandro, he stood if possible stiller than before, and said in a low voice, " How know you it was the mother that was the Indian?"

Juan laughed again, maliciously: " Ha, it is the Ortegna face she has; and that Ortegna, why, he was the scandal byword of the whole coast. There was not a decent woman would have spoken to him, except for his wife's sake."

" But did you not say that it was in the Señora Ortegna's keeping that the child was? " asked Alessandro, breathing harder and faster each moment now; stupid old Juan Can so absorbed in relish of his gossip, that he noticed nothing.

" Ay, ay. So I said," he went on; " and so it was. There be such saints, you know; though the Lord knows if she had been minded to give shelter to all her husband's bastards, she might have taken lease of a church to hold them. But there was a story about a man's coming with this infant and leaving it in the Señora's room; and she, poor lady, never having had a child of her own, did warm to it at first sight, and kept it with her to the last; and I wager me, a hard time she had to get our Señora to take the child when she died; except that it was to spite Ortegna, I think our Señora would as soon the child had been dead."

" Has she not treated her kindly? " asked Alessandro, in a husky voice.

Juan Can's pride resented this question. " Do you suppose the Señora Moreno would do an unkindness to one under her roof? " he asked loftily. " The Señorita has been always, in all things, like Señor Felipe himself. It was so that she promised the Señora Ortegna, I have heard."

" Does the Señorita know all this? " asked Alessandro.

Juan Can crossed himself. " Saints save us, no! " he exclaimed. " I 'll not forget, to my longest day, what it cost me, once I spoke in her hearing, when she was yet small. I did not know she heard; but she went to the Señora, asking who was her mother. And she said I had said her mother was no good, which in faith I did, and no wonder. And the Señora came to me, and said she, ' Juan Canito, you have been a long time in our house; but if ever I hear of your mentioning aught concerning the Señorita Ramona, on this estate or anywhere else in the country, that day you leave my service! ' — And

The Old Bench where Juan Can sat. —Photograph by V.C. Vroman. Circa 1913.

Laura, said to be 102, with Benjamina, 117, much venerated. Indians painted during Jackson's visit in 1881. —Painting by Henry Sandham 3

you 'd not do me the ill-turn to speak of it, Alessandro, now?" said the old man, anxiously. "My tongue runs away with me, lying here on this cursed bed, with nothing to do, — an active man like me."

"No, I 'll not speak of it, you may be assured," said Alessandro, walking away slowly.

"Here! Here!" called Juan. "What about that plan you had for making a bed for Señor Felipe on the veranda? Was it of raw-hide you meant?"

"Ah, I had forgotten," said Alessandro, returning. "Yes, that was it. There is great virtue in a raw-hide, tight stretched; my father says that it is the only bed the Fathers would ever sleep on, in the Mission days. I myself like the ground even better; but my father sleeps always on the raw-hide. He says it keeps him well. Do you think I might speak of it to the Señora?"

"Speak of it to Señor Felipe himself," said Juan. "It will be as he says. He rules this place now, from beginning to end; and it is but yesterday I held him on my knee. It is soon that the old are pushed to the wall, Alessandro."

"Nay, Juan Canito," replied Alessandro, kindly. "It is not so. My father is many years older than you are, and he rules our people to-day as firmly as ever. I myself obey him, as if I were a lad still."

"What else, then, but a lad do you call yourself, I wonder," thought Juan; but he answered, "It is not so with us. The old are not held in such reverence."

"That is not well," replied Alessandro. "We have been taught differently. There is an old man in our village who is many, many years older than my father. He helped to carry the mortar at the building of the San Diego Mission, I do not know how many years ago. He is long past a hundred years of age. He is blind and childish, and cannot walk;
3 but he is cared for by every one. And we bring him in our arms to every council, and set him by my father's side. He talks very foolishly sometimes, but my father will not let him be interrupted. He says it brings bad luck to affront the aged. We will presently be aged ourselves."

"Ay, ay!" said Juan, sadly. "We must all come to it. It is beginning to look not so far off to me!"

Alessandro stared, no less astonished at Juan Can's unconscious revelation of his standard of measurement of years than Juan had been at his. "Faith, old man, what name dost give to yourself to-day!" he thought; but went on with the topic of the raw-hide bed. "I may not so soon get speech with Señor Felipe," he said. "It is usually when he is sleepy that I go to play for him or to sing. But it makes my heart heavy to see him thus languishing day by day, and all for lack of the air and the sun, I do believe, indeed, Juan."

"Ask the Señorita, then," said Juan. "She has his ear at all times."

Alessandro made no answer. Why was it that it did not please him, — this suggestion of speaking to Ramona of his plan for Felipe's welfare? He could not have told; but he did not wish to speak of it to her.

"I will speak to the Señora," he said; and as luck would have it, at that moment the Señora stood in the doorway, come to ask after Juan Can's health.

The suggestion of the raw-hide bed struck her favorably. She herself had, in her youth, heard much of their virtues, and slept on them. "Yes," she said, "they are good. We will try it. It was only yesterday that Señor Felipe was complaining of the bed he lies on; and when he was well, he thought nothing could be so good; he brought it here, at a great price, for me, but I could not lie on it. It seemed as if it would throw me off as soon as I lay down; it is a cheating device, like all these innovations the Americans have brought into the country. But Señor Felipe till now thought it a luxury; now he tosses on it, and says it is throwing him all the time."

Alessandro smiled, in spite of his reverence for the Señora. "I once lay down on one myself, Señora," he said, "and that was what I said to my father. It was like a wild horse under me, making himself ready to buck. I thought perhaps the invention was of the saints, that men should not sleep too long."

"There is a pile of raw-hides," said Juan, "well cured, but not too stiff; Juan José was to have sent them off to-day to be sold; one of those will be just right. It must not be too dry." 4

"The fresher the better," said Alessandro, "so it have no dampness. Shall I make the bed, Señora?" he asked, "and will the Señora permit that I make it on the veranda? I was just asking Juan Can if he thought I might be so bold as to ask you to let me bring Señor Felipe into the outer air. With us, it is thought death to be shut up in walls, as he has been so long. Not till we are sure to die, do we go into the dark like that."

The Señora hesitated. She did not share Alessandro's prejudice in favor of fresh air.

"Night and day both?" she said. "Surely it is not well to sleep out in the night?"

"That is the best of all, Señora," replied Alessandro, earnestly. "I beg the Señora to try it. If Señor Felipe have not mended greatly after the first night he have so slept, then Alessandro will be a liar."

"No, only mistaken," said the Señora, gently. She felt herself greatly drawn to this young man by his devotion, as she thought, to Felipe. "When I die and leave Felipe here," she had more than once said to herself, "it would be a great good to him to have such a servant as this on the place."

"Very well, Alessandro," she replied; "make the bed, and we will try it at once."

This was early in the forenoon. The sun was still high in the west, when Ramona, sitting as usual in the veranda, at her embroidery, saw Alessandro coming, followed by two men, bearing the raw-hide bed.

4 The raw hides known as "California dollars" had been until recently used as legal tender up and down the coast.

The inner courtyard at Guajome. — Photograph by George Wharton James. Circa 1911.

"What can that be?" she said. "Some new invention of Alessandro's, but for what?"

"A bed for the Señor Felipe, Señorita," said Alessandro, running lightly up the steps. "The Señora has given permission to place it here on the veranda, and Señor Felipe is to lie here day and night; and it will be a marvel in your eyes how he will gain strength. It is the close room which is keeping him weak now; he has no illness."

"I believe that is the truth, Alessandro," exclaimed Ramona; "I have been thinking the same thing. My head aches after I am in that room but an hour, and when I come here I am well. But the nights too, Alessandro? Is it not harmful to sleep out in the night air?"

"Why, Señorita?" asked Alessandro, simply.

And Ramona had no answer, except, "I do not know; I have always heard so."

"My people do not think so," replied Alessandro; "unless it is cold, we like it better. It is good, Señorita, to look up at the sky in the night."

"I should think it would be," cried Ramona. "I never thought of it. I should like to do it."

Alessandro was busy, with his face bent down, arranging the bedstead in a sheltered corner of the veranda. If his face had been lifted, Ramona would have seen a look on it that would have startled her more than the one she had surprised a few days previous, after the incident with Margarita. All day there had been coming and going in Alessandro's brain a confused procession of thoughts, vague yet intense. Put in words, they would have been found to be little more than ringing changes on this idea: "The Señorita Ramona has Indian blood in her veins. The Señorita Ramona is alone. The Señora loves her not. Indian blood! Indian blood!" These, or something like them, would have been the words; but Alessandro did not put them in words. He only worked away on the rough posts for Señor Felipe's bedstead, hammered, fitted, stretched the raw-hide and made it tight and firm, driving every nail, striking every blow, with a bounding sense of exultant strength, as if there were suddenly all around him a new heavens and a new earth.

Now, when he heard Ramona say suddenly in her girlish, eager tone, "It must be; I never thought of it; I should like to try it," these vague confused thoughts of the day, and the day's bounding sense of exultant strength, combined in a quick vision before Alessandro's eyes, — a vision of starry skies overhead, Ramona and himself together, looking up to them. But when he raised his head, all he said was, "There, Señorita! That is all firm, now. If Señor Felipe will let me lay him on this bed, he will sleep as he has not slept since he fell ill."

Ramona ran eagerly into Felipe's room. "The bed is all ready on the veranda," she exclaimed. "Shall Alessandro come in and carry you out?"

Felipe looked up, startled. The Señora turned

on Ramona that expression of gentle, resigned displeasure, which always hurt the girl's sensitive nature far worse than anger. "I had not spoken to Felipe yet of the change, Ramona," she said. "I supposed that Alessandro would have informed me when the bed was ready; I am sorry you came in so suddenly. Felipe is still very weak, you see."

"What is it? What is it?" exclaimed Felipe, impatiently.

As soon as it was explained to him, he was like a child in his haste to be moved.

"That's just what I needed!" he exclaimed. "This cursed bed racks every bone in my body, and I have longed for the sun more than ever a thirsty man longed for water. Bless you, Alessandro," he went on, seeing Alessandro in the doorway. "Come here, and take me up in those long arms of yours, and carry me quick. Already I feel myself better."

Alessandro lifted him as if he were a baby; indeed, it was but a light burden now, Felipe's wasted body, for a man much less strong than Alessandro to lift.

Ramona, chilled and hurt, ran in advance, carrying pillows and blankets. As she began to arrange them on the couch, the Señora took them from her hands, saying, "I will arrange them myself;" and waved Ramona away.

It was a little thing. Ramona was well used to such. Ordinarily it would have given her no pain she could not conceal. But the girl's nerves were not now in equilibrium. She had had hard work to keep back her tears at the first rebuff. This second was too much. She turned, and walked swiftly away, the tears rolling down her cheeks.

Alessandro saw it; Felipe saw it.

To Felipe the sight was, though painful, not a surprise. He knew but too well how often his mother hurt Ramona. All he thought now, in his weakness, was, "Alas! what a pity my mother does not love Ramona!"

To Alessandro the sight was the one drop too much in the cup. As he stooped to lay Felipe on the bed, he trembled so that Felipe looked up, half afraid.

"Am I still so heavy, Alessandro?" he said, smiling.

"It is not your weight, Señor Felipe," answered Alessandro, off guard, still trembling, his eyes following Ramona.

Felipe saw. In the next second, the eyes of the two young men met. Alessandro's fell before Felipe's. Felipe gazed on, steadily, at Alessandro.

"Ah!" he said; and as he said it, he closed his eyes, and let his head sink back into the pillow.

"Is that comfortable? Is that right?" asked the Señora, who had seen nothing.

"The first comfortable moment I have had, mother," said Felipe. "Stay, Alessandro. I want to speak to you as soon as I am rested. This move has shaken me up a good deal. Wait."

"Yes, Señor," replied Alessandro, and seated himself on the veranda steps.

"If you are to stay, Alessandro," said the Señora, "I will go and look after some matters that need my attention. I feel always at ease about Señor Felipe when you are with him. You will stay till I come back?"

"Yes, Señora," said Alessandro, in a tone cold as the Señora's own had been to Ramona. He was no longer in heart the Señora Moreno's servant. In fact, he was at that very moment revolving confusedly in his mind whether there could be any possibility of his getting away before the expiration of the time for which he had agreed to stay.

It was a long time before Felipe opened his eyes. Alessandro thought he was asleep.

At last Felipe spoke. He had been watching Alessandro's face for some minutes. "Alessandro," he said.

Alessandro sprang to his feet, and walked swiftly to the bedside. He did not know what the next word might be. He felt that the Señor Felipe had seen straight into his heart in that one moment's look, and Alessandro was prepared for anything.

"Alessandro," said Felipe, "my mother has been speaking to me about your remaining with us permanently. Juan Can is now very old, and after this accident will go on crutches the rest of his days, poor soul! We are in great need of some man who understands sheep, and the care of the place generally."

As he spoke, he watched Alessandro's face closely. Swift changing expressions passed over it. Surprise predominated. Felipe misunderstood the surprise. "I knew you would be surprised," he said. "I told my mother that you would not think of it; that you had stayed now only because we were in trouble."

Alessandro bowed his head gratefully. This recognition from Felipe gave him pleasure.

"Yes, Señor," he said, "that was it. I told Father Salvierderra it was not for the wages. But my father and I have need of all the money we can earn. Our people are very poor, Señor. I do not know whether my father would think I ought to take the place you offer me, or not, Señor. It would be as he said. I will ask him."

"Then you would be willing to take it?" asked Felipe.

"Yes, Señor, if my father wished me to take it," replied Alessandro, looking steadily and gravely at Felipe; adding, after a second's pause, "if you are sure that you desire it, Señor Felipe, it would be a pleasure to me to be of help to you."

And yet it was only a few moments ago that Alessandro had been turning over in his mind the possibility of leaving the Señora Moreno's service immediately. This change had not been a caprice, not been an impulse of passionate desire to remain near Ramona; it had come from a sudden consciousness that the Señor Felipe would be his friend. And Alessandro was not mistaken.

Chapter IX

WHEN the Señora came back to the veranda, she found Felipe asleep, Alessandro standing at the foot of the bed, with his arms crossed on his breast, watching him. As the Señora drew near, Alessandro felt again the same sense of dawning hatred which had seized him at her harsh speech to Ramona. He lowered his eyes, and waited to be dismissed.

"You can go now, Alessandro," said the Señora. "I will sit here. You are quite sure that it will be safe for Señor Felipe to sleep here all night?"

"It will cure him before many nights," replied Alessandro, still without raising his eyes, and turning to go.

"Stay," said the Señora. Alessandro paused. "It will not do for him to be alone here in the night, Alessandro."

Alessandro had thought of this, and had remembered that if he lay on the veranda floor by Señor Felipe's side, he would also lie under the Señorita's window.

"No, Señora," he replied. "I will lie here by his side. That was what I had thought, if the Señora is willing."

"Thank you, Alessandro," said the Señora, in a tone which would have surprised poor Ramona, still sitting alone in her room, with sad eyes. She did not know the Señora could speak thus sweetly to any one but Felipe. "Thank you! You are kind. I will have a bed made for you."

"Oh, no!" cried Alessandro; "if the Señora will excuse me, I could not lie on a bed. A raw-hide like Señor Felipe's, and my blanket, are all I want. I could not lie on any bed."

"To be sure," thought the Señora; "what was I thinking of! How the boy makes one forget he is an Indian! But the floor is harder than the ground, Alessandro," she said kindly.

"No, Señora," he said, "it is all one; and to-night I will not sleep. I will watch Señor Felipe, in case there should be a wind, or he should wake and need something."

"I will watch him myself till midnight," said the Señora. "I should feel easier to see how he sleeps at first."

It was the balmiest of summer nights, and as still as if no living thing were on the earth. There was a full moon, which shone on the garden, and on the white front of the little chapel among the trees. Ramona, from her window, saw Alessandro pacing up and down the walk. She had seen him spread down the raw-hide by Felipe's bed, and had seen the Señora take her place in one of the big carved chairs. She wondered if they were both going to watch; she wondered why the Señora would never let her sit up and watch with Felipe.

"I am not of any use to anybody," she thought sadly. She dared not go out and ask any questions about the arrangements for the night. At supper the Señora had spoken to her only in the same cold and distant manner which always made her dumb and afraid. She had not once seen Felipe alone during the day. Margarita, who, in the former times, — ah, how far away those former times looked now! — had been a greater comfort to Ramona than she realized, — Margarita now was sulky and silent, never came into Ramona's presence if she could help it, and looked at her sometimes with an expression which made Ramona tremble, and say to herself, "She hates me. She has always hated me since that morning."

It had been a long, sad day to Ramona; and as she sat in her window leaning her head against the sash, and looked at Alessandro pacing up and down, she felt for the first time, and did not shrink from it nor in any wise disavow or disguise it to herself, that she was glad he loved her. More than this she did not think; beyond this she did not go. Her mind was not like Margarita's, full of fancies bred of freedom in intercourse with men. But distinctly, tenderly glad that Alessandro loved her, and distinctly, tenderly aware how well he loved her, she was, as she sat at her window this night, looking out into the moonlit garden; after she had gone to bed, she could still hear his slow, regular steps on the garden-walk, and the last thought she had, as she fell asleep, was that she was glad Alessandro loved her.

The moon had been long set, and the garden, chapel-front, trees, vines, were all wrapped in impenetrable darkness, when Ramona awoke, sat up in her bed, and listened. All was so still that the sound of Felipe's low, regular breathing came in through her open window. After hearkening to it for a few moments, she rose noiselessly from her bed, and creeping to the window parted the curtains and looked out; noiselessly, she thought; but it was not noiselessly enough to escape Alessandro's quick ear; without a sound, he sprang to his feet, and stood looking at Ramona's window.

"I am here, Señorita," he whispered. "Do you want anything?"

"Has he slept all night like this?" she whispered back.

"Yes, Señorita. He has not once moved."

"How good!" said Ramona. "How good!"

Then she stood still; she wanted to speak again to

Alessandro, to hear him speak again, but she could think of no more to say. Because she could not, she gave a little sigh.

Alessandro took one swift step towards the window. " May the saints bless you, Señorita," he whispered fervently.

"Thank you, Alessandro," murmured Ramona, and glided back to her bed, but not to sleep. It lacked not much of dawn; as the first faint light filtered through the darkness, Ramona heard the Señora's window open.

" Surely she will not strike up the hymn and wake Felipe," thought Ramona; and she sprang again to the window to listen. A few low words between the Señora and Alessandro, and then the Señora's window closed again, and all was still.

" I thought she would not have the heart to wake him," said Ramona to herself. "The Virgin would have had no pleasure in our song, I am sure; but I will say a prayer to her instead;" and she sank on her knees at the head of her bed, and began saying a whispered prayer. The footfall of a spider in Ramona's room had not been light enough to escape the ear of that watching lover outside. Again Alessandro's tall figure arose from the floor, turning towards Ramona's window; and now the darkness was so far softened to dusk, that the outline of his form could be seen. Ramona felt it rather than saw it, and stopped praying. Alessandro was sure he had heard her voice.

"Did the Señorita speak?" he whispered, his face close at the curtain. Ramona, startled, dropped her rosary, which rattled as it fell on the wooden floor.

" No, no, Alessandro," she said, " I did not speak." And she trembled, she knew not why. The sound of the beads on the floor explained to Alessandro what had been the whispered words he heard.

" She was at her prayers," he thought, ashamed and sorry. " Forgive me," he whispered, " I thought you called;" and he stepped back to the outer edge of the veranda, and seated himself on the railing. He would lie down no more. Ramona remained on her knees, gazing at the window. Through the transparent muslin curtain the dawning light came slowly, steadily, till at last she could see Alessandro distinctly. Forgetful of all else, she knelt gazing at him. The rosary lay on the floor, forgotten. Ramona would not finish that prayer, that day. But her heart was full of thanksgiving and gratitude, and the Madonna had a better prayer than any in the book.

The sun was up, and the canaries, finches, and linnets had made the veranda ring with joyous racket, before Felipe opened his eyes. The Señora had come and gone and come again, looking at him anxiously, but he stirred not. Ramona had stolen timidly out, glancing at Alessandro only long enough to give him one quick smile, and bent over Felipe's bed, holding her breath, he lay so still.

"Ought he to sleep so long?" she whispered.

"Till the noon, it may be," answered Alessandro; " and when he wakes, you will see by his eye that he is another man."

It was indeed so. When Felipe first looked about him, he laughed outright with pure pleasure. Then catching sight of Alessandro at the steps, he called, in a stronger voice than had yet been heard from him, " Alessandro, you are a famous physician. Why could n't that fool from Ventura have known as much? With all his learning, he had had me in the next world before many days, except for you. Now, Alessandro, breakfast! I am hungry. I had forgotten what the thought of food was like to a hungry stomach. And plenty! plenty!" he called, as Alessandro ran towards the kitchen. "Bring all they have."

When the Señora saw Felipe bolstered up in the bed, his eye bright, his color good, his voice clear, eating heartily like his old self, she stood like a statue in the middle of the veranda for a moment; then turning to Alessandro, she said chokingly, "May Heaven reward you!" and disappeared abruptly in her own room. When she came out, her eyes were red. All day she moved and spoke with a softness unwonted, indeed inconceivable. She even spoke kindly and without constraint to Ramona. She felt like one brought back from the dead.

After this, a new sort of life began for them all. Felipe's bed on the veranda was the rallying point for everything and everybody. The servants came to look up at him, and wish him well, from the garden-walk below. Juan Can, when he first hobbled out on the stout crutches Alessandro had made him of manzanita wood, dragged himself all the way round the house, to have a look at Señor Felipe and a word with him. The Señora sat there, in the big carved chair, looking like a sibyl with her black silk banded head-dress severely straight across her brow, and her large dark eyes gazing out, past Felipe, into the far south sky. Ramona lived there too, with her embroidery or her book, sitting on cushions on the floor in a corner, or at the foot of Felipe's bed, always so placed, however, — if anybody had noticed, but nobody did, — so placed that she could look at Felipe without looking full at the Señora's chair, even if the Señora were not in it.

Here also came Alessandro many times a day, — sometimes sent for, sometimes of his own accord. He was freely welcome. When he played or sang, he sat on the upper step of the stairs leading down to the garden. He also had a secret, which he thought all his own, in regard to the positions he chose. He sat always, when Ramona was there, in the spot which best commanded a view of her face. The secret was not all his own. Felipe knew it. Nothing was escaping Felipe in these days. A bomb-shell exploding at their feet would not have more astonished the different members of this circle, the Señora, Ramona, Alessandro, than it would to have been made suddenly aware of the thoughts which were going on in Felipe's mind now, from day to day, as he lay there placidly looking at them all.

It is probable that if Felipe had been in full health and strength when the revelation suddenly came to him that Alessandro loved Ramona, and that Ramona might love Alessandro, he would have been instantly filled with jealous antagonism. But at the time when this revelation came, he was prostrate, feeble, thinking many times a day that he must soon die; it did not seem to Felipe that a man could be so weak as he was, and ever again be strong and well. Side by side with these forebodings of his own death, always came the thought of Ramona. What would become of her, if he were gone? Only too well he knew that the girl's heart would be broken; that she could not live on alone with his mother. Felipe adored his mother; but he understood her feeling about Ramona.

With his feebleness had also come to Felipe, as is often the case in long illnesses, a greater clearness of perception. Ramona had ceased to puzzle him. He no longer asked himself what her long, steady look into his eyes meant. He knew. He saw it meant that as a sister she loved him, had always loved him, and could love him in no other way. He wondered a little at himself that this gave him no more pain; only a sort of sweet, mournful tenderness towards her. It must be because he was so soon going out of the world, he thought. Presently he began to be aware that a new quality was coming into his love for her. He himself was returning to the brother love which he had had for her when they were children together, and in which he had felt no change until he became a man and Ramona a woman. It was strange what a peace fell upon Felipe when this was finally clear and settled in his mind. No doubt he had had more misgiving and fear about his mother in the matter than he had ever admitted to himself; perhaps also the consciousness of Ramona's unfortunate birth had rankled at times; but all this was past now. Ramona was his sister. He was her brother. What course should he pursue in the crisis which he saw drawing near? How could he best help Ramona? What would be best for both her and Alessandro? Long before the thought of any possible union between himself and Ramona had entered into Alessandro's mind, still longer before it had entered into Ramona's to think of Alessandro as a husband, Felipe had spent hours in forecasting, plotting, and planning for them. For the first time in his life he felt himself in the dark as to his mother's probable action. That any concern as to Ramona's personal happiness or welfare would influence her, he knew better than to think for a moment. So far as that was concerned, Ramona might wander out the next hour, wife of a homeless beggar, and his mother would feel no regret. But Ramona had been the adopted daughter of the Señora Ortegna, bore the Ortegna name, and had lived as foster-child in the house of the Morenos. Would the Señora permit such a one to marry an Indian?

Felipe doubted. The longer he thought, the more he doubted. The more he watched, the more he saw that the question might soon have to be decided. Any hour might precipitate it. He made plan after plan for forestalling trouble, for preparing his mother; but Felipe was by nature indolent, and now he was, in addition, feeble. Day after day slipped by. It was exceedingly pleasant on the veranda. Ramona was usually with him; his mother was gentler, less sad, than he had ever seen her. Alessandro was always at hand, ready for any service, — in the field, in the house, — his music a delight, his strength and fidelity a repose, his personal presence always agreeable. "If only my mother could think it," reflected Felipe, "it would be the best thing, all round, to have Alessandro stay here as overseer of the place, and then they might be married. Perhaps before the summer is over she will come to see it so."

And the delicious, languid, semi-tropic summer came hovering over the valley. The apricots turned golden, the peaches glowed, the grapes filled and hardened, like opaque emeralds hung thick under the canopied vines. The garden was a shade brown, and the roses had all fallen; but there were lilies, and orange-blossoms, and poppies, and carnations, and geraniums in the pots, and musk, — oh, yes, ever and always musk. It was like an enchanter's spell, the knack the Señora had of forever keeping relays of musk to bloom all the year; and it was still more like an enchanter's spell, that Felipe would never confess that he hated it. But the bees liked it, and the humming-birds, — the butterflies also; and the air was full of them. The veranda was a quieter place now as the season's noon grew near. The linnets were all nesting, and the finches and the canaries too; and the Señora spent hours, every day, tirelessly feeding the mothers. The vines had all grown and spread out to their thickest; no need any longer of the gay blanket Alessandro had pinned up that first morning to keep the sun off Felipe's head.

What was the odds between a to-day and a to-morrow in such a spot as this? "To-morrow," said Felipe, "I will speak to my mother," and "to-morrow," and "to-morrow;" but he did not.

There was one close observer of these pleasant veranda days that Felipe knew nothing about. That was Margarita. As the girl came and went about her household tasks, she was always on the watch for Alessandro, on the watch for Ramona. She was biding her time. Just what shape her revenge was going to take, she did not know. It was no use plotting. It must be as it fell out; but that the hour and the way for her revenge would come, she never doubted.

When she saw the group on the veranda, as she often did, all listening to Alessandro's violin, or to his singing, Alessandro himself now at his ease and free in the circle, as if he had been there always, her anger was almost beyond bounds.

"Oh, ho! like a member of the family; quite so!" she sneered. "It is new times when a head shepherd spends his time with the ladies of the house, and sits in their presence like a guest who is invited! We shall see; we shall see what comes of all this!" And she knew not which she hated the more of the two, Alessandro or Ramona.

Since the day of the scene at the artichoke-field she had never spoken to Alessandro, and had avoided, so far as was possible, seeing him. At first Alessandro was sorry for this, and tried to be friendly with her. As soon as he felt assured that the incident had not hurt him at all in the esteem of Ramona, he began to be sorry for Margarita. "A man should not be rude to any maiden," he thought; and he hated to remember how he had pushed Margarita from him, and snatched his hand away, when he had in the outset made no objection to her taking it. But Margarita's resentment was not to be appeased. She understood only too clearly how little Alessandro's gentle advances meant, and she would none of them. "Let him go to his Señorita," she said bitterly, mocking the reverential tone in which she had overheard him pronounce the word. "She is fond enough of him, if only the fool had eyes to see it. She'll be ready to throw herself at his head before long, if this kind of thing keeps up. 'It is not well to speak thus freely of young men, Margarita!' Ha, ha! Little I thought that day which way the wind set in my mistress's temper! I'll wager she reproves me no more, under this roof or any other! Curse her! What did she want of Alessandro, except to turn his head, and then bid him go his way!"

To do Margarita justice, she never once dreamed of the possibility of Ramona's wedding Alessandro. A clandestine affair, an intrigue of more or less intensity, such as she herself might have carried on with any one of the shepherds, — this was the utmost stretch of Margarita's angry imaginations in regard to her young mistress's liking for Alessandro. There was not, in her way of looking at things, any impossibility of such a thing as that. But marriage! It might be questioned whether that idea would have been any more startling to the Señora herself than to Margarita.

Little had passed between Alessandro and Ramona which Margarita did not know. The girl was always like a sprite, — here, there, everywhere, in an hour, and with eyes which, as her mother often told her, saw on all sides of her head. Now, fired by her new purpose, new passion, she moved swifter than ever, and saw and heard even more. There were few hours of any day when she did not know to a certainty where both Alessandro and Ramona were; and there had been few meetings between them which she had not either seen or surmised.

In the simple life of such a household as the

—Illustration by Henry Sandham.

The grape arbor at Guajome. —Photograph by George Wharton James. Circa 1911.

1

The chapel door. —Photograph by V.C. Vroman. Circa 1913.

2

—Courtesy of the San Diego Historical Society - Ticor Collection

Helen Hunt Jackson loved Indian handicrafts and was an avid collector. She took her treasures along on most

Señora's, it was not strange that this was possible; nevertheless, it argued and involved untiring vigilance on Margarita's part. Even Felipe, who thought himself, from his vantage-post of observation on the veranda, and from his familiar relation with Ramona, well informed of most that happened, would have been astonished to hear all that Margarita could have told him. In the first days Ramona herself had guilelessly told him much, — had told him how Alessandro, seeing her trying to sprinkle and bathe and keep alive the green ferns with which she had decorated the chapel for Father Salvierderra's coming, had said: "Oh, Señorita, they are dead! Do not take trouble with them! I will bring you fresh ones;" and the next morning she had found, lying
1 at the chapel door, a pile of such ferns as she had never before seen; tall ones, like ostrich-plumes, six and eight feet high; the feathery maiden-hair, and the gold fern, and the silver, twice as large as she ever had found them. The chapel was beautiful, like a conservatory, after she had arranged them in vases and around the high candlesticks.

It was Alessandro, too, who had picked up in the artichoke-patch all of the last year's seed-vessels which had not been trampled down by the cattle, and bringing one to her, had asked shyly if she did not think it prettier than flowers made out of paper. His people, he said, made wreaths of them. And so they were, more beautiful than any paper flowers which ever were made, — great soft round disks of fine straight threads like silk, with a kind of saint's halo around them of sharp, stiff points, glossy as satin, and of a lovely creamy color. It was the strangest thing in the world nobody had ever noticed them as they lay there on the ground. She had put a great wreath of them around Saint Joseph's head, and a bunch in the Madonna's hand; and when the Señora saw them, she exclaimed in admiration, and thought they must have been made of silk and satin.

2 And Alessandro had brought her beautiful baskets, made by the Indian women at Pala, and one which had come from the North, from the Tulare country; it had gay feathers woven in with the reeds, — red and yellow, in alternate rows, round and round. It was like a basket made out of a bright-colored bird.

And a beautiful stone bowl Alessandro had brought her, glossy black, that came all the way from Catalina Island; a friend of Alessandro's got it. For the first few weeks it had seemed as if hardly a day passed that there was not some new token to be chronicled of Alessandro's thoughtfulness and good-will. Often, too, Ramona had much to tell that Alessandro had said, — tales of the old Mission days that he had heard from his father; stories of saints, and of the early Fathers, who were more like saints than like men, Alessandro said, — Father Junipero, who founded the first Missions, and Father Crespi, his friend. Alessandro's grandfather had journeyed with

Father Crespi as his servant, and many a miracle he had with his own eyes seen Father Crespi perform. There was a cup out of which the Father always took his chocolate for breakfast, — a beautiful cup, which was carried in a box, the only luxury the Father had; and one morning it was broken, and everybody was in terror and despair. "Never mind, never mind," said the Father; "I will make it whole;" and taking the two pieces in his hands, he held them tight together, and prayed over them, and 3
they became one solid piece again, and it was used all through the journey, just as before.

But now, Ramona never spoke voluntarily of Alessandro. To Felipe's sometimes artfully put questions or allusions to him, she made brief replies, and never continued the topic; and Felipe had observed another thing: she now rarely looked at Alessandro. When he was speaking to others she kept her eyes on the ground. If he addressed her, she looked quickly up at him, but lowered her eyes after the first glance. Alessandro also observed this, and was glad of it. He understood it. He knew how differently she could look in his face in the rare moments when they were alone together. He fondly thought he alone knew this; but he was mistaken. Margarita knew. She had more than once seen it.

It had happened more than once that he had found Ramona at the willows by the brook, and had talked with her there. The first time it happened, it was a chance; after that never a chance again, for Alessandro went often seeking the spot, hoping to find her. In Ramona's mind too, not avowed, but half consciously, there was, if not the hope of seeing him there, at least the memory that it was there they had met. It was a pleasant spot, — cool and shady even at noon, and the running water always full of music. Ramona often knelt there of a morn- 4
ing, washing out a bit of lace or a handkerchief; and when Alessandro saw her, it went hard with him to stay away. At such moments the vision returned to him vividly of that first night when, for the first second, seeing her face in the sunset glow, he had thought her scarce mortal. It was not that he even now thought her less a saint; but ah, how well he knew her to be human! He had gone alone in the dark to this spot many a time, and, lying on the grass, put his hands into the running water, and played with it dreamily, thinking, in his poetic Indian fashion, thoughts like these: "Whither have gone the drops that passed beneath her hands, just here? These drops will never find those in the sea; but I love this water!"

Margarita had seen him thus lying, and without dreaming of the refined sentiment which prompted his action, had yet groped blindly towards it, thinking to herself: "He hopes his Señorita will come down to him there. A nice place it is for a lady to meet her lover, at the washing-stones! It will take swifter water than any in that brook, Señorita Ramona, to wash you white in the Señora's eyes, if ever

of her travels and took pleasure in displaying them, hoping always that by demonstrating the artistry of native workmanship she could help to reveal the Indian culture to skeptical Anglos.

* * *

3 The child of rigid Calvinists raised to regard the Pope as an Anti-Christ, Jackson was perhaps more enthralled by the mission mystique than if she'd been reared a Catholic. "The tales still told by old people of festal occasions at the missions sound like tales of the Old World rather than the new," she wrote in *Century*. "There was a strange difference fifty years ago (the 1830s), between the atmosphere on the east and the west sides of the American continent: On the Atlantic shore, the descendants of the Puritans weighed down by serious purpose, half grudging the time for their one staid yearly Thanksgiving, and driving the Indians farther and farther into the wilderness every year, fighting and killing them; on the Pacific shore, the merry people of Mexican and Spanish blood, troubling themselves about nothing, dancing away whole days and nights like children, while their priests were gathering the Indians by thousands into communities and feeding and teaching them."

4 

Indian women washing. Circa 1880.
—Courtesy of the San Diego Histroical Society - Ticor Collection

she come upon you there with the head shepherd, making free with him, maybe! Oh, but if that could only happen, I'd die content!" And the more Margarita watched, the more she thought it not unlikely that it might turn out so. It was oftener at the willows than anywhere else that Ramona and Alessandro met; and, as Margarita noticed with malicious satisfaction, they talked each time longer, each time parted more lingeringly. Several times it had happened to be near supper-time; and Margarita, with one eye on the garden-walk, had hovered restlessly near the Señora, hoping to be ordered to call the Señorita to supper.

"If but I could come on them of a sudden, and say to her as she did to me, 'You are wanted in the house'! Oh, but it would do my soul good! I'd say it so it would sting like a lash laid on both their faces! It will come! It will come! It will be there that she'll be caught one of these fine times she's having! I'll wait! It will come!"

The willows. — Photograph by A.C. Vroman, 1913

Chapter X

IT came. And when it came, it fell out worse for Ramona than Margarita's most malicious hopes had pictured; but Margarita had no hand in it. It was the Señora herself.

Since Felipe had so far gained as to be able to be dressed, sit in his chair on the veranda, and walk about the house and garden a little, the Señora, at ease in her mind about him, had resumed her old habit of long, lonely walks on the place. It had been well said by her servants, that there was not a blade of grass on the estate that the Señora had not seen. She knew every inch of her land. She had a special purpose in walking over it now. She was carefully examining to see whether she could afford to sell to the Ortegas a piece of pasture-land which they greatly desired to buy, as it joined a pasturage tract of theirs. This bit of land lay farther from the house than the Señora realized, and it had taken more time than she thought it would, to go over it; and it was already sunset on this eventful day, when, hurrying home, she turned off from the highway into the same short-cut path in which Father Salvierderra had met Ramona in the spring. There was no difficulty now in getting through the mustard tangle. It was parched and dry, and had been trampled by cattle. The Señora walked rapidly, but it was dusky twilight when she reached the willows; so dusky that she saw nothing — and she stepped so lightly on the smooth brown path that she made no sound — until suddenly, face to face with a man and a woman standing locked in each other's arms, she halted, stepped back a pace, gave a cry of surprise, and, in the same second, recognized the faces of the two, who, stricken dumb, stood apart, each gazing into her face with terror.

Strangely enough, it was Ramona who spoke first. Terror for herself had stricken her dumb; terror for Alessandro gave her a voice.

"Señora," she began.

"Silence! Shameful creature!" cried the Señora. "Do not dare to speak! Go to your room!"

Ramona did not move.

"As for you," the Señora continued, turning to Alessandro, "you," — she was about to say, "You

are discharged from my service from this hour," but
recollecting herself in time, said, — "you will answer
to Señor Felipe. Out of my sight!" And the Señora
Moreno actually, for once in her life beside herself
with rage, stamped her foot on the ground. "Out 1
of my sight!" she repeated.

Alessandro did not stir, except to turn towards Ramona with an inquiring look. He would run no risk of doing what she did not wish. He had no idea what she would think it best to do in this terrible dilemma.

"Go, Alessandro," said Ramona, calmly, still looking the Señora full in the eye. Alessandro obeyed; before the words had left her lips, he had walked away.

Ramona's composure, and Alessandro's waiting for further orders than her own before stirring from the spot, were too much for Señora Moreno. A wrath, such as she had not felt since she was young, took possession of her. As Ramona opened her lips again, saying, "Señora," the Señora did a shameful deed; she struck the girl on the mouth, a cruel blow.

"Speak not to me!" she cried again; and seizing her by the arm, she pushed rather than dragged her up the garden-walk.

"Señora, you hurt my arm," said Ramona, still in the same calm voice. "You need not hold me. I will go with you. I am not afraid."

Was this Ramona? The Señora, already ashamed, let go the arm, and stared in the girl's face. Even in the twilight she could see upon it an expression of transcendent peace, and a resolve of which no one would have thought it capable. "What does this mean?" thought the Señora, still weak, and trembling all over, from rage. "The hussy, the hypocrite!" and she seized the arm again.

This time Ramona did not remonstrate, but submitted to being led like a prisoner, pushed into her 2
own room, the door slammed violently and locked on
the outside.

All of which Margarita saw. She had known for an hour that Ramona and Alessandro were at the willows, and she had been consumed with impatience at the Señora's prolonged absence. More than once she had gone to Felipe, and asked with assumed interest if he were not hungry, and if he and the Señorita would not have their supper.

"No, no, not till the Señora returns," Felipe had answered. He, too, happened this time to know where Ramona and Alessandro were. He knew also where the Señora had gone, and that she would be late home; but he did not know that there would be any chance of her returning by way of the willows at the brook; if he had known it, he would have contrived to summon Ramona.

When Margarita saw Ramona shoved into her room by the pale and trembling Señora, saw the key turned, taken out, and dropped into the Señora's pocket, she threw her apron over her head, and ran into the back porch. Almost a remorse seized her. She remem-

1 

—Painting by Henry Sandham. Circa, 1900.

2 Like her heroine, Helen Hunt Jackson was virtually imprisoned during her stay at Rancho Guajome. Furious that her activist guest had encouraged the servants to seek better food and pay, Señora Couts literally locked the author into her room each night and did not allow her out until the following morning.

A barred window at Camulos. —Photograph by George Wharton James. Circa 1911.

3 Aside from her passion for the Indians, the love of Helen Hunt Jackson's life was her son, Rennie. "They were intimate friends when he was just a baby," an acquaintance recalled. She described the relationship between mother and son as "the best and happiest" she'd ever seen. Though only nine years old when stricken with diphtheria, Rennie reacted with amazing tenderness, courage and perception. Jackson had always found it difficult to reprimand him and could never insist that he obey her without first giving him a careful explanation of why the act was necessary. Now he showed the same affection and understanding of her. Realizing that he was dying, the child pleaded: "Promise me, Mama, that you won't kill yourself." In the long years that followed, throughout all her travels, Jackson was never without a photograph of Rennie.

An Indian dwelling typical of the time.
— Photograph by George Wharton James. Circa 1900.

bered in a flash how often Ramona had helped her in times gone by, — sheltered her from the Señora's displeasure. She recollected the torn altar-cloth. " Holy Virgin! what will be done to her now?" she exclaimed, under her breath. Margarita had never conceived of such an extremity as this. Disgrace, and a sharp reprimand, and a sundering of all relations with Alessandro, — this was all Margarita had meant to draw down on Ramona's head. But the Señora looked as if she might kill her.

" She always did hate her, in her heart," reflected Margarita; " she shan't starve her to death, anyhow. I'll never stand by and see that. But it must have been something shameful the Señora saw, to have brought her to such a pass as this; " and Margarita's jealousy again got the better of her sympathy. " Good enough for her. No more than she deserved. An honest fellow like Alessandro, that would make a good husband for any girl! " Margarita's short-lived remorse was over. She was an enemy again.

It was an odd thing, how identical were Margarita's and the Señora's view and interpretation of the situation. The Señora looking at it from above, and Margarita looking at it from below, each was sure, and they were both equally sure, that it could be nothing more nor less than a disgraceful intrigue. Mistress and maid were alike incapable either of conjecturing or of believing the truth.

As ill luck would have it, — or was it good luck? — Felipe also had witnessed the scene in the garden-walk. Hearing voices, he had looked out of his window, and, almost doubting the evidence of his senses, had seen his mother violently dragging Ramona by the arm, — Ramona pale, but strangely placid; his mother with rage and fury in her white face. The sight told its own tale to Felipe. Smiting his forehead with his hand, he groaned out: " Fool that I was, to let her be surprised; she has come on them unawares; now she will never, never forgive it! " And Felipe threw himself on his bed, to think what should be done. Presently he heard his mother's voice, still agitated, calling his name. He remained silent, sure she would soon seek him in his room. When she entered, and, seeing him on the bed, came swiftly towards him, saying, " Felipe, dear, are you ill?" he replied in a feeble voice, " No, mother, only tired a little to-night; " and as she bent over him, anxious,
4 alarmed, he threw his arms around her neck and
3 kissed her warmly. " Mother mia! " he said passionately, " what should I do without you? " The caress, the loving words, acted like oil on the troubled waters. They restored the Señora as nothing else could. What mattered anything, so long as she had her adoring and adorable son! And she would not speak to him, now that he was so tired, of this disgraceful and vexing matter of Alessandro. It could wait till morning. She would send him his supper in his room, and he would not miss Ramona, perhaps.

" I will send your supper here, Felipe," she said; " you must not overdo; you have been walking too much. Lie still." And kissing him affectionately, she went to the dining-room, where Margarita, vainly trying to look as if nothing had happened, was standing, ready to serve supper. When the Señora entered, with her countenance composed, and in her ordinary tones said, "Margarita, you can take Señor Felipe's supper into his room; he is lying down, and will not get up; he is tired," Margarita was ready to doubt if she had not been in a nightmare dream. Had she, or had she not, within the last half-hour, seen the Señora, shaking and speechless with rage, push the Señorita Ramona into her room, and lock her up there? She was so bewildered that she stood still and gazed at the Señora, with her mouth wide open.

"What are you staring at, girl?" asked the Señora, so sharply that Margarita jumped.

"Oh, nothing, nothing, Señora! And the Señorita, will she come to supper? Shall I call her?" she said.

The Señora eyed her. Had she seen? Could she have seen? The Señora Moreno was herself again. So long as Ramona was under her roof, no matter what she herself might do or say to the girl, no servant should treat her with disrespect, or know that aught was wrong.

"The Señorita is not well," she said coldly. "She is in her room. I myself will take her some supper later, if she wishes it. Do not disturb her." And the Señora returned to Felipe

Margarita chuckled inwardly, and proceeded to clear the table she had spread with such malicious punctuality two short hours before. In those two short hours how much had happened!

"Small appetite for supper will our Señorita have, I reckon," said the bitter Margarita, "and the Señor Alessandro also! I'm curious to see how he will carry himself."

But her curiosity was not gratified. Alessandro came not to the kitchen. The last of the herdsmen had eaten and gone; it was past nine o'clock, and no Alessandro. Slyly Margarita ran out and searched in some of the places where she knew he was in the habit of going; but Alessandro was not to be found. Once she brushed so near his hiding-place that he thought he was discovered, and was on the point of speaking, but luckily held his peace, and she passed on. Alessandro was hid behind the geranium clump at the chapel door; sitting on the ground, with his knees drawn up to his chin, watching Ramona's window. He intended to stay there all night. He felt that he might be needed; if Ramona wanted him, she would either open her window and call, or would come out and go down through the garden-walk to the willows. In either case, he would see her from the hiding-place he had chosen. He was racked by his emotions; mad with joy one minute, sick at heart with misgiving the next. Ramona loved him. She had told him so. She had said she would go away with him and be his wife. The words had but just passed her lips, at that dreadful moment when the Señora appeared in their presence. As he lived the scene over again, he re-experienced the joy and the terror equally.

What was not that terrible Señora capable of doing? Why did she look at him and at Ramona with such loathing scorn? Since she knew that the Señorita was half Indian, why should she think it so dreadful a thing for her to marry an Indian man? It did not once enter into Alessandro's mind, that the Señora could have had any other thought, seeing them as she did, in each other's arms. And again, what had he to give to Ramona? Could she live in a house such as he must live in, — live as the Temecula
4 women lived? No! for her sake he must leave his people; must go to some town, must do — he knew not what — something to earn more money. Anguish seized him as he pictured to himself Ramona suffering deprivations. The more he thought of the future in this light, the more his joy faded and his fear grew. He had never had sufficient hope that she could be his, to look forward thus to the practical details of life; he had only gone on loving, and in a vague way dreaming and hoping; and now, — now, in a moment, all had been changed; in a moment he had spoken, and she had spoken, and such words once spoken, there was no going back; and he had put his arms around her, and felt her head on his shoulder, and kissed her! Yes, he, Alessandro, had kissed the Señorita Ramona, and she had been glad of it, and had kissed him on the lips, as no maiden kisses a man unless she will wed with him, — him, Alessandro! Oh, no wonder the man's brain whirled, as he sat there in the silent darkness, wondering, afraid, helpless; his love wrenched from him, in the very instant of their first kiss, — wrenched from him, and he himself ordered, by one who had the right to order him, to begone! What could an Indian do against a Moreno!

Would Felipe help him? Ay, there was Felipe! That Felipe was his friend, Alessandro knew with a knowledge as sure as the wild partridge's instinct for the shelter of her brood; but could Felipe move the Señora? Oh, that terrible Señora! What would become of them?

As in the instant of drowning, men are said to review in a second the whole course of their lives, so in this supreme moment of Alessandro's love there flashed through his mind vivid pictures of every word and act of Ramona's since he first knew her. He recollected the tone in which she had said, and the surprise with which he heard her say it, at the time of Felipe's fall, "You are Alessandro, are you not?" He heard again her soft-whispered prayers the first night Felipe slept on the veranda. He recalled her tender distress because the shearers had had no dinner; the evident terribleness to her of a person going one whole day without food. "O God! will she always have food each day if she comes with me?" he said. And at the bare thought he was ready to flee away from her forever. Then he recalled her look and her words only a few hours ago, when he first told her he loved her; and his heart took courage. She had said, "I know you love me, Alessandro, and I am glad of it," and had lifted her eyes to his, with all the love that a woman's eyes can carry; and when he threw his arms around her, she had of her own accord come closer, and laid one hand on his shoulder, and turned her face to his. Ah, what else mattered! There was the whole world; if she loved him like this, nothing could make them wretched; his love would be enough for her, — and for him hers was an empire.

It was indeed true, though neither the Señora nor Margarita would have believed it, that this had been the first word of love ever spoken between Alessandro and Ramona, the first caress ever given, the first moment of unreserve. It had come about, as lovers' first words, first caresses, are so apt to do, unexpectedly, with no more premonition, at the instant, than there is of the instant of the opening of a flower. Alessandro had been speaking to Ramona of the conversation Felipe had held with him in regard to remaining on the place, and asked her if she knew of the plan.

"Yes," she said; "I heard the Señora talking about it with Felipe, some days ago."

"Was she against my staying?" asked Alessandro, quickly.

"I think not," said Ramona, "but I am not sure. It is not easy to be sure what the Señora wishes, till afterward. It was Felipe that proposed it."

This somewhat enigmatical statement as to the difficulty of knowing the Señora's wishes was like Greek to Alessandro's mind.

"I do not understand, Señorita," he said. "What do you mean by 'afterward'?"

"I mean," replied Ramona, "that the Señora never says she wishes anything; she says she leaves everything to Felipe to decide, or to Father Salvierderra. But I think it is always decided as she wishes to have it, after all. The Señora is wonderful, Alessandro; don't you think so?"

"She loves Señor Felipe very much," was Alessandro's evasive reply.

"Oh, yes," exclaimed Ramona. "You do not begin to know how much. She does not love any other human being. He takes it all. She has n't any left. If he had died, she would have died too. That is the reason she likes you so much; she thinks you saved Felipe's life. I mean, that is one reason," added Ramona, smiling, and looking up confidingly at Alessandro, who smiled back, not in vanity, but honest gratitude that the Señorita was pleased to intimate that he was not unworthy of the Señora's regard.

"I do not think she likes me," he said. "I cannot tell why; but I do not think she likes any one in the world. She is not like any one I ever saw, Señorita."

"No," replied Ramona, thoughtfully. "She is not. I am, oh, so afraid of her, Alessandro! I have always been, ever since I was a little girl. I used to think she hated me; but now I think she does not care one way or the other, if I keep out of her way."

While Ramona spoke these words, her eyes were fixed on the running water at her feet. If she had looked up, and seen the expression in Alessandro's eyes as he listened, the thing which was drawing near would have drawn near faster, would have arrived at that moment; but she did not look up. She went on, little dreaming how hard she was making it for Alessandro.

"Many 's the time I've come down here, at night, to this brook, and looked at it, and wished it was a big river, so I could throw myself in, and be carried away out to the sea, dead. But it is a fearful sin, Father Salvierderra says, to take one's own life; and always the next morning, when the sun came out, and the birds sang, I've been glad enough I had not done it. Were you ever so unhappy as that, Alessandro?"

"No, Señorita, never," replied Alessandro; "and it is thought a great disgrace, among us, to kill one's self. I think I could never do it. But, oh, Señorita, it is a grief to think of your being unhappy. Will you always be so? Must you always stay here?"

"Oh, but I am not always unhappy!" said Ramona, with her sunny little laugh. "Indeed, I am generally very happy. Father Salvierderra says that if one does no sin, one will be always happy, and that it is a sin not to rejoice every hour of the day in the sun and the sky and the work there is to do; and there is always plenty of that." Then, her face clouding, she continued: "I suppose I shall always stay here. I have no other home; you know I was the Señora's sister's adopted child. She died when I was little, and the Señora kindly took me. Father Salvierderra says I must never forget to be grateful to her for all she has done for me, and I try not to."

Alessandro eyed her closely. The whole story, as Juan Can had told it to him, of the girl's birth, was burning in his thoughts. How he longed to cry out, "O my loved one, they have made you homeless in your home. They despise you. The blood of my race is in your veins; come to me; come to me! be surrounded with love!" But he dared not. How could he dare?

Some strange spell seemed to have unloosed Ramona's tongue to-night. She had never before spoken to Alessandro of her own personal history or burdens; but she went on: "The worst thing is, Alessandro, that she will not tell me who my mother was; and I do not know if she is alive or not, or anything about her. Once I asked the Señora, but she forbade me ever to ask her again. She said she herself would tell me when it was proper for me to know. But she never has."

How the secret trembled on Alessandro's lips now.

Ramona had never seemed so near, so intimate, so trusting. What would happen if he were to tell her the truth? Would the sudden knowledge draw her closer to him, or repel her?

"Have you never asked her again?" he said.

Ramona looked up astonished. "No one ever disobeyed the Señora," she said quickly.

"I would!" exclaimed Alessandro.

"You may think so," said Ramona, "but you could n't. When you tried, you would find you could n't. I did ask Father Salvierderra once."

"What did he say?" asked Alessandro, breathless.

"The same thing. He said I must not ask; I was not old enough. When the time came, I would be told," answered Ramona, sadly. "I don't see what they can mean by the time's coming. What do you suppose they meant?"

"I do not know the ways of any people but my own, Señorita," replied Alessandro. "Many things that your people do, and still more that these Americans do, are to me so strange, I know nothing what they mean. Perhaps they do not know who was your mother?"

"I am sure they do," answered Ramona, in a low tone, as if the words were wrung from her. "But let us talk about something else, Alessandro; not about sad things, about pleasant things. Let us talk about your staying here."

"Would it be truly a pleasure to the Señorita Ramona, if I stayed?" said Alessandro.

"You know it would," answered Ramona, frankly, yet with a tremor in her voice, which Alessandro felt. "I do not see what we could any of us do without you. Felipe says he shall not let you go."

Alessandro's face glowed. "It must be as my father says, Señorita," he said. "A messenger came from him yesterday, and I sent him back with a letter telling him what the Señor Felipe had proposed to me, and asking him what I should do. My father is very old, Señorita, and I do not see how he can well spare me. I am his only child, and my mother died years ago. We live alone together in our house, and when I am away he is very lonely. But he would like to have me earn the wages, I know, and I hope he will think it best for me to stay. There are many things we want to do for the village; most of our people are poor, and can do little more than get what they need to eat day by day, and my father wishes to see them better off before he dies. Now that the Americans are coming in all around us, he is afraid and anxious all the time. He wants to get a big fence built around our land, so as to show where it is; but the people cannot take much time to work on the fence; they need all their time to work for themselves and their families. Indians
have a hard time to live now, Señorita. Were you 5
ever in Temecula?"

"No," said Ramona. "Is it a large town?"

Alessandro sighed. "Dear Señorita, it is not a town; it is only a little village not more than twenty

In 1923 Bruce Botteler and Dorise Schukow portrayed Alessandro and Ramona in the first presentation of what was to be an annual outdoor pageant presented by the People of Hemet and San Jacinto. —Courtesy of the Ramona Pageant Assoc., Inc.

5 

Temecula village. — Drawing by Henry Sandham, 1913.

6 The Indians living at Temecula, children and grandchildren of the San Luis Rey neophytes, had most of their valley under cultivation. Their valley was a fertile one, watered by two streams. Though poorly paid for their work, they nonetheless possessed cattle, horses, and sheep.

Loretta Young and Don Ameche as Ramona and Alessandro in the 20th Century-Fox production.

7 The soft coo of the wood dove haunted Jackson in the New York apartment where she'd settled in to write *Ramona.* "What is the Indian word for 'wild wood dove'? she asked a friend in California, then responded to his reply: "The word for wood dove, if I read your word correctly is, mayel—is that it? To that I shall add the termina, making it Majella, an exceedingly pretty name with a charming significance."

houses in all, and some of those are built only of tule. There is a chapel, and a graveyard. We built an adobe wall around the graveyard last year. That my father said we would do, before we built the fence around the village."

"How many people are there in the village?" asked Ramona.

6 "Nearly two hundred, when they are all there; but many of them are away most of the time. They must go where they can get work; they are hired by the farmers, or to do work on the great ditches, or to go as shepherds; and some of them take their wives and children with them. I do not believe the Señorita has ever seen any very poor people."

"Oh, yes, I have, Alessandro, at Santa Barbara. There were many poor people there, and the Sisters used to give them food every week."

"Indians?" said Alessandro.

Ramona colored. "Yes," she said, "some of them were, but not like your men, Alessandro. They were very different; miserable looking; they could not read nor write, and they seemed to have no ambition."

"That is the trouble," said Alessandro, "with so many of them; it is with my father's people, too. They say, 'What is the use?' My father gets in despair with them, because they will not learn better. He gives them a great deal, but they do not seem to be any better off for it. There is only one other man in our village who can read and write, besides my father and me, Señorita; and yet my father is all the time begging them to come to his house and learn of him. But they say they have no time; and indeed there is much truth in that, Señorita. You see everybody has troubles, Señorita."

Ramona had been listening with sorrowful face. All this was new to her. Until to-night, neither she nor Alessandro had spoken of private and personal matters.

"Ah, but these are real troubles," she said. "I do not think mine were real troubles at all. I wish I could do something for your people, Alessandro. If the village were only near by, I could teach them, could I not? I could teach them to read. The Sisters always said, that to teach the ignorant and the poor was the noblest work one could do. I wish I could teach your people. Have you any relatives there besides your father? Is there any one in the village that you — love, Alessandro?"

Alessandro was too much absorbed in thoughts of his people to observe the hesitating emphasis with which Ramona asked this question.

"Yes, Señorita, I love them all. They are like my brothers and sisters, all of my father's people," he said; "and I am unhappy about them all the time."

During the whole of this conversation Ramona had had an undercurrent of thought going on, which was making her uneasy. The more Alessandro said about his father and his people, the more she realized that he was held to Temecula by bonds that would be hard to break, the more she feared his father would not let him remain away from home for any length of time. At the thought of his going away, her very heart sickened. Taking a sudden step towards him, she said abruptly, "Alessandro, I am afraid your father will not give his consent to your staying here."

"So am I, Señorita," he replied sadly.

"And you would not stay if he did not approve of it, of course," she said.

"How could I, Señorita?"

"No," she said, "it would not be right;" but as she said these words, the tears filled her eyes.

Alessandro saw them. The world changed in that second. "Señorita! Señorita Ramona!" he cried, "tears have come in your eyes! O Señorita, then you will not be angry if I say that I love you!" and Alessandro trembled with the terror and delight of having said the words.

Hardly did he trust his palpitating senses to be telling him true the words that followed, quick, firm, though only in a whisper,—"I know that you love me, Alessandro, and I am glad of it!" Yes, this was what the Señorita Ramona was saying! And when he stammered, "But you, Señorita, you do not —you could not—" "Yes, Alessandro, I do—I love you!" in the same clear, firm whisper; and the next minute Alessandro's arms were around Ramona, and he had kissed her, sobbing rather than saying, "O Señorita, do you mean that you will go with me? that you are mine? Oh, no, beloved Señorita, you cannot mean that!" But he was kissing her. He knew she did mean it; and Ramona, whispering, "Yes, Alessandro, I do mean it; I will go with you," clung to him with her hands, and kissed him, and repeated it, "I will go with you, I love you." And then, just then, came the Señora's step, and her sharp cry of amazement, and there she stood, no more than an arm's-length away, looking at them with her indignant, terrible eyes.

What an hour this for Alessandro to be living over and over, as he crouched in the darkness, watching! But the bewilderment of his emotions did not dull his senses. As if stalking deer in a forest, he listened for sounds from the house. It seemed strangely still. As the darkness deepened, it seemed still stranger that no lamps were lit. Darkness in the Señora's room, in the Señorita's; a faint light in the dining-room, soon put out,—evidently no supper going on there. Only from under Felipe's door streamed a faint radiance; and creeping close to the veranda, Alessandro heard voices fitfully talking,—the Señora's and Felipe's; no word from Ramona. Piteously he fixed his eyes on her window; it was open, but the curtains tight drawn; no stir, no sound. Where was she? What had been done to his love? Only the tireless caution and infinite patience of his Indian blood kept Alessandro from going to her window. But he would imperil nothing by acting on his own responsibility. He would wait, if it were till daylight, till his love made a sign. Certainly before long Señor Felipe would come to his veranda bed, and then he could venture to speak to him. But it was near midnight when the door of Felipe's room opened, and he and his mother came out, still speaking in low tones. Felipe lay down on his couch; his mother, bending over, kissed him, bade him good-night, and went into her own room.

It had been some time now since Alessandro had left off sleeping on the veranda floor by Felipe's side. Felipe was so well it was not needful. But Felipe felt sure he would come to-night, and was not surprised when, a few minutes after the Señora's door closed, he heard a low voice through the vines, "Señor Felipe?"

"Hush, Alessandro," whispered Felipe. "Do not make a sound. To-morrow morning early I will see you, behind the little sheepfold. It is not safe to talk here."

"Where is the Señorita?" Alessandro breathed rather than said.

"In her room," answered Felipe.

"Well?" said Alessandro.

"Yes," said Felipe, hoping he was not lying; and this was all Alessandro had to comfort himself with, through his long night of watching. No, not all; one other thing comforted him,—the notes of two wood-doves, that at intervals he heard, cooing to each other; just the two notes, the call and the answer, "Love?" "Here," "Love?" "Here,"— and long intervals of silence between. Plain as if written on a page was the thing they told.

"That is what my Ramona is like," thought he, "the gentle wood-dove. If she is my wife my people
7 will call her Majel, the Wood-Dove."

An advertisement from the Los Angeles Times, February 18, 1916.

Chapter XI

WHEN the Señora bade Felipe good-night, she did not go to bed. After closing her door, she sat down to think what should be done about Ramona. It had been a hard task she had set herself, talking all the evening with Felipe without alluding to the topic uppermost in her mind. But Felipe was still nervous and irritable. She would not spoil his night's rest, she thought, by talking of disagreeable things. Moreover, she was not clear in her own mind what she wished to have done about Alessandro. If Ramona were to be sent away to the nuns, which was the only thing the Señora could think of as yet, there would be no reason for discharging Alessandro. And with him the Señora was by no means ready to part, though in her first anger she had been ready to dismiss him on the spot. As she pursued her reflections, the whole situation cleared itself in her mind; so easily do affairs fall into line, in the plottings and plannings of an arbitrary person, who makes in his formula no allowance for a human element which he cannot control.

Ramona should be sent in disgrace to the Sisters' School, to be a servant there for the rest of her life. The Señora would wash her hands of her forever. Even Father Salvierderra himself could not expect her any longer to keep such a shameless creature under her roof. Her sister's written instructions had provided for the possibility of just such a contingency. Going to a secret closet in the wall, behind a life-size statue of Saint Catharine, the Señora took out an iron box, battered and rusty with age, and set it on the bed. The key turned with difficulty in the lock. It was many years since the Señora had opened this box. No one but herself knew of its existence. There had been many times in the history of the Moreno house when the price of the contents of that box would have averted loss and misfortune; but the Señora no more thought of touching the treasure than if it had been guarded by angels with fiery swords. There they lay, brilliant and shining even in the dim light of the one candle, — rubies, emeralds, pearls, and yellow diamonds. The Señora's lip curled as she looked at them.

"Fine dowry, truly, for a creature like this!" she said. "Well I knew in the beginning no good would come of it; base begotten, base born, she has but carried out the instincts of her nature. I suppose I may be grateful that my own son was
too pure to be her prey!" "To be given to my 1
adopted daughter, Ramona Ortegna, on her wedding day," — so the instructions ran, — "if she weds worthily and with your approval. Should such a misfortune occur, which I do not anticipate, as that she should prove unworthy, then these jewels, and all I have left to her of value, shall be the property of the Church."

"No mention as to what I am to do with the girl herself if she proves unworthy," thought the Señora,
bitterly; "but the Church is the place for her; no 2
other keeping will save her from the lowest depths of disgrace. I recollect my sister said that Angus had at first intended to give the infant to the Church. Would to God he had done so, or left it with its Indian mother!" and the Señora rose, and paced the floor. The paper of her dead sister's handwriting fell at her feet. As she walked, her long skirt swept it rustling to and fro. She stooped, picked it up, read it again, with increasing bitterness. No softness at the memory of her sister's love for the little child; no relenting. "Unworthy!" Yes, that was a mild word to apply to Ramona, now. It was all settled; and when the girl was once out of the house, the Señora would breathe easier. She and Felipe would lead their lives together, and Felipe would wed some day. Was there a woman fair enough, good enough, for Felipe to wed? But he must wed; and the place would be gay with children's voices, and Ramona would be forgotten.

The Señora did not know how late it was. "I will tell her to-night," she said. "I will lose no time; and now she shall hear who her mother was!"

It was a strange freak of just impulse in the Señora's angry soul, which made her suddenly remember that Ramona had had no supper, and led her to go to the kitchen, get a jug of milk and some bread, and take them to the room. Turning the key cautiously, that Felipe might not hear, she opened the door and glided in. No voice greeted her; she held her candle high up; no Ramona in sight; the bed was empty. She glanced at the window. It was open. A terror seized the Señora; fresh anger also. "She has run off with Alessandro," she thought. "What horrible disgrace!" Standing motionless, she heard a faint, regular breathing from the other side of the bed. Hastily crossing the room, she saw a sight which had melted a heart that was only ice; but the Señora's was stone towards Ramona. There lay Ramona on the floor, her head on a pillow at the feet of the big Madonna which stood in the corner. Her left hand was under her cheek, her right arm flung tight around the base of the statue. She was sound

1

Drawing by Henry Sandham. Circa 1913.

2 Governor Pedro Fages set the California precedent for confining uppity women to convents in 1784, when Señora Fages — angered by his open liaison with an Indian woman — locked her bedroom door. The governor's response was to break it down and carry his wife bodily to Mission Carmel where she was incarcerated for several months. The custom continued, the last resort of frustrated husbands, fathers and guardians, for more than one hundred years.

asleep. Her face was wet with tears. Her whole attitude was full of significance. Even helpless in sleep, she was one who had taken refuge in sanctuary. This thought had been distinct in the girl's mind when she found herself, spite of all her woe and terror, growing sleepy. "She won't dare to hurt me at the Virgin's feet," she had said; "and the window is open. Felipe would hear if I called; and Alessandro will watch." And with a prayer on her lips she fell asleep.

It was Felipe's nearness more than the Madonna's, which saved her from being roused to hear her doom. The Señora stood for some moments looking at her, and at the open window. With a hot rush of disgraceful suspicions, she noted what she had never before thought of, that Alessandro, through all his watching with Felipe, had had close access to Ramona's window. "Shameful creature!" she repeated to herself. "And she can sleep! It is well she prayed, if the Virgin will hear such!" and she turned away, first setting down the jug of milk and the bread on a table. Then, with a sudden and still more curious mingling of justness in her wrath, she returned, and lifting the coverlet from the bed, spread it over Ramona, covering her carefully from head to foot. Then she went out and again locked the door.

Felipe, from his bed, heard and divined all, but made no sound. "Thank God, the poor child is asleep!" he said; "and my poor dear mother feared to awake me by speaking to her! What will become of us all to-morrow!" And Felipe tossed and turned, and had barely fallen into an uneasy sleep, when his mother's window opened, and she sang the first line of the sunrise hymn. Instantly Ramona joined, evidently awake and ready; and no sooner did the watching Alessandro hear the first note of her voice, than he struck in; and Margarita, who had been up for an hour, prowling, listening, peering, wondering, her soul racked between her jealousy and her fears, — even Margarita delayed not to unite; and Felipe, too, sang feebly; and the volume of the song went up as rounded and melodious as if all hearts were at peace and in harmony, instead of being all full of sorrow, confusion, or hatred. But there was no one of them all who was not the better for the singing; Ramona and Alessandro most of all.

"The saints be praised," said Alessandro. "There is my wood-dove's voice. She can sing!" And, "Alessandro was near. He watched all night. I am glad he loves me," said Ramona.

"To hear those two voices!" said the Señora; "would one suppose they could sing like that? Perhaps it is not so bad as I think."

As soon as the song was done, Alessandro ran to the sheepfold, where Felipe had said he would see him. The minutes would be like years to Alessandro till he had seen Felipe.

Ramona, when she waked and found herself carefully covered, and bread and milk standing on the table, felt much reassured. Only the Señora's own hand had done this, she felt sure, for she had heard her the previous evening turn the key in the lock, then violently take it out; and Ramona knew well that the fact of her being thus a prisoner would be known to none but the Señora herself. The Señora would not set servants to gossiping. She ate her bread and milk thankfully, for she was very hungry. Then she set her room in order, said her prayers, and sat down to wait. For what? She could not imagine; in truth, she did not much try. Ramona had passed now into a country where the Señora did not rule. She felt little fear. Felipe would not see her harmed, and she was going away presently with Alessandro. It was wonderful what peace and freedom lay in the very thought. The radiance on her face of these two new-born emotions was the first thing the Señora observed as she opened the door, and slowly, very slowly, eying Ramona with a steady look, entered the room. This joyous composure on Ramona's face angered the Señora, as it had done before, when she was dragging her up the garden-walk. It seemed to her like nothing less than brazen effrontery, and it changed the whole tone and manner of her address.

Seating herself opposite Ramona, but at the farthest side of the room, she said, in a tone scornful and insulting, "What have you to say for yourself?"

Returning the Señora's gaze with one no less steady, Ramona spoke in the same calm tone in which she had twice the evening before attempted to stay the Señora's wrath. This time, she was not interrupted.

"Señora," she said slowly, "I tried to tell you last night, but you would not hear me. If you had listened, you would not have been so angry. Neither Alessandro nor I have done anything wrong, and we were not ashamed. We love each other, and we are going to be married, and go away. I thank you, Señora, for all you have done for me; I am sure you will be a great deal happier when I am away;" and Ramona looked wistfully, with no shade of resentment, into the Señora's dark, shrunken face. "You have been very good to do so much for a girl you did not love. Thank you for the bread and milk last night. Perhaps I can go away with Alessandro to-day. I do not know what he will wish. We had only just that minute spoken of being married, when you found us last night."

The Señora's face was a study during the few moments that it took to say these words. She was dumb with amazement. Instantaneously, on the first sense of relief that the disgrace had not been what she supposed, followed a new wrath, if possible hotter than the first; not so much scorn, but a bitterer anger. "Marry! Marry that Indian!" she cried, as soon as she found voice. "You marry an Indian? Never! Are you mad? I will never permit it."

Ramona looked anxiously at her. "I have never disobeyed you, Señora," she said, "but this is different from all other things; you are not my mother. I have promised to marry Alessandro."

The girl's gentleness deceived the Señora.

"No," she said icily, "I am not your mother; but I stand in a mother's place to you. You were my sister's adopted child, and she gave you to me. You cannot marry without my permission, and I forbid you ever to speak again of marrying this Indian."

The moment had come for the Señora Moreno to find out, to her surprise and cost, of what stuff this girl was made, — this girl, who had for fourteen years lived by her side, docile, gentle, sunny, and uncomplaining in her loneliness. Springing to her feet, and walking swiftly till she stood close face to face with the Señora, who, herself startled by the girl's swift motion, had also risen to her feet, Ramona said, in a louder, firmer voice: "Señora Moreno, you may forbid me as much as you please. The whole world cannot keep me from marrying Alessandro. I love him. I have promised, and I shall keep my word." And with her young lithe arms straight down at her sides, her head thrown back, Ramona flashed full in the Señora's face a look of proud defiance. It was the first free moment her soul had ever known. She felt herself buoyed up as by wings in air. Her old terror of the Señora fell from her like a garment thrown off.

"Pshaw!" said the Señora, contemptuously, half amused, in spite of her wrath, by the girl's, as she thought, bootless vehemence, "you talk like a fool. Do you not know that I can shut you up in the nunnery to-morrow, if I choose?"

"No, you cannot!" replied Ramona.

"Who, then, is to hinder me?" said the Señora, insolently.

"Alessandro!" answered Ramona, proudly.

"Alessandro!" the Señora sneered. "Alessandro! Ha! a beggarly Indian, on whom my servants will set the dogs, if I bid them! Ha, ha!"

The Señora's sneering tone but roused Ramona more. "You would never dare!" she cried; "Felipe would not permit it!" A most unwise retort for Ramona.

"Felipe!" cried the Señora, in a shrill voice. "How dare you pronounce his name! He will none of you, from this hour! I will forbid him to speak to you. Indeed, he will never desire to set eyes on you when he hears the truth."

"You are mistaken, Señora," answered Ramona, more gently. "Felipe is Alessandro's friend, and — mine," she added, after a second's pause.

"So, ho! the Señorita thinks she is all-powerful in the house of Moreno!" cried the Señora. "We will see! we will see! Follow me, Señorita Ramona!" And throwing open the door, the Señora strode out, looking back over her shoulder.

"Follow me!" she cried again sharply, seeing that Ramona hesitated; and Ramona went; across the

In 1923 Dorise Schukow, left, and Adelaide Clarke appeared as Ramona and the Señora in the first production of *Ramona*, presented by the People of Hemet and San Jacinto. —Courtesy of the Ramona Pageant Assoc., Inc.

Mary Pickford was the first to portray Ramona in a movie. Here she is shown in the 1910 Biograph film with Kate Brure as the Señora.

passage-way leading to the dining-room, out into the veranda, down the entire length of it, to the Señora's room, — the Señora walking with a quick, agitated step, strangely unlike her usual gait; Ramona walking far slower than was her habit, and with her eyes bent on the ground. As they passed the dining-room door, Margarita, standing just inside, shot at Ramona a vengeful, malignant glance.

"She would help the Señora against me in anything," thought Ramona; and she felt a thrill of fear, such as the Señora with all her threats had not stirred.

The Señora's windows were open. She closed them both, and drew the curtains tight. Then she locked the door, Ramona watching her every movement.

"Sit down in that chair," said the Señora, pointing to one near the fireplace. A sudden nervous terror seized Ramona.

"I would rather stand, Señora," she said.

"Do as I bid you!" said the Señora, in a husky tone; and Ramona obeyed. It was a low, broad armchair, and as she sank back into it, her senses seemed leaving her. She leaned her head against the back and closed her eyes. The room swam. She was roused by the Señora's strong smelling-salts held for her to breathe, and a mocking taunt from the Señora's iciest voice: "The Señorita does not seem so over-strong as she did a few moments back!"

Ramona tried to reason with herself; surely no ill could happen to her, in this room, within call of the whole house. But an inexplicable terror had got possession of her; and when the Señora, with a sneer on her face, took hold of the Saint Catharine statue, and wheeling it half around, brought into view a door in the wall, with a big iron key in the key-hole, which she proceeded to turn, Ramona shook with fright. She had read of persons who had been shut up alive in cells in the wall, and starved to death. With dilating eyes she watched the Señora, who, all unaware of her terror, was prolonging it and intensifying it by her every act. First she took out the small iron box, and set it on a table. Then, kneeling, she drew out from an inner recess in the closet a large leather-covered box, and pulled it, grating and scraping along the floor, till it stood in front of Ramona. All this time she spoke no word, and the cruel expression of her countenance deepened each moment. The fiends had possession of the Señora Moreno this morning, and no mistake. A braver heart than Ramona's might have indeed been fearful, at being locked up alone with a woman who looked like that.

Finally, she locked the door and wheeled the statue back into its place. Ramona breathed freer. She was not, after all, to be thrust into the wall closet and left to starve. She gazed with wonder at the old battered boxes. What could it all mean?

"Señorita Ramona Ortegna," began the Señora,

drawing up a chair, and seating herself by the table on which stood the iron box, " I will now explain to you why you will not marry the Indian Alessandro."

At these words, this name, Ramona was herself again, — not her old self, her new self, Alessandro's promised wife. The very sound of his name, even on an enemy's tongue, gave her strength. The terrors fled away. She looked up, first at the Señora, then at the nearest window. She was young and strong; at one bound, if worst came to worst, she could leap through the window, and fly for her life, calling on Alessandro.

" I shall marry the Indian Alessandro, Señora Moreno," she said, in a tone as defiant, and now almost as insolent, as the Señora's own.

The Señora paid no heed to the words, except to say, " Do not interrupt me again. I have much to tell you; " and opening the box, she lifted out and placed on the table tray after tray of jewels. The sheet of written paper lay at the bottom of the box.

" Do you see this paper, Señorita Ramona?" she asked, holding it up. Ramona bowed her head. " This was written by my sister, the Señora Ortegna, who adopted you and gave you her name. These were her final instructions to me, in regard to the disposition to be made of the property she left to you."

Ramona's lips parted. She leaned forward, breathless, listening, while the Señora read sentence after sentence. All the pent-up pain, wonder, fear of her childhood and her girlhood, as to the mystery of her birth, swept over her anew, now. Like one hearkening for life or death, she listened. She forgot Alessandro. She did not look at the jewels. Her eyes never left the Señora's face. At the close of the reading, the Señora said sternly, " You see, now, that my sister left to me the entire disposition of everything belonging to you."

" But it has n't said who was my mother," cried Ramona. " Is that all there is in the paper?"

The Señora looked stupefied. Was the girl feigning? Did she care nothing that all these jewels, almost a little fortune, were to be lost to her forever?

" Who was your mother?" she exclaimed scornfully. " There was no need to write that down. Your mother was an Indian. Everybody knew that!"

At the word " Indian," Ramona gave a low cry.

The Señora misunderstood it. " Ay," she said, " a low, common Indian. I told my sister, when she took you, the Indian blood in your veins would show some day; and now it has come true."

Ramona's cheeks were scarlet. Her eyes flashed. " Yes, Señora Moreno," she said, springing to her feet; " the Indian blood in my veins shows to-day. I understand many things I never understood before. Was it because I was an Indian that you have always hated me?"

" You are not an Indian, and I have never hated you," interrupted the Señora.

Ramona heeded her not, but went on, more and more impetuously. " And if I am an Indian, why do you object to my marrying Alessandro? Oh, I am glad I am an Indian! I am of his people. He will be glad!" The words poured like a torrent out of her lips. In her excitement she came closer and closer to the Señora. " You are a cruel woman," she said. " I did not know it before; but now I do. If you knew I was an Indian, you had no reason to treat me so shamefully as you did last night, when you saw me with Alessandro. You have always hated me. Is my mother alive? Where does she live? Tell me; and I will go to her to-day. Tell me! She will be glad that Alessandro loves me!"

It was a cruel look, indeed, and a crueller tone, with which the Señora answered: " I have not the least idea who your mother was, or if she is still alive. Nobody ever knew anything about her, — some low, vicious creature, that your father married when he was out of his senses, as you are now, when you talk of marrying Alessandro!"

" He married her, then?" asked Ramona, with emphasis. " How know you that, Señora Moreno?"

" He told my sister so," replied the Señora, reluctantly. She grudged the girl even this much of consolation.

" What was his name?" asked Ramona.

" Phail; Angus Phail," the Señora replied almost mechanically. She found herself strangely constrained by Ramona's imperious earnestness, and she chafed under it. The tables were being turned on her, she hardly knew how. Ramona seemed to tower in stature, and to have the bearing of the one in authority, as she stood before her pouring out passionate question after question. The Señora turned to the larger box, and opened it. With unsteady hands she lifted out the garments which for so many years had rarely seen the light. Shawls and rebosos of damask, laces, gowns of satin, of velvet. As the Señora flung one after another on the chairs, it was a glittering pile of shining, costly stuffs. Ramona's eyes rested on them dreamily.

" Did my adopted mother wear all these?" she asked, lifting in her hand a fold of lace, and holding it up to the light, in evident admiration.

Again the Señora misconceived her. The girl seemed not insensible to the value and beauty of this costly raiment. Perhaps she would be lured by it.

" All these are yours, Ramona, you understand, on your wedding day, if you marry worthily, with my permission," said the Señora, in a voice a shade less cold than had hitherto come from her lips. " Did you understand what I read you?"

The girl did not answer. She had taken up in her hand a ragged, crimson silk handkerchief, which, tied in many knots, lay in one corner of the jewel-box.

" There are pearls in that," said the Señora; " that came with the things your father sent to my sister when he died."

Ramona's eyes gleamed. She began untying the

knots. The handkerchief was old, the knots tied tight, and undisturbed for years. As she reached the last knot, and felt the hard stones, she paused. "This was my father's, then?" she said.

"Yes," said the Señora, scornfully. She thought she had detected a new baseness in the girl. She was going to set up a claim to all which had been her father's property. "They were your father's, and all these rubies, and these yellow diamonds;" and she pushed the tray towards her.

Ramona had untied the last knot. Holding the handkerchief carefully above the tray, she shook the pearls out. A strange, spicy fragrance came from the silk. The pearls fell in among the rubies, rolling right and left, making the rubies look still redder by contrast with their snowy whiteness.

"I will keep this handkerchief," she said, thrusting it, as she spoke, by a swift resolute movement into her bosom. "I am very glad to have one thing that belonged to my father. The jewels, Señora, you can give to the Church, if Father Salvierderra thinks that is right. I shall marry Alessandro;" and still keeping one hand in her bosom where she had thrust the handkerchief, she walked away and seated herself again in her chair.

Father Salvierderra! The name smote the Señora like a spear-thrust. There could be no stronger evidence of the abnormal excitement under which she had been laboring for the last twenty-four hours, than the fact that she had not once, during all this time, thought to ask herself what Father Salvierderra would say, or might command, in this crisis. Her religion and the long habit of its outward bonds had alike gone from her in her sudden wrath against Ramona. It was with a real terror that she became conscious of this.

"Father Salvierderra?" she stammered; "he has nothing to do with it."

But Ramona saw the change in the Señora's face, at the word, and followed up her advantage. "Father Salvierderra has to do with everything," she said boldly. "He knows Alessandro. He will not forbid me to marry him, and if he did —" Ramona stopped. She also was smitten with a sudden terror at the vista opening before her, — of a disobedience to Father Salvierderra.

"And if he did," repeated the Señora, eying Ramona keenly, "would you disobey him?"

"Yes," said Ramona.

"I will tell Father Salvierderra what you say," retorted the Señora, sarcastically, "that he may spare himself the humiliation of laying any commands on you, to be thus disobeyed."

Ramona's lip quivered, and her eyes filled with the tears which no other of the Señora's taunts had been strong enough to bring. Dearly she loved the old monk; had loved him since her earliest recollection. His displeasure would be far more dreadful to her than the Señora's. His would give her grief; the Senora's, at utmost, only terror.

Clasping her hands, she said: "Oh, Señora, have mercy! Do not say that to the Father!"

"It is my duty to tell the Father everything that happens in my family," answered the Señora, chillingly. "He will agree with me, that if you persist in this disobedience you will deserve the severest punishment. I shall tell him all;" and she began putting the trays back in the box.

"You will not tell him as it really is, Señora," persisted Ramona. "I will tell him myself."

"You shall not see him! I will take care of that!" cried the Señora, so vindictively that Ramona shuddered.

"I will give you one more chance," said the Señora, pausing in the act of folding up one of the damask gowns. "Will you obey me? Will you promise to have nothing more to do with this Indian?"

"Never, Señora," replied Ramona; "never!"

"Then the consequences be on your own head," cried the Señora. "Go to your room! And, hark! I forbid you to speak of all this to Señor Felipe. Do you hear?"

Ramona bowed her head. "I hear," she said; and gliding out of the room, closed the door behind her, and instead of going to her room, sped like a hunted creature down the veranda steps, across the garden, calling in a low tone, "Felipe! Felipe! Where are you, Felipe?"

Chapter XII

"What shall we do?"
—Painting by Henry Sandham. Circa 1900.

THE little sheepfold, or corral, was beyond the artichoke-patch, on that southern slope whose sunshine had proved so disastrous a temptation to Margarita in the matter of drying the altar-cloth. It was almost like a terrace, this long slope; and the sheepfold, being near the bottom, was wholly out of sight of the house. This was the reason Felipe had selected it as the safest spot for his talk with Alessandro.

When Ramona reached the end of the trellised walk in the garden, she halted and looked to the right and left. No one was in sight. As she had entered the Señora's room an hour before, she had caught a glimpse of some one, she felt almost positive it was Felipe, turning off in the path to the left, leading down to the sheepfold. She stood irresolute for a moment, gazing earnestly down this path. "If the saints would only tell me where he is!" she said aloud. She trembled as she stood there, fearing each second to hear the Señora's voice calling her. But fortune was favoring Ramona, for once; even as the words passed her lips, she saw Felipe coming slowly up the bank. She flew to meet him. "Oh, Felipe, Felipe!" she began.

"Yes, dear, I know it all," interrupted Felipe; "Alessandro has told me."

"She forbade me to speak to you, Felipe," said Ramona, "but I could not bear it. What are we to do? Where is Alessandro?"

"My mother forbade you to speak to me!" cried Felipe, in a tone of terror. "Oh, Ramona, why did you disobey her? If she sees us talking, she will be even more displeased. Fly back to your room. Leave it all to me. I will do all that I can."

"But, Felipe," began Ramona, wringing her hands in distress.

"I know! I know!" said Felipe; "but you must not make my mother any more angry. I don't know what she will do till I talk with her. Do go back to your room! Did she not tell you to stay there?"

"Yes," sobbed Ramona, "but I cannot. Oh, Felipe, I am so afraid! Do help us! Do you think you can? You won't let her shut me up in the convent, will you,

Onslow Stevens, left, played Alessandro, Harry Hofmann, Felipe in the 1940 Hemet production of Ramona. —Courtesy of the Ramona Pageant Assoc., Inc.

Felipe? Where is Alessandro? Why can't I go away with him this minute? Where is he? Dear Felipe, let me go now."

Felipe's face was horror-stricken. "Shut you in the convent!" he gasped. "Did she say that? Ramona, dear, fly back to your room. Let me talk to her. Fly, I implore you. I can't do anything for you if she sees me talking with you now;" and he turned away, and walked swiftly down the terrace.

Ramona felt as if she were indeed alone in the world. How could she go back into that house! Slowly she walked up the garden-path again, meditating a hundred wild plans of escape. Where, where was Alessandro? Why did he not appear for her rescue? Her heart failed her; and when she entered her room, she sank on the floor in a paroxysm of hopeless weeping. If she had known that Alessandro was already a good half-hour's journey on his way to Temecula, galloping farther and farther away from her each moment, she would have despaired indeed.

This was what Felipe, after hearing the whole story, had counselled him to do. Alessandro had given him so vivid a description of the Señora's face and tone, when she had ordered him out of her sight, that Felipe was alarmed. He had never seen his mother angry like that. He could not conceive why her wrath should have been so severe. The longer he talked with Alessandro, the more he felt that it would be wiser for him to be out of sight till the first force of her anger had been spent. "I will say that I sent you," said Felipe, "so she cannot feel that you have committed any offence in going. Come back in four days, and by that time it will be all settled what you shall do."

It went hard with Alessandro to go without seeing Ramona; but it did not need Felipe's exclamation of surprise, to convince him that it would be foolhardy to attempt it. His own judgment had told him that it would be out of the question.

"But you will tell her all, Señor Felipe? You will tell her that it is for her sake I go?" the poor fellow said piteously, gazing into Felipe's eyes as if he would read his inmost soul.

"I will, indeed, Alessandro; I will," replied Felipe; and he held his hand out to Alessandro, as to a friend and equal. "You may trust me to do all I can do for Ramona and for you."

"God bless you, Señor Felipe," answered Alessandro, gravely, a slight trembling of his voice alone showing how deeply he was moved.

"He 's a noble fellow," said Felipe to himself, as he watched Alessandro leap on his horse, which had been tethered near the corral all night, — "a noble fellow! There is n't a man among all my friends who would have been manlier or franker than he has been in this whole business. I don't in the least wonder that Ramona loves him. He 's a noble fellow! But what is to be done! What is to be done!"

Felipe was sorely perplexed. No sharp crisis of disagreement had ever arisen between him and his mother, but he felt that one was coming now. He was unaware of the extent of his influence over her. He doubted whether he could move her very far. The threat of shutting Ramona up in the convent terrified him more than he liked to admit to himself. Had she power to do that? Felipe did not know. She must believe that she had, or she would not have made the threat. Felipe's whole soul revolted at the cruel injustice of the idea.

"As if it were a sin for the poor girl to love Alessandro!" he said. "I 'd help her to run away with him, if worse comes to worst. What can make my mother feel so!" And Felipe paced back and forth till the sun was high, and the sharp glare and heat reminded him that he must seek shelter; then he threw himself down under the willows. He dreaded to go into the house. His instinctive shrinking from the disagreeable, his disposition to put off till another time, held him back, hour by hour. The longer he thought the situation over, the less he knew how to broach the subject to his mother; the more uncertain he felt whether it would be wise for him to broach it at all. Suddenly he heard his name called. It was Margarita, who had been sent to call him to dinner. "Good heavens! dinner already!" he cried, springing to his feet.

"Yes, Señor," replied Margarita, eying him observantly. She had seen him talking with Alessandro, had seen Alessandro galloping away down the river road. She had also gathered much from the Señora's look, and Ramona's, as they passed the dining-room door together soon after breakfast. Margarita could have given a tolerably connected account of all that had happened within the last twenty-four hours to the chief actors in this tragedy which had so suddenly begun in the Moreno household. Not supposed to know anything, she yet knew nearly all; and her every pulse was beating high with excited conjecture and wonder as to what would come next.

Dinner was a silent and constrained meal, — Ramona absent, the fiction of her illness still kept up; Felipe embarrassed, and unlike himself; the Señora silent, full of angry perplexity. At her first glance in Felipe's face, she thought to herself, "Ramona has spoken to him. When and how did she do it?" For it had been only a few moments after Ramona had left her presence, that she herself had followed, and, seeing the girl in her own room, had locked the door as before, and had spent the rest of the morning on the veranda within hands' reach of Ramona's window. How, when, and where had she contrived to communicate with Felipe? The longer the Señora studied over this, the angrier and more baffled she felt; to be outwitted was even worse to her than to be disobeyed. Under her very eyes, as it were, something evidently had happened, not only against her will, but which she could not explain. Her anger even rippled out towards Felipe, and was fed by the recollection of Ramona's unwise retort, "Felipe would not let you!"

What had Felipe done or said to make the girl so sure that he would be on her side and Alessandro's? Was it come to this, that she, the Señora Moreno, was to be defied in her own house by children and servants!

It was with a tone of severe displeasure that she said to Felipe, as she rose from the dinner-table, "My son, I would like to have some conversation with you in my room, if you are at leisure."

"Certainly, mother," said Felipe, a load rolling off his mind at her having thus taken the initiative, for which he lacked courage; and walking swiftly towards her, he attempted to put his arm around her waist, as it was his affectionate habit frequently to do. She repulsed him gently, but bethinking herself, passed her hand through his arm, and leaning on it heavily as she walked, said: "This is the most fitting way, my son. I must lean more and more heavily on you each year now. Age is telling on me fast. Do you not find me greatly changed, Felipe, in the last year?"

"No, madre mia," replied Felipe, "indeed I do not. I see not that you have changed in the last ten years." And he was honest in this. His eyes did not note the changes so clear to others, and for the best of reasons. The face he saw was one no one else ever beheld; it was kindled by emotion, transfigured by love, whenever it was turned towards him.

The Señora sighed deeply as she answered: "That must be because you so love me, Felipe. I myself see the changes even day by day. Troubles tell on me as they did not when I was younger. Even within the last twenty-four hours I seem to myself to have aged frightfully;" and she looked keenly at Felipe as she seated herself in the arm-chair where poor Ramona had swooned a few hours before. Felipe remained standing before her, gazing, with a tender expression, upon her features, but saying nothing.

"I see that Ramona has told you all!" she continued, her voice hardening as she spoke. What a fortunate wording of her sentence!

"No, mother; it was not Ramona, it was Alessandro, who told me this morning, early," Felipe answered hastily, hurrying on, to draw the conversation as far away from Ramona as possible. "He came and spoke to me last night after I was in bed; but I told him to wait till morning, and then I would hear all he had to say."

"Ah!" said the Señora, relieved. Then, as Felipe remained silent, she asked, "And what did he say?"

"He told me all that had happened."

"All!" said the Señora, sneeringly. "Do you suppose that he told you all?"

"He said that you had bidden him begone out of your sight," said Felipe, "and that he supposed he must go. So I told him to go at once. I thought you would prefer not to see him again."

"Ah!" said the Señora again, startled, gratified that Felipe had so promptly seconded her action, but sorry that Alessandro had gone. "Ah, I did not know whether you would think it best to discharge him at once or not; I told him he must answer to you. I did not know but you might devise some measures by which he could be retained on the estate."

Felipe stared. Could he believe his ears? This did not sound like the relentless displeasure he had expected. Could Ramona have been dreaming? In his astonishment, he did not weigh his mother's words carefully; he did not carry his conjecture far enough; he did not stop to make sure that retaining Alessandro on the estate might not of necessity bode any good to Ramona; but with his usual impetuous ardor, sanguine, at the first glimpse of hope, that all was well, he exclaimed joyfully, "Ah, dear mother, if that could only be done, all would be well;" and, never noting the expression of his mother's face, nor pausing to take breath, he poured out all he thought and felt on the subject.

"That is just what I have been hoping for ever since I saw that he and Ramona were growing so fond of each other. He is a splendid fellow, and the best hand we have ever had on the place. All the men like him; he would make a capital overseer; and if we put him in charge of the whole estate, there would not be any objection to his marrying Ramona. That would give them a good living here with us."

"Enough!" cried the Señora, in a voice which fell on Felipe's ears like a voice from some other world, — so hollow, so strange. He stopped speaking, and uttered an ejaculation of amazement. At the first words he had uttered, the Señora had fixed her eyes on the floor, — a habit of hers when she wished to listen with close attention. Lifting her eyes now, and fixing them full on Felipe, she regarded him with a look which not all his filial reverence could bear without resentment. It was nearly as scornful as that with which she had regarded Ramona. Felipe colored.

"Why do you look at me like that, mother?" he exclaimed. "What have I done?"

The Señora waved her hand imperiously. "Enough!" she reiterated. "Do not say any more. I wish to think for a few moments;" and she fixed her eyes on the floor again.

Felipe studied her countenance. A more nearly rebellious feeling than he had supposed himself capable of slowly arose in his heart. Now he for the first time perceived what terror his mother must inspire in a girl like Ramona.

"Poor little one!" he thought. "If my mother looked at her as she did at me just now, I wonder she did not die."

A great storm was going on in the Señora's bosom. Wrath against Ramona was uppermost in it. In addition to all else, the girl had now been the cause, or at least the occasion, of Felipe's having, for the first time in his whole life, angered her beyond her control.

"As if I had not suffered enough by reason of

Janet Scott portrayed the relentless Señora from 1936-39 in the Hemet production of Ramona. —Courtesy of the Ramona Pageant Assoc., Inc.

that creature," she thought bitterly to herself, "without her coming between me and Felipe!"

But nothing could long come between the Señora and Felipe. Like a fresh lava-stream flowing down close on the track of its predecessor, came the rush of the mother's passionate love for her son close on the passionate anger at his words.

When she lifted her eyes they were full of tears, which it smote Felipe to see. As she gazed at him, they rolled down her cheeks, and she said in trembling tones: "Forgive me, my child; I had not thought anything could make me thus angry with you. That shameless creature is costing us too dear. She must leave the house."

Felipe's heart gave a bound; Ramona had not been mistaken, then. A bitter shame seized him at his mother's cruelty. But her tears made him tender; and it was in a gentle, even pleading voice that he replied: "I do not see, mother, why you call Ramona shameless. There is nothing wrong in her loving Alessandro."

"I found her in his arms!" exclaimed the Señora.

"I know," said Felipe; "Alessandro told me that he had just at that instant told her he loved her, and she had said she loved him, and would marry him, just as you came up."

"Humph!" retorted the Señora; "do you think that Indian would have dared to speak a word of love to the Señorita Ramona Ortegna, if she had not conducted herself shamelessly? I wonder that he concerned himself to speak about marriage to her at all."

"Oh, mother! mother!" was all that Felipe could say to this. He was aghast. He saw now, in a flash, the whole picture as it lay in his mother's mind, and his heart sank within him. "Mother!" he repeated, in a tone which spoke volumes.

"Ay," she continued, "that is what I say. I see no reason why he hesitated to take her, as he would take any Indian squaw, with small ceremony of marrying."

"Alessandro would not take any woman that way any quicker than I would, mother," said Felipe, courageously; "you do him injustice." He longed to add, "And Ramona too," but he feared to make bad matters worse by pleading for her at present.

"No, I do not," said the Señora; "I do Alessandro full justice. I think very few men would have behaved as well as he has under the same temptation. I do not hold him in the least responsible for all that has happened. It is all Ramona's fault."

Felipe's patience gave way. He had not known, till now, how very closely this pure and gentle girl, whom he had loved as a sister in his boyhood, and had come near loving as a lover in his manhood, had twined herself around his heart. He could not remain silent another moment, and hear her thus wickedly accused.

"Mother!" he exclaimed, in a tone which made

the Señora look up at him in sudden astonishment. "Mother, I cannot help it if I make you very angry; I must speak; I can't bear to hear you say such things of Ramona. I have seen for a long time that Alessandro loved the very ground under her feet; and Ramona would not have been a woman if she had not seen it too! She has seen it, and has felt it, and has come to love him with all her soul, just as I hope some woman will love me one of these days. If I am ever loved as well as she loves Alessandro, I shall be lucky. I think they ought to be married; and I think we ought to take Alessandro on to the estate, so that they can live here. I don't see anything disgraceful in it, nor anything wrong, nor anything but what was perfectly natural. You know, mother, it is n't as if Ramona really belonged to our family; you know she is half Indian." A scornful ejaculation from his mother interrupted him here; but Felipe hurried on, partly because he was borne out of himself at last by impetuous feeling, partly that he dreaded to stop, because if he did, his mother would speak; and already he felt a terror of what her next words might be. "I have often thought about Ramona's future, mother. You know a great many men would not want to marry her, just because she is half Indian. You, yourself, would never have given your consent to my marrying her, if I had wanted to." Again an exclamation from the Señora, this time more of horror than of scorn. But Felipe pressed on. "No, of course you would not, I always knew that; except for that, I might have loved her myself, for a sweeter girl never drew breath in this God's earth." Felipe was reckless now; having entered on this war, he would wage it with every weapon that lay within his reach; if one did not tell, another might. "You have never loved her. I don't know that you have ever even liked her; I don't think you have. I know, as a little boy, I always used to see how much kinder you were to me than to her, and I never could understand it. And you are unjust to her now. I've been watching her all summer; I've seen her and Alessandro together continually. You know yourself, mother, he has been with us on the veranda, day after day, just as if he were one of the family. I've watched them by the hour, when I lay there so sick; I thought you must have seen it too. I don't believe Alessandro has ever looked or said or done a thing I would n't have done in his place; and I don't believe Ramona has ever looked, said, or done a thing I would not be willing to have my own sister do!" Here Felipe paused. He had made his charge; like a young impetuous general, massing all his forces at the onset; he had no reserves. It is not the way to take Gibraltars.

When he paused, literally breathless, he had spoken so fast, — and even yet Felipe was not quite strong, so sadly had the fever undermined his constitution, — the Señora looked at him interrogatively, and said in a now composed tone: "You do not believe that Ramona has done anything that you would not be willing to have your own sister do? Would you be willing that your own sister should marry Alessandro?"

Clever Señora Moreno! During the few moments that Felipe had been speaking, she had perceived certain things which it would be beyond her power to do; certain others that it would be impolitic to try to do. Nothing could possibly compensate her for antagonizing Felipe. Nothing could so deeply wound her, as to have him in a resentful mood towards her; or so weaken her real control of him, as to have him feel that she arbitrarily overruled his preference or his purpose. In presence of her imperious will, even her wrath capitulated and surrendered. There would be no hot words between her and her son. He should believe that he determined the policy of the Moreno house, even in this desperate crisis.

Felipe did not answer. A better thrust was never seen on any field than the Señora's question. She repeated it, still more deliberately, in her wonted gentle voice. The Señora was herself again, as she had not been for a moment since she came upon Alessandro and Ramona at the brook. How just and reasonable the question sounded, as she repeated it slowly, with an expression in her eyes, of poising and weighing matters. "Would you be willing that your own sister should marry Alessandro?"

Felipe was embarrassed. He saw whither he was being led. He could give but one answer to this question. "No, mother," he said, "I should not; but — "

"Never mind buts," interrupted his mother; "we have not got to those yet;" and she smiled on Felipe, — an affectionate smile, but it somehow gave him a feeling of dread. "Of course I knew you could make but one answer to my question. If you had a sister, you would rather see her dead than married to any one of these Indians."

Felipe opened his lips eagerly, to speak. "Not so," he said.

"Wait, dear!" exclaimed his mother. "One thing at a time. I see how full your loving heart is, and I was never prouder of you as my son than when listening just now to your eloquent defence of Ramona. Perhaps you may be right and I wrong as to her character and conduct. We will not discuss those points." It was here that the Señora had perceived some things that it would be out of her power to do. "We will not discuss those, because they do not touch the real point at issue. What it is our duty to do by Ramona, in such a matter as this, does not turn on her worthiness or unworthiness. The question is, Is it right for you to allow her to do what you would not allow your own sister to do?" The Señora paused for a second, noted with secret satisfaction how puzzled and unhappy Felipe looked; then, in a still gentler voice, she went on, "You surely would not think that right, my son, would you?" And now the Señora waited for an answer.

"No, mother," came reluctantly from Felipe's lips. "I suppose not; but—"

"I was sure my own son could make no other reply," interrupted the Señora. She did not wish Felipe at present to do more than reply to her questions. "Of course it would not be right for us to let Ramona do anything which we would not let her do if she were really of our own blood. That is the way I have always looked at my obligation to her. My sister intended to rear her as her own daughter. She had given her her own name. When my sister died, she transferred to me all her right and responsibility in and for the child. You do not suppose that if your aunt had lived, she would have ever given her consent to her adopted daughter's marrying an Indian, do you?"

Again the Señora paused for a reply, and again the reluctant Felipe said, in a low tone, "No, I suppose she would not."

"Very well. Then that lays a double obligation on us. It is not only that we are not to permit Ramona to do a thing which we would consider disgraceful to one of our own blood; we are not to betray the trust reposed in us by the only person who had a right to control her, and who transferred that trust to us. Is not that so?"

"Yes, mother," said the unhappy Felipe.

He saw the meshes closing around him. He felt that there was a flaw somewhere in his mother's reasoning, but he could not point it out; in fact, he could hardly make it distinct to himself. His brain was confused. Only one thing he saw clearly, and that was, that after all had been said and done, Ramona would still marry Alessandro. But it was evident that it would never be with his mother's consent. "Nor with mine either, openly, the way she puts it. I don't see how it can be; and yet I have promised Alessandro to do all I could for him. Curse the luck, I wish he had never set foot on the place!" said Felipe in his heart, growing unreasonable, and tired with the perplexity.

The Señora continued: "I shall always blame myself bitterly for having failed to see what was going on. As you say, Alessandro has been with us a great deal since your illness, with his music, and singing, and one thing and another; but I can truly say that I never thought of Ramona's being in danger of looking upon him in the light of a possible lover, any more than of her looking thus upon Juan Canito, or Luigo, or any other of the herdsmen or laborers. I regret it more than words can express, and I do not know what we can do, now that it has happened."

"That's it, mother! That's it!" broke in Felipe. "You see, you see it is too late now."

The Señora went on as if Felipe had not spoken. "I suppose you would really very much regret to part with Alessandro, and your word is in a way pledged to him, as you had asked him if he would stay on the place. Of course, now that all this has happened, it would be very unpleasant for Ramona to stay here, and see him continually—at least for a time, until she gets over this strange passion she seems to have conceived for him. It will not last. Such sudden passions never do." The Señora artfully interpolated, "What should you think, Felipe, of having her go back to the Sisters' school for a time? She was very happy there."

The Señora had strained a point too far. Felipe's self-control suddenly gave way, and as impetuously as he had spoken in the beginning, he spoke again now, nerved by the memory of Ramona's face and tone as she had cried to him in the garden, "Oh, Felipe, you won't let her shut me up in the convent, will you?" "Mother!" he cried, "you would never do that. You would not shut the poor girl up in the convent!"

The Señora raised her eyebrows in astonishment. "Who spoke of shutting up?" she said. "Ramona has already been there at school. She might go again. She is not too old to learn. A change of scene and occupation is the best possible cure for a girl who has a thing of this sort to get over. Can you propose anything better, my son? What would you advise?" And a third time the Señora paused for an answer.

These pauses and direct questions of the Señora's were like nothing in life so much as like that stage in a spider's processes when, withdrawing a little way from a half-entangled victim, which still supposes himself free, it rests from its weaving, and watches the victim flutter. Subtle questions like these, assuming, taking for granted as settled, much which had never been settled at all, were among the best weapons in the Señora's armory. They rarely failed her.

"Advise!" cried Felipe, excitedly. "Advise! This is what I advise—to let Ramona and Alessandro marry. I can't help all you say about our obligations. I dare say you're right; and it's a cursedly awkward complication for us, anyhow, the way you put it."

"Yes, awkward for you, as the head of our house," interrupted the Señora, sighing. "I don't quite see how you would face it."

"Well, I don't propose to face it," continued Felipe, testily. "I don't propose to have anything to do with it, from first to last. Let her go away with him, if she wants to."

"Without our consent?" said the Señora, gently.

"Yes, without it, if she can't go with it; and I don't see, as you have stated it, how we could exactly take any responsibility about marrying her to Alessandro. But for heaven's sake, mother, let her go! She will go, anyway. You haven't the least idea how she loves Alessandro, or how he loves her. Let her go!"

"Do you really think she would run away with him, if it came to that?" asked the Señora, earnestly. "Run away and marry him, spite of our refusing to consent to the marriage?"

"I do," said Felipe.

"Then it is your opinion, is it, that the only thing left for us to do, is to wash our hands of it altogether, and leave her free to do what she pleases?"

"That 's just what I do think, mother," replied Felipe, his heart growing lighter at her words. "That 's just what I do think. We can't prevent it, and it is of no use to try. Do let us tell them they can do as they like."

"Of course, Alessandro must leave us, then," said the Señora. "They could not stay here."

"I don't see why!" said Felipe, anxiously.

"You will, my son, if you think a moment. Could we possibly give a stronger indorsement to their marriage than by keeping them here? Don't you see that would be so?"

Felipe's eyes fell. "Then I suppose they could n't be married here, either," he said.

"What more could we do than that, for a marriage that we heartily approved of, my son?"

"True, mother;" and Felipe clapped his hand to his forehead. "But then we force them to run away!"

"Oh, no!" said the Señora, icily. "If they go, they will go of their own accord. We hope they will never do anything so foolish and wrong. If they do, I suppose we shall always be held in a measure responsible for not having prevented it. But if you think it is not wise, or of no use to attempt that, I do not see what there is to be done."

Felipe did not speak. He felt discomfited; felt as if he had betrayed his friend Alessandro, his sister Ramona; as if a strange complication, network of circumstances, had forced him into a false position; he did not see what more he could ask, what more could be asked, of his mother; he did not see, either, that much less could have been granted to Alessandro and Ramona; he was angry, wearied, perplexed.

The Señora studied his face. "You do not seem satisfied, Felipe dear," she said tenderly. "As, indeed, how could you be in this unfortunate state of affairs? But can you think of anything different for us to do?"

"No," said Felipe, bitterly. "I can't, that 's the worst of it. It is just turning Ramona out of the house, that 's all."

"Felipe! Felipe!" exclaimed the Señora, "how unjust you are to yourself! You know you would never do that! You know that she has always had a home here as if she were a daughter, and always will have, as long as she wishes it. If she chooses to turn her back on it, and go away, is it our fault? Do not let your pity for this misguided girl blind you to what is just to yourself and to me. Turn Ramona out of the house! You know I promised my sister to bring her up as my own child; and I have always felt that

—Illustration by Henry Sandham. Circa 1883.

—Illustration by Henry Sandham. Circa 1900.

my son would receive the trust from me, when I died. Ramona has a home under the Moreno roof so long as she will accept it. It is not just, Felipe, to say that we turn her out;" and tears stood in the Señora's eyes.

"Forgive me, dear mother," cried the unhappy Felipe. "Forgive me for adding one burden to all you have to bear. Truth is, this miserable business has so distraught my senses, I can't seem to see anything as it is. Dear mother, it is very hard for you. I wish it were done with."

"Thanks for your precious sympathy, my Felipe," replied the Señora. "If it were not for you, I should long ago have broken down beneath my cares and burdens. But among them all, have been few so grievous as this. I feel myself and our home dishonored. But we must submit. As you say, Felipe, I wish it were done with. It would be as well, perhaps, to send for Ramona at once, and tell her what we have decided. She is no doubt in great anxiety; we will see her here."

Felipe would have greatly preferred to see Ramona alone; but as he knew not how to bring this about, he assented to his mother's suggestion.

Opening her door, the Señora walked slowly down the passage-way, unlocked Ramona's door, and said: "Ramona, be so good as to come to my room. Felipe and I have something to say to you."

Ramona followed, heavy-hearted. The words, "Felipe and I," boded no good.

"The Señora has made Felipe think just as she does herself," thought Ramona. "Oh, what will become of me!" and she stole a reproachful, imploring look at Felipe. He smiled back in a way which reassured her; but the reassurance did not last long.

"Señorita Ramona Ortegna," began the Señora. Felipe shivered. He had had no conception that his mother could speak in that way. The words seemed to open a gulf between Ramona and all the rest of the world, so cold and distant they sounded, — as the Señora might speak to an intruding stranger.

"Señorita Ramona Ortegna," she said, "my son and I have been discussing what it is best for us to do in the mortifying and humiliating position in which you place us by your relation with the Indian Alessandro. Of course you know — or you ought to know — that it is utterly impossible for us to give our consent to your making such a marriage; we should be false to a trust, and dishonor our own family name, if we did that."

Ramona's eyes dilated, her cheeks paled; she opened her lips, but no sound came from them; she looked towards Felipe, and seeing him with downcast eyes, and an expression of angry embarrassment on his face, despair seized her. Felipe had deserted their cause. Oh, where, where was Alessandro! Clasping her hands, she uttered a low cry, — a cry that cut Felipe to the heart. He was finding out, in thus being witness of Ramona's suffering, that she was far nearer and dearer to him than he had realized. It would have taken very little, at such moments as these, to have made Felipe her lover again; he felt now like springing to her side, folding his arms around her, and bidding his mother defiance. It took all the self-control he could gather, to remain silent, and trust to Ramona's understanding him later.

Ramona's cry made no break in the smooth, icy flow of the Señora's sentences. She gave no sign of having heard it, but continued: "My son tells me that he thinks our forbidding it would make no difference; that you would go away with the man all the same. I suppose he is right in thinking so, as you yourself told me that even if Father Salvierderra forbade it, you would disobey him. Of course, if this is your determination, we are powerless. Even if I were to put you in the keeping of the Church, which is what I am sure my sister, who adopted you as her child, would do, if she were alive, you would devise some means of escape, and thus bring a still greater and more public scandal on the family. Felipe thinks that it is not worth while to attempt to bring you to reason in that way; and we shall therefore do nothing. I wished to impress it upon you that my son, as head of this house, and I, as my sister's representative, consider you a member of our own family. So long as we have a home for ourselves, that home is yours, as it always has been. If you choose to leave it, and to disgrace yourself and us by marrying an Indian, we cannot help ourselves."

The Señora paused. Ramona did not speak. Her eyes were fixed on the Señora's face, as if she would penetrate to her inmost soul; the girl was beginning to recognize the Señora's true nature; her instincts and her perceptions were sharpened by love.

"Have you anything to say to me or to my son?" asked the Señora.

"No, Señora," replied Ramona; "I do not think of anything more to say than I said this morning. Yes," she added, "there is. Perhaps I shall not speak with you again before I go away. I thank you once more for the home you have given me for so many years. And you too, Felipe," she continued, turning towards Felipe, her face changing, all her pent-up affection and sorrow looking out of her tearful eyes, — "you too, dear Felipe. You have always been so good to me. I shall always love you as long as I live;" and she held out both her hands to him. Felipe took them in his, and was about to speak, when the Señora interrupted him. She did not intend to have any more of this sort of affectionate familiarity between her son and Ramona.

"Are we to understand that you are taking your leave now?" she said. "Is it your purpose to go at once?"

"I do not know, Señora," stammered Ramona; "I have not seen Alessandro; I have not heard —" And she looked up in distress at Felipe, who answered compassionately, —

"Alessandro has gone."

"Gone!" shrieked Ramona. "Gone! not gone, Felipe!"

"Only for four days," replied Felipe. "To Temecula. I thought it would be better for him to be away for a day or two. He is to come back immediately. Perhaps he will be back day after to-morrow."

"Did he want to go? What did he go for? Why did n't you let me go with him? Oh, why, why did he go?" cried Ramona.

"He went because my son told him to go," broke in the Señora, impatient of this scene, and of the sympathy she saw struggling in Felipe's expressive features. "My son thought, and rightly, that the sight of him would be more than I could bear just now; so he ordered him to go away, and Alessandro obeyed."

Like a wounded creature at bay, Ramona turned suddenly away from Felipe, and facing the Señora, her eyes resolute and dauntless spite of the streaming tears, exclaimed, lifting her right hand as she spoke, "You have been cruel; God will punish you!" and without waiting to see what effect her words had produced, without looking again at Felipe, she walked swiftly out of the room.

"You see," said the Señora, "you see she defies us."

"She is desperate," said Felipe. "I am sorry I sent Alessandro away."

"No, my son" replied the Señora, "you were wise, as you always are. It may bring her to her senses, to have a few days' reflection in solitude."

"You do not mean to keep her locked up, mother, do you?" cried Felipe.

The Señora turned a look of apparently undisguised amazement on him. "You would not think that best, would you? Did you not say that all we could do, was simply not to interfere with her in any way? To wash our hands, so far as is possible, of all responsibility about her?"

"Yes, yes," said the baffled Felipe; "that was what I said. But, mother—" He stopped. He did not know what he wanted to say.

The Señora looked tenderly at him, her face full of anxious inquiry.

"What is it, Felipe dear? Is there anything more you think I ought to say or do?" she asked.

"What is it you are going to do, mother?" said Felipe. "I don't seem to understand what you are going to do."

"Nothing, Felipe! You have entirely convinced me that all effort would be thrown away. I shall do nothing," replied the Señora. "Nothing whatever."

"Then as long as Ramona is here, everything will be just as it always has been?" said Felipe.

The Señora smiled sadly. "Dear Felipe, do you think that possible? A girl who has announced her determination to disobey not only you and me, but Father Salvierderra, who is going to bring disgrace both on the Moreno and the Ortegna name, — we can't feel exactly the same towards her as we did before, can we?"

Felipe made an impatient gesture. "No, of course not. But I mean, is everything to be just the same, outwardly, as it was before?"

"I supposed so," said the Señora. "Was not that your idea? We must try to have it so, I think. Do not you?"

"Yes," groaned Felipe, "if we can!"

Chapter XIII

THE Señora Moreno had never before been so discomfited as in this matter of Ramona and Alessandro. It chafed her to think over her conversation with Felipe; to recall how far the thing she finally attained was from the thing she had in view when she began. To have Ramona sent to the convent, Alessandro kept as overseer of the place, and the Ortegna jewels turned into the treasury of the Church, — this was the plan she had determined on in her own mind. Instead of this, Alessandro was not to be overseer on the place; Ramona would not go to the convent: she would be married to Alessandro, and they would go away together; and the Ortegna jewels, — well, that was a thing to be decided in the future; that should be left to Father Salvierderra to decide. Bold as the Señora was, she had not quite the courage requisite to take that question wholly into her own hands.

One thing was clear, Felipe must not be consulted in regard to them. He had never known of them, and need not now. Felipe was far too much in sympathy with Ramona to take a just view of the situation. He would be sure to have a quixotic idea of Ramona's right of ownership. It was not impossible that Father Salvierderra might have the same feeling. If so, she must yield; but that would go harder with her than all the rest. Almost the Señora would have been ready to keep the whole thing a secret from the Father, if he had not been at the time of the Señora Ortegna's death fully informed of all the particulars of her bequest to her adopted child. At any rate, it would be nearly a year before the Father came again, and in the meantime she would not risk writing about it. The treasure was as safe in Saint Catharine's keeping as it had been all these fourteen years; it should still lie hidden there. When Ramona went away with Alessandro, she would write to Father Salvierderra, simply stating the facts in her own way, and telling him that all further questions must wait for decision until they met.

And so she plotted and planned, and mapped out the future in her tireless weaving brain, till she was somewhat soothed for the partial failure of her plans.

There is nothing so skilful in its own defence as imperious pride. It has an ingenious system of its own, of reprisals, — a system so ingenious that the defeat must be sore indeed, after which it cannot still find some booty to bring off! And even greater than this ingenuity at reprisals is its capacity for self-deception. In this regard, it outdoes vanity a thousandfold. Wounded vanity knows when it is mortally hurt; and limps off the field, piteous, all disguises thrown away. But pride carries its banner to the last; and fast as it is driven from one field unfurls it in another, never admitting that there is a shade less honor in the second field than in the first, or in the third than in the second; and so on till death. It is impossible not to have a certain sort of admiration for this kind of pride. Cruel, those who have it, are to all who come in their way; but they are equally cruel to themselves, when pride demands the sacrifice. Such pride as this has led many a forlorn hope, on the earth, when all other motives have died out of men's breasts; has won many a crown, which has not been called by its true name.

Before the afternoon was over, the Señora had her plan, her chart of the future, as it were, all reconstructed; the sting of her discomfiture soothed; the placid quiet of her manner restored; her habitual occupations also, and little ways, all resumed. She was going to do "nothing" in regard to Ramona. Only she herself knew how much that meant; how bitterly much! She wished she were sure that Felipe also would do "nothing;" but her mind still misgave her about Felipe. Unpityingly she had led him on, and entangled him in his own words, step by step, till she had brought him to the position she wished him to take. Ostensibly, his position and hers were one, their action a unit; all the same, she did not deceive herself as to his real feeling about the affair. He loved Ramona. He liked Alessandro. Barring the question of family pride, which he had hardly thought of till she suggested it, and which he would not dwell on apart from her continuing to press it, — barring this, he would have liked to have Alessandro marry Ramona and remain on the place. All this would come uppermost in Felipe's mind again when he was removed from the pressure of her influence. Nevertheless, she did not intend to speak with him on the subject again, or to permit him to speak to her. Her ends would be best attained by taking and keeping the ground that the question of their non-interference having been settled once for all, the painful topic should never be renewed between them. In patient silence they must await Ramona's action; must bear whatever of disgrace and pain she chose to inflict on the family which had sheltered her from her infancy till now.

The details of the "nothing" she proposed to do, slowly arranged themselves in her mind. There should be no apparent change in Ramona's position in the house. She should come and go as freely as ever; no watch on her movements; she should eat,

sleep, rise up and sit down with them, as before; there should be not a word, or act, that Felipe's sympathetic sensitiveness could construe into any provocation to Ramona to run away. Nevertheless, Ramona should be made to feel, every moment of every hour, that she was in disgrace; that she was with them, but not of them; that she had chosen an alien's position, and must abide by it. How this was to be done, the Señora did not put in words to herself, but she knew very well. If anything would bring the girl to her senses, this would. There might still be a hope, the Señora believed, so little did she know Ramona's nature, or the depth of her affection for Alessandro, that she might be in this manner brought to see the enormity of the offence she would commit if she persisted in her purpose. And if she did perceive this, confess her wrong, and give up the marriage, — the Señora grew almost generous and tolerant in her thoughts as she contemplated this contingency, — if she did thus humble herself and return to her rightful allegiance to the Moreno house, the Señora would forgive her, and would do more for her than she had ever hitherto done. She would take 1
her to Los Angeles and to Monterey; would show her a little more of the world; and it was by no means unlikely that there might thus come about for her a satisfactory and honorable marriage. Felipe should see that she was not disposed to deal unfairly by Ramona in any way, if Ramona herself would behave properly.

Ramona's surprise, when the Señora entered her room just before supper, and, in her ordinary tone, asked a question about the chili which was drying on the veranda, was so great, that she could not avoid showing it both in her voice and look.

The Señora recognized this immediately, but gave no sign of having done so, continuing what she had to say about the chili, the hot sun, the turning of the grapes, etc., precisely as she would have spoken to Ramona a week previous. At least, this was what Ramona at first thought; but before the sentences were finished, she had detected in the Señora's eye and tone the weapons which were to be employed against her. The emotion of half-grateful wonder with which she had heard the first words changed quickly to heart-sick misery before they were concluded; and she said to herself: "That's the way she is going to break me down, she thinks! But she can't do it. I can bear anything for four days; and the minute Alessandro comes, I will go away with him." This train of thought in Ramona's mind was reflected in her face. The Señora saw it, and hardened herself still more. It was to be war, then. No hope of surrender. Very well. The girl had made her choice.

Margarita was now the most puzzled person in the household. She had overheard snatches of the conversation between Felipe and his mother and Ramona, having let her curiosity get so far the better of her discretion as to creep to the door and listen.

1

Illustration by Henry Sandham. Circa 1913.

El Puebla de Nuestra Señora la Reina de Los Angeles (The Town of Our Lady the Queen of the Angels) was changing almost overnight from a sleepy Mexican village to a bustling American city. Within a month of Jackson's arrival on December 21, 1882, electric lights were introduced and a few cement sidewalks. An influx of Easterners had swollen the population to 12,000, but the atmosphere was still predominantly Latin.

In fact, she narrowly escaped being caught, having had barely time to begin her feint of sweeping the passage-way, when Ramona, flinging the door wide open, came out, after her final reply to the Señora, the words of which Margarita had distinctly heard: "God will punish you."

"Holy Virgin! how dare she say that to the Señora?" ejaculated Margarita, under her breath; and the next second Ramona rushed by, not even seeing her. But the Señora's vigilant eyes, following Ramona, saw her; and the Señora's voice had a ring of suspicion in it, as she called, "How comes it you are sweeping the passage-way at this hour of the day, Margarita?"

It was surely the devil himself that put into Margarita's head the quick lie which she instantaneously told. "There was early breakfast, Señora, to be cooked for Alessandro, who was setting off in haste, and my mother was not up, so I had it to cook."

As Margarita said this, Felipe fixed his eyes steadily upon her. She changed color. Felipe knew this was a lie. He had seen Margarita peering about among the willows while he was talking with Alessandro at the sheepfold; he had seen Alessandro halt for a moment and speak to her as he rode past, — only for a moment; then, pricking his horse sharply, he had galloped off down the valley road. No breakfast had Alessandro had at Margarita's hands, or any other's, that morning. What could have been Margarita's motive for telling this lie?

But Felipe had too many serious cares on his mind to busy himself long with any thought of Margarita or her fibs. She had said the first thing which came into her head, most likely, to shelter herself from the Señora's displeasure; which was indeed very near the truth, only there was added a spice of malice against Alessandro. A slight undercurrent of jealous antagonism towards him had begun to grow up among the servants of late; fostered, if not originated, by Margarita's sharp sayings as to his being admitted to such strange intimacy with the family.

While Felipe continued ill, and was so soothed to rest by his music, there was no room for cavil. It was natural that Alessandro came and went as a physician might. But after Felipe had recovered, why should this freedom and intimacy continue? More than once there had been sullen mutterings of this kind on the north veranda, when all the laborers and servants were gathered there of an evening, Alessandro alone being absent from the group, and the sounds of his voice or his violin coming from the south veranda, where the family sat.

"It would be a good thing if we too had a bit of music now and then," Juan Canito would grumble; "but the lad 's chary enough of his bow on this side the house."

"Ho! we 're not good enough for him to play to!" Margarita would reply; "'Like master, like servant,' is a good proverb sometimes, but not always. But there 's a deal going on, on the veranda yonder, besides fiddling!" and Margarita's lips would purse themselves up in an expression of concentrated mystery and secret knowledge, well fitted to draw from everybody a fire of questions, none of which, however, would she answer. She knew better than to slander the Señorita Ramona, or to say a word even reflecting upon her unfavorably. Not a man or a woman there would have borne it. They all had loved Ramona ever since she came among them as a toddling baby. They petted her then, and idolized her now. Not one of them whom she had not done good offices for, — nursed them, cheered them, remembered their birthdays and their saints'-days. To no one but her mother had Margarita unbosomed what she knew, and what she suspected; and old Marda, frightened at the bare pronouncing of such words, had terrified Margarita into the solemnest of promises never, under any circumstances whatever, to say such things to any other member of the family. Marda did not believe them. She could not. She believed that Margarita's jealousy had imagined all.

"And the Señora; she 'd send you packing off this place in an hour, and me too, long 's I 've lived here, if ever she was to know of you blackening the Señorita. An Indian, too! You must be mad, Margarita!"

When Margarita, in triumph, had flown to tell her that the Señora had just dragged the Señorita Ramona up the garden-walk, and shoved her into her room and locked the door, and that it was because she had caught her with Alessandro at the washing-stones, Marda first crossed herself in sheer mechanical fashion at the shock of the story, and then cuffed Margarita's ears for telling her.

"I 'll take the head off your neck, if you say that aloud again! Whatever 's come to the Señora! Forty years I 've lived under this roof, and I never saw her lift a hand to a living creature yet. You 're out of your senses, child!" she said, all the time gazing fearfully towards the room.

"You 'll see whether I am out of my senses or not," retorted Margarita, and ran back to the dining-room. And after the dining-room door was shut, and the unhappy pretence of a supper had begun, old Marda had herself crept softly to the Señorita's door and listened, and heard Ramona sobbing as if her heart would break. Then she knew that what Margarita had said must be true, and her faithful soul was in sore straits what to think. The Señorita misdemean herself! Never! Whatever happened, it was not that! There was some horrible mistake somewhere. Kneeling at the keyhole, she had called cautiously to Ramona, "Oh, my lamb, what is it?" But Ramona had not heard her, and the danger was too great of remaining; so scrambling up with difficulty from her rheumatic knees, the old woman had hobbled back to the kitchen as much in the dark as before, and, by a curiously illogical consequence, crosser than ever to her daughter. All the next day she watched for herself, and could not but see that all appearances bore out Margarita's statements. Alessandro's sudden departure had been a tremendous corroboration of the story. Not one of the men had had an inkling of it; Juan Canito, Luigo, both alike astonished; no word left, no message sent; only Señor Felipe had said carelessly to Juan Can, after breakfast, "You'll have to look after things yourself for a few days, Juan. Alessandro has gone to Temecula."

"For a few days!" exclaimed Margarita, sarcastically, when this was repeated to her. "That's easy said! If Alessandro Assis is seen here again, I'll eat my head! He's played his last tune on the south veranda, I wager you."

But when at supper-time of this same eventful day the Señora was heard, as she passed the Señorita's door, to say in her ordinary voice, "Are you ready for supper, Ramona?" and Ramona was seen to come out and walk by the Señora's side to the dining-room; silent, to be sure, — but then that was no strange thing, the Señorita always was more silent in the Señora's presence, — when Marda, standing in the court-yard, feigning to be feeding her chickens, but keeping a close eye on the passage-ways, saw this, she was relieved, and thought: "It's only a dispute there has been. There will be disputes in families sometimes. It is none of our affair. All is settled now."

And Margarita, standing in the dining-room, when she saw them all coming in as usual, — the Señora, Felipe, Ramona, — no change, even to her scrutinizing eye, in anybody's face, was more surprised than she had been for many a day; and began to think again, as she had more than once since this tragedy began, that she must have dreamed much that she remembered.

But surfaces are deceitful, and eyes see little. Considering its complexity, the fineness and delicacy of its mechanism, the results attainable by the human eye seem far from adequate to the expenditure put upon it. We have flattered ourselves by inventing proverbs of comparison in matter of blindness, — "blind as a bat," for instance. It would be safe to say that there cannot be found in the animal kingdom a bat, or any other creature, so blind in its own range of circumstance and connection, as the greater majority of human beings are in the bosoms of their families. Tempers strain and recover, hearts break and heal, strength falters, fails, and comes near to giving way altogether, every day, without being noted by the closest lookers-on.

Before night of this second day since the trouble had burst like a storm-cloud on the peaceful Moreno household, everything had so resumed the ordinary expression and routine, that a shrewder observer and reasoner than Margarita might well be excused for doubting if any serious disaster could have occurred to any one. Señor Felipe sauntered about in his usual fashion, smoking his cigarettes, or lay on his

The servants' quarters. — Photograph by A. C. Vroman. Circa 1913.

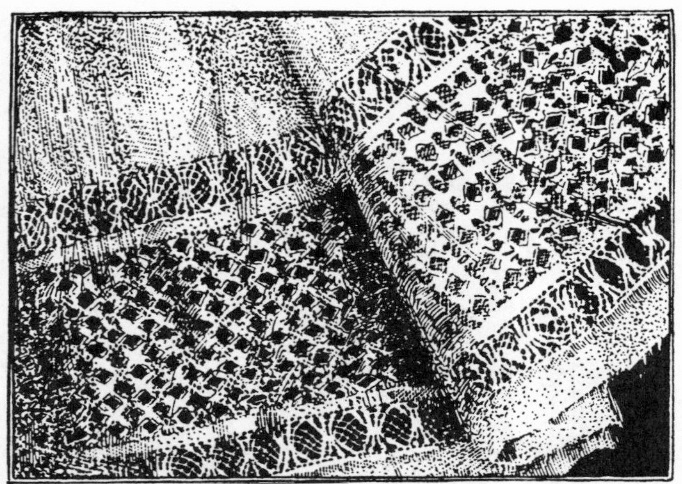

The altar cloth, at Ranch Camulos. — Drawing by Henry Sandham. Circa 1913. 2

bed in the veranda, dozing. The Señora went her usual rounds of inspection, fed her birds, spoke to every one in her usual tone, sat in her carved chair with her hands folded, gazing out on the southern sky. Ramona busied herself with her usual duties, dusted the chapel, put fresh flowers before all the Madonnas,
2 and then sat down at her embroidery. Ramona had been for a long time at work on a beautiful altar-cloth for the chapel. It was to have been a present to the Señora. It was nearly done. As she held up the frame in which it was stretched, and looked at the delicate tracery of the pattern, she sighed. It had been with a mingled feeling of interest and hopelessness that she had for months been at work on it, often saying to herself, "She won't care much for it, beautiful as it is, just because I did it; but Father Salvierderra will be pleased when he sees it."

Now, as she wove the fine threads in and out, she thought: "She will never let it be used on the altar. I wonder if I could any way get it to Father Salvierderra, at Santa Barbara. I would like to give it to him. I will ask Alessandro. I'm sure the Señora would never use it, and it would be a shame to leave it here. I shall take it with me." But as she thought these things, her face was unruffled. A strange composure had settled on Ramona. "Only four days; only four days; I can bear anything for four days!" these words were coming and going in her mind like refrains of songs which haunt one's memory and will not be still. She saw that Felipe looked anxiously at her, but she answered his inquiring looks always with a gentle smile. It was evident that the Señora did not intend that she and Felipe should have any private conversation; but that did not so much matter. After all, there was not so much to be said. Felipe knew all. She could tell him nothing; Felipe had acted for the best, as he thought, in sending Alessandro away till the heat of the Señora's anger should have spent itself.

After her first dismay at suddenly learning that Alessandro had gone, had passed, she had reflected that it was just as well. He would come back prepared to take her with him. How, or where, she did not know; but she would go with no question. Perhaps she would not even bid the Señora good-by; she wondered how that would arrange itself, and how far Alessandro would have to take her, to find a priest to marry them. It was a terrible thing to have to do, to go out of a home in such a way: no wedding — no wedding clothes — no friends — to go unmarried, and journey to a priest's house, to have the ceremony performed; "but it is not my fault," said Ramona to herself; "it is hers. She drives me to do it. If it is wrong, the blame will be hers. Father Salvierderra would gladly come here and marry us, if she would send for him. I wish we could go to him, Alessandro and I; perhaps we can. I would not be afraid to ride so far; we could do it in two days." The more Ramona thought of this, the more it appeared to her the natural thing for them to do. "He will be on our side, I know he will," she thought. "He always liked Alessandro, and he loves me."

It was strange how little bitterness towards the Señora was in the girl's mind; how comparatively little she thought of her. Her heart was too full of Alessandro and of their future; and it had never been Ramona's habit to dwell on the Señora in her thoughts. As from her childhood up she had accepted the fact of the Señora's coldness towards her, so now she accepted her injustice and opposition as part of the nature of things, and not to be altered.

During all these hours, during the coming and going of these crowds of fears, sorrows, memories, anticipations in Ramona's heart, all that there was to be seen to the eye was simply a calm, quiet girl, sitting on the veranda, diligently working at her lace-frame. Even Felipe was deceived by her calmness, and wondered what it meant, — if it could be that she was undergoing the change that his mother had thought possible, and designated as coming "to her senses." Even Felipe did not know the steadfast fibre of the girl's nature; neither did he realize what a bond had grown between her and Alessandro. In fact, he sometimes wondered of what this bond had been made. He had himself seen the greater part of their intercourse with each other; nothing could have been farther removed from anything like love-making. There had been no crises of incident, or marked moments of experience such as in Felipe's imaginations of love were essential to the fulness of its growth. This is a common mistake on the part of those who have never felt love's true bonds. Once in those chains, one perceives that they are not of the sort full forged in a day. They are made as the great iron cables are made, on which bridges are swung across the widest water-channels, — not of single huge rods, or bars, which would be stronger, perhaps, to look at; but of myriads of the finest wires, each one by itself so fine, so frail, it would barely hold a child's kite in the wind: by hundreds, hundreds of thousands of such, twisted, re-twisted together, are made the mighty cables, which do not any more swerve from their place in the air, under the weight and jar of the ceaseless traffic and tread of two cities, than the solid earth swerves under the same ceaseless weight and jar. Such cables do not break.

Even Ramona herself would have found it hard to tell why she thus loved Alessandro; how it began, or by what it grew. It had not been a sudden adoration, like his passion for her; it was, in the beginning, simply a response; but now it was as strong a love as his, — as strong, and as unchangeable. The Señora's harsh words had been like a forcing-house air to it, and the sudden knowledge of the fact of her own Indian descent seemed to her like a revelation, pointing out the path in which destiny called her to walk. She thrilled with pleasure at the thought of the joy with which Alessandro would hear this, — the joy and the surprise. She imagined to herself, in hundreds of ways, the time, place, and phrase in which she would tell him. She could not satisfy herself as to the best; as to which would give keenest pleasure to him and to her. She would tell him, as soon as she saw him; it should be her first word of greeting. No! There would be too much of trouble and embarrassment then. She would wait till they were far away, till they were alone, in the wilderness; and then she would turn to him, and say, "Alessandro, my people are your people!" Or she would wait, and keep her secret until she had reached Temecula, and they had begun their life there, and Alessandro had been astonished to see how readily and kindly she took to all the ways of the Indian village; and then, when he expressed some such emotion, she would quietly say, "But I too am an Indian, Alessandro!"

Strange, sad bride's dreams these; but they made Ramona's heart beat with happiness as she dreamed them.

Chapter XIV

THE first day had gone, it was near night of the second, and not a word had passed between Felipe and Ramona, except in the presence of the Señora. It would have been beautiful to see, if it had not been so cruel a thing, the various and devious methods by which the Señora had brought this about. Felipe, oddly enough, was more restive under it than Ramona. She had her dreams. He had nothing but his restless consciousness that he had not done for her what he hoped; that he must seem to her to have been disloyal; this, and a continual wonder what she could be planning or expecting which made her so placid, kept Felipe in a fever of unrest, of which his mother noted every sign, and redoubled her vigilance.

Felipe thought perhaps he could speak to Ramona in the night, through her window. But the August heats were fierce now; everybody slept with wide-open windows; the Señora was always wakeful; if she should chance to hear him thus holding secret converse with Ramona, it would indeed make bad matters worse. Nevertheless, he decided to try it. At the first sound of his footsteps on the veranda floor, "My son, are you ill? Can I do anything?" came from the Señora's window. She had not been asleep at all. It would take more courage than Felipe possessed, to try that plan again; and he lay on his veranda bed, this afternoon, tossing about with sheer impatience at his baffled purpose. Ramona sat at the foot of the bed, taking the last stitches in the nearly completed altar-cloth. The Señora sat in her usual seat, dozing, with her head thrown back. It was very hot; a sultry south-wind, with dust from the desert, had been blowing all day, and every living creature was more or less prostrated by it.

As the Señora's eyes closed, a sudden thought struck Felipe. Taking out a memorandum-book in which he kept his accounts, he began rapidly writing. Looking up, and catching Ramona's eye, he made a sign to her that it was for her. She glanced apprehensively at the Señora. She was asleep. Presently Felipe, folding the note, and concealing it in his hand, rose, and walked towards Ramona's window, Ramona terrifiedly watching him; the sound of Felipe's steps roused the Señora, who sat up instantly, and gazed about her with that indescribable expression peculiar to people who hope they have not been asleep, but know they have. "Have I been asleep?" she asked.

"About one minute, mother," answered Felipe, who was leaning, as he spoke, against Ramona's open window, his arms crossed behind him. Stretching them out, and back and forth a few times, yawning idly, he said, "This heat is intolerable!" Then he sauntered leisurely down the veranda steps into the garden-walk, and seated himself on the bench under the trellis there.

The note had been thrown into Ramona's room. She was hot and cold with fear lest she might not be able to get it unobserved. What if the Señora were to go first into the room! She hardly dared look at her. But fortune is not always on the side of tyrants. The Señora was fast dozing off again, relieved that Felipe was out of speaking distance of Ramona. As soon as her eyes were again shut, Ramona rose to go. The Señora opened her eyes. Ramona was crossing the threshold of the door; she was going into the house. Good! Still farther away from Felipe.

"Are you going to your room, Ramona?" said the Señora.

"I was," replied Ramona, alarmed. "Did you want me here?"

"No," said the Señora; and she closed her eyes again.

In a second more the note was safe in Ramona's hands.

"Dear Ramona," Felipe had written, "I am distracted because I cannot speak with you alone. Can you think of any way? I want to explain things to you. I am afraid you do not understand. Don't be unhappy. Alessandro will surely be back in four days. I want to help you all I can, but you saw I could not do much. Nobody will hinder your doing what you please; but, dear, I wish you would not go away from us!"

Tearing the paper into small fragments, Ramona thrust them into her bosom, to be destroyed later. Then looking out of the window, and seeing that the Señora was now in a sound sleep, she ventured to write a reply to Felipe, though when she would find a safe opportunity to give it to him, there was no telling. "Thank you, dear Felipe. Don't be anxious. I am not unhappy. I understand all about it. But I must go away as soon as Alessandro comes." Hiding this also safe in her bosom, she went back to the veranda. Felipe rose, and walked towards the steps. Ramona, suddenly bold, stooped, and laid her note on the second step. Again the tired eyes of the Señora opened. They had not been shut five minutes; Ramona was at her work; Felipe was coming up the steps from the garden. He nodded laughingly to his mother, and laid his finger on his lips.

All was well. The Señora dozed again. Her nap had cost her more than she would ever know. This one secret interchange between Felipe and Ramona then, thus making, as it were, common cause with each other as against her, and in fear of her, was a step never to be recalled, — a step whose significance could scarcely be overestimated. Tyrants, great and small, are apt to overlook such possibilities as this; to forget the momentousness which the most trivial incident may assume when forced into false proportions and relations. Tyranny can make liars and cheats out of the honestest souls. It is done oftener than any except close students of human nature realize. When kings and emperors do this, the world cries out with sympathy, and holds the plotters more innocent than the tyrant who provoked the plot. It is Russia that stands branded in men's thoughts, and not Siberia.

The Señora had a Siberia of her own, and it was there that Ramona was living in these days. The Señora would have been surprised to know how little the girl felt the cold. To be sure, it was not as if she had ever felt warmth in the Señora's presence; yet between the former chill and this were many degrees, and except for her new life, and new love, and hope in the thought of Alessandro, Ramona could not have borne it for a day.

The fourth day came; it seemed strangely longer than the others had. All day Ramona watched and listened. Felipe, too; for, knowing what Alessandro's impatience would be, he had, in truth, looked for him on the previous night. The horse he rode was a fleet one, and would have made the journey with ease in half the time. But Felipe reflected that there might be many things for Alessandro to arrange at Temecula. He would doubtless return prepared to take Ramona back with him, in case that proved 1
the only alternative left them. Felipe grew wretched as his fancy dwelt on the picture of Ramona's future. He had been in the Temecula village. He knew its poverty; the thought of Ramona there was monstrous. To the indolent, ease-loving Felipe it was incredible that a girl reared as Ramona had been, could for a moment contemplate leading the life of a poor laboring man's wife. He could not conceive of love's making one undertake any such life. Felipe 2
had much to learn of love. Night came; no Alessandro. Till the darkness settled down, Ramona sat, watching the willows. When she could no longer see, she listened. The Señora, noting all, also listened. She was uneasy as to the next stage of affairs, but she would not speak. Nothing should induce her to swerve from the line of conduct on which she had determined. It was the full of the moon. When the first broad beam of its light came over the hill, and flooded the garden and the white front of the little chapel, just as it had done on that first night when Alessandro watched with Felipe on the veranda, Ramona pressed her face against the window-panes, and gazed out into the garden. At

1 The interior of an Indian home. — Illustration by Henry Sandham. Circa 1900.

2 An Indian dwelling. Circa 1880. —Courtesy of the San Diego Historical Society – Tico Collection

each flickering motion of the shadows she saw the form of a man approaching. Again and again she saw it. Again and again the breeze died, and the shadow ceased. It was near morning before, weary, sad, she crept to bed; but not to sleep. With wide-open, anxious eyes, she still watched and listened. Never had the thought once crossed her mind that Alessandro might not come at the time Felipe had said. In her childlike simplicity she had accepted this as unquestioningly as she had accepted other facts in her life. Now that he did not come, unreasoning and unfounded terror took possession of her, and she asked herself continually, "Will he ever come! They sent him away; perhaps he will be too proud to come back!" Then faith would return, and saying to herself, "He would never, never forsake me; he knows I have no one in the whole world but him; he knows how I love him," she would regain composure, and remind herself of the many detentions which might have prevented his coming at the time set. Spite of all, however, she was heavy at heart; and at breakfast her anxious eyes and absent look were sad to see. They hurt Felipe. Too well he knew what it meant. He also was anxious. The Señora saw it in his face, and it vexed her. The girl might well pine, and be mortified if her lover did not appear. But why should Felipe disquiet himself? The Señora disliked it. It was a bad symptom. There might be trouble ahead yet. There was, indeed, trouble ahead, — of a sort the Señora's imaginings had not pictured.

Another day passed; another night; another, and another. One week now since Alessandro, as he leaped on his horse, had grasped Felipe's hand, and said: "You will tell the Señorita; you will make sure that she understands why I go; and in four days I will be back." One week, and he had not come. The three who were watching and wondering looked covertly into each other's faces, each longing to know what the others thought.

Ramona was wan and haggard. She had scarcely slept. The idea had taken possession of her that Alessandro was dead. On the sixth and seventh days she had walked each afternoon far down the river road, by which he would be sure to come; down the meadows, and by the cross-cut, out to the highway; at each step straining her tearful eyes into the distance, — the cruel, blank, silent distance. She had come back after dark, whiter and more wan than she went out. As she sat at the supper-table, silent, making no feint of eating, only drinking glass after glass of milk, in thirsty haste, even Margarita pitied her. But the Señora did not. She thought the best thing which could happen, would be that the Indian should never come back. Ramona would recover from it in a little while; the mortification would be the worst thing, but even that, time would heal. She wondered that the girl had not more pride than to let her wretchedness be so plainly seen. She herself would have died before she would go about with such a woe-begone face, for a whole household to see and gossip about.

On the morning of the eighth day, Ramona, desperate, waylaid Felipe, as he was going down the veranda steps. The Señora was in the garden, and saw them; but Ramona did not care. "Felipe!" she cried, "I must, I must speak to you! Do you think Alessandro is dead? What else could keep him from coming?" Her lips were dry, her cheeks scarlet, her voice husky. A few days more of this, and she would be in a brain fever, Felipe thought, as he looked compassionately at her.

"Oh, no, no, dear! Do not think that!" he replied. "A thousand things might have kept him."

"Ten thousand things would not! Nothing could!" said Ramona. "I know he is dead. Can't you send a messenger, Felipe, and see?"

The Señora was walking towards them. She overheard the last words. Looking towards Felipe, no more regarding Ramona than if she had not been within sight or hearing, the Señora said, "It seems to me that would not be quite consistent with dignity. How does it strike you, Felipe? If you thought best, we might spare a man as soon as the vintage is done, I suppose."

3 Ramona walked away. The vintage would not be over for a week. There were several vineyards yet which had not been touched; every hand on the place was hard at work, picking the grapes, treading them out in tubs, emptying the juice into stretched raw-hides swung from cross-beams in a long shed. In the willow copse the brandy-still was in full blast; it took one man to watch it; this was Juan Can's favorite work; for reasons of his own he liked best to do it alone; and now that he could no longer tread grapes in the tubs, he had a better chance for uninterrupted work at the still. "No ill but has its good," he thought sometimes, as he lay comfortably stretched out in the shade, smoking his pipe day after day, and breathing the fumes of the fiery brandy.

As Ramona disappeared in the doorway, the Señora, coming close to Felipe, and laying her hand on his arm, said in a confidential tone, nodding her head in the direction in which Ramona had vanished: "She looks badly, Felipe. I don't know what we can do. We surely cannot send to summon back a lover we do not wish her to marry, can we? It is very perplexing. Most unfortunate, every way. What do you think, my son?" There was almost a diabolical art in the manner in which the Señora could, by a single phrase or question, plant in a person's mind the precise idea she wished him to think he had originated himself.

"No; of course we can't send for him," replied Felipe, angrily; "unless it is to send for him to marry her; I wish he had never set foot on the place. I am sure I don't know what to do. Ramona's looks frighten me. I believe she will die."

"I cannot wish Alessandro had never set foot on the place," said the Señora, gently, "for I feel that I owe your life to him, my Felipe; and he is not to blame for Ramona's conduct. You need not fear her dying. She may be ill; but people do not die of love like hers for Alessandro."

"Of what kind do they die, mother?" asked Felipe, impatiently.

The Señora looked reproachfully at him. "Not often of any," she said; "but certainly not of a sudden passion for a person in every way beneath them, in position, in education, in all points which are essential to congeniality of tastes or association of life."

The Señora spoke calmly, with no excitement, as if she were discussing an abstract case. Sometimes, when she spoke like this, Felipe for the moment felt as if she were entirely right, as if it were really a disgraceful thing in Ramona to have thus loved Alessandro. It could not be gainsaid that there was this gulf of which she spoke. Alessandro was undeniably Ramona's inferior in position, education, in all the external matters of life; but in nature, in true nobility of soul, no! Alessandro was no man's inferior in these; and in capacity to love, — Felipe sometimes wondered whether he had ever known Alessandro's equal in that. This thought had occurred to him more than once, as from his sick-bed he had, unobserved, studied the expression with which Alessandro gazed at Ramona. But all this made no difference in the perplexity of the present dilemma, in the embarrassment of his and his mother's position now. Send a messenger to ask why Alessandro did not return! Not even if he had been an accepted and publicly recognized lover, would Felipe do that! Ramona ought to have more pride. She ought of herself to know that. And when Felipe, later in the day, saw Ramona again, he said as much to her. He said it as gently as he could; so gently that she did not at first comprehend his idea. It was so foreign, so incompatible with her faith, how could she?

When she did understand, she said slowly: "You mean that it will not do to send to find out if Alessandro is dead, because it will look as if I wished him to marry me whether he wished it or not?" and she fixed her eyes on Felipe's, with an expression he could not fathom.

"Yes, dear," he answered, "something like that, though you put it harshly."

"Is it not true," she persisted, "that is what you mean?"

Reluctantly Felipe admitted that it was.

Ramona was silent for some moments; then she said, speaking still more slowly, "If you feel like that, we had better never talk about Alessandro again. I suppose it is not possible that you should know, as I do, that nothing but his being dead would keep him from coming back. Thanks, dear Felipe;" and after this she did not speak again of Alessandro.

3

Harvest time. — Illustration by Henry Sandham. Circa 1880.

4

In the mission garden, San Juan Bautista. —Illustration by Henry Sandham. Circa 1880.

Days went by; a week. The vintage was over. The Señora wondered if Ramona would now ask again for a messenger to go to Temecula. Almost even the Señora relented, as she looked into the girl's white and wasted face, as she sat silent, her hands folded in her lap, her eyes fixed on the willows. The altar-cloth was done, folded and laid away. It would never hang in the Moreno chapel. It was promised, in Ramona's mind, to Father Salvierderra. She had resolved to go to him; if he, a feeble old man, could walk all the way between Santa Barbara and their home, she could surely do the same. She would not lose the way. There were not many roads; she could ask. The convent, the bare thought of which had been so terrible to Ramona fourteen days ago, when the Señora had threatened her with it, now seemed a heavenly refuge, the only shelter she craved. There was a school for orphans attached
4 to the convent at San Juan Bautista, she knew; she
would ask the Father to let her go there, and she would spend the rest of her life in prayer, and in teaching the orphan girls. As hour after hour she sat revolving this plan, her fancy projected itself so vividly into the future, that she lived years of her life. She felt herself middle-aged, old. She saw the procession of nuns, going to vespers, leading the children by the hand; herself wrinkled and white-haired, walking between two of the little ones. The picture gave her peace. As soon as she grew a little stronger, she would set off on her journey to the Father; she could not go just yet, she was too weak; her feet trembled if she did but walk to the foot of the garden. Alessandro was dead; there could be no doubt of that. He was buried in that little walled graveyard of which he had told her. Sometimes she thought she would try to go there and see his grave, perhaps see his father; if Alessandro had told him of her, the old man would be glad to see her; perhaps, after all, her work might lie there, among Alessandro's people. But this looked hard; she had not courage for it; shelter and rest were what she wanted,—the sound of the Church's prayers, and the Father's blessing every day. The convent was the best.

She thought she was sure that Alessandro was dead; but she was not, for she still listened, still watched. Each day she walked out on the river road, and sat waiting till dusk. At last came a day when she could not go; her strength failed her. She lay all day on her bed. To the Señora, who asked frigidly if she were ill, she answered: "No, Señora, I do not think I am ill. I have no pain, but I cannot get up. I shall be better to-morrow."

"I will send you strong broth and a medicine," the Señora said; and sent her both by the hands of Margarita, whose hatred and jealousy broke down at the first sight of Ramona's face on the pillow; it looked so much thinner and sharper there than it had when she was sitting up. "Oh, Señorita! Señorita!" she cried, in a tone of poignant grief, "are you going to die? Forgive me, forgive me!"

"I have nothing to forgive you, Margarita," replied Ramona, raising herself on her elbow, and lifting her eyes kindly to the girl's face as she took the broth from her hands. "I do not know why you ask me to forgive you."

Margarita flung herself on her knees by the bed, in a passion of weeping. "Oh, but you do know, Señorita, you do know! Forgive me!"

"No, I know nothing," replied Ramona; "but if you know anything, it is all forgiven. I am not going to die, Margarita. I am going away," she added, after a second's pause. Her inmost instinct told her that she could trust Margarita now. Alessandro being dead, Margarita would no longer be her enemy, and Margarita could perhaps help her. "I am going away, Margarita, as soon as I feel a little stronger. I am going to a convent; but the Señora does not know. You will not tell?"

"No, Señorita!" whispered Margarita, — thinking in her heart, "Yes, she is going away, but it will be with the angels." — "No, Señorita, I will not tell. I will do anything you want me to."

"Thanks, Margarita mia," replied Ramona. "I thought you would;" and she lay back on her pillow, and closed her eyes, looking so much more like death than like life that Margarita's tears flowed faster than before, and she ran to her mother, sobbing out, "Mother, mother! the Señorita is ill to death. I am sure she is. She has taken to her bed; and she is as white as Señor Felipe was at the worst of the fever."

"Ay," said old Marda, who had seen all this for days back; "ay, she has wasted away, this last week, like one in a fever, sure enough; I have seen it. It must be she is starving herself to death."

"Indeed, she has not eaten for ten days, — hardly since that day;" and Margarita and her mother exchanged looks. It was not necessary to further define the day.

"Juan Can says he thinks he will never be seen here again," continued Margarita.

"The saints grant it, then," said Marda, hotly; "if it is he has cost the Señorita all this! I am that turned about in my head with it all, that I've no thoughts to think; but plain enough it is, he is mixed up with whatever 't is has gone wrong."

"I could tell what it is," said Margarita, her old pertness coming uppermost for a moment; "but I've got no more to say, now the Señorita's lying on her bed, with the face she's got. It's enough to break your heart to look at her. I could just go down on my knees to her for all I've said; and I will, and to Saint Francis too! She's going to be with him before long; I know she is."

"No," said the wiser, older Marda. "She is not so ill as you think. She is young. It's the heart's gone out of her; that's all. I've been that way myself. People are, when they're young."

"I'm young!" retorted Margarita. "I've never been that way."

"There's many a mile to the end of the road, my girl," said Marda, significantly; "and 'It's ill boasting the first day out,' was a proverb when I was your age!"

Marda had never been much more than half-way fond of this own child of hers. Their natures were antagonistic. Traits which, in Margarita's father, had embittered many a day of Marda's early married life, were perpetually cropping out in Margarita, making between the mother and daughter a barrier which even parental love was not always strong enough to surmount. And, as was inevitable, this antagonism was constantly leading to things which seemed to Margarita, and in fact were, unjust and ill-founded.

"She's always flinging out at me, whatever I do," thought Margarita. "I know one thing; I'll never tell her what the Señorita's told me; never, — not till after she's gone."

A sudden suspicion flashed into Margarita's mind. She seated herself on the bench outside the kitchen door, to wrestle with it. What if it were not to a convent at all, but to Alessandro, that the Señorita meant to go! No; that was preposterous. If it had been that, she would have gone with him in the outset. Nobody who was plotting to run away with a lover ever wore such a look as the Señorita wore now. Margarita dismissed the thought; yet it left its trace. She would be more observant for having had it; her resuscitated affection for her young mistress was not yet so strong that it would resist the assaults of jealousy, if that passion were to be again aroused in her fiery soul. Though she had never been deeply in love with Alessandro herself, she had been enough so, and she remembered him vividly enough, to feel yet a sharp emotion of displeasure at the recollection of his devotion to the Señorita. Now that the Señorita seemed to be deserted, unhappy, prostrated, she had no room for anything but pity for her; but let Alessandro come on the stage again, and all would be changed. The old hostility would return. It was but a dubious sort of ally, after all, that Ramona had so unexpectedly secured in Margarita. She might prove the sharpest of broken reeds.

It was sunset of the eighteenth day since Alessandro's departure. Ramona had lain for four days well-nigh motionless on her bed. She herself began to think she must be going to die. Her mind seemed to be vacant of all thought. She did not even sorrow for Alessandro's death; she seemed torpid, body and soul. Such prostrations as these are Nature's enforced rests. It is often only by help of them that our bodies tide over crises, strains, in which, if we continued to battle, we should be slain.

As Ramona lay half unconscious, — neither awake nor yet asleep, — on this evening, she was suddenly aware of a vivid impression produced upon her; it was not sound, it was not sight. She was alone; the house was still as death; the warm September twilight silence reigned outside. She sat up in her bed, intent — half alarmed — half glad — bewildered — alive. What had happened? Still there was no sound, no stir. The twilight was fast deepening; not a breath of air moving. Gradually her bewildered senses and faculties awoke from their long-dormant condition; she looked around the room; even the walls seemed revivified; she clasped her hands, and leaped from the bed. "Alessandro is not dead!" she said aloud; and she laughed hysterically. "He is not dead!" she repeated. "He is not dead! He is somewhere near!"

With quivering hands she dressed, and stole out of the house. After the first few seconds she found herself strangely strong; she did not tremble; her feet trod firm on the ground. "Oh, miracle!" she thought, as she hastened down the garden-walk; "I am well again! Alessandro is near!" So vivid was the impression, that when she reached the willows and found the spot silent, vacant, as when she had last sat there, hopeless, broken-hearted, she experienced a revulsion of disappointment. "Not here!" she cried; "not here!" and a swift fear shook her. "Am I mad? Is it this way, perhaps, people lose their senses, when they are as I have been?"

But the young, strong blood was running swift in her veins. No! this was no madness; rather a newly discovered power; a fulness of sense; a revelation. Alessandro was near.

Swiftly she walked down the river road. The farther she went, the keener grew her expectation, her sense of Alessandro's nearness. In her present mood she would have walked on and on, even to Temecula itself, sure that she was at each step drawing nearer to Alessandro. As she approached the second willow copse, which lay perhaps a quarter of a mile west of the first, she saw the figure of a man, standing, leaning against one of the trees. She halted. It could not be Alessandro. He would not have paused for a moment so near the house where he was to find her. She was afraid to go on. It was late to meet a stranger in this lonely spot. The figure was strangely still; so still that, as she peered through the dusk, she half fancied it might be an optical illusion. She advanced a few steps, hesitatingly, then stopped. As she did so, the man advanced a few steps, then stopped. As he came out from the shadows of the trees, she saw that he was of Alessandro's height. She quickened her steps, then suddenly stopped again. What did this mean? It could not be Alessandro. Ramona wrung her hands in agony of suspense. An almost unconquerable instinct urged her forward; but terror held her back. After standing irresolute for some minutes, she turned to walk back to the house, saying, "I must not run the risk of its being a stranger. If it is Alessandro, he will come."

But her feet seemed to refuse to move in the opposite direction. Slower and slower she walked for a few paces, then turned again. The man had returned to his former place, and stood as at first, leaning against the tree.

"It may be a messenger from him," she said; "a messenger who has been told not to come to the house until after dark."

Her mind was made up. She quickened her pace to a run. A few moments more brought her so near that she could see distinctly. It was — yes, it was Alessandro. He did not see her. His face was turned partially away, his head resting against the tree; he must be ill. Ramona flew, rather than ran. In a moment more, Alessandro had heard the light steps, turned, saw Ramona, and, with a cry, bounded forward, and they were clasped in each other's arms before they had looked in each other's faces. Ramona spoke first. Disengaging herself gently, and looking up, she began: "Alessandro —" But at the first sight of his face she shrieked. Was this Alessandro, this haggard, emaciated, speechless man, who gazed at her with hollow eyes, full of misery, and no joy! "O God," cried Ramona, "you have been ill! you are ill! My God, Alessandro, what is it?"

Alessandro passed his hand slowly over his forehead, as if trying to collect his thoughts before speaking, all the while keeping his eyes fixed on Ramona, with the same anguished look, convulsively holding both her hands in his.

"Señorita," he said, "my Señorita!" Then he stopped. His tongue seemed to refuse him utterance; and this voice, — this strange, hard, unresonant voice, — whose voice was it? Not Alessandro's.

"My Señorita," he began again, "I could not go without one sight of your face; but when I was here, I had not courage to go near the house. If you had not come, I should have gone back without seeing you."

Ramona heard these words in fast-deepening terror. What did they mean? Her look seemed to suggest a new thought to Alessandro.

"Heavens, Señorita!" he cried, "have you not heard? Do you not know what has happened?"

"I know nothing, love," answered Ramona. "I have heard nothing since you went away. For ten days I have been sure you were dead; but to-night something told me that you were near, and I came to meet you."

At the first words of Ramona's sentence, Alessandro threw his arms around her again. As she said "love," his whole frame shook with emotion.

"My Señorita!" he whispered, "my Señorita! how shall I tell you! How shall I tell you!"

"What is there to tell, Alessandro?" she said. "I am afraid of nothing, now that you are here, and not dead, as I thought."

But Alessandro did not speak. It seemed impossible. At last, straining her closer to his breast, he cried: "Dearest Señorita! I feel as if I should die when I tell you,-- I have no home; my father is dead; my people are driven out of their village. I am only a beggar now, Señorita; like those you used to feed and pity in Los Angeles convent!" As he spoke the last words, he reeled, and, supporting himself against the tree, added: "I am not strong, Señorita; we have been starving." 5

Ramona's face did not reassure him. Even in the dusk he could see its look of incredulous horror. He misread it.

"I only came to look at you once more," he continued. "I will go now. May the saints bless you, my Señorita, always. I think the Virgin sent you to me to-night. I should never have seen your face if you had not come."

While he was speaking, Ramona had buried her face in his bosom. Lifting it now, she said, "Did you mean to leave me to think you were dead, Alessandro?"

"I thought that the news about our village must have reached you," he said, "and that you would know I had no home, and could not come, to seem to remind you of what you had said. Oh, Señorita, it was little enough I had before to give you! I don't know how I dared to believe that you could come to be with me; but I loved you so much, I had thought of many things I could do; and—" lowering his voice and speaking almost sullenly—"it is the saints, I believe, who have punished me thus for having resolved to leave my people, and take all I had for myself and you. Now they have left me nothing;" and he groaned.

"Who?" cried Ramona. "Was there a battle? Was your father killed?" She was trembling with horror.

"No," answered Alessandro. "There was no battle. There would have been, if I had had my way; but my father implored me not to resist. He said it would only make it worse for us in the end. The sheriff, too, he begged me to let it all go on peaceably, and help him keep the people quiet. He felt terribly to have to do it. It was Mr. Rothsaker, from San Diego. We had often worked for him on his ranch. He knew all about us. Don't you recollect, Señorita, I told you about him,—how fair he always was, and kind too? He has the biggest wheat-ranch in Cajon; we 've harvested miles and miles of wheat for him. He said he would have rather died, almost, than have had it to do; but if we resisted, he would have to order his men to shoot. He had twenty men with him. They thought there would be trouble; and well they might,—turning a whole village full of men and women and children out of their houses, and driving them off like foxes. If it had been any man but Mr. Rothsaker, I would have shot him dead, if I had hung for it; but I knew if he thought we must go, there was no help for us."

"But, Alessandro," interrupted Ramona, "I can't

5 Jackson had no need to exaggerate the drama here. When she, as a fact finding commissioner, first sought the Indian village of Temecula, she found only its graveyard. Upon investigation, Jackson learned that the grant conceded to the Indians in 1852 by the United States Peace and Freedom Treaty had proved useless. In 1869 five white settlers from San Francisco saw the land and set out to get it. An action was filed ordering the Indians to move. They appealed to an activist priest in San Diego who in turn appealed to one of the judges in the case. These efforts merely postponed the inevitable. In 1875 the sheriff of San Diego arrived with a posse of determined men and a warrant which deprived the Indians of their homes and crops just maturing for harvest. Their personal possessions were confiscated as well—in payment for the cost of the suit.

understand. Who was it made Mr. Rothsaker do it? Who has the land now?"

"I don't know who they are," Alessandro replied, his voice full of anger and scorn. "They 're Americans, — eight or ten of them. They all got together and brought a suit, they call it, up in San Francisco; and it was decided in the court that they owned all our land. That was all Mr. Rothsaker could tell about it. It was the law, he said, and nobody could go against the law."

"Oh," said Ramona, "that 's the way the Americans took so much of the Señora's land away from her. It was in the court up in San Francisco; and they decided that miles and miles of her land, which the General had always had, was not hers at all. They said it belonged to the United States Government."

"They are a pack of thieves and liars, every one of them!" cried Alessandro. "They are going to steal all the land in this country; we might all just as well throw ourselves into the sea, and let them have it. My father has been telling me this for years. He saw it coming; but I did not believe him. I did not think men could be so wicked; but he was right. I am glad he is dead. That is the only thing I have to be thankful for now. One day I thought he was going to get well, and I prayed to the Virgin not to let him. I did not want him to live. He never knew anything clear after they took him out of his house. That was before I got there. I found him sitting on the ground outside. They said it was the sun that had turned him crazy; but it was not. It was his heart breaking in his bosom. He would not come out of his house, and the men lifted him up and carried him out by force, and threw him on the ground; and then they threw out all the furniture we had; and when he saw them doing that, he put his hands up to his head, and called out, 'Alessandro! Alessandro!' and I was not there! Señorita, they said it was a voice to make the dead hear, that he called with; and nobody could stop him. All that day and all the night he kept on calling. God! Señorita, I wonder I did not die when they told me! When I got there, some one had built up a little booth of tule over his head, to keep the sun off. He did not call any more, only for water, water. That was what made them think the sun had done it. They did all they could; but it was such a dreadful time, nobody could do much; the sheriff's men were in great hurry; they gave no time. They said the people must all be off in two days. Everybody was running hither and thither. Everything out of the houses in piles on the ground. The people took all the roofs off their houses too. They were made of the tule reeds; so they would do again. Oh, Señorita, don't ask me to tell you any more! It is like death. I can't!"

Ramona was crying bitterly. She did not know what to say. What was love, in face of such calamity? What had she to give to a man stricken like this?

"Don't weep, Señorita," said Alessandro, drearily. "Tears kill one, and do no good."

"How long did your father live?" asked Ramona, clasping her arms closer around his neck. They were sitting on the ground now, and Ramona, yearning over Alessandro, as if she were the strong one and he the one to be sheltered, had drawn his head to her bosom, caressing him as if he had been hers for years. Nothing could have so clearly shown his enfeebled and benumbed condition, as the manner in which he received these caresses, which once would have made him beside himself with joy. He leaned against her breast as a child might.

"He! He died only four days ago. I stayed to bury him, and then I came away. I have been three days on the way; the horse, poor beast, is almost weaker than I. The Americans took my horse," Alessandro said.

"Took your horse!" cried Ramona, aghast. "Is that the law, too?"

"So Mr. Rothsaker told me. He said the judge had said he must take enough of our cattle and horses to pay all it had cost for the suit up in San Francisco. They did n't reckon the cattle at what they were worth, I thought; but they said cattle were selling very low now. There were not enough in all the village to pay it, so we had to make it up in horses; and they took mine. I was not there the day they drove the cattle away, or I would have put a ball into Benito's head before any American should ever have had him to ride. But I was over in Pachanga with my father. He would not stir a step for anybody but me; so I led him all the way; and then after he got there he was so ill I never left him a minute. He did not know me any more, nor know anything that had happened. I built a little hut of tule, and he lay on the ground till he died. When I put him in his grave, I was glad."

"In Temecula?" asked Ramona.

"In Temecula!" exclaimed Alessandro, fiercely. "You don't seem to understand, Señorita. We have no right in Temecula, not even to our graveyard full of the dead. Mr. Rothsaker warned us all not to be hanging about there; for he said the men who were coming in were a rough set, and they would shoot any Indian at sight, if they saw him trespassing on their property."

"Their property!" ejaculated Ramona.

"Yes; it is theirs," said Alessandro, doggedly. "That is the law. They've got all the papers to show it. That is what my father always said, — if the Señor Valdez had only given him a paper! But they never did in those days. Nobody had papers. The American law is different."

"It 's a law of thieves!" cried Ramona.

"Yes, and of murderers too," said Alessandro. "Don't you call my father murdered just as much as if they had shot him? I do! And, O Señorita, my Señorita, there was José! You recollect José, who went for my violin? But, my beloved one, I am killing you with these terrible things! I will speak no more."

"No, no, Alessandro. Tell me all, all. You must have no grief I do not share. Tell me about José," cried Ramona, breathlessly.

"Señorita, it will break your heart to hear. José was married a year ago. He had the best house in Temecula, next to my father's. It was the only other one that had a shingled roof. And he had a barn too, and that splendid horse he rode, and oxen, and a flock of sheep. He was at home when 6
the sheriff came. A great many of the men were away, grape-picking. That made it worse. But José was at home; for his wife had a little baby only a few weeks old, and the child seemed sickly and not like to live, and José would not leave it. José was the first one that saw the sheriff riding into the village, and the band of armed men behind him, and José knew what it meant. He had often talked it over with me and with my father, and now he saw that it had come; and he went crazy in one minute, and fell on the ground all froth at his mouth. He had had a fit like that once before; and the doctor said if he had another, he would die. But he did not. They picked him up, and presently he was better; and Mr. Rothsaker said nobody worked so well in the moving the first day as José did. Most of the men would not lift a hand. They sat on the ground with the women, and covered up their faces, and would not see. But José worked; and, Señorita, one of the first things he did, was to run with my father's violin to the store, to Mrs. Hartsel, and ask her to hide it for us; José knew it was worth money. But before noon the second day he had another fit, and died in it,—died right in his own door, carrying out some of the things; and after Carmena—that's his wife's name—saw he was dead, she never spoke, but sat rocking back and forth on the ground, with the baby in her arms. She went over to Pachanga at the same time I did with my father. It was a long procession of us."

"Where is Pachanga?" asked Ramona.

"About three miles from Temecula, a little sort 7
of cañon. I told the people they'd better move over there; the land did not belong to anybody, and perhaps they could make a living there. There is n't any water; that's the worst of it."

"No water!" cried Ramona.

"No running water. There is one little spring, and they dug a well by it as soon as they got there; so there was water to drink, but that is all. I saw Carmena could hardly keep up, and I carried the baby for her on one arm, while I led my father with the other hand; but the baby cried, so she took it back. I thought then it would n't live the day out; but it did live till the morning of the day

6 Helen Hunt Jackson's original title for Ramona was to have been *In the Name of the Law* — which the author finally rejected because she was certain such a good title must certainly have been used before.

—Illustration by Henry Sandham. Circa 1883.

7 The Indian word, Temecula, means grief or mourning. It seems to have had a strangely prophetic fitness for the valley to which it was given.

Ann Daniels and Maurice Jara appeared as Ramona and Alessandro in the 1960 Hemet production.
—Courtesy of the Ramona Pageant Assoc., Inc.

my father died. Just a few hours before he died, Carmena came along with the baby rolled up in her shawl, and sat down by me on the ground, and did not speak. When I said, 'How is the little one?' she opened her shawl and showed it to me, dead. 'Good, Carmena!' said I. 'It is good! My father is dying too. We will bury them together.' So she sat by me all that morning, and at night she helped me dig the graves. I wanted to put the baby on my father's breast; but she said, no, it must have a little grave. So she dug it herself; and we put them in; and she never spoke, except that once. She was sitting there by the grave when I came away. I made a cross of two little trees with the boughs chopped off, and set it up by the graves. So that is the way our new graveyard was begun, — my father and the little baby; it is the very young and the very old that have the blessed fortune to die. I cannot die, it seems!"

"Where did they bury José?" gasped Ramona.

"In Temecula," said Alessandro. "Mr. Rothsaker made two of his men dig a grave in our old graveyard for José. But I think Carmena will go at night and bring his body away. I would! But, my Señorita, it is very dark, I can hardly see your beloved eyes. I think you must not stay longer. Can I go as far as the brook with you, safely, without being seen? The saints bless you, beloved, for coming. I could not have lived, I think, without one more sight of your face;" and, springing to his feet, Alessandro stood waiting for Ramona to move. She remained still. She was in a sore strait. Her heart held but one impulse, one desire, — to go with Alessandro; nothing was apparently farther from his thoughts than this. Could she offer to go? Should she risk laying a burden on him greater than he could bear? If he were indeed a beggar, as he said, would his life be hindered or helped by her? She felt herself strong and able. Work had no terrors for her; privations she knew nothing of, but she felt no fear of them.

"Alessandro!" she said, in a tone which startled him.

"My Señorita!" he said tenderly.

"You have never once called me Ramona."

"I cannot, Señorita!" he replied.

"Why not?"

"I do not know. I sometimes think 'Ramona,'" he added faintly; "but not often. If I think of you by any other name than as my Señorita, it is usually by a name you never heard."

"What is it?" exclaimed Ramona, wonderingly.

"An Indian word, my dearest one, the name of the bird you are like, — the wood-dove. In the Luiseno tongue that is Majel; that was what I thought my people would have called you, if you had come to dwell among us. It is a beautiful name, Señorita, and is like you."

Alessandro was still standing. Ramona rose; coming close to him, she laid both her hands on his breast, and her head on her hands, and said: "Alessandro, I have something to tell you. I am an Indian. I belong to your people."

Alessandro's silence astonished her. "You are surprised," she said. "I thought you would be glad."

"The gladness of it came to me long ago, my Señorita," he said. "I knew it!"

"How?" cried Ramona. "And you never told me, Alessandro!"

"How could I?" he replied. "I dared not. Juan Canito, it was, told me."

"Juan Canito!" said Ramona, musingly. "How could he have known?" Then in a few rapid words she told Alessandro all that the Señora had told her. "Is that what Juan Can said?" she asked.

"All except the father's name," stammered Alessandro.

"Who did he say was my father?" she asked.

Alessandro was silent.

"It matters not," said Ramona. "He was wrong. The Señora, of course, knew. He was a friend of hers, and of the Señora Ortegna, to whom he gave me. But I think, Alessandro, I have more of my mother than of my father."

"Yes, you have, my Señorita," replied Alessandro, tenderly. "After I knew it, I then saw what it was in your face had always seemed to me like the faces of my own people."

"Are you not glad, Alessandro?"

"Yes, my Señorita."

What more should Ramona say? Suddenly her heart gave way; and without premeditation, without resolve, almost without consciousness of what she was doing, she flung herself on Alessandro's breast, and cried: "Oh, Alessandro, take me with you! take me with you! I would rather die than have you leave me again!"

Chapter XV

ALESSANDRO'S first answer to this cry of Ramona's was a tightening of his arms around her; closer and closer he held her, till it was almost pain; she could hear the throbs of his heart, but he did not speak. Then, letting his arms fall, taking her hand in his, he laid it on his forehead reverently, and said, in a voice which was so husky and trembling she could barely understand his words: "My Señorita knows that my life is hers. She can ask me to go into the fire or into the sea, and neither the fire nor the sea would frighten me; they would but make me glad for her sake. But I cannot take my Señorita's life to throw it away. She is tender; she would die; she cannot lie on the earth for a bed, and have no food to eat. My Señorita does not know what she says."

His solemn tone; this third-person designation, as if he were speaking of her, not with her, almost as if he were thinking aloud to God rather than speaking to her, merely calmed and strengthened, did not deter Ramona. "I am strong; I can work too, Alessandro. You do not know. We can both work. I am not afraid to lie on the earth; and God will give us food," she said.

"That was what I thought, my Señorita, until now. When I rode away that morning, I had it in my thoughts, as you say, that if you were not afraid, I would not be; and that there would at least always be food, and I could make it that you should never suffer; but, Señorita, the saints are displeased. They do not pray for us any more. It is as my father said, they have forsaken us. These Americans will destroy us all. I do not know but they will presently begin to shoot us and poison us, to get us all out of the country, as they do the rabbits and the gophers; it would not be any worse than what they have done. Would not you rather be dead, Señorita, than be as I am to-day?"

Each word he spoke but intensified Ramona's determination to share his lot. "Alessandro," she interrupted, "there are many men among your people who have wives, are there not?"

"Yes, Señorita!" replied Alessandro, wonderingly.

Karen Grant Thompson appeared as Ramona and Crist Thomas as Alessandro in the 1981 Ramona Outdoor Play presented by the people of Hemet and San Jacinto.
—Courtesy of the Ramona Pageant Assoc., Inc.

— Illustration by Henry Sandham. Circa 1913.

1

Helen Hunt Jackson, visiting San Juan Bautista Mission in 1881, had a mystical vision of Father Junipero Serra as she listened to the singing of the orphans. Later she talked with a Californio woman, eighty-five years old, who recalled the good old days. Portly, jolly, keen-eyed, keen-tongued, she was the widow of one of the soldiers in the old mission guard and the mother of twelve. Jackson likened her memory to a magic glass, reproducing the pictures of the past. Sixty years back she remembered, "The Indians used to be in San Juan Bautista like sheep by the thousand and thousand. They were always good and the padres were always kind. Fifty oxen were killed for food every eight days, and everybody had plenty to eat. There was much more water then than now, plenty of rain, and the streams always full."

An arrangement for banjo and ukulele.

"Have their wives left them and gone away, now that this trouble has come?"

"No, Señorita!" still more wonderingly; "how could they?"

"They are going to stay with them, help them to earn money, try to make them happier, are they not?"

"Yes, Señorita." Alessandro began to see whither these questions tended. It was not unlike the Señora's tactics, the way in which Ramona narrowed in her lines of interrogation.

"Do the women of your people love their husbands very much?"

"Very much, Señorita." A pause. It was very dark now. Alessandro could not see the hot currents running swift and red over Ramona's face; even her neck changed color as she asked her last question. "Do you think any one of them loves her husband more than I love you, Alessandro?"

Alessandro's arms were again around her, before the words were done. Were not such words enough to make a dead man live? Almost; but not enough to make such a love as Alessandro's selfish. Alessandro was silent.

"You know there is not one!" said Ramona, impetuously.

"Oh, it is too much!" cried Alessandro, throwing his arms up wildly. Then, drawing her to him again, he said, the words pouring out breathless: "My Señorita, you take me to the door of heaven, but I dare not go in. I know it would kill you, Señorita, to live the life we must live. Let me go, dearest Señorita; let me go! It had been better if you had never seen me."

"Do you know what I was going to do, Alessandro, if you had not come?" said Ramona. "I was going to run away from the Señora's house, all alone, and walk all the way to Santa Barbara, to Father
1 Salvierderra, and ask him to put me in the convent at San Juan Bautista; and that is what I will do now if you leave me!"

"Oh, no, no, Señorita, my Señorita, you will not do that! My beautiful Señorita in the convent! No, no!" cried Alessandro, greatly agitated.

"Yes, if you do not let me come with you, I shall do it. I shall set out to-morrow."

Her words carried conviction to Alessandro's soul. He knew she would do as she said. "Even that would not be so dreadful as to be hunted like a wild beast, Señorita; as you may be, if you come with me."

"When I thought you were dead, Alessandro, I did not think the convent would be dreadful at all. I thought it would be peace; and I could do good, teaching the children. But if I knew you were alive, I could never have peace; not for one minute have peace, Alessandro! I would rather die, than not be where you are. Oh, Alessandro, take me with you!"

Alessandro was conquered. "I will take you, my most beloved Señorita," he said gravely, — no lover's gladness in his tone, and his voice was hollow; "I will take you. Perhaps the saints will have mercy on you, even if they have forsaken me and my people!"

"Your people are my people, dearest; and the saints never forsake any one who does not forsake them. You will be glad all our lives long, Alessandro," cried Ramona; and she laid her head on his breast in solemn silence for a moment, as if registering a vow.

Well might Felipe have said that he would hold himself fortunate if any woman ever loved him as Ramona loved Alessandro.

When she lifted her head, she said timidly, now that she was sure, "Then you will take your Ramona with you, Alessandro?"

"I will take you with me till I die; and may the Madonna guard you, my Ramona," replied Alessandro, clasping her to his breast, and bowing his head upon hers. But there were tears in his eyes, and they were not tears of joy; and in his heart he said, as in his rapturous delight when he first saw Ramona bending over the brook under the willows he had said aloud, "My God! what shall I do!"

It was not easy to decide on the best plan of procedure now. Alessandro wished to go boldly to the house, see Señor Felipe, and if need be the Señora. Ramona quivered with terror at the bare mention of it. "You do not know the Señora, Alessandro," she cried, "or you would never think of it. She has been terrible all this time. She hates me so that she would kill me if she dared. She pretends that she will do nothing to prevent my going away; but I believe at the last minute she would throw me in the well in the court-yard, rather than have me go with you."

"I would never let her harm you," said Alessandro. "Neither would Señor Felipe."

"She turns Felipe round her finger as if he were soft wax," answered Ramona. "She makes him of a hundred minds in a minute, and he can't help himself. Oh, I think she is in league with the fiends, Alessandro! Don't dare to come near the house; I will come here as soon as every one is asleep. We must go at once."

Ramona's terrors overruled Alessandro's judgment, and he consented to wait for her at the spot where they now stood. She turned back twice to embrace him again. "Oh, my Alessandro, promise me that you will not stir from this place till I come," she said.

"I will be here when you come," he said.

"It will not be more than two hours," she said, "or three, at the utmost. It must be nine o'clock now."

She did not observe that Alessandro had evaded the promise not to leave the spot. That promise Alessandro would not have given. He had something to do in preparation for this unexpected flight of Ramona. In her innocence, her absorption in her thoughts of Alessandro and of love, she had never seemed to consider how she would make this long journey. As Alessandro had ridden towards Temecula, eighteen days ago, he had pictured himself riding back on his fleet, strong Benito, and bringing Antonio's matchless little dun mare for Ramona to ride. Only eighteen short days ago; and as he was dreaming that very dream, he had looked up and seen Antonio on the little dun mare, galloping towards him like the wind, the overridden creature's breath coming from her like pants of a steam-engine, and her sides dripping blood, where Antonio, who loved her, had not spared the cruel spurs; and Antonio, seeing him, had uttered a cry, and flinging himself off, came with a bound to his side, and with gasps between his words told him. Alessandro could not remember the words, only that after them he set his teeth, and dropping the bridle, laid his head down between Benito's ears, and whispered to him; and Benito never stopped, but galloped on all that day, till he came into Temecula; and there Alessandro saw the roofless houses, and the wagons being loaded, and the people running about, the women and children wailing; and then they showed him the place where his father lay on the ground, under the tule, and jumping off Benito he let him go, and that was the last he ever saw of him. Only eighteen days ago! And now here he was, under the willows,—the same copse where he first halted, at his first sight of Ramona; and it was night, dark night, and Ramona had been there, in his arms; she was his; and she was coming back presently to go away with him,—where? He had no home in the wide world to which to take her,—and this poor beast he had ridden from Temecula, had it strength enough left to carry her? Alessandro doubted. He had himself walked more than half the distance, to spare the creature, and yet there had been good pasture all the way; but the animal had been too long starved to recover quickly. In the Pachanga cañon, where they had found refuge, the grass was burned up by the sun, and the few horses taken over there had suffered wretchedly; some had died. But Alessandro, even while his arms were around Ramona, had revolved in his mind a project he would not have dared to confide to her. If Baba, Ramona's own horse, was still in the corral, Alessandro could without difficulty lure him out. He thought it would be no sin. At any rate, if it were, it could not be avoided. The Señorita must have a horse, and Baba had always been her own; had followed her about like a dog ever since he could run; in fact, the only taming he had ever had, had been done by Ramona, with bread and honey. He was intractable to others; but Ramona could guide him by a wisp of his silky mane. Alessandro also had nearly as complete control over him; for it had been one of his greatest pleasures, during the summer, when he could not see Ramona, to caress and fondle her horse, till Baba knew and loved him next to his young mistress. If only Baba were in the corral, all would be well. As soon as the sound of Ramona's footsteps had died away, Alessandro followed with quick but stealthy steps; keeping well down in the bottom, below the willows, he

A scene from the 20th Century-Fox production of *Ramona*.

An Indian house in Pachanga Canyon.
—Photograph by George Wharton James. Circa 1911.

—Illustration by Henry Sandham. Circa 1900.

skirted the terrace where the artichoke-patch and the sheepfolds lay, and then turned up to approach the corral from the farther side. There was no light in any of the herdsmen's huts. They were all asleep. That was good. Well Alessandro knew how sound they slept; many a night while he slept there with them he had walked twice over their bodies as they lay stretched on skins on the floor, — out and in without rousing them. If only Baba would not give a loud whinny. Leaning on the corral-fence, Alessandro gave a low, hardly audible whistle. The horses were all in a group together at the farther end of the corral. At the sound there was a slight movement in the group; and one of them turned and came a pace or two towards Alessandro.

" I believe that is Baba himself," thought Alessandro; and he made another low sound. The horse quickened his steps; then halted, as if he suspected some mischief.

" Baba," whispered Alessandro. The horse knew his name as well as any dog; knew Alessandro's voice too, but the sagacious creature seemed instinctively to know that here was an occasion for secrecy and caution. If Alessandro whispered, he, Baba, would whisper back; and it was little more than a whispered whinny which he gave, as he trotted quickly to the fence, and put his nose to Alessandro's face, rubbing and kissing and giving soft whinnying sighs.

" Hush! hush! Baba," whispered Alessandro, as if he were speaking to a human being. " Hush!" and he proceeded cautiously to lift off the upper rails and bushes of the fence. The horse understood instantly; and as soon as the fence was a little lowered, leaped over it and stood still by Alessandro's side, while he replaced the rails, smiling to himself, spite of his grave anxiety, to think of Juan Can's wonder in the morning as to how Baba had managed to get out of the corral.

This had taken only a few moments. It was better luck than Alessandro had hoped for; emboldened by it, he began to wonder if he could not get the saddle too. The saddles, harnesses, bridles, and all such things hung on pegs in an open barn, such as is constantly to be seen in Southern California; as significant a testimony, in matter of climate, as any Signal Service Report could be, — a floor and a roof; no walls, only corner posts to hold the roof. Nothing but summer-houses on a large scale are the South California barns. Alessandro stood musing. The longer he thought, the greater grew his desire for that saddle.

" Baba, if only you knew what I wanted of you, you 'd lie down on the ground here and wait while I got the saddle. But I dare not risk leaving you.
2 Come, Baba! " and he struck down the hill again, the horse following him softly. When he got down below the terrace, he broke into a run, with his hand in Baba's mane, as if it were a frolic; and in a few moments they were safe in the willow copse, where

Alessandro's poor pony was tethered. Fastening Baba with the same lariat, Alessandro patted him on the neck, pressed his face to his nose, and said aloud, "Good Baba, stay here till the Señorita comes." Baba whinnied.

"Why should n't he know the Señorita's name! I believe he does!" thought Alessandro, as he turned and again ran swiftly back to the corral. He felt strong now, — felt like a new man. Spite of all the terror, joy thrilled him. When he reached the corral, all was yet still. The horses had not moved from their former position. Throwing himself flat on the ground, Alessandro crept on his breast from the corral to the barn, several rods' distance. This was the most hazardous part of his adventure; every other moment he paused, lay motionless for some seconds, then crept a few paces more. As he neared the corner where Ramona's saddle always hung, his heart beat. Sometimes, of a warm night, Luigo slept on the barn floor. If he were there to-night, all was lost. Groping in the darkness, Alessandro pulled himself up on the post, felt for the saddle, found it, lifted it, and in a trice was flat on the ground again, drawing the saddle along after him. Not a sound had he made, that the most watchful of sheep-dogs could hear.

"Ha, old Capitan, caught you napping this time!" said Alessandro to himself, as at last he got safe to the bottom of the terrace, and, springing to his feet, bounded away with the saddle on his shoulders. It was a weight for a starving man to carry, but he felt it not, for the rejoicing he had in its possession. Now his Señorita would go in comfort. To ride Baba was to be rocked in a cradle. If need be, Baba would carry them both, and never know it; and it might come to that, Alessandro thought, as he knelt by the side of his poor beast, which was stretched out on the ground exhausted; Baba standing by, looking down in scornful wonder at this strange new associate.

"The saints be praised!" thought Alessandro, as he seated himself to wait. "This looks as if they would not desert my Señorita."

Thoughts whirled in his brain. Where should they go first? What would be best? Would they be pursued? Where could they hide? Where should he seek a new home?

It was bootless thinking, until Ramona was by his side. He must lay each plan before her. She must decide. The first thing was to get to San Diego, to the priest, to be married. That would be three days' hard ride; five for the exhausted Indian pony. What should they eat on the way? Ah! Alessandro bethought him of the violin at Hartsel's. Mr. Hartsel would give him money on that; perhaps buy it. Then Alessandro remembered his own violin. He had not once thought of it before. It lay in its case on a table in Señor Felipe's room when he came away. Was it possible? No, of course it could not be possible that the Señorita would think to bring it. What would she bring? She would be wise, Alessandro was sure.

How long the hours seemed as he sat thus plotting and conjecturing; more and more thankful, as each hour went by, to see the sky still clouded, the darkness dense. "It must have been the saints, too, that brought me on a night when there was no moon," he thought; and then he said again, devout and simple-minded man that he was, "They mean to protect my Señorita; they will let me take care of her."

Ramona was threading a perilous way, through great difficulties. She had reached her room unobserved, so far as she could judge. Luckily for her, Margarita was in bed with a terrible toothache, for which her mother had given her a strong sleeping-draught. Margarita was disposed of. If she had not been, Ramona would never have got away, for Margarita would have known that she had been out of the house for two hours, and would have watched to see what it meant.

Ramona came in through the court-yard; she dared not go by the veranda, sure that Felipe and his mother were sitting there still, for it was not late.

As she entered her room, she heard them talking. She closed one of her windows, to let them know she was there. Then she knelt at the Madonna's feet, and in an inaudible whisper told her all she was going to do, and prayed that she would watch over her and Alessandro, and show them where to go.

"I know she will! I am sure she will!" whispered Ramona to herself as she rose from her knees.

Then she threw herself on her bed, to wait till the Señora and Felipe should be asleep. Her brain was alert, clear. She knew exactly what she wished to do. She had thought that all out, more than two weeks ago, when she was looking for Alessandro hour by hour.

Early in the summer Alessandro had given to her, as curiosities, two of the large nets which the Indian
2 women use for carrying all sorts of burdens. They are woven out of the fibres of a flax-like plant, and are strong as iron. The meshes being large, they are very light; are gathered at each end, and fastened to a band which goes around the forehead. In these can be carried on the back, with comparative ease, heavier loads than could be lifted in any other way. Until Ramona recollected these, she had been perplexed to know how she should carry the things which she had made up her mind it would be right for her to take, — only a few; simply necessaries; one stuff gown and her shawls; the new altar-cloth, and two changes of clothes; that would not be a great deal; she had a right to so much, she thought, now that she had seen the jewels in the Señora's keeping. "I will tell Father Salvierderra exactly what I took," she thought, "and ask him if it was too much." She did not like to think that all these clothes she must take had been paid for with the Señora Moreno's money.

And Alessandro's violin. Whatever else she left, that must go. What would life be to Alessandro without a violin! And if they went to Los Angeles, he might earn money by playing at dances. Already Ramona had devised several ways by which they could both earn money.

There must be also food for the journey. And it must be good food, too; wine for Alessandro. Anguish filled her heart as she recalled how gaunt he looked. "Starving," he said they had been. Good God! Starving! And she had sat down each day at loaded tables, and seen, each day, good food thrown to the dogs to eat.

It was long before the Señora went to her room; and long after that before Felipe's breathing had become so deep and regular that Ramona dared feel sure that he was asleep. At last she ventured out. All was dark; it was past midnight.

"The violin first!" she said; and creeping into the dining-room, and through the inner door to Felipe's room, she brought it out, rolled it in shawl after shawl, and put it in the net with her clothes. Then she stole out, with this net on her back, "like a true Indian woman as I am," she said, almost gayly, to herself, — through the court-yard, around the southeast corner of the house, past the garden, down to the willows, where she laid down her load, and went back for the second.

This was harder. Wine she was resolved to have and bread and cold meat. She did not know so well where to put her hand on old Marda's possessions as on her own, and she dared not strike a light. She made several journeys to the kitchen and pantry before she had completed her store. Wine, luckily, she found in the dining-room, — two full bottles; also milk, which she poured into a leathern flask which hung on the wall in the veranda.

Now all was ready. She leaned from her window, and listened to Felipe's breathing. "How can I go without bidding him good-by?" she said. "How can I?" and she stood irresolute.

"Dear Felipe! Dear Felipe! He has always been so good to me! He has done all he could for me! I wish I dared kiss him. I will leave a note for him."

Taking a pencil and paper, and a tiny wax taper, whose light would hardly be seen across a room, she slipped once more into the dining-room, knelt on the floor behind the door, lighted her taper, and wrote:

"Dear Felipe, — Alessandro has come, and I am going away with him to-night. Don't let anything be done to us, if you can help it. I don't know where we are going. I hope, to Father Salvierderra. I shall love you always. Thank you, dear Felipe, for all your kindness.

"Ramona."

It had not taken a moment. She blew out her taper, and crept back into her room. Felipe's bed was now moved close to the wall of the house. From her window she could reach its foot. Slowly, cautiously, she stretched out her arm and dropped the little paper on the coverlet, just over Felipe's feet. There was a risk that the Señora would come out in the morning, before Felipe awaked, and see the note first; but that risk she would take.

"Farewell, dear Felipe!" she whispered, under her breath, as she turned from the window.

The delay had cost her dear. The watchful Capitan, from his bed at the upper end of the court, had half heard, half scented something strange going on. As Ramona stepped out, he gave one short, quick bark, and came bounding down.

"Holy Virgin, I am lost!" thought Ramona; but, crouching on the ground, she quickly opened her net, and as Capitan came towards her, gave him a piece of meat, fondling and caressing him. While he ate it, wagging his tail, and making great demonstrations of joy, she picked up her load again, and still fondling him, said, "Come on, Capitan!" It was her last chance. If he barked again, somebody would be waked; if he went by her side quietly, she might escape. A cold sweat of terror burst on her forehead as she took her first step cautiously. The dog followed. She quickened her pace; he trotted along, still smelling the meat in the net. When she reached the willows, she halted, debating whether she should give him a large piece of meat, and try to run away while he was eating it, or whether she should let him go quietly along. She decided on the latter course; and, picking up her other net, walked on. She was safe now. She turned, and looked back towards the house; all was dark and still. She could hardly see its outline. A great wave of emotion swept over her. It was the only home she had ever known. All she had experienced of happiness, as well as of bitter pain, had been there, — Felipe, Father Salvierderra, the servants, the birds, the garden, the dear chapel! Ah, if she could have once more prayed in the chapel! Who would put fresh flowers and ferns in the chapel now? How Felipe would miss her, when he knelt before the altar! For fourteen years she had knelt by his side. And the Señora, — the hard, cold Señora! She would alone be glad. Everybody else would be sorry. "They will all be sorry I have gone, — all but the Señora! I wish it had been so that I could have bidden them all good-by, and had them all bid me good-by, and wish us good fortune!" thought the gentle, loving girl, as she drew a long sigh, and, turning her back on her home, went forward in the path she had chosen.

She stooped and patted Capitan on the head. "Will you come with me, Capitan?" she said; and Capitan leaped up joyfully, giving two or three short, sharp notes of delight. "Good Capitan, come! They will not miss him out of so many," she thought, "and it will always seem like something from home, as long as I have Capitan."

When Alessandro first saw Ramona's figure dimly in the gloom, drawing slowly nearer, he did not recognize it, and he was full of apprehension at the sight. What stranger could it be, abroad in these lonely meadows at this hour of the night? Hastily he led the horses farther back into the copse, and hid himself behind a tree, to watch. In a few moments more he thought he recognized Capitan, bounding by the side of this bent and slow-moving figure. Yet this was surely an Indian woman toiling along under a heavy load. But what Indian woman would have so superb a colley as Capitan? Alessandro strained his eyes through the darkness. Presently he saw the figure halt, — drop part of its burden.

"Alessandro!" came in a sweet, low call.

He bounded like a deer, crying, "My Señorita! my Señorita! Can that be you? To think that you have brought these heavy loads!"

Ramona laughed. "Do you remember the day you showed me how the Indian women carried so much on their backs, in these nets? I did not think then I would use it so soon. But it hurts my forehead, Alessandro. It is n't the weight, but the strings cut. I could n't have carried them much farther!"

"Ah, you had no basket to cover the head," replied Alessandro, as he threw up the two nets on his shoulders as if they had been feathers. In doing so, he felt the violin-case.

"Is it the violin?" he cried. "My blessed one, where did you get it?"

"Off the table in Felipe's room," she answered. "I knew you would rather have it than anything else. I brought very little, Alessandro; it seemed nothing while I was getting it; but it is very heavy to carry. Will it be too much for the poor tired horse? You and I can walk. And see, Alessandro, here is Capitan. He waked up, and I had to bring him, to keep him still. Can't he go with us?"

Capitan was leaping up, putting his paws on Alessandro's breast, licking his face, yelping, doing all a dog could do, to show welcome and affection.

Alessandro laughed aloud. Ramona had not more than two or three times heard him do this. It frightened her. "Why do you laugh, Alessandro?" she said.

"To think what I have to show you, my Señorita," he said. "Look here;" and turning towards the willows, he gave two or three low whistles, at the first note of which Baba came trotting out of the copse to the end of his lariat, and began to snort and whinny with delight as soon as he perceived Ramona.

Ramona burst into tears. The surprise was too great.

"Are you not glad, Señorita?" cried Alessandro, aghast. "Is it not your own horse? If you do not wish to take him, I will lead him back. My pony can carry you, if we journey very slowly. But I thought it would be joy to you to have Baba."

"Oh, it is! it is!" sobbed Ramona, with her head on Baba's neck. "It is a miracle, — a miracle. How did he come here? And the saddle too!" she cried, for the first time observing that. "Alessandro," in

The altar in the chapel. —Phtotograph by A.C. Vroman. Circa 1913

—Illustration by Henry Sandham. Cica 1883.

an awe-struck whisper, "did the saints send him? Did you find him here?" It would have seemed to Ramona's faith no strange thing, had this been so.

"I think the saints helped me to bring him," answered Alessandro, seriously, "or else I had not done it so easily. I did but call, near the corral-fence, and he came to my hand, and leaped over the rails at my word, as quickly as Capitan might have done. He is yours, Señorita. It is no harm to take him?"

"Oh, no!" answered Ramona. "He is more mine than anything else I had; for it was Felipe gave him to me when he could but just stand on his legs; he was only two days old; and I have fed him out of my hand every day till now; and now he is five. Dear Baba, we will never be parted, never!" and she took his paw in both her hands, and laid her cheek against it lovingly.

Alessandro was busy, fastening the two nets on either side the saddle. "Baba will never know he has a load at all; they are not so heavy as my Señorita thought," he said. "It was the weight on the forehead, with nothing to keep the strings from the skin, which gave her pain."

Alessandro was making all haste. His hands trembled. "We must make all the speed we can, dearest Señorita," he said, "for a few hours. Then we will rest. Before light, we will be in a spot where we can hide safely all day. We will journey only by night, lest they pursue us."

"They will not," said Ramona. "There is no danger. The Señora said she should do nothing. 'Nothing!'" she repeated, in a bitter tone. "That is what she made Felipe say, too. Felipe wanted to help us. He would have liked to have you stay with us; but all he could get was, that she would do 'nothing!' But they will not follow us. They will wish never to hear of me again. I mean, the Señora will wish never to hear of me. Felipe will be sorry. Felipe is very good, Alessandro."

They were all ready now, — Ramona on Baba, the two packed nets swinging from her saddle, one on either side. Alessandro, walking, led his tired pony. It was a sad sort of procession for one going to be wed, but Ramona's heart was full of joy.

"I don't know why it is, Alessandro," she said; "I should think I would be afraid, but I have not the least fear, — not the least; not of anything that can come, Alessandro," she reiterated with emphasis. "Is it not strange?"

"Yes, Señorita," he replied solemnly, laying his hand on hers as he walked close at her side. "It is strange. I am afraid, — afraid for you, my Señorita! But it is done, and we will not go back; and perhaps the saints will help you, and will let me take care of you. They must love you, Señorita; but they do not love me, nor my people."

"Are you never going to call me by my name?" asked Ramona. "I hate your calling me Señorita. That was what the Señora always called me when she was displeased."

"I will never speak the word again!" cried Alessandro. "The saints forbid I should speak to you in the words of that woman!"

"Can't you say Ramona?" she asked.

Alessandro hesitated. He could not have told why it seemed to him difficult to say Ramona.

"What was that other name, you said you always thought of me by?" she continued. "The Indian name, — the name of the dove?"

"Majel," he said. "It is by that name I have oftenest thought of you since the night I watched all night for you, after you had kissed me, and two wood-doves were calling and answering each other in the dark; and I said to myself, that is what my love is like, the wood-dove: the wood-dove's voice is low like hers, and sweeter than any other sound in the earth; and the wood-dove is true to one mate always —" He stopped.

"As I to you, Alessandro," said Ramona, leaning from her horse, and resting her hand on Alessandro's shoulder.

Baba stopped. He was used to knowing by the most trivial signs what his mistress wanted; he did not understand this new situation; no one had ever before, when Ramona was riding him, walked by his side so close that he touched his shoulders, and rested his hand in his mane. If it had been anybody else than Alessandro, Baba would not have permitted it even now. But it must be all right, since Ramona was quiet; and now she had stretched out her hand and rested it on Alessandro's shoulder. Did that mean halt for a moment? Baba thought it might, and acted accordingly; turning his head round to the right, and looking back to see what came of it.

Alessandro's arms around Ramona, her head bent down to his, their lips together, — what could Baba think? As mischievously as if he had been a human being or an elf, Baba bounded to one side and tore the lovers apart. They both laughed, and cantered on, — Alessandro running; the poor Indian pony feeling the contagion, and loping as it had not done for many a day.

"Majel is my name, then," said Ramona, "is it? It is a sweet sound, but I would like it better Majella. Call me Majella."

"That will be good," replied Alessandro, "for the reason that never before had any one the same name. It will not be hard for me to say Majella. I know not why your name of Ramona has always been hard to my tongue."

"Because it was to be that you should call me Majella," said Ramona. "Remember, I am Ramona no longer. That also was the name the Señora called me by — and dear Felipe too," she added thoughtfully. "He would not know me by my new name. I would like to have *him* always call me Ramona. But for all the rest of the world I am Majella, now, — Alessandro's Majel!"

Chapter XVI

AFTER they reached the highway, and had trotted briskly on for a mile, Alessandro suddenly put out his hand, and taking Baba by the rein, began turning him round and round in the road.

"We will not go any farther in the road," he said, "but I must conceal our tracks here. We will go backwards for a few paces." The obedient Baba backed slowly, half dancing, as if he understood the trick; the Indian pony, too, curvetted awkwardly, then by a sudden bound under Alessandro's skilful guidance, leaped over a rock to the right, and stood waiting further orders. Baba followed, and Capitan; and there was no trail to show where they had left the road.

After trotting the pony round and round again in ever-widening circles, cantering off in one direction after another, then backing over the tracks for a few moments, Ramona docilely following, though much bewildered as to what it all meant, Alessandro said: "I think now they will never discover where we left the road. They will ride along, seeing our tracks plain, and then they will be so sure that we would have kept straight on, that they will not notice for a time; and when they do, they will never be able to see where the trail ended. And now my Majella has a very hard ride before her. Will she be afraid?"

"Afraid!" laughed Ramona. "Afraid, — on Baba, and with you!"

But it was indeed a hard ride. Alessandro had decided to hide for the day in a cañon he knew, from which a narrow trail led direct to Temecula, — a trail which was known to none but Indians. Once in this cañon, they would be safe from all possible pursuit. Alessandro did not in the least share Ramona's confidence that no effort would be made to overtake them. To his mind, it appeared certain that the Señora would never accept the situation without making an attempt to recover at least the horse and the dog. "She can say, if she chooses, that I have stolen one of her horses," he thought to himself bitterly; "and everybody would believe her. Nobody would believe us, if we said it was the Señorita's own horse."

From the Hemet program—

Raquel Tejada, 18 year old La Jolla beauty, assumes the leading role of the Ramona Outdoor Play. The youngest Ramona in the 32 year history of the pagent, Miss Tejada is also the tenth actress to play the leading role since the pagent was founded. A straight 'A' student at La Jolla High, she is also maintaining a high average at San Diego State College. She is a life member of the California Scholarship Federation. Hailed as one of the State's prettiest girls, her winsome beauty won her the title of 'Maid of California' at the 1958 State Fair in Sacramento, and the 'Fairest of the Fair' at the California Exposition and San Diego County Fair. Miss Tejada has appeared in two major productions of the La Jolla's widely recognized Drury Lane productions 'Bullfight' and 'Trial of Joshua Tripp'. Raquel Tejada is thrilled in having been selected to portray the heroine of California's Greatest Outdoor Play.

Photograph as it appeared in the Hemet program of Raquel Tejada (Welch).
—Courtesy of the Ramona Pageant Assoc., Inc.

A turning point in Raquel Welch's career was her starring role in the Ramona Pageant.

The head of the cañon was only a couple of miles from the road; but it was in a nearly impenetrable thicket of chaparral, where young oaks had grown up so high that their tops made, as it were, a second stratum of thicket. Alessandro had never ridden through it; he had come up on foot once from the other side, and, forcing his way through the tangle, had found, to his surprise, that he was near the highway. It was from this cañon that he had brought the ferns which it had so delighted Ramona to arrange for the decoration of the chapel. The place was filled with them, growing almost in tropical luxuriance; but this was a mile or so farther down, and to reach that spot from above, Alessandro had had to let himself down a sheer wall of stone. The cañon at its head was little more than a rift in the rocks, and the stream which had its rise in it was only a trickling spring at the beginning. It was this precious water, as well as the inaccessibility of the spot, which had decided Alessandro to gain the place at all hazards and costs. But a wall of granite would not have seemed a much more insuperable obstacle than did this wall of chaparral, along which they rode, vainly searching for a break in it. It appeared to Alessandro to have thickened and knit even since the last spring. At last they made their way down a small side cañon, — a sort of wing to the main cañon; a very few rods down this, and they were as hidden from view from above as if the earth had swallowed them. The first red tints of the dawn were coming. From the eastern horizon to the zenith, the whole sky was like a dappled crimson fleece.

"Oh, what a lovely place!" exclaimed Ramona. "I am sure this was not a hard ride at all, Alessandro! Is this where we are to stay?"

Alessandro turned a compassionate look upon her. "How little does the wood-dove know of rough places!" he said. "This is only the beginning; hardly is it even the beginning."

Fastening his pony to a bush, he reconnoitred the place, disappearing from sight the moment he entered the chaparral in any direction. Returning at last, with a grave face, he said, "Will Majella let me leave her here for a little time? There is a way, but I can find it only on foot. I will not be gone long. I know it is near."

Tears came into Ramona's eyes. The only thing she dreaded was the losing sight of Alessandro. He gazed at her anxiously. "I must go, Majella," he said with emphasis. "We are in danger here."

"Go! go! Alessandro," she cried. "But, oh, do not be long!"

As he disappeared in the thicket, the tough boughs crackling and snapping before him, it seemed to Ramona that she was again alone in the world. Capitan, too, bounded after Alessandro, and did not return at her call. All was still. Ramona laid her head on Baba's neck. The moments seemed hours. At last, just as the yellow light streamed across the sky, and the crimson fleeces turned in one second to gold, she heard Alessandro's steps, the next moment saw his face. It was aglow with joy.

"I have found the trail!" he exclaimed; "but we must climb up again out of this; and it is too light. I like it not."

With fear and trembling they urged their horses up and out into the open again, and galloped a half-mile farther west, still keeping as close to the chaparral thicket as possible. Here Alessandro, who led the way, suddenly turned into the very thicket itself; no apparent opening; but the boughs parted and closed, and his head appeared above them; still the little pony was trotting bravely along. Baba snorted with displeasure as he plunged into the same bristling pathway. The thick-set, thorny branches smote Ramona's cheeks. What was worse, they caught the nets swung on Baba's sides; presently these were held fast, and Baba began to rear and kick. Here was a real difficulty. Alessandro dismounted, cut the strings, and put both the packages securely on the back of his own pony. "I will walk," he said. "It was only a little way longer I would have ridden. I shall lead Baba, where it is narrow."

"Narrow," indeed. It was from sheer terror, soon, that Ramona shut her eyes. A path, it seemed to her only a hand's-breadth wide, — a stony, crumbling path, — on the side of a precipice, down which the stones rolled, and rolled, and rolled, echoing, far out of sight, as they passed; at each step the beasts took, the stones rolled and fell. Only the yucca-plants, with their sharp bayonet-leaves, had made shift to keep foothold on this precipice. Of these there were thousands; and their tall flower-stalks, fifteen, twenty feet high, set thick with the shining, smooth seed-cups, glistened like satin chalices in the sun. Below — hundreds of feet below — lay the cañon bottom, a solid bed of chaparral, looking soft and even as a bed of moss. Giant sycamore-trees lifted their heads, at intervals, above this; and far out in the plain glistened the loops of the river, whose sources, unknown to the world, seen of but few human eyes, were to be waters of comfort to these fugitives this day.

Alessandro was cheered. The trail was child's play to him. At the first tread of Baba's dainty steps on the rolling stones, he saw that the horse was as sure-footed as an Indian pony. In a few short hours, now, they would be all at rest. He knew where, under a sycamore-clump, there was running water, clear as crystal, and cold, — almost colder than one could drink, — and green grass too; plenty for two days' feed for the horses, or even three; and all California might be searched over in vain for them, once they were down this trail. His heart full of joy at these thoughts, he turned, to see Ramona pallid, her lips parted, her eyes full of terror. He had forgotten that her riding had hitherto been only on the smooth ways of the valley and the plain. There she was so fearless, that he had had no misgiving about her nerves here; but she had dropped the reins, was clutching Baba's mane with both hands, and sitting unsteadily in her saddle. She had been too proud to cry out; but she was nearly beside herself with fright. Alessandro halted so suddenly that Baba, whose nose was nearly on his shoulder, came to so sharp a stop that Ramona uttered a cry. She thought he had lost his footing.

Alessandro looked at her in dismay. To dismount on that perilous trail was impossible; moreover, to walk there would take more nerve than to ride. Yet she looked as if she could not much longer keep her seat.

"Carita," he cried, "I was stupid not to have told you how narrow the way is; but it is safe. I can run in it. I ran all this way with the ferns on my back I brought for you."

"Oh, did you?" gasped Ramona, diverted, for the moment, from her contemplation of the abyss, and more reassured by that change of her thoughts than she could have been by anything else. "Did you? It is frightful, Alessandro. I never heard of such a trail. I feel as if I were on a rope in the air. If I could get down and go on my hands and knees, I think I would like it better. Could I?"

"I would not dare to have you get off, just here, Majella," answered Alessandro, sorrowfully. "It is dreadful to me to see you suffer so; I will go very slowly. Indeed, it is safe; we all came up here, the whole band, for the sheep-shearing, — old Fernando on his horse all the way."

"Really," said Ramona, taking comfort at each word, "I will try not to be so silly. Is it far, dearest Alessandro?"

"Not much more as steep as this, dear, nor so narrow; but it will be an hour yet before we stop."

But the worst was over for Ramona now, and long before they reached the bottom of the precipice she was ready to laugh at her fears; only, as she looked back at the zigzag lines of the path over which she had come, — little more than a brown thread, they seemed, flung along the rock, — she shuddered.

Down in the bottom of the cañon it was still the dusky gloaming when they arrived. Day came late to this fairy spot. Only at high noon did the sun fairly shine in. As Ramona looked around her, she uttered an exclamation of delight, which satisfied Alessandro. "Yes," he said, "when I came here for the ferns, I wished to myself many times that you could see it. There is not in all this country so beautiful a place. This is our first home, my Majella," he added, in a tone almost solemn; and throwing his arms around her, he drew her to his breast, with the first feeling of joy he had experienced.

"I wish we could live here always," cried Ramona.

"Would Majella be content?" said Alessandro.

"Very," she answered.

He sighed. "There would not be land enough, to live here," he said. "If there were, I too would like to stay here till I died, Majella, and never see the face of a white man again!" Already the instinct of the hunted and wounded animal to seek hiding, was striving in Alessandro's blood. "But there would be no food. We could not live here." Ramona's exclamation had set Alessandro to thinking, however. "Would Majella be content to stay here three days now?" he asked. "There is grass enough for the horses for that time. We should be very safe here; and I fear very much we should not be safe on any road. I think, Majella, the Señora will send men after Baba."

"Baba!" cried Ramona, aghast at the idea. "My own horse! She would not dare to call it stealing a horse, to take my own Baba!" But even as she spoke, her heart misgave her. The Señora would dare anything; would misrepresent anything; only too well Ramona knew what the very mention of the phrase "horse-stealing" meant all through the country. She looked piteously at Alessandro. He read her thoughts.

"Yes, that is it, Majella," he said. "If she sent men after Baba, there is no knowing what they might do. It would not do any good for you to say he was yours. They would not believe you; and they might take me too, if the Señora had told them to, and put me into Ventura jail."

"She's just wicked enough to do it!" cried Ramona. "Let us not stir out of this spot, Alessandro, — not for a week! Could n't we stay a week? By that time she would have given over looking for us."

"I am afraid not a week. There is not feed for the horses; and I do not know what we could eat. I have my gun, but there is not much, now, to kill."

"But I have brought meat and bread, Alessandro," said Ramona, earnestly, "and we could eat very little each day, and make it last!" She was like a child, in her simplicity and eagerness. Every other thought was for the time being driven out of her mind by the terror of being pursued. Pursuit of her, she knew, would not be in the Señora's plan; but the reclaiming of Baba and Capitan, that was another thing. The more Ramona thought of it, the more it seemed to her a form of vengeance which would be likely to commend itself to the Señora's mind. Felipe might possibly prevent it. It was he who had given Baba to her. He would feel that it would be shameful to recall or deny the gift. Only in Felipe lay Ramona's hope.

If she had thought to tell Alessandro that in her farewell note to Felipe she had said that she supposed they were going to Father Salvierderra, it would have saved both her and Alessandro much disquietude. Alessandro would have known that men pursuing them, on that supposition, would have gone straight down the river road to the sea, and struck northward along the coast. But it did not occur to Ramona to mention this; in fact, she hardly recollected it after the first day. Alessandro had explained to her his plan, which was to go by way

San Pasqual had been set apart by executive order 1
in 1870. At that time between two and three hundred Indians lived in the valley. Some had been members of the original pueblo established there in 1835. White settlers were incensed by the action. One newspaper article railed: "This act on the part of the government is no better than highway robbery, and the persons engaged in it too base to be called men. There is not a person in either of these valleys that will not be ruined pecunarily if these orders are enforced."

Another of the newspaper articles gleaned by Helen 2
Hunt Jackson angrily complained: "These Indians are as fixed in their habitations as the whites, and have fruit trees, buildings and other valuable improvements to make them contented and comfortable. There is, belonging to an Indian family there, a fig tree that is the largest in the State, covering a space sixty paces in diameter."

of Temecula to San Diego, to be married there by Father Gaspara, the priest of that parish, and then
1 go to the village or pueblo of San Pasquale, about fifteen miles northwest of San Diego. A cousin of Alessandro's was the head man of this village, and had many times begged him to come there to live; but Alessandro had steadily refused, believing it to be his duty to remain at Temecula with his father. San Pasquale was a regularly established pueblo, founded by a number of the Indian neophytes of the San Luis Rey Mission at the time of the breaking up of that Mission. It was established by a decree of the Governor of California, and the lands of the San Pasquale Valley given to it. A paper recording this establishment and gift, signed by the Governor's own hand, was given to the Indian who was the first Alcalde of the pueblo. He was Chief Pablo's brother. At his death the authority passed into the hands of his son, Ysidro, the cousin of whom Alessandro had spoken.

"Ysidro has that paper still," Alessandro said, "and he thinks it will keep them their village. Perhaps it will; but the Americans are beginning to come in at the head of the valley, and I do not believe, Majella, there is any safety anywhere. Still, for a few years we can perhaps stay there. There are nearly two hundred Indians in the valley; it is much better than Temecula, and Ysidro's people are much better off than ours were. They have splendid herds of cattle and horses, and large wheat-
2 fields. Ysidro's house stands under a great fig-tree; they say it is the largest fig-tree in the country."

"But, Alessandro," cried Ramona, "why do you think it is not safe there, if Ysidro has the paper? I thought a paper made it all right."

"I don't know," replied Alessandro. "Perhaps it may be; but I have got the feeling now that nothing will be of any use against the Americans. I don't believe they will mind the paper."

"They did n't mind the papers the Señora had for all that land of hers they took away," said Ramona, thoughtfully. "But Felipe said that was because Pïo Pico was a bad man, and gave away lands he had no right to give away."

"That 's just it," said Alessandro. "Can't they say that same thing about any governor, especially if he has given lands to us? If the Señora could n't keep hers, with Señor Felipe to help her, and he knows all about the law, and can speak the American language, what chance is there for us? We can't take care of ourselves any better than the wild beasts can, my Majella. Oh, why, why did you come with me? Why did I let you?"

After such words as these, Alessandro would throw himself on the ground, and for a few moments not even Ramona's voice would make him look up. It was strange that the gentle girl, unused to hardship, or to the thought of danger, did not find herself terrified by these fierce glooms and apprehensions of her lover. But she was appalled by nothing. Saved from the only thing in life she had dreaded, sure that Alessandro lived, and that he would not leave her, she had no fears. This was partly from her inexperience, from her utter inability to conceive of the things Alessandro's imagination painted in colors only too true; but it was also largely due to the inalienable loyalty and quenchless courage of her soul, — qualities in her nature never yet tested; qualities of which she hardly knew so much as the name, but which were to bear her steadfast and buoyant through many sorrowful years.

Before nightfall of this their first day in the wilder- 3
ness, Alessandro had prepared for Ramona a bed of finely broken twigs of the manzanita and ceanothus, both of which grew in abundance all through the cañon. Above these he spread layers of glossy ferns, five and six feet long; when it was done, it was a couch no queen need have scorned. As Ramona seated herself on it, she exclaimed: "Now I shall see how it feels to lie and look up at the stars at night! Do you recollect, Alessandro, the night you put Felipe's bed on the veranda, when you told me how beautiful it was to lie at night out of doors and look up at the stars?"

Indeed did Alessandro remember that night, — the first moment he had ever dared to dream of the Señorita Ramona as his own. "Yes, I remember it, my Majella," he answered slowly; and in a 3
moment more added, "That was the day Juan Can had told me that your mother was of my people; and that was the night I first dared in my thoughts to say that perhaps you might some day love me."

"But where are you going to sleep, Alessandro?" said Ramona, seeing that he spread no more boughs. "You have made yourself no bed."

Alessandro laughed. "I need no bed," he said. "We think it is on our mother's lap we lie, when we lie on the ground. It is not hard, Majella. It is soft, and rests one better than beds. But to-night I shall not sleep. I will sit by this tree and watch."

"Why, what are you afraid of?" asked Ramona.

"It may grow so cold that I must make a fire for Majella," he answered. "It sometimes gets very cold before morning in these cañons; so I shall feel safer to watch to-night."

This he said, not to alarm Ramona. His real reason for watching was, that he had seen on the edge of the stream tracks which gave him uneasiness. They were faint and evidently old; but they looked like the tracks of a mountain lion. As soon as it was dark enough to prevent the curl of smoke from being seen from below, he would light a fire, and keep it blazing all night, and watch, gun in hand, lest the beast return.

"But you will be dead, Alessandro, if you do not sleep. You are not strong," said Ramona, anxiously.

"I am strong now, Majella," answered Alessandro. And indeed he did already look like a renewed man, spite of all his fatigue and anxiety. "I am no

—Illustration by Henry Sandham. Circa 1883.

longer weak; and to-morrow I will sleep, and you shall watch."

"Will you lie on the fern-bed then?" asked Ramona, gleefully.

"I would like the ground better," said honest Alessandro.

Ramona looked disappointed. "That is very strange," she said. "It is not so soft, this bed of boughs, that one need fear to be made tender by lying on it," she continued, throwing herself down; "but oh, how sweet, how sweet it smells!"

"Yes, there is spice-wood in it," he answered. "I put it in at the head, for Majella's pillow."

Ramona was very tired, and she was happy. All night long she slept like a child. She did not hear Alessandro's steps. She did not hear the crackling of the fire he lighted. She did not hear the barking of Capitan, who more than once, spite of all Alessandro could do to quiet him, made the cañon echo with sharp, quick notes of warning, as he heard the stealthy steps of wild creatures in the chaparral. Hour after hour she slept on. And hour after hour Alessandro sat leaning against a huge sycamore-trunk, and watched her. As the fitful firelight played over her face, he thought he had never seen it so beautiful. Its expression of calm repose insensibly soothed and strengthened him. She looked like a saint, he thought; perhaps it was as a saint of help and guidance, the Virgin was sending her to him and his people. The darkness deepened, became blackness; only the red gleams from the fire broke it, in swaying rifts, as the wind makes rifts in black storm-clouds in the heavens. With the darkness, the stillness also deepened. Nothing broke that, except an occasional motion of Baba or the pony, or an alert signal from Capitan; then all seemed stiller than ever. Alessandro felt as if God himself were in the cañon. Countless times in his life before he had lain in lonely places under the sky and watched the night through, but he never felt like this. It was ecstasy, and yet it was pain. What was to come on the morrow, and the next morrow, and the next, and the next, all through the coming years? What was to come to this beloved and loving woman who lay there sleeping, so confident, so trustful, guarded only by him, — by him, Alessandro, the exile, fugitive, homeless man?

Before the dawn, wood-doves began their calling. The cañon was full of them, no two notes quite alike, it seemed to Alessandro's sharpened sense; pair after pair, he fancied that he recognized; speaking and replying, as did the pair whose voices had so comforted him the night he watched under the geranium hedge by the Moreno chapel, — "Love?" "Here!" "Love?" "Here!" They comforted him still more now. "They too have only each other," he thought, as he bent his eyes lovingly on Ramona's face.

It was dawn, and past dawn, on the plains, before it was yet morning twilight in the cañon; but the birds in the upper boughs of the sycamores caught the tokens of the coming day, and began to twitter in the dusk. Their notes fell on Ramona's sleeping ear, like the familiar sound of the linnets in the veranda-thatch at home, and waked her instantly. Sitting up bewildered, and looking about her, she exclaimed, "Oh, is it morning already, and so dark? The birds can see more sky than we! Sing, Alessandro," and she began the hymn: —

"'Singers at dawn
From the heavens above
People all regions;
Gladly we too sing.'"

Never went up truer invocation, from sweeter spot.

"Sing not so loud, my Majel," whispered Alessandro, as her voice went carolling like a lark's in the pure ether. "There might be hunters near who would hear;" and he joined in with low and muffled tones.

As she dropped her voice at this caution, it seemed even sweeter than before: —

"'Come, O sinners,
Come, and we will sing
Tender hymns
To our refuge.'"

"Ah, Majella, there is no sinner here, except me!" said Alessandro. "My Majella is like one of the Virgin's own saints." And indeed he might have been forgiven the thought, as he gazed at Ramona, sitting there in the shimmering light, her face thrown out into relief by the gray wall of fern-draped rock behind her; her splendid hair, unbound, falling in tangled masses to her waist; her cheeks flushed, her face radiant with devout and fervent supplication, her eyes uplifted to the narrow belt of sky overhead, where filmy vapors were turning to gold, touched by a sun she could not see.

"Hush, my love," she breathed rather than said. "That would be a sin, if you really thought it.

'O beautiful Queen,
Princess of Heaven,'"

she continued, repeating the first lines of the song; and then, sinking on her knees, reached out one hand for Alessandro's, and glided, almost without a break in the melodious sound, into a low recitative of the morning prayers. Her rosary was of fine-chased gold beads, with an ivory crucifix; a rare and precious relic of the Missions' olden times. It had belonged to Father Peyri himself, was given by him to Father Salvierderra, and by Father Salvierderra to the "blessed child," Ramona, at her confirmation. A warmer token of his love and trust he could not have bestowed upon her, and to Ramona's religious and affectionate heart it had always seemed a bond and an assurance, not only of Father Salvierderra's love, but of the love and protection of the now sainted Peyri.

As she pronounced the last words of her trusting prayer, and slipped the last of the golden beads along on its string, a thread of sunlight shot into the cañon through a deep narrow gap in its rocky eastern crest, — shot in for a second, no more; fell aslant the rosary, lighted it; by a flash as if of fire, across the fine-cut facets of the beads, on Ramona's hands, and on the white face of the ivory Christ. Only a flash, and it was gone! To both Ramona and Alessandro it came like an omen, — like a message straight from the Virgin. Could she choose better messenger, — she, the compassionate one, the loving woman in heaven; mother of the Christ to whom they prayed, through her, — mother, for whose sake He would regard their least cry, — could she choose better messenger, or swifter, than the sunbeam, to say that she heard and would help them in these sore straits?

Perhaps there were not, in the whole great world, at that moment to be found, two souls who were experiencing so vivid a happiness as thrilled the veins of these two friendless ones, on their knees, alone in the wilderness, gazing half awe-stricken at the shining rosary.

Scene from "Ramona," Clune's Auditorium.

Photo favorites and film features,

Whose sparkle will illuminate local screens this

Today is the last day of Billie Burke in "Peggy."

Garrick.

May Allison, one of the most popular of film stars, even as she was one of the most popular of musical comedy stars a few seasons ago, and Harold Lockwood, well-known screen idol, will appear at the Garrick tomorrow and Tuesday in "The Other Side of the Door," said to be an exceptionally strong photodrama.

Wednesday and Thursday the offering will be "The Five Faults of Flo," a matrimonial comedy drama, and on Friday the bill will be changed to make room for the David Horsley production of "Vengeance is Mine," starring Crane Wilbur.

Miller's.

"The Fool's Revenge," a dramatic feature photoplay, is to be the offering at Miller's Theater starting tomorrow. The original play served as a starring vehicle for such famous ac-

Chapter XVII

BEFORE the end of their second day in the cañon, the place had become to Ramona so like a friendly home, that she dreaded to leave its shelter. Nothing is stronger proof of the original intent of Nature to do more for man than civilization in its arrogance will long permit her to do, than the quick and sure way in which she reclaims his affection, when by weariness, idle chance, or disaster, he is returned, for an interval, to her arms. How soon he rejects the miserable subterfuges of what he had called habits; sheds the still more miserable pretences of superiority, makeshifts of adornment, and chains of custom! "Whom the gods love, die young," has been too long carelessly said. It is not true, in the sense in which men use the words. Whom the gods love, dwell with nature; if they are ever lured away, return to her before they are old. Then, however long they live before they die, they die young. Whom the gods love, live young—forever.

With the insight of a lover added to the instinct of the Indian, Alessandro saw how, hour by hour, there grew in Ramona's eyes the wonted look of one at home; how she watched the shadows, and knew what they meant.

"If we lived here, the walls would be sun-dials for us, would they not?" she said, in a tone of pleasure. "I see that yon tall yucca has gone in shadow sooner than it did yesterday."

And, "What millions of things grow here, Alessandro! I did not know there were so many. Have they all names? The nuns taught us some names; but they were hard, and I forgot them. We might name them for ourselves, if we lived here. They would be our relations."

And, "For one year I should lie and look up at the sky, my Alessandro, and do nothing else. It hardly seems as if it would be a sin to do nothing for a year, if one gazed steadily at the sky all the while."

And, "Now I know what it is I have always seen in your face, Alessandro. It is the look from the sky. One must be always serious and not unhappy, but never too glad, I think, when he lives with nothing between him and the sky, and the saints can see him every minute."

And, "I cannot believe that it is but two days I have lived in the air, Alessandro. This seems to me the first home I have ever had. Is it because I am Indian, Alessandro, that it gives me such joy?"

It was strange how many more words Ramona spoke than Alessandro, yet how full she felt their intercourse to be. His silence was more than silent; it was taciturn. Yet she always felt herself answered. A monosyllable of Alessandro's, nay, a look, told what other men took long sentences to say, and said less eloquently.

After long thinking over this, she exclaimed, "You speak as the trees speak, and like the rock yonder, and the flowers, without saying anything!"

This delighted Alessandro's very heart. "And you, Majella," he exclaimed; "when you say that, you speak in the language of our people; you are as we are."

And Ramona, in her turn, was made happy by his words,—happier than she would have been made by any other praise or fondness.

Alessandro found himself regaining all his strength as if by a miracle. The gaunt look had left his face. Almost it seemed that its contour was already fuller. There is a beautiful old Gaelic legend of a Fairy who wooed a Prince, came again and again to him, and, herself invisible to all but the Prince, hovered in the air, sang loving songs to draw him away from the crowd of his indignant nobles, who heard her voice and summoned magicians to rout her by all spells and enchantments at their command. Finally they succeeded in silencing her and driving her off; but as she vanished from the Prince's sight she threw him an apple,—a magic golden apple. Once having tasted of this, he refused all other food. Day after day, night after night, he ate only this golden apple; and yet, morning after morning, evening after evening, there lay the golden fruit, still whole and shining, as if he had not fed upon it; and when the Fairy came the next time, the Prince leaped into her magic boat, sailed away with her, and never was seen in his kingdom again. It was only an allegory, this legend,—a beautiful allegory, and true,—of love and lovers. The food on which Alessandro was, hour by hour, now growing strong, was as magic and invisible as Prince Connla's apple, and just as strength-giving.

"My Alessandro, how is it you look so well, so soon?" said Ramona, studying his countenance with loving care. "I thought that night you would die. Now you look nearly strong as ever; your eyes shine, and your hand is not hot! It is the blessed air; it has cured you, as it cured Felipe of the fever."

"If the air could keep me well, I had not been ill, Majella," replied Alessandro. "I had been under no roof except the tule-shed, till I saw you. It is not the air;" and he looked at her with a gaze that said the rest.

At twilight of the third day, when Ramona saw Alessandro leading up Baba, saddled ready for the journey, the tears filled her eyes. At noon Alessandro had said to her: "To-night, Majella, we must go. There is not grass enough for another day. We must go while the horses are strong. I dare not lead them any farther down the cañon to graze, for there is a ranch only a few miles lower. To-day I found one of the man's cows feeding near Baba."

Ramona made no remonstrance. The necessity was too evident; but the look on her face gave Alessandro a new pang. He, too, felt as if exiled afresh in leaving the spot. And now, as he led the horses slowly up, and saw Ramona sitting in a dejected attitude beside the nets, in which were again carefully packed their small stores, his heart ached anew. Again the sense of his homeless and destitute condition settled like an unbearable burden on his soul. Whither and to what was he leading his Majella?

But once in the saddle, Ramona recovered cheerfulness. Baba was in such gay heart, she could not be wholly sad. The horse seemed fairly rollicking with satisfaction at being once more on the move. Capitan, too, was gay. He had found the cañon dull, spite of its refreshing shade and cool water. He longed for sheep. He did not understand this inactivity. The puzzled look on his face had made Ramona laugh more than once, as he would come and stand before her, wagging his tail and fixing his eyes intently on her face, as if he said in so many words, "What in the world are you about in this cañon, and do not you ever intend to return home? Or if you will stay here, why not keep sheep? Do you not see that I have nothing to do?"

"We must ride all night, Majella," said Alessandro, "and lose no time. It is a long way to the place where we shall stay to-morrow."

"Is it a cañon?" asked Ramona, hopefully.

"No," he replied, "not a cañon; but there are beautiful oak-trees. It is where we get our acorns for the winter. It is on the top of a high hill."

"Will it be safe there?" she asked.

"I think so," he replied; "though not so safe as here. There is no such place as this in all the country."

"And then where shall we go next?" she asked.

"That is very near Temecula," he said. "We must go into Temecula, dear Majella. I must go to Mr. Hartsel's. He is friendly. He will give me money for my father's violin. If it were not for that, I would never go near the place again."

"I would like to see it, Alessandro," she said gently.

"Oh, no, no, Majella!" he cried; "you would not. It is terrible; the houses all unroofed, — all but my father's and José's. They were shingled roofs; they will be just the same; all the rest are only walls. Antonio's mother threw hers down; I don't know

Loretta Young and Don Ameche as Ramona and Alessandro in the 1937 20th Century-Fox production.

—Illustration by Henry Sandham. Circa 1883.

how the old woman ever had the strength; they said she was like a fury. She said nobody should ever live in those walls again; and she took a pole, and made a great hole in one side, and then she ran Antonio's wagon against it with all her might, till it fell in. No, Majella. It will be dreadful."

"Would n't you like to go into the graveyard again, Alessandro?" she said timidly.

"The saints forbid!" he said solemnly. "I think it would make me a murderer to stand in that graveyard! If I had not you, my Majel, I should kill some white man when I came out. Oh, do not speak of it!" he added, after a moment's silence; "it takes the strength all out of my blood again, Majella. It feels as if I should die!"

And the word "Temecula" was not mentioned between them again until dusk the next day, when, as they were riding slowly along between low, wooded hills, they suddenly came to an opening, a green, marshy place, with a little thread of trickling water, at which their horses stopped, and drank thirstily; and Ramona, looking ahead, saw lights twinkling in the distance. "Lights, Alessandro, lights!" she exclaimed, pointing to them.

"Yes, Majella," he replied, "it is Temecula;" and springing off his pony he came to her side, and putting both his hands on hers, said: "I have been thinking, for a long way back, Carita, what is to be done here. I do not know. What does Majella think will be wise? If men have been sent out to pursue us, they may be at Hartsel's. His store is the place where everybody stops, everybody goes. I dare not have you go there, Majella; yet I must go. The only way I can get any money is from Mr. Hartsel."

"I must wait somewhere while you go!" said Ramona, her heart beating as she gazed ahead into the blackness of the great plain. It looked vast as the sea. "That is the only safe thing, Alessandro."

"I think so too," he said; "but, oh, I am afraid for you; and will not you be afraid?"

"Yes," she replied, "I am afraid. But it is not so dangerous as the other."

"If anything were to happen to me, and I could not come back to you, Majella, if you give Baba his reins he will take you safe home, — he and Capitan."

Ramona shrieked aloud. She had not thought of this possibility. Alessandro had thought of everything. "What could happen?" she cried.

"I mean if the men were there, and if they took me for stealing the horse," he said.

"But you would not have the horse with you," she said. "How could they take you?"

"That might n't make any difference," replied Alessandro. "They might take me, to make me tell where the horse was."

"Oh, Alessandro," sobbed Ramona, "what shall we do!" Then in another second, gathering her courage, she exclaimed, "Alessandro, I know what

I will do. I will stay in the graveyard. No one will come there. Shall I not be safest there?"

"Holy Virgin! would my Majel stay there?" exclaimed Alessandro.

"Why not?" she said. "It is not the dead that will harm us. They would all help us if they could. I have no fear. I will wait there while you go; and if you do not come in an hour, I will come to Mr. Hartsel's after you. If there are men of the Señora's there, they will know me; they will not dare to touch me. They will know that Felipe would punish them. I will not be afraid. And if they are ordered to take Baba, they can have him; we can walk when the pony is tired."

Her confidence was contagious. "My wood-dove has in her breast the heart of the lion," said Alessandro, fondly. "We will do as she says. She is wise;" and he turned their horses' heads in the direction of the graveyard. It was surrounded by a low adobe wall, with one small gate of wooden paling. As they reached it, Alessandro exclaimed, "The thieves have taken the gate!"

"What could they have wanted with that?" said Ramona.

"To burn," he said doggedly. "It was wood; but it was very little. They might have left the graves safe from wild beasts and cattle!"

As they entered the enclosure, a dark figure rose from one of the graves. Ramona started.

"Fear nothing," whispered Alessandro. "It must be one of our people. I am glad; now you will not be alone. It is Carmena, I am sure. That was the corner where they buried José. I will speak to her;" and leaving Ramona at the gate, he went slowly on, saying in a low voice, in the Luiseno language, "Carmena, is that you? Have no fear. It is I, Alessandro!"

It was Carmena. The poor creature, nearly crazed with grief, was spending her days by her baby's grave in Pachanga, and her nights by her husband's in Temecula. She dared not come to Temecula by day, for the Americans were there, and she feared them. After a short talk with her, Alessandro returned, leading her along. Bringing her to Ramona's side, he laid her feverish hand in Ramona's, and said: "Majella, I have told her all. She cannot speak a word of Spanish, but she is very glad, she says, that you have come with me, and she will stay close by your side till I come back."

Ramona's tender heart ached with desire to comfort the girl; but all she could do was to press her hand in silence. Even in the darkness she could see the hollow, mournful eyes and the wasted cheek. Words are less needful to sorrow than to joy. Carmena felt in every fibre how Ramona was pitying her. Presently she made a gentle motion, as if to draw her from the saddle. Ramona bent down and looked inquiringly into her face. Again she drew her gently with one hand, and with the other pointed to the corner from which she had come. Ramona

The entrance to the graveyard. — Drawing by Henry Sandham. Circa 1913.

understood. "She wants to show me her husband's grave," she thought. "She does not like to be away from it. I will go with her."

Dismounting, and taking Baba's bridle over her arm, she bowed her head assentingly, and still keeping firm hold of Carmena's hand, followed her. The graves were thick, and irregularly placed, each mound marked by a small wooden cross. Carmena led with the swift step of one who knew each inch of the way by heart. More than once Ramona stumbled and nearly fell, and Baba was impatient and restive at the strange inequalities under his feet. When they reached the corner, Ramona saw the fresh-piled earth of the new grave. Uttering a wailing cry, Carmena, drawing Ramona to the edge of it, pointed down with her right hand, then laid both hands on her heart, and gazed at Ramona piteously. Ramona burst into weeping, and again clasping Carmena's hand, laid it on her own breast, to show her sympathy. Carmena did not weep. She was long past that; and she felt for the moment lifted out of herself by the sweet, sudden sympathy of this stranger, — this girl like herself, yet so different, so wonderful, so beautiful, Carmena was sure she must be. Had the saints sent her from heaven to Alessandro? What did it mean? Carmena's bosom was heaving with the things she longed to say and to ask; but all she could do was to press Ramona's hand again and again, and occasionally lay her soft cheek upon it.

"Now, was it not the saints that put it into my head to come to the graveyard?" thought Ramona. "What a comfort to this poor heart-broken thing to see Alessandro! And she keeps me from all fear. Holy Virgin! but I had died of terror here all alone. Not that the dead would harm me; but simply from the vast, silent plain, and the gloom."

Soon Carmena made signs to Ramona that they would return to the gate. Considerate and thoughtful, she remembered that Alessandro would expect to find them there. But it was a long and weary watch they had, waiting for Alessandro to come.

After leaving them, and tethering his pony, he had struck off at a quick run for Hartsel's, which was perhaps an eighth of a mile from the graveyard. His own old home lay a little to the right. As he drew near, he saw a light in its windows. He stopped as if shot. "A light in our house!" he exclaimed; and he clenched his hands. "Those cursed robbers have gone into it to live already!" His blood seemed turning to fire. Ramona would not have recognized the face of her Alessandro now. It was full of implacable vengeance. Involuntarily he felt for his knife. It was gone. His gun he had left inside the graveyard, leaning against the wall. Ah! in the graveyard! Yes, and there also was Ramona waiting for him. Thoughts of vengeance fled. The world held now but one work, one hope, one passion, for him. But he would at least see who were these dwellers in his father's house. A fierce desire to see their faces burned within him. Why should he thus torture himself? Why, indeed? But he must. He would see the new home-life already begun on the grave of his. Stealthily creeping under the window from which the light shone, he listened. He heard children's voices; a woman's voice; at intervals the voice of a man, gruff and surly; various household sounds also. It was evidently the supper-hour. Cautiously raising himself till his eyes were on a level with the lowest panes in the window, he looked in.

A table was set in the middle of the floor, and there were sitting at it a man, woman, and two children. The youngest, little more than a baby, sat in its high chair, drumming with a spoon on the table, impatient for its supper. The room was in great confusion, — beds made on the floor, open boxes half unpacked, saddles and harness thrown down in corners; evidently there were new-comers into the house. The window was open by an inch. It had warped, and would not shut down. Bitterly Alessandro recollected how he had put off from day to day the planing of that window to make it shut tight. Now, thanks to that crack, he could hear all that was said. The woman looked weary and worn. Her face was a sensitive one, and her voice kindly; but the man had the countenance of a brute, — of a human brute. Why do we malign the so-called brute creation, making their names a unit of comparison for base traits which never one of them possessed?

"It seems as if I never should get to rights in this world!" said the woman. Alessandro understood enough English to gather the meaning of what she said. He listened eagerly. "When will the next wagon get here?"

"I don't know," growled her husband. "There's been a slide in that cursed cañon, and blocked the road. They won't be here for several days yet. Hain't you got stuff enough round now? If you'd clear up what's here now, then 'twould be time enough to grumble because you hadn't got everything."

"But, John," she replied, "I can't clear up till the bureau comes, to put the things away in, and the bedsteads. I can't seem to do anything."

"You can grumble, I take notice," he answered. "That's about all you women are good for, anyhow. There was a first-rate raw-hide bedstead in here. If Rothsaker hadn't been such a fool's to let those dogs of Indians carry off all their truck, we might have had that!"

The woman looked at him reproachfully, but did not speak for a moment. Then her cheeks flushed, and seeming unable to repress the speech, she exclaimed, "Well, I'm thankful enough he did let the poor things take their furniture. I'd never have slept a wink on that bedstead, I know, if it had ha' been left here. It's bad enough to take their houses this way!"

"Oh, you shut up your head for a blamed fool,

will you!" cried the man. He was half drunk, his worst and most dangerous state. She glanced at him half timorously, half indignantly, and turning to the children, began feeding the baby. At that second the other child looked up, and catching sight of the outline of Alessandro's head, cried out, "There 's a man there! There, at the window!"

Alessandro threw himself flat on the ground, and
held his breath. Had he imperilled all, brought
danger on himself and Ramona, by yielding to this
mad impulse to look once more inside the walls of
his home? With a fearful oath, the half-drunken
man exclaimed, "One of those damned Indians, I 1
expect. I 've seen several hangin' round to-day.
We 'll have to shoot two or three of 'em yet, before
we 're rid of 'em!" and he took his gun down from
the pegs above the fireplace, and went to the door
with it in his hand.

"Oh, don't fire, father, don't!" cried the woman. "They 'll come and murder us all in our sleep if you do! Don't fire!" and she pulled him back by the sleeve.

Shaking her off, with another oath, he stepped across the threshold, and stood listening, and peering into the darkness. Alessandro's heart beat like a hammer in his breast. Except for the thought of Ramona, he would have sprung on the man, seized his gun, and killed him.

"I don't believe it was anybody, after all, father," persisted the woman. "Bud 's always seein' things. I don't believe there was anybody there. Come in; supper 's gettin' all cold."

"Well, I 'll jest fire, to let 'em know there 's powder 'n' shot round here," said the fiend. "If it hits any on 'em roamin' round, he won't know what hurt him;" and levelling his gun at random, with his drunken, unsteady hand he fired. The bullet whistled away harmlessly into the empty darkness. Hearkening a few moments, and hearing no cry, he hiccupped, "Mi-i-issed him that time," and went in to his supper.

Alessandro did not dare to stir for a long time.
How he cursed his own folly in having brought himself into this plight! What needless pain of waiting
he was inflicting on the faithful one, watching for
him in that desolate and fearful place of graves! At
last he ventured, — sliding along on his belly a few
inches at a time, till, several rods from the house, he
dared at last to spring to his feet and bound away at 2
full speed for Hartsel's.

Hartsel's was one of those mongrel establishments to be seen nowhere except in Southern California. Half shop, half farm, half tavern, it gathered up to itself all the threads of the life of the whole region. Indians, ranchmen, travellers of all sorts, traded at Hartsel's, drank at Hartsel's, slept at Hartsel's. It was the only place of its kind within a radius of twenty miles; and it was the least bad place of its kind within a much wider radius.

Hartsel was by no means a bad fellow — when he

1 The Anglicization of California would have proceeded more slowly—and possibly more fairly—had gold not been discovered so soon after statehood was declared. As it was, the impact of thousands of people—most of them with no knowledge of Spanish, was overwhelming. Despite the intentions of early legislators, what was fair and proper quickly gave way to what was expedient. Most American settlers viewed California as conquered territory and saw no reason to allow government regulations to stand in their way. To their minds the land—and sometimes even its inhabitants— was clearly theirs to be exploited as they saw fit.

2 

Helen Hunt Jackson visited this mecca — actually the Wolfe Store — during her tenure as a Special Commissioner of Indian Affairs.

Photograph by George Wharton JAmes. Circa 1911.

was sober; but as that condition was not so frequent as it should have been, he sometimes came near being a very bad fellow indeed. At such times everybody was afraid of him, — wife, children, travellers, ranchmen, and all. "It was only a question of time and occasion," they said, "Hartsel's killing somebody sooner or later;" and it looked as if the time were drawing near fast. But, out of his cups, Hartsel was kindly, and fairly truthful; entertaining, too, to a degree which held many a wayfarer chained to his chair till small hours of the morning, listening to his landlord's talk. How he had drifted from Alsace to San Diego County, he could hardly have told in minute detail himself, there had been so many stages and phases of the strange journey; but he had come to his last halt now. Here, in this Temecula, he would lay his bones. He liked the country. He liked the wild life, and, for a wonder, he liked the Indians. Many a good word he spoke for them to travellers who believed no good of the race, and evidently listened with polite incredulity when he would say, as he often did: "I 've never lost a dollar off these Indians yet. They do all their trading with me. There 's some of them I trust as high 's a hundred dollars. If they can't pay this year, they 'll pay 3
next; and if they die, their relations will pay their debts for them, a little at a time, till they 've got it all paid off. They 'll pay in wheat, or bring a steer, maybe, or baskets or mats the women make; but they 'll pay. They 're honester 'n the general run of Mexicans about paying; I mean Mexicans that are as poor 's they are."

Hartsel's dwelling-house was a long, low adobe building, with still lower flanking additions, in which were bedrooms for travellers, the kitchen, and store-rooms. The shop was a separate building, of rough planks, a story and a half high, the loft of which was one great dormitory well provided with beds on the floor, but with no other article of bedroom furniture. They who slept in this loft had no fastidious standards of personal luxury. These two buildings, with some half-dozen out-houses of one sort and another, stood in an enclosure surrounded by a low white picket fence, which gave to the place a certain home-like look, spite of the neglected condition of the ground, which was bare sand, or sparsely tufted with weeds and wild grass. A few plants, parched and straggling, stood in pots and tin cans around the door of the dwelling-house. One hardly knew whether they made the place look less desolate or more so. But they were token of a woman's hand, and of a nature which craved something more than the unredeemed wilderness around her afforded.

A dull and lurid light streamed out from the wide-open door of the store. Alessandro drew cautiously near. The place was full of men, and he heard loud laughing and talking. He dared not go in. Stealing around to the rear, he leaped the fence, and went to the other house and opened the kitchen door. Here he was not afraid. Mrs. Hartsel had never any but Indian servants in her employ. The kitchen was lighted only by one dim candle. On the stove were sputtering and hissing all the pots and frying-pans it would hold. Much cooking was evidently going on for the men who were noisily rollicking in the other house.

Seating himself by the fire, Alessandro waited. In a few moments Mrs. Hartsel came hurrying back to her work. It was no uncommon experience to find an Indian quietly sitting by her fire. In the dim light she did not recognize Alessandro, but mistook him, as he sat bowed over, his head in his hands, for old Ramon, who was a sort of recognized hanger-on of the place, earning his living there by odd jobs of fetching and carrying, and anything else he could do.

"Run, Ramon," she said, "and bring me more wood; this cottonwood is so dry, it burns out like rotten punk; I 'm off my feet to-night, with all these men to cook for;" then turning to the table, she began cutting her bread, and did not see how tall and unlike Ramon was the man who silently rose and went out to do her bidding. When, a few moments later, Alessandro re-entered, bringing a huge armful of wood, which it would have cost poor old Ramon three journeys at least to bring, and throwing it down on the hearth, said, "Will that be enough, Mrs. Hartsel?" she gave a scream of surprise, and dropped her knife. "Why, who —" she began; then, seeing his face, her own lighting up with pleasure, she continued, "Alessandro! Is it you? Why, I took you in the dark for old Ramon! I thought you were in Pachanga."

"In Pachanga!" Then as yet no one had come from the Señora Moreno's to Hartsel's in search of him and the Señorita Ramona! Alessandro's heart felt almost light in his bosom. From the one immediate danger he had dreaded, they were safe; but no trace of emotion showed on his face, and he did not raise his eyes as he replied: "I have been in Pachanga. My father is dead. I have buried him there."

"Oh, Alessandro! Did he die?" cried the kindly woman, coming close to Alessandro, and laying her hand on his shoulder. "I heard he was sick." She paused; she did not know what to say. She had suffered so at the time of the ejectment of the Indians,
4 that it had made her ill. For two days she had kept her doors shut and her windows close curtained, that she need not see the terrible sights. She was not a woman of many words. She was a Mexican, but there were those who said that some Indian blood ran in her veins. This was not improbable; and it seemed more than ever probable now, as she stood still by Alessandro's side, her hand on his shoulder, her eyes fixed in distress on his face. How he had altered! How well she recollected his lithe figure, his alert motion, his superb bearing, his handsome face, when she last saw him in the spring!

"You were away all summer, Alessandro?" she said at last, turning back to her work.

"Yes," he said; "at the Señora Moreno's."

"So I heard," she said. "That is a fine great place, is it not? Is her son grown a fine man? He was a lad when I saw him. He went through here with a drove of sheep once."

"Ay, he is a man now," said Alessandro, and buried his face in his hands again.

"Poor fellow! I don't wonder he does not want to speak," thought Mrs. Hartsel. "I'll just let him alone;" and she spoke no more for some moments.

Alessandro sat still by the fire. A strange apathy seemed to have seized him; at last he said wearily: "I must be going now. I wanted to see Mr. Hartsel a minute, but he seems to be busy in the store."

"Yes," she said, "a lot of San Francisco men; they belong to the company that 's coming in here in the valley; they 've been here two days. Oh, Alessandro," she continued, bethinking herself, "Jim 's got your violin here; José brought it."

"Yes, I know it," answered Alessandro. "José told me; and that was one thing I stopped for."

"I 'll run and get it," she exclaimed.

"No," said Alessandro, in a slow, husky voice. "I do not want it. I thought Mr. Hartsel might buy it. I want some money. It was not mine; it was my father's. It is a great deal better than mine. My father said it would bring a great deal of money. It is very old."

"Indeed it is," she replied; "one of those men in there was looking at it last night. He was astonished at it, and he would not believe Jim when he told him about its having come from the Mission."

"Does he play? Will he buy it?" cried Alessandro.

"I don't know; I 'll call Jim," she said; and running out she looked in at the other door, saying, "Jim! Jim!"

Alas, Jim was in no condition to reply. At her first glance in his face, her countenance hardened into an expression of disgust and defiance. Returning to the kitchen, she said scornfully, disdaining all disguises, "Jim 's drunk. No use your talking to him to-night. Wait till morning."

"Till morning!" A groan escaped from Alessandro, in spite of himself. "I can't!" he cried. "I must go on to-night."

"Why, what for?" exclaimed Mrs. Hartsel, much astonished. For one brief second Alessandro revolved in his mind the idea of confiding everything to her; only for a second, however. No; the fewer knew his secret and Ramona's, the better.

"I must be in San Diego to-morrow," he said.

"Got work there?" she said.

"Yes; that is, in San Pasquale," he said; "and I ought to have been there three days ago."

Mrs. Hartsel mused. "Jim can't do anything to-night," she said; "that 's certain. You might see the man yourself, and ask him if he 'd buy it."

3 Wolfe, the owner of the store spoke admiringly of the Indians to Jackson. They were "good pay," he told her. "Give them their time and they'll always pay, and if they die their relations will pay the last cent."

When the author asked him how they earned their money, he seemed to have no distinct idea. Some of them had a little stock; they might now and then sell a horse or cow. They hired as laborers whenever they could get a chance, working at sheep-shearing in the spring and autumn, and at grape-picking in the vintage season. A few of them had a little wheat to sell; sometimes they paid him in wheat. There were not nearly as many of them as there used to be, he thought. Where had they all gone? He shrugged his shoulders. "Who knows?"

4 Jackson interviewed Ramona Wolfe who described the ordeal to her. It had taken the Indians three days to move. Procession after procession, with cries and tears, walked slowly behind the wagons carrying their household goods. The final two days Mrs. Wolfe had kept her doors and windows closed, for she could not bear the sight. Hearing these words spoken, looking at the ruins of the little adobe houses beside the silent graveyard, Jackson "realized forcibly how different a thing is history seen from history written or read."

Alessandro shook his head. An invincible repugnance withheld him. He could not face one of these Americans who were "coming in" to his valley. Mrs. Hartsel understood.

"I'll tell you, Alessandro," said the kindly woman, "I'll give you what money you need to-night, and then, if you say so, Jim 'll sell the violin to-morrow, if that man wants it, and you can pay me back out of that, and when you're along this way again you can have the rest. Jim 'll make as good a trade for you 's he can. He's a real good friend to all of you, Alessandro, when he's himself."

"I know it, Mrs. Hartsel. I'd trust Mr. Hartsel more than any other man in this country," said Alessandro. "He's about the only white man I do trust!"

Mrs. Hartsel was fumbling in a deep pocket in her under-petticoat. Gold-piece after gold-piece she drew out. "Humph! Got more 'n I thought I had," she said. "I've kept all that's been paid in here to-day, for I knew Jim'd be drunk before night."

Alessandro's eyes fastened on the gold. How he longed for an abundance of those little shining pieces for his Majella! He sighed as Mrs. Hartsel counted them out on the table, — one, two, three, four, bright five-dollar pieces.

"That is as much as I dare take," said Alessandro, when she put down the fourth. "Will you trust me for so much?" he added sadly. "You know I have nothing left now. Mrs. Hartsel, I am only a beggar, till I get some work to do."

The tears came into Mrs. Hartsel's eyes. "It's a shame!" she said, — "a shame, Alessandro! Jim and I haven't thought of anything else, since it happened. Jim says they'll never prosper, never. Trust you? Yes, indeed. Jim and I'll trust you, or your father, the last day of our lives."

"I'm glad he is dead," said Alessandro, as he knotted the gold into his handkerchief and put it into his bosom. "But he was murdered, Mrs. Hartsel, — murdered, just as much as if they had fired a bullet into him."

"That's true!" she exclaimed vehemently. "I say so too; and so was José. That's just what I said at the time, — that bullets would not be half so inhuman!"

The words had hardly left her lips, when the door from the dining-room burst open, and a dozen men, headed by the drunken Jim, came stumbling, laughing, reeling into the kitchen.

"Where's supper? Give us our supper! What are you about with your Indian here? I'll teach you how to cook ham!" stammered Jim, making a lurch towards the stove. The men behind caught him and saved him. Eying the group with slow scorn, Mrs. Hartsel, who had not a cowardly nerve in her body, said: "Gentlemen, if you will take your seats at the table, I will bring in your supper immediately. It is all ready."

One or two of the soberer ones, shamed by her tone, led the rest back into the dining-room, where, seating themselves, they began to pound the table and swing the chairs, swearing, and singing ribald songs.

"Get off as quick as you can, Alessandro," whispered Mrs. Hartsel, as she passed by him, standing like a statue, his eyes, full of hatred and contempt, fixed on the tipsy group. "You'd better go. There's no knowing what they'll do next."

"Are you not afraid?" he said in a low tone.

"No!" she said. "I'm used to it. I can always manage Jim. And Ramon's round somewhere, — he and the bull-pups; if worse comes to worst, I can call the dogs. These San Francisco fellows are always the worst to get drunk. But you'd better get out of the way!"

"And these are the men that have stolen our lands, and killed my father, and José, and Carmena's baby!" thought Alessandro, as he ran swiftly back towards the graveyard. "And Father Salvierderra says, God is good. It must be the saints no longer pray to Him for us!"

But Alessandro's heart was too full of other thoughts, now, to dwell long on past wrongs, however bitter. The present called him too loudly. Putting his hand in his bosom, and feeling the soft, knotted handkerchief, he thought: "Twenty dollars! It is not much! But it will buy food for many days for my Majella and for Baba!"

Chapter XVIII

EXCEPT for the reassuring help of Carmena's presence by her side, Ramona would never have had courage to remain during this long hour in the graveyard. As it was, she twice resolved to bear the suspense no longer, and made a movement to go. The chance of Alessandro's encountering at Hartsel's the men sent in pursuit of him and of Baba, loomed in her thoughts into a more and more frightful danger each moment she reflected upon it. It was a most unfortunate suggestion for Alessandro to have made. Her excited fancy went on and on, picturing the possible scenes which might be going on almost within stone's-throw of where she was sitting, helpless, in the midnight darkness,—Alessandro seized, tied, treated as a thief, and she, Ramona, not there to vindicate him, to terrify the men into letting him go. She could not bear it; she would ride boldly to Hartsel's door. But when she made a motion as if she would go, and said in the soft Spanish, of which Carmena knew no word, but which yet somehow conveyed Ramona's meaning, "I must go! It is too long! I cannot wait here!" Carmena had clasped her hand tighter, and said in the San Luiseno tongue, of which Ramona knew no word, but which yet somehow conveyed Carmena's meaning, "O beloved lady, you must not go! Waiting is the only safe thing. Alessandro said, to wait here. He will come." The word "Alessandro" was plain. Yes, Alessandro had said, wait; Carmena was right. She would obey, but it was a fearful ordeal. It was strange how Ramona, who felt herself preternaturally brave, afraid of nothing, so long as Alessandro was by her side, became timorous and wretched the instant he was lost to her sight. When she first heard his steps coming, she quivered with terror lest they might not be his. The next second she knew; and with a glad cry, "Alessandro! Alessandro!" she bounded to him, dropping Baba's reins.

Sighing gently, Carmena picked up the reins, and stood still, holding the horse, while the lovers clasped each other with breathless words. "How she loves Alessandro!" thought the widowed Carmena. "Will they leave him alive to stay with her? It is better not to love!" But there was no bitter envy in her mind for the two who were thus blest while she went desolate. All of Pablo's people had great affection for Alessandro. They had looked forward to his being over them in his father's place. They knew his goodness, and were proud of his superiority to themselves.

"Majella, you tremble," said Alessandro, as he threw his arms around her. "You have feared! Yet you were not alone." He glanced at Carmena's motionless figure, standing by Baba.

"No, not alone, dear Alessandro; but it was so long!" replied Ramona; "and I feared the men had taken you, as you feared. Was there any one there?"

"No! No one had heard anything. All was well. They thought I had just come from Pachanga," he answered.

"Except for Carmena, I should have ridden after you half an hour ago," continued Ramona. "But she told me to wait."

"She told you!" repeated Alessandro. "How did you understand her speech?"

"I do not know. Was it not a strange thing?" replied Ramona. "She spoke in your tongue, but I thought I understood her. Ask her if she did not say that I must not go; that it was safer to wait; that you had so said, and you would soon come."

Alessandro repeated the words to Carmena. "Did you say that?" he asked.

"Yes," answered Carmena.

"You see, then, she has understood the Luiseno words," he said delightedly. "She is one of us."

"Yes," said Carmena, gravely, "she is one of us!" Then, taking Ramona's hand in both of her own for farewell, she repeated, in a tone as of dire prophecy, "One of us, Alessandro! one of us!" And as she gazed after their retreating forms, almost immediately swallowed and lost in the darkness, she repeated the words again to herself,—"One of us! one of us! Sorrow came to me; she rides to meet it!" and she crept back to her husband's grave, and threw herself down, to watch till the dawn.

The road which Alessandro would naturally have taken would carry them directly by Hartsel's again. But, wishing to avoid all risk of meeting or being seen by any of the men on the place, he struck well out to the north, to make a wide circuit around it. This brought them past the place where Antonio's house had stood. Here Alessandro halted, and putting his hand on Baba's rein, walked the horses close to the pile of ruined walls. "This was Antonio's house, Majella," he whispered. "I wish every house in the valley had been pulled down like this. Old Juana was right. The Americans are living in my father's house, Majella," he went on, his whisper growing thick with rage. "That was what kept me so long. I was looking in at the window at them eating their supper. I thought I should go mad, Majella. If I had had my gun, I should have shot them all dead!"

An almost inarticulate gasp was Ramona's fir t reply to this. "Living in your house!" she said. "You saw them?"

"Yes," he said; "the man, and his wife, and two little children; and the man came out, with his gun, on the doorstep, and fired it. They thought they heard something moving, and it might be an Indian; so he fired. That was what kept me so long."

Just at this moment Baba tripped over some small object on the ground. A few steps farther, and he tripped again. "There is something caught round his foot, Alessandro," said Ramona. "It keeps moving."

Alessandro jumped off his horse, and kneeling down, exclaimed, "It 's a stake, — and the lariat fastened to it. Holy Virgin! what — " The rest of his ejaculation was inaudible. The next Ramona knew, he had run swiftly on, a rod or two. Baba had followed, and Capitan and the pony; and there stood a splendid black horse, as big as Baba, and Alessandro talking under his breath to him, and clapping both his hands over the horse's nose, to stop him, as often as he began whinnying; and it seemed hardly a second more before he had his saddle off the poor little Indian pony, and striking it sharply on its sides had turned it free, had saddled the black horse, and leaping on his back, said, with almost a sob in his voice: "My Majella, it is Benito, my own Benito. Now the saints indeed have helped us! Oh, the ass, the idiot, to stake out Benito with such a stake as that! A jack rabbit had pulled it up. Now, my Majella, we will gallop! Faster! faster! I will not breathe easy till we are out of this cursed valley. When we are once in the Santa Margarita Cañon, I know a trail they will never find!"

Like the wind galloped Benito, — Alessandro half lying on his back, stroking his forehead, whispering to him, the horse snorting with joy: which were gladder of the two, horse or man, could not be said. And neck by neck with Benito came Baba. How the ground flew away under their feet! This was companionship, indeed, worthy of Baba's best powers. Not in all the California herds could be found two superber horses than Benito and Baba. A wild, almost reckless joy took possession of Alessandro. Ramona was half terrified as she heard him still talking, talking to Benito. For an hour they did not draw rein. Both Benito and Alessandro knew every inch of the ground. Then, just as they had descended into the deepest part of the cañon, Alessandro suddenly reined sharply to the left, and began climbing the precipitous wall. "Can you follow, dearest Majella?" he cried.

"Do you suppose Benito can do anything that Baba cannot?" she retorted, pressing on closely.

But Baba did not like it. Except for the stimulus of Benito ahead, he would have given Ramona trouble.

"There is only a little, rough like this, dear," called Alessandro, as he leaped a fallen tree, and halted to see how Baba took it. "Good!" he cried, as Baba jumped it like a deer. "Good! Majella! We have got the two best horses in the country. You 'll see they are alike, when daylight comes. I have often wondered they were so much alike. They would go together splendidly."

After a few rods of this steep climbing they came out on the top of the cañon's south wall, in a dense oak forest comparatively free from underbrush. "Now," said Alessandro, "I can go from here to San Diego by paths that no white man knows. We will be near there before daylight."

Already the keen salt air of the ocean smote their faces. Ramona drank it in with delight. "I taste salt in the air, Alessandro," she cried.

"Yes, it is the sea," he said. "This cañon leads straight to the sea. I wish we could go by the shore, Majella. It is beautiful there. When it is still, the waves come as gently to the land as if they were in play; and you can ride along with your horse's feet in the water, and the green cliffs almost over your head; and the air off the water is like wine in one's head."

"Cannot we go there?" she said longingly. "Would it not be safe?"

"I dare not," he answered regretfully. "Not now, Majella; for on the shore-way, at all times, there are people going and coming."

"Some other time, Alessandro, we can come, after we are married, and there is no danger?" she asked.

"Yes, Majella," he replied; but as he spoke the words, he thought, "Will a time ever come when there will be no danger?"

The shore of the Pacific Ocean for many miles north of San Diego is a succession of rounding promontories, walling the mouths of cañons, down many of which small streams make to the sea. These cañons are green and rich at bottom, and filled with trees, chiefly oak. Beginning as little more than rifts in the ground, they deepen and widen, till at their mouths they have a beautiful crescent of shining beach from an eighth to a quarter of a mile long. The one which Alessandro hoped to reach before morning was not a dozen miles from the old town of San Diego, and commanded a fine view of the outer harbor. When he was last in it, he had found it a nearly impenetrable thicket of young oak-trees. Here, he believed, they could hide safely all day, and after nightfall ride into San Diego, be married at the priest's house, and push on to San Pasquale that same night. "All day, in that cañon, Majella can look at the sea," he thought; "but I will not tell her now, for it may be the trees have been cut down, and we cannot be so close to the shore."

It was near sunrise when they reached the place. The trees had not been cut down. Their tops, seen from above, looked like a solid bed of moss filling in the cañon bottom. The sky and the sea were both red. As Ramona looked down into the soft green pathway, it seemed, leading out to the wide and sparkling sea, she thought Alessandro had brought her into a fairy-land.

"What a beautiful world!" she cried; and riding up so close to Benito that she could lay her hand on Alessandro's, she said solemnly: "Do you not think we ought to be very happy, Alessandro, in such a beautiful world as this? Do you think we might sing our sunrise hymn here?"

Alessandro glanced around. They were alone on the breezy open; it was not yet full dawn; great masses of crimson vapor were floating upward from the hills behind San Diego. The light was still burning in the light-house on the promontory walling the inner harbor, but in a few moments more it would be day. "No, Majella, not here!" he said. "We must not stay. As soon as the sun rises, a man or a horse may be seen on this upper coast-line as far as eye can reach. We must be among the trees with all the speed we can make."

It was like a house with a high, thick roof of oak tree-tops, the shelter they found. No sun penetrated it; a tiny trickle of water still remained, and some grass along its rims was still green, spite of the long drought,—a scanty meal for Baba and Benito, but they ate it with relish in each other's company.

"They like each other, those two," said Ramona, laughing, as she watched them. "They will be friends."

"Ay," said Alessandro, also smiling. "Horses are friends, like men, and can hate each other, like men, too. Benito would never see Antonio's mare, the little yellow one, that he did not let fly his heels at her; and she was as afraid, at sight of him, as a cat is at a dog. Many a time I have laughed to see it."

"Know you the priest at San Diego?" asked Ramona.

"Not well," replied Alessandro. "He came seldom to Temecula when I was there; but he is a friend of Indians. I know he came with the men from San Diego at the time when there was fighting, and the whites were in great terror; and they said, except for Father Gaspara's words, there would not have been a white man left alive in Pala. My father had sent all his people away before that fight began. He knew it was coming, but he would have nothing to do with it. He said the Indians were all crazy. It was no use. They would only be killed themselves. That is the worst thing, my Majella. The stupid Indians fight and kill, and then what can we do? The white men think we are all the same. Father Gaspara has never been to Pala, I heard, since that time. There goes there now the San Juan Capistrano priest. He is a bad man. He takes money from the starving poor."

"A priest!" ejaculated Ramona, horror-stricken.

"Ay! a priest!" replied Alessandro. "They are not all good,— not like Father Salvierderra."

"Oh, if we could but have gone to Father Salvierderra!" exclaimed Ramona, involuntarily.

Holy water font, Pala. —Painting by Henry Sandham. Circa 1883.

Mission Indians. —Painting by Henry Sandham. Circa 1883.

Mission San Luis Rey. — Photograph by A.C. Vroman. Circa 1913.

Alessandro looked distressed. "It would have been much more danger, Majella," he said, "and I had no knowledge of work I could do there."

His look made Ramona remorseful at once. How cruel to lay one feather-weight of additional burden on this loving man! "Oh, this is much better, really," she said. "I did not mean what I said. It is only because I have always loved Father Salvierderra so. And the Señora will tell him what is not true. Could we not send him a letter, Alessandro?"

"There is a Santa Inez Indian I know," replied Alessandro, "who comes down with nets to sell, sometimes, to Temecula. I know not if he goes to San Diego. If I could get speech with him, he would go up from Santa Inez to Santa Barbara for me, I am sure; for once he lay in my father's house, sick for many weeks, and I nursed him, and since then he is always begging me to take a net from him, whenever he comes. It is not two days from Santa Inez to Santa Barbara."

"I wish it were the olden time now, Alessandro," sighed Ramona, "when the men like Father Salvierderra had all the country. Then there would be work for all, at the Missions. The Señora says the Missions were like palaces, and that there were thousands of Indians in every one of them; thousands and thousands, all working so happy and peaceful."

"The Señora does not know all that happened at the Missions," replied Alessandro. "My father says that at some of them were dreadful things, when bad men had power. Never any such things at San Luis Rey Father Peyri was like a father to all his Indians. My father says that they would all of them lie down in a fire for him, if he had commanded it. And when he went away, to leave the country, when his heart was broken, and the Mission all ruined, he had to fly by night, Majella, just as you and I have done; for if the Indians had known it, they would have risen up to keep him. There was a ship here in San Diego harbor, to sail for Mexico, and the Father made up his mind to go in it; and it was over this same road we have come, my Majella, that he rode, and by night; and my father was the only one he trusted to know it. My father came with him; they took the swiftest horses, and they rode all night, and my father carried in front of him, on the horse, a box of the sacred things of the altar, very heavy. And many a time my father has told me the story, how they got to San Diego at daybreak, and the Father was rowed out to the ship in a little boat; and not much more than on board was he, my father standing like one dead on the shore, watching, he loved him so, when, lo! he heard a great crying, and shouting, and trampling of horses' feet, and there came galloping down to the water's edge three hundred of the Indians from San Luis Rey, who had found out that the Father had gone to San Diego to take ship, and they had ridden all night on his track, to fetch him back. And when my father pointed to the ship, and told them he was already on board, they

set up a cry fit to bring the very sky down; and some of them flung themselves into the sea, and swam out to the ship, and cried and begged to be taken on board and go with him. And Father Peyri stood on the deck, blessing them, and saying farewell, with the tears running on his face; and one of the Indians — how they never knew — made shift to climb up on the chains and ropes, and got into the ship itself; and they let him stay, and he sailed away with the Father. And my father said he was all his life sorry that he himself had not thought to do the same thing; but he was like one dumb and deaf and with no head, he was so unhappy at the Father's 1
going."

"Was it here, in this very harbor?" asked Ramona, in breathless interest, pointing out towards the blue water of which they could see a broad belt framed by their leafy foreground arch of oak tops.

"Ay, just there he sailed, — as that ship goes now," he exclaimed, as a white-sailed schooner sailed swiftly by, going out to sea. "But the ship lay at first inside the bar; you cannot see the inside harbor from here. It is the most beautiful water I have 2
ever seen, Majella. The two high lands come out like two arms to hold it and keep it safe, as if they loved it."

"But, Alessandro," continued Ramona, "were there really bad men at the other Missions? Surely not the Franciscan Fathers?"

"Perhaps not the Fathers themselves, but the men under them. It was too much power, Majella. When my father has told me how it was, it has seemed to me I should not have liked to be as he was. It is not right that one man should have so much power. There was one at the San Gabriel Mission; he was 3
an Indian. He had been set over the rest; and when a whole band of them ran away one time, and went back into the mountains, he went after them; and he brought back a piece of each man's ear; the pieces were strung on a string; and he laughed, and said that was to know them by again, — by their clipped ears. An old woman, a Gabrieleno, who came over to Temecula, told me she saw that. She lived at the Mission herself. The Indians did not all want to come to the Missions; some of them preferred to stay in the woods, and live as they always had lived; and I think they had a right to do that if they preferred, Majella. It was stupid of them to stay and be like beasts, and not know anything; but do you not think they had the right?"

"It is the command to preach the gospel to every creature," replied the pious Ramona. "That is what Father Salvierderra said was the reason the Franciscans came here. I think they ought to have made the Indians listen. But that was dreadful about the ears, Alessandro. Do you believe it?"

"The old woman laughed when she told it," he answered. "She said it was a joke; so I think it was true. I know I would have killed the man who tried to crop my ears that way."

1 Many of the priests contrived to compensate themselves for the loss of their feudal empires. Don Mariano Vallejo noted one example when escorting Luis Martinez, a padre from Mission Santa Barbara, onto the Thomas Nowlan. Several times the priest staggered, but once safely in the cabin assigned him, Martinez smiled, "Perhaps you thought me drunk?" Obviously pleased with his cleverness at outwitting the port officials, he threw open his robe revealing garments heavily lined with gold.

2 The author allowed her hero to speak for her. Visiting San Diego for the first time on March 4, 1882, Jackson was struck by the beauty of the bay and the surrounding hills. When friends took her riding in their carriage out to the tip of Point Loma, the inveterate traveler called the drive "the most beautiful in America."

3

San Gabriel Mission. —Photograph by A. C. Vroman. Circa 1913.

During the regime of Father José Maria Zalvdea an Indian woman who had suffered a miscarriage was charged with infanticide and punished by having her head shaved, by being flogged every day for fifteen days, by wearing irons on her feet for three months and by "having to appear every Sunday in church on the steps leading up to the altar, wtih a hideous painted wooden child in her arms."

Casa de Estudillo, the grand dame of San Diego's Old 4
Town has gone through many vicissitudes. Built in 1829 by the dashing 26-year-old José Antonio Estudillo, the house was designed as a showplace for his wife, Maria Victoria.

As was the custom with grand mansions, the four foot adobe walls were coated with whitewash and the tile roof layed over mud, matted seaweed and reeds supported by rough rafters bound together by leather thongs. The twelve spacious rooms opening directly onto the central courtyard included a chapel and a grand sala where balls were held.

The son of the former commander of the San Diego presidio and one of the wealthiest landowners in the region, Estudillo served in the military and later as the town's revenue collector and treasurer. When the American government was established, he was appointed county treasurer and assessor. In addition to the Old Town property—a prime piece of real estate in the center of town—he held title to land grants in Temecula, San Jacinto, San Juan Capistrano and the Otay Rancho.

For years the house was a social mecca, accommodating not only the Estudillos' eleven children, but frequent guests from all over the state. Widowed in 1852, Maria Estudillo not only kept the family together but added to it by adopting nine orphaned relatives and several Indian children whose parents had died.

After the matriarch's death the Estudillo clan resided in the house until 1887 when the last family member moved out. Before long the caretaker was selling bits of wood and tile ripped from the walls to tourists who believed that Ramona had really been married there. Since there was no Catholic church in Old Town at the time of the Ramona episode, it was assumed that any marriage would have been performed in the chapel of the Estudillo home where Mass was still celebrated.

Casa Estudillo in 1890. —Photograph by author.

A promise that the property would always be known as the Estudillo House and $500 bought the

"Did you ever tell that to Father Salvierderra?" asked Ramona.

"No, Majella. It would not be polite," said Alessandro.

"Well, I don't believe it," replied Ramona, in a relieved tone. "I don't believe any Franciscan ever could have permitted such things."

The great red light in the light-house tower had again blazed out, and had been some time burning, before Alessandro thought it prudent to resume their journey. The road on which they must go into old San Diego, where Father Gaspara lived, was the public road from San Diego to San Luis Rey, and they were almost sure to meet travellers on it.

But their fleet horses bore them so well, that it
4 was not late when they reached the town. Father Gaspara's house was at the end of a long, low adobe building, which had served no mean purpose in the old Presidio days, but was now fallen into decay; and all its rooms, except those occupied by the Father, had been long uninhabited. On the opposite side of the way, in a neglected, weedy open, stood his chapel, — a poverty-stricken little place, its walls imperfectly whitewashed, decorated by a few coarse pictures and by broken sconces of looking-glass, rescued in their dilapidated condition from the Mission buildings now gone utterly to ruin. In these had been put candle-holders of common tin, in which a few cheap candles dimly lighted the room. Everything about it was in unison with the atmosphere of the place, — the most profoundly melancholy in all Southern California. Here was the spot where that grand old Franciscan, Padre Junipero Serra, began his work, full of the devout and ardent purpose to reclaim the wilderness and its peoples to his country and his Church; on this very beach he went up and down for those first terrible weeks, nursing the sick, praying with the dying, and burying the dead, from the pestilence-stricken Mexican ships lying in the harbor. Here he baptized his first Indian converts, and founded his first Mission. And the only traces now remaining of his heroic labors and hard-won successes were a pile of crumbling ruins, a few old olive-trees and palms; in less than another century even these would be gone; returned into the keeping of that mother, the earth, who puts no headstones at the sacredest of her graves.

Father Gaspara had been for many years at San Diego. Although not a Franciscan, having, indeed, no especial love for the order, he had been from the first deeply impressed by the holy associations of the place. He had a nature at once fiery and poetic; there were but three things he could have been, — a soldier, a poet, or a priest. Circumstances had made him a priest; and the fire and the poetry which would have wielded the sword or kindled the verse, had he found himself set either to fight or to sing, had all gathered into added force in his priestly vocation. The look of a soldier he had never quite lost, — neither the look nor the tread; and his flashing dark eyes, heavy black hair and beard, and quick elastic step, seemed sometimes strangely out of harmony with his priest's gown. And it was the sensitive soul of the poet in him which had made him withdraw within himself more and more, year after year, as he found himself comparatively powerless to do anything for the hundreds of Indians that he would fain have seen gathered once more, as of old, into the keeping of the Church. He had made frequent visits to them in their shifting refuges, following up family after family, band after band, that he knew; he had written bootless letter after letter to the Government officials of one sort and another, at Washington. He had made equally bootless efforts to win some justice, some protection for them, from officials nearer home; he had endeavored to stir the Church itself to greater efficiency in their behalf. Finally, weary, disheartened, and indignant with that intense, suppressed indignation which the poetic temperament alone can feel, he had ceased, — had said, "It is of no use; I will speak no word; I am done; I can bear no more!" and settling down into the routine of his parochial duties to the little Mexican and Irish congregation of his charge in San Diego, he had abandoned all effort to do more for the Indians than visit their chief settlements once or twice a year, to administer the sacraments. When fresh outrages were brought to his notice, he paced his room, plucked fiercely at his black beard, with ejaculations, it is to be feared, savoring more of the camp than the altar; but he made no effort to do anything. Lighting his pipe, he would sit down on the old bench in his tile-paved veranda, and smoke by the hour, gazing out on the placid water of the deserted harbor, brooding, ever brooding, over the wrongs he could not redress.

A few paces off from his door stood the just begun walls of a fine brick church, which it had been the dream and pride of his heart to see builded, and full of worshippers. This, too, had failed. With San Diego's repeatedly vanishing hopes and dreams of prosperity had gone this hope and dream of Father Gaspara's. It looked, now, as if it would be indeed a waste of money to build a costly church on this site. Sentiment, however sacred and loving towards the dead, must yield to the demands of the living. To build a church on the ground where Father Junipero first trod and labored, would be a work to which no Catholic could be indifferent; but there were other and more pressing claims to be met first. This was right. Yet the sight of these silent walls, only a few feet high, was a sore one to Father Gaspara, — a daily cross, which he did not find grow lighter as he paced up and down his veranda, year in and year out, in the balmy winter and cool summer of that magic climate.

"Majella, the chapel is lighted; but that is good!" exclaimed Alessandro, as they rode into the silent plaza. "Father Gaspara must be there;" and jumping off his horse, he peered in at the uncurtained window. "A marriage, Majella, — a marriage!" he

crumbling adobe in 1906. Within a year the place changed hands again, this time for only $10. John Spreckels, the new owner, who also owned the Hotel del Coronado and the San Diego Electric Railway Line, had a grand design. His hotel guests needed something more than the beach to keep them sunny and he needed a terminus for his electric railway line. The Ramona legend solved both problems.

Casa Estudillo today — Ramona's marriage place.
—Photograph by author.

Hazel Waterman, San Diego's first woman architect, was hired to restore the building to its former glory. She began her task by studying early photographs, interviewing oldtimers who recalled the house from the 1870s, and visiting adobes of the same period around the state. Ready at last to begin, Waterman hired Mexican workers to make and sun-bake adobe bricks, mold and kiln-fire new roof tiles and brick paving, and reframe the entire roof system with new log rafters and beams. Workmen mixed cactus juice with whitewash to give the walls an old appearance and age the new roof timbers by soaking them in the bay mud flats. The result was an exquisitely restored mansion.

But what Spreckels wanted was a tourist mecca. He decorated the chapel with Indian style trinkets and brought in a minister to marry couples in the same spot that Ramona and Alessandro supposedly stood. Souvenirs were sold in an adjoining shop and outside in the courtyard hopefuls tossed pennies into a wishing well.

The enterprise was a dazzling success from the very beginning; more than 125,000 people visited Ramona's Marriage Place during the 1915 Panama-California International Exhibition. Four movies and a steady stream of tourists continued to swell attendance. Then in 1968, Legler Benbough, a civic leader, purchased the property and deeded it to the State of California. The San Diego chapter of the Colonial Dames of America took on the task of refurnishing the historic adobe with early California antiques. After much controversy, the name "Ramona's Marriage Place" was finally dropped.

It took more than sixty years, but a promise was finally honored. The place is once again known as The Estudillo House.

The founding of Mission San Diego. — © Automobile Club of Southern California. Reproduced by permission.

Father Anthony Ubach —Photograph by Goerge Wharton James. Circa 1911.

A cigar-smoking militant 5
with an outspoken tongue and a strong taste for Spanish wine, Father Anthony Ubach couldn't have been more surprised to find himself woven into the pages of a romance. The soldier-type priest who angrily protested the treatment of the Indians whose responsibility he'd shouldered was delighted to find a potential ally in the equally outspoken Eastern writer. He was only too happy to drive her about the countryside in his two-horse double seated carriage. Jackson traveled with him from early morning to late at night, visiting the remnants of missions and locating mission Indians. With Ubach's assistance, Jackson attended trials involving Indian offenders and visited hovels on hills and in canyons where the dispossessed just barely managed to survive.

Ubach regaled Jackson with stories of San Diego and its
past. One that left a lasting impression was about a 6
young couple who'd appeared at his door late one night. The woman was the daughter of a prominent Californio family, the man an Indian sheepherder. They begged him to marry them immediately, which he did. Soon after, the couple was apprehended by the bride's angry family. The union was annulled, the woman subsequently forced into marriage with another, and the Indian beaten nearly to death. It was tragic, romantic, a tale a writer would not forget.

cried, hastily returning. "This, too, is good fortune. We need not to wait long."

5 When the sacristan whispered to Father Gaspara that an Indian couple had just come in, wishing to be married, the Father frowned. His supper was waiting; he had been out all day, over at the old Mission olive-orchard, where he had not found things to his mind; the Indian man and wife whom he hired to take care of the few acres the Church yet owned there had been neglecting the Church lands and trees, to look after their own. The Father was vexed, tired, and hungry, and the expression with which he regarded Alessandro and Ramona, as they came towards him, was one of the least prepossessing of which his dark face was capable. Ramona, who had never knelt to any priest save the gentle Father Salvierderra, and who had supposed that all priests must look, at least, friendly, was shocked at the sight of the impatient visage confronting her. But, as his first glance fell on Ramona, Father Gaspara's expression changed.

"What is all this?" he thought; and as quick as he thought it, he exclaimed, in a severe tone, looking at Ramona, "Woman, are you an Indian?"

"Yes, Father," answered Ramona, gently. "My mother was an Indian."

"Ah! half-breed!" thought Father Gaspara. "It is strange how sometimes one of the types will conquer, and sometimes another! But this is no common creature;" and it was with a look of new interest and sympathy on his face that he proceeded with the ceremony, — the other couple, a middle-aged Irishman, with his more than middle-aged bride, standing quietly by, and looking on with a vague sort of wonder in their ugly, impassive faces, as if it struck them oddly that Indians should marry.

6 The book of the marriage-records was kept in Father Gaspara's own rooms, locked up and hidden even from his old housekeeper. He had had bitter reason to take this precaution. It had been for more than one man's interest to cut leaves out of this old record, which dated back to 1769, and had many pages written full in the hand of Father Junipero himself.

As they came out of the chapel, Father Gaspara leading the way, the Irish couple shambling along shamefacedly apart from each other, Alessandro, still holding Ramona's hand in his, said, "Will you ride, dear? It is but a step."

"No, thanks, dear Alessandro, I would rather walk," she replied; and Alessandro slipping the bridles of the two horses over his left arm, they walked on. Father Gaspara heard the question and answer, and was still more puzzled.

"He speaks as a gentleman speaks to a lady," he mused. "What does it mean? Who are they?"

Father Gaspara was a well-born man, and in his home in Spain had been used to associations far superior to any which he had known in his Californian life. A gentle courtesy of tone and speech, such as that with which Alessandro had addressed Ramona, was not often heard in his parish. When they entered his house, he again regarded them both attentively. Ramona wore on her head the usual black shawl of the Mexican women. There was nothing distinctive, to the Father's eye, in her figure or face. In the dim light of the one candle, — Father Gaspara allowed himself no luxuries, — the exquisite coloring of her skin and the deep blue of her eyes were not to be seen. Alessandro's tall figure and dignified bearing were not uncommon. The Father had seen many as fine-looking Indian men. But his voice was remarkable, and he spoke better Spanish than was wont to be heard from Indians.

"Where are you from?" said the Father, as he 7
held his pen poised in hand, ready to write their names in the old raw-hide-bound book.

"Temecula, Father," replied Alessandro.

Father Gaspara dropped his pen. "The village the Americans drove out the other day?" he cried.

"Yes, Father."

Father Gaspara sprang from his chair, took refuge from his excitement, as usual, in pacing the floor. "Go! go! I'm done with you! It's all over," he said fiercely to the Irish bride and groom, who had given him their names and their fee, but were still hanging about irresolute, not knowing if all were ended or not. "A burning shame! The most dastardly thing I have seen yet in this land forsaken of God!" cried the Father. "I saw the particulars of it in the San Diego paper yesterday." Then, coming to a halt in front of Alessandro, he exclaimed: "The paper said that the Indians were compelled to pay all the costs of the suit; that the sheriff took their cattle to do it. Was that true?"

"Yes, Father," replied Alessandro.

The Father strode up and down again, plucking at his beard. "What are you going to do?" he said. "Where have you all gone? There were two hundred in your village the last time I was there."

"Some have gone over into Pachanga," replied Alessandro, "some to San Pasquale, and the rest to San Bernardino."

"Body of Jesus! man! But you take it with philosophy!" stormed Father Gaspara.

Alessandro did not understand the word "philosophy," but he knew what the Father meant. "Yes, Father," he said doggedly. "It is now twenty-one days ago. I was not so at first. There is nothing to be done."

Ramona held tight to Alessandro's hand. She was afraid of this fierce, black-bearded priest, who dashed
back and forth, pouring out angry invectives. 8
"The United States Government will suffer for it!" he continued. "It is a Government of thieves and robbers! God will punish them. You will see; they will be visited with a curse, — a curse in their borders; their sons and their daughters shall be desolate! But why do I prate in these vain words? My son, tell me your names again;" and he seated himself once more

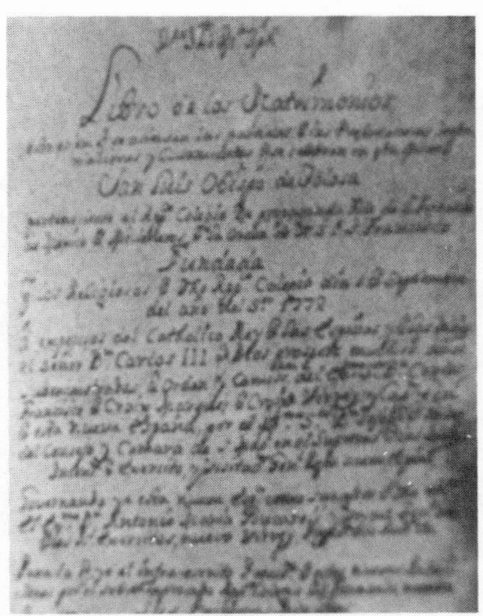
Libro de los Matrimonios

7 Father Junipera Serra's handwriting on a mission marriage register.

Helen Hunt Jackson first heard of the Temecula displacement from Father Ubach. The priest had tried to intercede for the Indians by appealing to the judges but his efforts had merely delayed the inevitable.

8 The federal government had followed a "removal policy since the 1820s as a means of solving "the Indian problem." It had been decided that the "Great American Desert"—an area from Texas to the Canadian border—was unfit for white people so it was designated as a permanent Indian frontier. Through a series of treaties, the Indians were persuaded to move west of this line to new lands which the American government promised to give them in perpetuity. The process was scarcely completed before the extension of the American boundary to the Pacific in the 1840s made the line obsolete.

Many settlers in California, finding that they could no longer move the Indians westward argued that the only solution was to move them off the face of the earth. Peter H. Burnett, first American governor of California, informed the legislature that a "war of extermination will continue to be waged between the races until the Indian race becomes extinct," and that it was "beyond the power of wisdom of man" to avert the "inevitable destiny of this race."

Estudillo House —Photograph by author.

Room at the Estudillo House. —Photograph by author.

at the table where the ancient marriage-record lay open.

After writing Alessandro's name, he turned to Ramona. "And the woman's?" he said.

Alessandro looked at Ramona. In the chapel he had said simply, "Majella." What name should he give more?

Without a second's hesitation, Ramona answered, "Majella. Majella Phail is my name."

She pronounced the word "Phail," slowly. It was new to her. She had never seen it written; as it lingered on her lips, the Father, to whom also it was a new word, misunderstood it, took it to be in two syllables, and so wrote it.

The last step was taken in the disappearance of Ramona. How should any one, searching in after years, find any trace of Ramona Ortegna, in the woman married under the name of "Majella Fayeel"?

"No, no! Put up your money, son," said Father Gaspara, as Alessandro began to undo the knots of the handkerchief in which his gold was tied. "Put up your money. I'll take no money from a Temecula Indian. I would the Church had money to give you. Where are you going now?"

"To San Pasquale, Father."

"Ah! San Pasquale! The head man there has the old pueblo paper," said Father Gaspara. "He was showing it to me the other day. That will, it may be, save you there. But do not trust to it, son. Buy yourself a piece of land as the white man buys his Trust to nothing."

Alessandro looked anxiously in the Father's face. "How is that, Father?" he said. "I do not know."

"Well, their rules be thick as the crabs here on the beach," replied Father Gaspara; "and, faith, they appear to me to be backwards of motion also, like the crabs: but the lawyers understand. When you have picked out your land, and have the money, come to me, and I will go with you and see that you are not cheated in the buying, so far as I can tell; but I myself am at my wit's ends with their devices. Farewell, son! Farewell, daughter!" he said, rising from his chair. Hunger was again getting the better of sympathy in Father Gaspara, and as he sat down to his long-deferred supper, the Indian couple faded from his mind; but after supper was over, as he sat smoking his pipe on the veranda, they returned again, and lingered in his thoughts,—lingered strangely, it seemed to him; he could not shake off the impression that there was something unusual about the woman. "I shall hear of them again, some day," he thought. And he thought rightly.

Chapter XIX

San Diego Mission. —Illustration by Henry Sandham. Circa 1913

AFTER leaving Father Gaspara's door, Alessandro and Ramona rode slowly through the now deserted plaza, and turned northward, on the river road, leaving the old Presidio walls on their right. The river was low, and they forded it without difficulty.

"I have seen this river so high that there was no fording it for many days," said Alessandro; "but that was in spring."

"Then it is well we came not at that time," said Ramona. "All the times have fallen out well for us, Alessandro, — the dark nights, and the streams low; but look! as I say it, there comes the moon!" and she pointed to the fine threadlike arc of the new moon, just visible in the sky. "Not big enough to do us any harm, however," she added. "But, dear Alessandro, do you not think we are safe now?"

"I know not, Majella, if ever we may be safe; but I hope so. I have been all day thinking I had gone foolish last night, when I told Mrs. Hartsel that I was on my way to San Pasquale. But if men should come there asking for us, she would understand, I think, and keep a still tongue. She would keep harm from us if she could."

Their way from San Diego to San Pasquale lay at first along a high mesa, or table-land, covered with 1
low shrub growths; after some ten or twelve miles of this, they descended among winding ridges, into a narrow valley, — the Poway valley. It was here that the Mexicans made one of their few abortive efforts to repel the American forces.

"Here were some Americans killed, in a fight with the Mexicans, Majella," said Alessandro. "I myself have a dozen bullets which I picked up in the ground about here. Many a time I have looked at them and thought if there should come another war against the Americans, I would fire them again, if I could. Does Señor Felipe think there is any likelihood that his people will rise against them any more? If they would, they would have all the Indians to help them, now. It would be a mercy if they might be driven out of the land, Majella."

"Yes," sighed Majella. "But there is no hope.

1 *Viva California!*
Californios were justly proud of their record in this, the most intense battle ever fought on California soil. General Kearny had 160 men—twice the number of Captain Pico's forces—yet it was the Californios who carried the day. Eighteen Americans were killed, 19 wounded in the fierce hand-to-hand combat. There were no serious casualties among the Californios who were fighting for their homes. Just off Highway 395 on Highway 78, a bronze marker on a large rock halfway up the hillside marks the spot where the historic event occurred.

Indian justice was indeed severe. Juan Antonio, chief of 2
the Cahuillas, once demanded the release of an Indian awaiting trial by the Americans for killing another Indian. "I come not here as a child," he said. "I wish to punish my people my own way. If they deserve hanging, I will hang them. If a white man deserves hanging, let the white man hang him. I am done."

The prisoner was released. The chief then strapped him on a horse and rode back to his village where the body of the murdered man had been laid in an open grave. With his own hands, Juan Antonio flung the murderer alive into this grave and ordered it to be instantly filled with earth.

In the days of the Spanish and Mexican land grants, 3
rancho boundaries were measured with *reatas*, or cattleman's ropes, which were of generally uniform length. Huge land grant parcels could be measured quite accurately by pulling lengths of rope end over end while on horseback. The first *vaquero*, or cowboy, holding one length of rope, would stand still, while the other, riding at a gallop, would pull out the *reata*. The first rider would then gallop off past the second, stretching his rope tight.

The rancho owner submitted a hand drawn map showing the permanent landmarks or acceptable points for boundaries. Americans couldn't honestly object to this method since they'd used it themselves, making use of a creek, a boulder or sometimes merely a wooden stake to lay out boundaries as they crossed and settled a continent. But honesty had very little to do with the forfeiture of existing Mexican titles. What the Americans wanted was to move in and develop California without competition from its natives.

I have heard the Señora speak of it with Felipe. There is no hope. They have power, and great riches, she said. Money is all that they think of. To get money, they will commit any crime, even murder. Every day there comes the news of their murdering each other for gold. Mexicans kill each other only for hate, Alessandro, — for hate, or in anger; never for gold."

"Indians, also," replied Alessandro. "Never one Indian killed another, yet, for money. It is for vengeance, always. For money! Bah! Majella, they are dogs!"

Rarely did Alessandro speak with such vehemence; but this last outrage on his people had kindled in his veins a fire of scorn and hatred which would never die out. Trust in an American was henceforth to him impossible. The name was a synonym for fraud and cruelty.

"They cannot all be so bad, I think, Alessandro," said Ramona. "There must be some that are honest; do you not think so?"

"Where are they, then," he cried fiercely, — "the
ones who are good? Among my people there are
always some that are bad; but they are in disgrace.
2 My father punished them, the whole people punished
them. If there are Americans who are good, who
will not cheat and kill, why do they not send after
these robbers and punish them? And how is it that
they make laws which cheat? It was the American
law which took Temecula away from us, and gave
it to those men! The law was on the side of the
thieves. No, Majella, it is a people that steals!
That is their name, — a people that steals, and that
kills for money. Is not that a good name for a great
people to bear, when they are like the sands in the
sea, they are so many?"

3 "That is what the Señora says," answered Ramona.
"She says they are all thieves; that she knows not,
each day, but that on the next will come more of
them, with new laws, to take away more of her land.
She had once more than twice what she has now,
Alessandro."

"Yes," he replied; "I know it. My father has told me. He was with Father Peyri at the place, when General Moreno was alive. Then all was his to the sea, — all that land we rode over the second night, Majella."

"Yes," she said, "all to the sea! That is what the Señora is ever saying: 'To the sea!' Oh, the beautiful sea! Can we behold it from San Pasquale, Alessandro?"

"No, my Majella, it is too far. San Pasquale is in the valley; it has hills all around it like walls. But it is good. Majella will love it; and I will build a house, Majella. All the people will help me. That is the way with our people. In two days it will be done. But it will be a poor place for my Majella," he said sadly. Alessandro's heart was ill at ease. Truly a strange bride's journey was this; but Ramona felt no fear.

"No place can be so poor that I do not choose it, if you are there, rather than the most beautiful place in the world where you are not, Alessandro," she said.

"But my Majella loves things that are beautiful," said Alessandro. "She has lived like a queen."

"Oh, Alessandro," merrily laughed Ramona, "how little you know of the way queens live! Nothing was fine at the Señora Moreno's, only comfortable; and any house you will build, I can make as comfortable as that was; it is nothing but trouble to have one so large as the Señora's. Margarita used to be tired to death, sweeping all those rooms in which nobody lived except the blessed old San Luis Rey saints. Alessandro, if we could have had just one statue, either Saint Francis or the Madonna, to bring luck to our house! That is what I would like better than all other things in the world. It is beautiful to sleep with the Madonna close to your bed. She speaks often to you in dreams."

Alessandro fixed serious, questioning eyes on Ramona as she uttered these words. When she spoke like this, he felt indeed as if a being of some other sphere had come to dwell by his side. "I cannot find how to feel towards the saints as you do, my Majella," he said. "I am afraid of them. It must be because they love you, and do not love us. That is what I believe, Majella. I believe they are displeased with us, and no longer make mention of us in heaven. That is what the Fathers taught that the saints were ever doing,—praying to God for us, and to the Virgin and Jesus. It is not possible, you see, that they could have been praying for us, and yet such things have happened, as happened in Temecula. I do not know how it is my people have displeased them."

"I think Father Salvierderra would say that it is a sin to be afraid of the saints, Alessandro," replied Ramona, earnestly. "He has often told me that it was a sin to be unhappy; and that withheld me many times from being wretched because the Señora would not love me. And, Alessandro," she went on, growing more and more fervent in tone, "even if nothing but misfortune comes to people, that does not prove that the saints do not love them; for when the saints were on earth themselves, look what they suffered: martyrs they were, almost all of them. Look at what holy Saint Catharine endured, and the blessed Saint Agnes. It is not by what happens to us here in this world that we can tell if the saints love us, or if we will see the Blessed Virgin."

"How can we tell, then?" he asked.

"By what we feel in our hearts, Alessandro," she replied; "just as I knew all the time, when you did not come,—I knew that you loved me. I knew that in my heart; and I shall always know it, no matter what happens. If you are dead, I shall know that you love me. And you,—you will know that I love you, the same."

"Yes," said Alessandro, reflectively, "that is true. But, Majella, it is not possible to have the same thoughts about a saint as about a person that one has seen, and heard the voice, and touched the hand."

"No, not quite," said Ramona; "not quite, about a saint; but one can for the Blessed Virgin, Alessandro! I am sure of that. Her statue, in my room at the Señora's, has been always my mother. Ever since I was little I have told her all I did. It was she helped me to plan what I should bring away with us. She reminded me of many things I had forgotten, except for her."

"Did you hear her speak?" said Alessandro, awe-stricken.

"Not exactly in words; but just the same as in words," replied Ramona, confidently. "You see when you sleep in the room with her, it is very different from what it is if you only see her in a chapel. Oh, I could never be very unhappy with her in my room!"

"I would almost go and steal it for you, Majella," cried Alessandro, with sacrilegious warmth.

"Holy Virgin!" cried Ramona, "never speak such a word. You would be struck dead if you laid your hand on her! I fear even the thought was a sin."

"There was a small figure of her in the wall of our house," said Alessandro. "It was from San Luis Rey. I do not know what became of it,—if it were left behind, or if they took it with my father's things to Pachanga. I did not see it there. When I go again, I will look."

"Again!" cried Ramona. "What say you? You go again to Pachanga? You will not leave me, Alessandro?"

At the bare mention of Alessandro's leaving her, Ramona's courage always vanished. In a moment, in the twinkling of an eye, she was transformed from the dauntless, confident, sunny woman, who bore him up as it were on wings of hope and faith, to a timid, shrinking, despondent child, crying out in alarm, and clinging to the hand.

"After a time, dear Majella, when you are wonted to the place, I must go, to fetch the wagon and the few things tha were ours. There is the rawhide bed which was Father Peyri's, and he gave to my father. Majella will like to lie on that. My father believed it had great virtue."

"Like that you made for Felipe?" she asked.

"Yes; but it is not so large. In those days the cattle were not so large as they are now: this is not so broad as Señor Felipe's. There are chairs, too, from the Mission, three of them, one almost as fine as those on your veranda at home. They were given to my father. And music-books,—beautiful parchment books! Oh, I hope those are not lost, Majella! If José had lived, he would have looked after it all. But in the confusion, all the things belonging to the village were thrown into wagons together, and no one knew where anything was. But all the people knew my father's chairs and the books of the music. If the Americans did not steal them, everything will be safe. My people do not steal. There was never but one thief in our village, and my father had him so whipped, he ran away and never came back. I heard he was living in San Jacinto, and was a thief yet, spite of all that whipping he had. I think if it is in the blood to be a thief, not even whipping will take it out, Majella."

"Like the Americans," she said, half laughing, but with tears in the voice. "Whipping would not cure them."

It wanted yet more than an hour of dawn when they reached the crest of the hill from which they looked down on the San Pasquale valley. Two such crests and valleys they had passed; this was the broadest of the three valleys, and the hills walling it were softer and rounder of contour than any they had yet seen. To the east and northeast lay ranges of high mountains, their tops lost in the clouds. The whole sky was overcast and gray.

"If it were spring, this would mean rain," said Alessandro; "but it cannot rain, I think, now."

"No!" laughed Ramona, "not till we get our house done. Will it be of adobe, Alessandro?"

"Dearest Majella, not yet! At first it must be of the tule. They are very comfortable while it is warm, and before winter I will build one of adobe."

"Two houses! Wasteful Alessandro! If the tule house is good, I shall not let you, Alessandro, build another."

Ramona's mirthful moments bewildered Alessandro. To his slower temperament and saddened nature they seemed preternatural; as if she were all of a sudden changed into a bird, or some gay creature outside the pale of human life, — outside and above it.

"You speak as the birds sing, my Majella," he said slowly. "It was well to name you Majel; only the wood-dove has not joy in her voice, as you have. She says only that she loves and waits."

"I say that, too, Alessandro!" replied Ramona, reaching out both her arms towards him.

The horses were walking slowly, and very close side by side. Baba and Benito were now such friends they liked to pace closely side by side; and Baba and Benito were by no means without instinctive recognitions of the sympathy between their riders. Already Benito knew Ramona's voice, and answered it with pleasure; and Baba had long ago learned to stop when his mistress laid her hand on Alessandro's shoulder. He stopped now, and it was long minutes before he had the signal to go on again.

"Majella! Majella!" cried Alessandro, as, grasping both her hands in his, he held them to his cheeks, to his neck, to his mouth, "if the saints would ask Alessandro to be a martyr for Majella's sake, like those she was telling of, then she would know if Alessandro loved her! But what can Alessandro do now? What, oh, what? Majella gives all; Alessandro gives nothing!" and he bowed his forehead on her hands, before he put them back gently on Baba's neck.

Tears filled Ramona's eyes. How should she win this saddened man, this distrusting lover, to the joy which was his desert? "Alessandro can do one thing," she said, insensibly falling into his mode of speaking, — "one thing for his Majella: never, never, never say that he has nothing to give her. When he says that, he makes Majella a liar; for she has said that he is all the world to her, — he himself all the world which she desires. Is Majella a liar?"

But it was even now with an ecstasy only half joy, the other half anguish, that Alessandro replied: "Majella cannot lie. Majella is like the saints. Alessandro is hers."

When they rode down into the valley, the whole village was astir. The vintage-time had nearly passed; everywhere were to be seen large, flat baskets of grapes drying in the sun. Old women and children were turning these, or pounding acorns in the deep stone bowls; others were beating the yucca-stalks, and putting them to soak in water; the oldest women were sitting on the ground, weaving baskets. There were not many men in the village now; two large bands were away at work, — one at the autumn sheep-shearing, and one working on a large irrigating ditch at San Bernardino.

In different directions from the village slow-moving herds of goats or of cattle could be seen, being driven to pasture on the hills; some men were ploughing; several groups were at work building houses of bundles of the tule reeds.

"These are some of the Temecula people," said Alessandro; "they are building themselves new houses here. See those piles of bundles darker-colored than the rest. Those are their old roofs they brought from Temecula. There, there comes Ysidro!" he cried joyfully, as a man, well-mounted, who had been riding from point to point in the village, came galloping towards them. As soon as Ysidro recognized Alessandro, he flung himself from his horse. Alessandro did the same, and both running swiftly towards each other till they met, they embraced silently. Ramona, riding up, held out her hand, saying, as she did so, "Ysidro?"

Pleased, yet surprised, at this confident and assured greeting, Ysidro saluted her, and turning to Alessandro, said in their own tongue, "Who is this woman whom you bring, that has heard my name?"

"My wife!" answered Alessandro, in the same tongue. "We were married last night by Father Gaspara. She comes from the house of the Señora Moreno. We will live in San Pasquale, if you have land for me, as you have said."

Whatever astonishment Ysidro felt, he showed none. Only a grave and courteous welcome was in his face and in his words as he said, "It is well. There is room. You are welcome." But when he heard the soft Spanish syllables in which Ramona spoke to Alessandro, and Alessandro, translating her words to him, said, "Majel speaks only in the Spanish tongue, but she will learn ours," a look of disquiet passed over his countenance. His heart feared for Alessandro, and he said, "Is she, then, not Indian? Whence got she the name of Majel?"

A look of swift intelligence from Alessandro reassured him. "Indian on the mother's side!" said Alessandro, "and she belongs in heart to our people. She is alone, save for me. She is one blessed of the Virgin, Ysidro. She will help us. The name Majel I have given her, for she is like the wood-dove; and she is glad to lay her old name down forever, to bear this new name in our tongue."

And this was Ramona's introduction to the Indian village, — this and her smile; perhaps the smile did most. Even the little children were not afraid of her. The women, though shy, in the beginning, at sight of her noble bearing, and her clothes of a kind and quality they associated only with superiors, soon felt her friendliness, and, what was more, saw by her every word, tone, look, that she was Alessandro's. If Alessandro's, theirs. She was one of them. Ramona would have been profoundly impressed and touched, could she have heard them speaking among themselves about her; wondering how it had come about that she, so beautiful, and nurtured in the Moreno house, of which they all knew, should be Alessandro's loving wife. It must be, they thought in their simplicity, that the saints had sent it as an omen of good to the Indian people. Towards night they came, bringing in a hand-barrow the most aged woman in the village to look at her. She wished to see the beautiful stranger before the sun went down, they said, because she was now so old she believed each night that before morning her time would come to die. They also wished to hear the old woman's verdict on her. When Alessandro saw them coming, he understood, and made haste to explain it to Ramona. While he was yet speaking, the procession arrived, and the aged woman in her strange litter was placed silently on the ground in front of Ramona, who was sitting under Ysidro's great fig-tree. Those who had borne her withdrew, and seated themselves a few paces off. Alessandro spoke first. In a few words he told the old woman of Ramona's birth, of their marriage, and of her new name of adoption; then he said, "Take her hand, dear Majella, if you feel no fear."

There was something scarcely human in the shrivelled arm and hand outstretched in greeting; but Ramona took it in hers with tender reverence: "Say to her for me, Alessandro," she said, "that I bow down to her great age with reverence, and that I hope, if it is the will of God that I live on the earth so long as she has, I may be worthy of such reverence as these people all feel for her." 4

Alessandro turned a grateful look on Ramona as

Old Indian woman weaving, —Illustration by Henry Sandham. Circa 1883.

4 The passage of time had possibly brought the author a reverence for age. Certainly her own feelings as a young woman bore little resemblance to Ramona's. In 1824, Helen—then the 23-year-old bride of an army officer—paid a New Year's Day call on Mrs. Alexander Hamilton. The widow of the Federalist patriot was then 96. The author thought the visit eerie and dismal. "Like," she confided to a friend, "hearing Ecclesiastes read in the middle of a forest." Mrs. Hamilton was "very old, so feeble, so much of another world that it seemed almost a mockery to have her bear any part in the ceremonies of the day. She is very deaf and could not stand to welcome her callers but had a daughter with her to lead them up one by one and introduce them. She is the most ancient woman in the country and this gives her a peculiar interest but I should hate to live so long that people would come to see me as they would go to a relic. It would seem like being some sort of live mummy!"

5

A dove-coat. — Illustration by Henry Sandham. Circa 1883.

6

Woven granaries. —Illustration by Henry Snadham. Circa 1883.

he translated this speech, so in unison with Indian modes of thought and feeling. A murmur of pleasure rose from the group of women sitting by. The aged woman made no reply; her eyes still studied Ramona's face, and she still held her hand.

"Tell her," continued Ramona, "that I ask if there is anything I can do for her. Say I will be her daughter if she will let me."

"It must be the Virgin herself that is teaching Majella what to say," thought Alessandro, as he repeated this in the San Luiseno tongue.

Again the women murmured pleasure, but the old woman spoke not. "And say that you will be her son," added Ramona.

Alessandro said it. It was perhaps for this that the old woman had waited. Lifting up her arm, like a sibyl, she said: "It is well; I am your mother. The winds of the valley shall love you, and the grass shall dance when you come. The daughter looks on her mother's face each day. I will go;" and making a sign to her bearers, she was lifted, and carried to her house.

The scene affected Ramona deeply. The simplest acts of these people seemed to her marvellously profound in their meanings. She was not herself sufficiently educated or versed in life to know why she was so moved, — to know that such utterances, such symbolisms as these, among primitive peoples, are thus impressive because they are truly and grandly dramatic; but she was none the less stirred by them, because she could not analyze or explain them.

"I will go and see her every day," she said; "she shall be like my mother, whom I never saw."

"We must both go each day," said Alessandro. "What we have said is a solemn promise among my people; it would not be possible to break it."

Ysidro's home was in the centre of the village, on a slightly rising ground; it was a picturesque group of four small houses, three of tule reeds and one of adobe, — the latter a comfortable little house of two rooms, with a floor and a shingled roof, both luxuries in San Pasquale. The great fig-tree, whose luxuriance and size were noted far and near throughout the country, stood half-way down the slope; but its boughs shaded all three of the tule houses. On
5 one of its lower branches was fastened a dove-cote, ingeniously made of willow wands, plastered with adobe, and containing so many rooms that the whole tree seemed sometimes a-flutter with doves and dovelings. Here and there, between the houses, were huge baskets, larger than barrels, woven of twigs, as
6 the eagle weaves its nest, only tighter and thicker. These were the outdoor granaries; in these were kept acorns, barley, wheat, and corn. Ramona thought them, as well she might, the prettiest things she ever saw.

"Are they hard to make?" she asked. "Can you make them, Alessandro? I shall want many."

"All you want, my Majella," replied Alessandro.

"We will go together to get the twigs; I can, I dare say, buy some in the village. It is only two days to make a large one."

"No. Do not buy one," she exclaimed. "I wish everything in our house to be made by ourselves." In which, again, Ramona was unconsciously striking one of the keynotes of pleasure in the primitive harmonics of existence.

The tule house which stood nearest to the dove-cote was, by a lucky chance, now empty, Ysidro's brother Ramon, who had occupied it, having gone with his wife and baby to San Bernardino, for the winter, to work; this house Ysidro was but too happy to give to Alessandro till his own should be done. It was a tiny place, though it was really two houses joined together by a roofed passage-way. In this passage-way the tidy Juana, Ramon's wife, kept her few pots and pans, and a small stove. It looked to Ramona like a baby-house. Timidly Alessandro said: "Can Majella live in this small place for a time? It will not be very long; there are adobes already made."

His countenance cleared as Ramona replied gleefully, "I think it will be very comfortable, and I shall feel as if we were all doves together in the dove-cote!"

"Majel!" exclaimed Alessandro; and that was all he said.

Only a few rods off stood the little chapel; in front of it swung on a cross-bar from two slanting 7
posts an old bronze bell which had once belonged to the San Diego Mission. When Ramona read the date, "1790," on its side, and heard that it was from the San Diego Mission church it had come, she felt a sense of protection in its presence.

"Think, Alessandro," she said; "this bell, no doubt, has rung many times for the mass for the holy 8
Father Junipero himself. It is a blessing to the village. I want to live where I can see it all the time. It will be like a saint's statue in the house."

With every allusion that Ramona made to the saints' statues, Alessandro's desire to procure one for her deepened. He said nothing; but he revolved it in his mind continually. He had once gone with his shearers to San Fernando, and there he had seen in a room of the old Mission buildings a dozen statues of saints huddled in dusty confusion. The San Fernando church was in crumbled ruins, and such of the church properties as were left there were in the keeping of a Mexican not over-careful, and not in the least devout. It would not trouble him to part with a saint or two, Alessandro thought, and no irreverence to the saint either; on the contrary, the greatest of reverence, since the statue was to be taken from a place where no one cared for it, and brought into one where it would be tenderly cherished, and worshipped every day. If only San Fernando were not so far away, and the wooden saints so heavy! However, it should come about yet. Majella should have a saint; nor distance nor difficulty should keep

7

The bells from the San Diego Mission.
—Photograph be Goerge Wharton James. Circa 1911.

8 In early 1776, Indians angered by the Spaniards' treatment of their women rebelled against Serra's Mission San Diego. To their rescue came Captain Juan Bautista de Anza, a third generation frontier soldier from Mexico. Anza had just successfullly accomplished one of the most remarkable movements in western history—a massive march of colonists from the northern station of Tabac, near present day Nogales, Arizona along what was then known as El Camino del Diablo (The Trail of the Devil). Anza began on October 23, 1775 with 240 men, women and children, and more than 1000 animals and arrived in San Gabriel on January 4, 1776 with more people than he'd begun with. One colonist had died en route, but numerous births along the way had more than made up for the casualty. News of the uprising greeted him upon arrival. Anza was dispatched with thirty-five soldiers to subdue the Indians.

Alessandro from procuring for his Majel the few things that lay within his power. But he held his peace about it. It would be a sweeter gift, if she did not know it beforehand. He pleased himself as subtly and secretly as if he had come of civilized generations, thinking how her eyes would dilate, if she waked up some morning and saw the saint by her bedside; and how sure she would be to think, at first, it was a miracle, — his dear, devout Majella, who, with all her superior knowledge, was yet more credulous than he. All her education had not taught her to think, as he, untaught, had learned, in his solitude with nature.

Before Alessandro had been two days in San Pasquale, he had heard of a piece of good-fortune which almost passed his belief, and which startled him for once out of his usual impassive demeanor.

"You know I have a herd of cattle of your father's, and near a hundred sheep?" said Ysidro.

"Holy Virgin!" cried Alessandro, "you do not mean that! How is that? They told me all our stock was taken by the Americans."

"Yes, so it was, all that was in Temecula," replied Ysidro; "but in the spring your father sent down to know if I would take a herd for him up into the mountains, with ours, as he feared the Temecula pasture would fall short, and the people there, who could not leave, must have their cattle near home; so he sent a herd over, — I think, near fifty head; and many of the cows have calved; and he sent, also, a little flock of sheep, — a hundred, Ramon said; he herded them with ours all summer, and he left a man up there with them. They will be down next week. It is time they were sheared."

Before he had finished speaking, Alessandro had vanished, bounding like a deer. Ysidro stared after him; but seeing him enter the doorway of the little tule hut, he understood, and a sad smile passed over his face. He was not yet persuaded that this marriage of Alessandro's would turn out a blessing. "What are a handful of sheep to her!" he thought.

Breathless, panting, Alessandro burst into Ramona's presence. "Majella! my Majella! There are cattle — and sheep," he cried. "The saints be praised! We are not like the beggars, as I said."

"I told you that God would give us food, dear Alessandro," replied Ramona, gently.

"You do not wonder! You do not ask!" he cried, astonished at her calm. "Does Majella think that a sheep or a steer can come down from the skies?"

"Nay, not as our eyes would see," she answered; "but the holy ones who live in the skies can do anything they like on the earth. Whence came these cattle, and how are they ours?"

When he told her, her face grew solemn. "Do you remember that night in the willows," she said, "when I was like one dying, because you would not bring me with you? You had no faith that there would be food. And I told you then that the saints never forsook those who loved them, and that God would give food. And even at that moment, when you did not know it, there were your cattle and your sheep feeding in the mountains, in the keeping of God! Will my Alessandro believe after this?" and she threw her arms around his neck and kissed him.

"It is true," said Alessandro. "I will believe, after this, that the saints love my Majella."

But as he walked at a slower pace back to Ysidro, he said to himself: "Majella did not see Temecula. What would she have said about the saints, if she had seen that, and seen the people dying for want of food? It is only for her that the saints pray. They are displeased with my people."

An Indian house. —Photograph by George Wharton James. Circa 1911.

Kelly Young, a mother of two young sons and a full time student at Long Beach State with television aspirations, portrayed Ramona opposite Brian Smith, a part time actor-full time counselor in the 1987 production of the Hemet Pageant
— Courtesy of the Ramona Pageant Assoc., Inc.

Chapter XX

ONE year, and a half of another year, had passed. Sheep-shearings and vintages had been in San Pasquale; and Alessandro's new house, having been beaten on by the heavy spring rains, looked no longer new. It stood on the south side of the valley, — too far, Ramona felt, from the blessed bell; but there had not been land enough for wheat-fields any nearer, and she could see the chapel, and the posts, and, on a clear day, the bell itself. The house was small. "Small to hold so much joy," she said, when Alessandro first led her to it, and said deprecatingly, "It is small, Majella, — too small;" and he recollected bitterly, as he spoke, the size of Ramona's own room at the Señora's house. "Too small," he repeated.

"Very small to hold so much joy, my Alessandro," she laughed; "but quite large enough to hold two persons."

It looked like a palace to the San Pasquale people, after Ramona had arranged their little possessions in it; and she herself felt rich as she looked around her two small rooms. The old San Luis Rey chairs and the raw-hide bedstead were there, and, most precious of all, the statuette of the Madonna. For this Alessandro had built a niche in the wall, between the head of the bed and the one window. The niche was deep enough to hold small pots in front of the statuette; and Ramona kept constantly growing there wild-cucumber plants, which wreathed and re-wreathed the niche till it looked like a bower. Below it hung her gold rosary and the ivory Christ; and many a woman of the village, when she came to see Ramona, asked permission to go into the bedroom and say her prayers there; so that it finally came to be a sort of shrine for the whole village.

A broad veranda, as broad as the Señora's, ran across the front of the little house. This was the only thing for which Ramona had asked. She could not quite fancy life without a veranda, and linnets in the thatch. But the linnets had not yet come. In vain Ramona strewed food for them, and laid little trains of crumbs to lure them inside the posts; they would not build nests inside. It was not their way in San Pasquale. They lived in the cañons, but this part of the valley was too bare of trees for them. "In a year or two more, when we have orchards, they will come," Alessandro said.

With the money from that first sheep-shearing, and from the sale of part of his cattle, Alessandro had bought all he needed in the way of farming implements, — a good wagon and harnesses, and a plough. Baba and Benito, at first restive and indignant, soon made up their minds to work. Ramona had talked to Baba about it as she would have talked to a brother. In fact, except for Ramona's help, it would have been a question whether even Alessandro could have made Baba work in harness. "Good Baba!" Ramona said, as she slipped piece after piece of the harness over his neck, — "Good Baba, you must help us; we have so much work to do, and you are so strong! Good Baba, do you love me?" and with one hand in his mane, and her cheek, every few steps, laid close to his, she led Baba up and down the first furrows he ploughed.

"My Señorita!" thought Alessandro to himself, half in pain, half in pride, as, running behind with the unevenly jerked plough, he watched her laughing face and blowing hair, — "my Señorita!"

But Ramona would not run with her hand in Baba's mane this winter. There was a new work for her, indoors. In a rustic cradle, which Alessandro had made, under her directions, of the woven twigs, like the great outdoor acorn-granaries, only closer woven, and of an oval shape, and lifted from the floor by four uprights of red manzanita stems, — in this cradle, on soft white wool fleeces, covered with white homespun blankets, lay Ramona's baby, six months old, lusty, strong, and beautiful, as only children born of great love and under healthful conditions can be. This child was a girl, to Alessandro's delight; to Ramona's regret, — so far as a loving mother can feel regret connected with her first-born. Ramona had wished for an Alessandro; but the disappointed wish faded out of her thoughts, hour by hour, as she gazed into her baby-girl's blue eyes, — eyes so blue that their color was the first thing noticed by each person who looked at her.

"Eyes of the sky," exclaimed Ysidro, when he first saw her.

"Like the mother's," said Alessandro; on which Ysidro turned an astonished look upon Ramona, and saw for the first time that her eyes, too, were blue.

"Wonderful!" he said. "It is so. I never saw it;" and he wondered in his heart what father it had been, who had given eyes like those to one born of an Indian mother.

"Eyes of the sky," became at once the baby's name in the village; and Alessandro and Ramona, before they knew it, had fallen into the way of so calling her. But when it came to the christening, they demurred. The news was brought to the village, one Saturday, that Father Gaspara would hold services in the valley the next day, and that he wished all the new-born babes to be brought for christening. Late into the night, Alessandro and Ramona sat by their sleeping baby and discussed what should be her name. Ramona wondered that Alessandro did not wish to name her Majella.

"No! Never but one Majella," he said, in a tone which gave Ramona a sense of vague fear, it was so solemn.

They discussed "Ramona," "Isabella." Alessandro suggested Carmena. This had been his mother's name.

At the mention of it Ramona shuddered, recollecting the scene in the Temecula graveyard. "Oh, no, no! Not that!" she cried. "It is ill-fated;" and Alessandro blamed himself for having forgotten her only association with the name.

At last Alessandro said: "The people have named her, I think, Majella. Whatever name we give her in the chapel, she will never be called anything but 'Eyes of the Sky,' in the village."

"Let that name be her true one, then," said Ramona. And so it was settled; and when Father 1
Gaspara took the little one in his arms, and made the sign of the cross on her brow, he pronounced with some difficulty the syllables of the Indian name, which meant "Blue Eyes," or "Eyes of the Sky."

Heretofore, when Father Gaspara had come to San Pasquale to say mass, he had slept at Lomax's, the store and post-office, six miles away, in the Bernardo valley. But Ysidro, with great pride, had this time ridden to meet him, to say that his cousin Alessandro, who had come to live in the valley, and had a good new adobe house, begged that the Father would do him the honor to stay with him.

"And indeed, Father," added Ysidro, "you will be far better lodged and fed than in the house of Lomax. My cousin's wife knows well how all should be done."

"Alessandro! Alessandro!" said the Father, musingly. "Has he been long married?"

"No, Father," answered Ysidro. "But little more than two years. They were married by you, on their way from Temecula here."

"Ay, ay! I remember," said Father Gaspara. "I will come;" and it was with no small interest that he looked forward to meeting again the couple that had so strongly impressed him.

Ramona was full of eager interest in her preparations for entertaining the priest. This was like the olden time; and as she busied herself with her cooking and other arrangements, the thought of Father Salvierderra was much in her mind. She could, perhaps, hear news of him from Father Gaspara. It was she who had suggested the idea to Alessandro; and when he said, "But where will you sleep yourself, with the child, Majella, if we give our room to the Father? I can lie on the floor outside; but you?"—"I will go to Ysidro's, and sleep with

Ramona's bedroom, San Pasquale. —Illustration by Henry Sandham. Circa 1883.

1 Jackson experienced the same difficulties naming the child. "I want very much to know what would be an Indian name for 'Blue Eyes,'" she wrote a California friend from New York. "Can you find out for me?" Whatever his answer, it didn't suit her. She wrote back, "The name for Blue Eyes will not do. I am sorry. Will you ask the old woman what it would be for 'Eyes of the Sky'? I dare say that would be no less dissonant and complicated, but I would be exceedingly glad if I could get an explicit word that would be melodious and pleasing for a child's name and yet *mean* blue eyes." Judging from Father Gaspara's problem, she never found it.

Juana," she replied. "For two nights, it is no matter; and it is such shame to have the Father sleep in the house of an American, when we have a good bed like this!"

Seldom in his life had Alessandro experienced such a sense of gratification as he did when he led Father Gaspara into his and Ramona's bedroom. The clean whitewashed walls, the bed neatly made, with broad lace on sheets and pillows, hung with curtains and a canopy of bright red calico, the old carved chairs, the Madonna shrine in its bower of green leaves, the shelves on the walls, the white-curtained window, — all made up a picture such as Father Gaspara had never before seen in his pilgrimages among the Indian villages. He could not restrain an ejaculation of surprise. Then his eye falling on the golden rosary, he exclaimed, "Where got you that?"

"It is my wife's," replied Alessandro, proudly. "It was given to her by Father Salvierderra."

"Ah!" said the Father. "He died the other day."

"Dead! Father Salvierderra dead!" cried Alessandro. "That will be a terrible blow. Oh, Father, I implore you not to speak of it in her presence. She must not know it till after the christening. It will make her heart heavy, so that she will have no joy."

Father Gaspara was still scrutinizing the rosary and crucifix. "To be sure, to be sure," he said absently; "I will say nothing of it; but this is a work of art, this crucifix; do you know what you have here? And this, — is this not an altar-cloth?" he added, lifting up the beautiful wrought altar-cloth, which Ramona, in honor of his coming, had pinned on the wall below the Madonna's shrine.

"Yes, Father, it was made for that. My wife made it. It was to be a present to Father Salvierderra; but she has not seen him, to give it to him. It will take the light out of the sun for her, when first she hears that he is dead."

Father Gaspara was about to ask another question, when Ramona appeared in the doorway, flushed with running. She had carried the baby over to Juana's and left her there, that she might be free to serve the Father's supper.

"I pray you tell her not," said Alessandro, under his breath; but it was too late. Seeing the Father with her rosary in his hand, Ramona exclaimed: —

"That, Father, is my most sacred possession. It once belonged to Father Peyri, of San Luis Rey, and he gave it to Father Salvierderra, who gave it to me. Know you Father Salvierderra? I was hoping to hear news of him through you."

"Yes, I knew him, — not very well; it is long since I saw him," stammered Father Gaspara. His hesitancy alone would not have told Ramona the truth; she would have set that down to the secular priest's indifference, or hostility, to the Franciscan order; but looking at Alessandro, she saw terror and sadness on his face. No shadow there ever escaped her eye. "What is it, Alessandro?" she exclaimed. "Is it something about Father Salvierderra? Is he ill?"

Alessandro shook his head. He did not know what to say. Looking from one to the other, seeing the confused pain in both their faces, Ramona, laying both her hands on her breast, in the expressive gesture she had learned from the Indian women, cried out in a piteous tone: "You will not tell me! You do not speak! Then he is dead!" and she sank on her knees.

"Yes, my daughter, he is dead," said Father Gaspara, more tenderly than that brusque and warlike priest often spoke. "He died a month ago, at Santa Barbara. I am grieved to have brought you tidings to give you such sorrow. But you must not mourn for him. He was very feeble, and he longed to die, I heard. He could no longer work, and he did not wish to live."

Ramona had buried her face in her hands. The Father's words were only a confused sound in her ears. She had heard nothing after the words, "a month ago." She remained silent and motionless for some moments; then rising, without speaking a word, or looking at either of the men, she crossed the room and knelt down before the Madonna. By a common impulse, both Alessandro and Father Gaspara silently left the room. As they stood together outside the door, the Father said, "I would go back to Lomax's if it were not so late. I like not to be here when your wife is in such grief."

"That would but be another grief, Father," said Alessandro. "She has been full of happiness in making ready for you. She is very strong of soul. It is she who makes me strong often, and not I who give strength to her."

"My faith, but the man is right," thought Father Gaspara, a half-hour later, when, with a calm face, Ramona summoned them to supper. He did not know, as Alessandro did, how that face had changed in the half-hour. It wore a look Alessandro had never seen upon it. Almost he dreaded to speak to her.

When he walked by her side, later in the evening, as she went across the valley to Fernando's house, he ventured to mention Father Salvierderra's name. Ramona laid her hand on his lips. "I cannot talk about him yet, dear," she said. "I never believed that he would die without giving us his blessing. Do not speak of him till to-morrow is over."

Ramona's saddened face smote on all the women's hearts as they met her the next morning. One by one they gazed, astonished, then turned away, and spoke softly among themselves. They all loved her, and half revered her too, for her great kindness, and readiness to teach and to help them. She had been like a sort of missionary in the valley ever since she came, and no one had ever seen her face without a smile. Now she smiled not. Yet there was the beautiful baby in its white dress, ready to be christened; and the sun shone, and the bell had been ringing for half an hour, and from every corner of the valley the people were gathering, and Father Gaspara, in his gold and green cassock, was praying before the altar; it was a joyous day in San Pasquale. Why did Alessandro and Ramona kneel apart in a corner, with such heart-stricken countenances, not even looking glad when their baby laughed, and reached up her hands? Gradually it was whispered about what had happened. Some one had got it from Antonio, of Temecula, Alessandro's friend. Then all the women's faces grew sad too. They all had heard of Father Salvierderra, and many of them had prayed to the ivory Christ in Ramona's room, and knew that he had given it to her.

As Ramona passed out of the chapel, some of them came up to her, and taking her hand in theirs, laid it on their hearts, speaking no word. The gesture was more than any speech could have been.

When Father Gaspara was taking leave, Ramona said, with quivering lips, "Father, if there is anything you know of Father Salvierderra's last hours, I would be grateful to you for telling me."

"I heard very little," replied the Father, "except that he had been feeble for some weeks; yet he would persist in spending most of the night kneeling on the stone floor in the church, praying."

"Yes," interrupted Ramona; "that he always did."

"And the last morning," continued the Father, "the Brothers found him there, still kneeling on the stone floor, but quite powerless to move; and they lifted him, and carried him to his room, and there they found, to their horror, that he had had no bed; he had lain on the stones; and then they took him to the Superior's own room, and laid him in the bed, and he did not speak any more, and at noon he died."

"Thank you very much, Father," said Ramona, without lifting her eyes from the ground; and in the same low, tremulous tone, "I am glad that I know that he is dead."

"Strange what a hold those Franciscans got on these Indians!" mused Father Gaspara, as he rode down the valley. "There 's none of them would look like that if I were dead, I warrant me! There," he exclaimed, "I meant to have asked Alessandro who this wife of his is! I don't believe she is a Temecula Indian. Next time I come, I will find out. She 's had some schooling somewhere, that 's plain. She 's quite superior to the general run of them. Next time I come, I will find out about her."

"Next time!" In what calendar are kept the records of those next times which never come? Long before Father Gaspara visited San Pasquale again, Alessandro and Ramona were far away, and strangers were living in their home.

It seemed to Ramona in after years, as she looked back over this life, that the news of Father Salvier-

Victor Jory as "Alessandro", 1924. —Courtesy of the Ramona Pageant Assoc., Inc.

Victor Jory, the most famous of all Alessandros, first portrayed the hero in 1924. His performance in the Hemet Pageant was a turning point for the young actor. Despite the demands of a burgeoning career, he performed the lead for ten years and later returned from Hollywood and Broadway to direct the outdoor production.

Though treated as non-persons, the Indians were nonetheless taxed. A bill introduced in Congress to provide homes for the Mission Indians on the reservation plan was reported upon unfavorably by a Senate committee on the grounds that the Indians were really American citizens. The following year the Pala Indian chief attempted to register to vote but was refused on the grounds that, being an Indian, he was not a citizen. At the same time a small band of San Diego County Indians was taxed $600. They paid, the sheriff said, "without a murmur."

2

derra's death was the first note of the knell of their happiness. It was but a few days afterward, when Alessandro came in one noon with an expression on his face that terrified her; seating himself in a chair, he buried his face in his hands, and would neither look up nor speak; not until Ramona was near crying from his silence, did he utter a word. Then, looking at her with a ghastly face, he said in a hollow voice, "It has begun!" and buried his face again. Finally Ramona's tears wrung from him the following story:

Ysidro, it seemed, had the previous year rented a cañon, at the head of the valley, to one Doctor Morong. It was simply as bee-pasture that the Doctor wanted it, he said. He put his hives there, and built a sort of hut for the man whom he sent up to look after the honey. Ysidro did not need the land, and thought it a good chance to make a little money. He had taken every precaution to make the transaction a safe one; had gone to San Diego, and got Father Gaspara to act as interpreter for him, in the interview with Morong; it had been a written agreement, and the rent agreed upon had been punctually paid. Now, the time of the lease having expired, Ysidro had been to San Diego to ask the Doctor if he wished to renew it for another year; and the Doctor had said that the land was his, and he was coming out there to build a house, and live.

Ysidro had gone to Father Gaspara for help, and Father Gaspara had had an angry interview with Doctor Morong; but it had done no good. The
2 Doctor said the land did not belong to Ysidro at all, but to the United States Government; and that he had paid the money for it to the agents in Los Angeles, and there would very soon come papers from Washington, to show that it was his. Father Gaspara had gone with Ysidro to a lawyer in San Diego, and had shown to this lawyer Ysidro's paper, — the old one from the Mexican Governor of California, establishing the pueblo of San Pasquale, and saying how many leagues of land the Indians were to have; but the lawyer had only laughed at Father Gaspara for believing that such a paper as that was good for anything. He said that was all very well when the country belonged to Mexico, but it was no good now; that the Americans owned it now; and everything was done by the American law now, not by the Mexican law any more.

"Then we do not own any land in San Pasquale at all," said Ysidro. "Is that what it means?"

And the lawyer had said, he did not know how it would be with the cultivated land, and the village where the houses were, — he could not tell about that; but he thought it all belonged to the men at Washington.

Father Gaspara was in such rage, Ysidro said, that he tore open his gown on his breast, and he smote himself, and he said he wished he were a soldier, and no priest, that he might fight this accursed United States Government; and the lawyer laughed at him, and told him to look after souls, — that was his business, — and let the Indian beggars alone! "Yes, that was what he said, — 'the Indian beggars!' and so they would be all beggars, presently."

Alessandro told this by gasps, as it were; at long intervals. His voice was choked; his whole frame shook. He was nearly beside himself with rage and despair.

"You see, it is as I said, Majella. There is no place safe. We can do nothing! We might better be dead!"

"It is a long way off, that cañon Doctor Morong had," said Ramona, piteously. "It would n't do any harm, his living there, if no more came."

"Majella talks like a dove, and not like a woman," said Alessandro, fiercely. "Will there be one to come, and not two? It is the beginning. To-morrow may come ten more, with papers to show that the land is theirs. We can do nothing, any more than the wild beasts. They are better than we."

From this day Alessandro was a changed man. Hope had died in his bosom. In all the village councils, — and they were many and long now, for the little community had been plunged into great anxiety and distress by this Doctor Morong's affair, — Alessandro sat dumb and gloomy. To whatever was proposed, he had but one reply: "It is of no use. We can do nothing."

"Eat your dinners to-day, to-morrow we starve," he said one night, bitterly, as the council broke up. When Ysidro proposed to him that they should journey to Los Angeles, where Father Gaspara had said the headquarters of the Government officers were, and where they could learn all about the new laws in regard to land, Alessandro laughed at him. "What more is it, then, which you wish to know,
my brother, about the American laws?" he said. "Is 3
it not enough that you know they have made a law which will take the land from Indians; from us who have owned it longer than any can remember; land that our ancestors are buried in, — will take that land and give it to themselves, and say it is theirs? Is it to hear this again said in your face, and to see the man laugh who says it, like the lawyer in San Diego, that you will journey to Los Angeles? I will not go!"

And Ysidro went alone. Father Gaspara gave him a letter to the Los Angeles priest, who went with him to the land-office, patiently interpreted for him all he had to say, and as patiently interpreted all that the officials had to say in reply. They did not laugh, as Alessandro in his bitterness had said. They were not inhuman, and they felt sincere sympathy for this man, representative of two hundred hard-working, industrious people, in danger of being turned out of house and home. But they were very busy; they had to say curtly, and in few words, all there was to be said: the San Pasquale district was certainly the property of the United States Government, and the lands were in market, to be filed on, and bought,

—Illustration by Henry Sandham. Circa 1883.

3 In 1870, President Grant set aside portions of the San Pasqual Valley for an Indian reservation. An Indian agency was established; and, shortly after his appointment, the agent posted official signs and made public announcements identifying designated lands as acreage for future Indian reservations. Anglo response was angry and immediate. Several irate settlers hired a lawyer, Charles P. Taggart, a recent owner of the influential *San Diego Union*. Taggart's first action was to publish inflammatory anti-reservation articles claiming that putting a reservation on such fertile land would ruin the honest and hardworking people of San Diego. Soon a vehement critic of the reservation system and, indirectly, of Grant's Peace Policy, the *Union* vowed to fight the plan until it was rescinded. And ultimately, it was.

according to the homestead laws. These officials had neither authority nor option in the matter. They were there simply to carry out instructions, and obey orders.

Ysidro understood the substance of all this, though the details were beyond his comprehension. But he did not regret having taken the journey; he had now made his last effort for his people. The Los Angeles priest had promised that he would himself write a letter to Washington, to lay the case before the head men there, and perhaps something would be done for their relief. It seemed incredible to Ysidro, as, riding along day after day, on his sad homeward journey, he reflected on the subject, — it seemed incredible to him that the Government would permit such a village as theirs to be destroyed. He reached home just at sunset; and looking down, as Alessandro and Ramona had done on the morning of their arrival, from the hill-crests at the west end of the valley, seeing the broad belt of cultivated fields and orchards, the peaceful little hamlet of houses, he groaned. "If the people who make these laws could only see this village, they would never turn us out, never! They can't know what is being done. I am sure they can't know."

"What did I tell you?" cried Alessandro, galloping up on Benito, and reining him in so sharply he reared and plunged. "What did I tell you? I saw by your face, many paces back, that you had come as you went, or worse! I have been watching for you these two days. Another American has come in with Morong in the cañon; they are making corrals; they will keep stock. You will see how long we have any pasture-lands in that end of the valley. I drive all my stock to San Diego next week. I will sell it for what it will bring, — both the cattle and the sheep. It is no use. You will see."

When Ysidro began to recount his interview with the land-office authorities, Alessandro broke in fiercely: "I wish to hear no more of it. Their names and their speech are like smoke in my eyes and my nose. I think I shall go mad, Ysidro. Go tell your story to the men who are waiting to hear it, and who yet believe that an American may speak truth!"

Alessandro was as good as his word. The very next week he drove all his cattle and sheep to San Diego, and sold them at great loss. "It is better than nothing," he said. "They will not now be sold by the sheriff, like my father's in Temecula." The money he got, he took to Father Gaspara. "Father," he said huskily, "I have sold all my stock. I would not wait for the Americans to sell it for me, and take the money. I have not got much, but it is better than nothing. It will make that we do not starve for one year. Will you keep it for me, Father? I dare not have it in San Pasquale. San Pasquale will be like Temecula, — it may be to-morrow."

To the Father's suggestion that he should put the money in a bank in San Diego, Alessandro cried: "Sooner would I throw it in the sea yonder! I trust no man, henceforth; only the Church I will trust. Keep it for me, Father, I pray you;" and the Father could not refuse his imploring tone.

"What are your plans now?" he asked.

"Plans!" repeated Alessandro, — "plans, Father! Why should I make plans? I will stay in my house so long as the Americans will let me. You saw our little house, Father!" His voice broke as he said this. "I have large wheat-fields; if I can get one more crop off them, it will be something; but my land is of the richest in the valley, and as soon as the Americans see it, they will want it. Farewell, Father. I thank you for keeping my money, and for all you said to the thief Morong. Ysidro told me. Farewell." And he was gone, and out of sight on the swift galloping Benito, before Father Gaspara bethought himself.

"And I remembered not to ask who his wife was. I will look back at the record," said the Father. Taking down the old volume, he ran his eye back over the year. Marriages were not so many in Father Gaspara's parish, that the list took long to read. The entry of Alessandro's marriage was blotted. The Father had been in haste that night. "Alessandro Assis. Majella Fa—" No more could be read. The name meant nothing to Father Gaspara. "Clearly an Indian name," he said to himself; "yet she seemed superior in every way. I wonder where she got it."

The winter wore along quietly in San Pasquale. The delicious soft rains set in early, promising a good grain year. It seemed a pity not to get in as much wheat as possible; and all the San Pasquale people went early to ploughing new fields, — all but Alessandro.

"If I reap all I have, I will thank the saints," he said. "I will plough no more land for the robbers." But after his fields were all planted, and the beneficent rains still kept on, and the hills all along the valley wall began to turn green earlier than ever before was known, he said to Ramona one morning, "I think I will make one more field of wheat. There will be a great yield this year. Maybe we will be left unmolested till the harvest is over."

"Oh, yes, and for many more harvests, dear Alessandro!" said Ramona, cheerily. "You are always looking on the black side."

"There is no other but the black side, Majella," he replied. "Strain my eyes as I may, on all sides all is black. You will see. Never any more harvests in San Pasquale for us, after this. If we get this, we are lucky. I have seen the white men riding up and down in the valley, and I found some of their cursed bits of wood with figures on them set up on my land the other day; and I pulled them up and burned them to ashes. But I will plough one more field this week; though, I know not why it is, my thoughts go against it even now. But I will do it; and I will not come home till night, Majella, for the field is too far to go and come twice. I shall be the whole day ploughing." So saying, he stooped and kissed the baby, and then kissing Ramona, went out.

Ramona stood at the door and watched him as he harnessed Benito and Baba to the plough. He did not once look back at her; his face seemed full of thought, his hands acting as it were mechanically. After he had gone a few rods from the house, he stopped, stood still for some minutes meditating, then went on irresolutely, halted again, but finally went on, and disappeared from sight among the low foot-hills to the east. Sighing deeply, Ramona turned back to her work. But her heart was too disquieted. She could not keep back the tears.

"How changed is Alessandro!" she thought. "It terrifies me to see him thus. I will tell the Blessed Virgin about it;" and kneeling before the shrine, she prayed fervently and long. She rose comforted, and drawing the baby's cradle out into the veranda, seated herself at her embroidery. Her skill with her needle had proved a not inconsiderable source of income, her fine lace-work being always taken by San Diego merchants, and at fairly good prices.

It seemed to her only a short time that she had been sitting thus, when, glancing up at the sun, she saw it was near noon; at the same moment she saw Alessandro approaching, with the horses. In dismay, she thought, "There is no dinner! He said he would not come!" and springing up, was about to run to meet him, when she observed that he was not alone. A short, thick-set man was walking by his side; they were talking earnestly. It was a white man. What did it bode? Presently they stopped. She saw Alessandro lift his hand and point to the house, then to the tule sheds in the rear. He seemed to be talking excitedly; the white man also; they were both speaking at once. Ramona shivered with fear. Motionless she stood, straining eye and ear; she could hear nothing, but the gestures told much. Had it come, — the thing Alessandro had said would come? Were they to be driven out, — driven out this very day, when the Virgin had only just now seemed to promise her help and protection?

The baby stirred, waked, began to cry. Catching the child up to her breast, she stilled her by convulsive caresses. Clasping her tight in her arms, she walked a few steps towards Alessandro, who, seeing her, made an imperative gesture to her to return. Sick at heart, she went back to the veranda and sat down to wait.

In a few moments she saw the white man counting out money into Alessandro's hand; then he turned and walked away, Alessandro still standing as if rooted to the spot, gazing into the palm of his hand, Benito and Baba slowly walking away from

Don Ameche as Alessandro in the 1937 20th Century Fox production of *Ramona*.

4 In the winter of 1883 the author visited the San Pasquale Valley with Father Ubach. She found only one remaining Indian who was doing day work for one of the Americans. The rest of the Indians, she was told, had fled into secret lairs like wild beasts. They had sought the most inaccessible spots in the hills or distant canyons, refuges reached only by miles of difficult trails.

5 In 1881, Jackson interviewed an American living in the San Pasqual valley who'd preempted the greater part of the Indians' village in just such a manner. He allowed that it was hard on the Indians to lose their homes and land, but justified his action by reminding her, "If I had not done it someone else would, for all agree that the Indian has no right to public lands."

him unnoticed; at last he seemed to rouse himself as from a trance, and picking up the horses' reins, came slowly towards her. Again she started to meet him; again he made the same authoritative gesture to her to return; and again she seated herself, trembling in every nerve of her body. Ramona was now sometimes afraid of Alessandro. When these fierce glooms seized him, she dreaded, she knew not what. He seemed no more the Alessandro she had loved.

Deliberately, lingeringly, he unharnessed the horses and put them in the corral. Then still more deliberately, lingeringly, he walked to the house; walked, without speaking, past Ramona, into the door. A lurid spot on each cheek showed burning red through the bronze of his skin. His eyes glittered. In silence Ramona followed him, and saw him draw from his pocket a handful of gold-pieces, fling them on the table, and burst into a laugh more terrible than any weeping, — a laugh which wrung from her instantly, involuntarily, the cry, "Oh, my Alessandro! my Alessandro! What is it? Are you mad?"

"No, my sweet Majel," he exclaimed, turning to her, and flinging his arms round her and the child together, drawing them so close to his breast that the embrace hurt, — "no, I am not mad; but I think I shall soon be! What is that gold? The price of this house, Majel, and of the fields, — of
4 all that was ours in San Pasquale! To-morrow we will go out into the world again. I will see if I can find a place the Americans do not want!"

It did not take many words to tell the story. Alessandro had not been ploughing more than an hour, when, hearing a strange sound, he looked up and saw a man unloading lumber a few rods off. Alessandro stopped midway in the furrow and watched him. The man also watched Alessandro. Presently he came towards him, and said roughly, "Look here! Be off, will you? This is my land. I'm going to build a house here."

Alessandro had replied, "This was my land yesterday. How comes it yours to-day?"

Something in the wording of this answer, or something in Alessandro's tone and bearing, smote the man's conscience, or heart, or what stood to him in the place of conscience and heart, and he said: "Come, now, my good fellow, you look like a reasonable kind of a fellow; you just clear out, will you, and not make me any trouble. You see the land's mine. I've got all this land round here;" and he waved his arm, describing a circle; "three hundred and twenty acres, me and my brother to-
5 gether, and we're coming in here to settle. We got our papers from Washington last week. It's all right, and you may just as well go peaceably, as make a fuss about it. Don't you see?"

Yes, Alessandro saw. He had been seeing this precise thing for months. Many times, in his dreams and in his waking thoughts, he had lived over scenes similar to this. An almost preternatural calm and wisdom seemed to be given him now.

"Yes, I see, Señor," he said. "I am not surprised. I knew it would come; but I hoped it would not be till after harvest. I will not give you any trouble, Señor, because I cannot. If I could, I would. But I have heard all about the new law which gives all the Indians' lands to the Americans. We cannot help ourselves. But it is very hard, Señor." He paused.

The man, confused and embarrassed, astonished beyond expression at being met in this way by an Indian, did not find words come ready to his tongue. "Of course, I know it does seem a little rough on fellows like you, that are industrious, and have done some work on the land. But you see the land's in the market; I've paid my money for it."

"The Señor is going to build a house?" asked Alessandro.

"Yes," the man answered. "I've got my family in San Diego, and I want to get them settled as soon as I can. My wife won't feel comfortable till she's in her own house. We're from the States, and she's been used to having everything comfortable."

"I have a wife and child, Señor," said Alessandro, still in the same calm, deliberate tone; "and we have a very good house of two rooms. It would save the Señor's building, if he would buy mine."

"How far is it?" said the man. "I can't tell exactly where the boundaries of my land are, for the stakes we set have been pulled up."

"Yes, Señor, I pulled them up and burned them. They were on my land," replied Alessandro. "My house is farther west than your stakes; and I have large wheat-fields there, too, — many acres, Señor, all planted."

Here was a chance, indeed. The man's eyes gleamed. He would do the handsome thing. He would give this fellow something for his house and wheat-crops. First he would see the house, however; and it was for that purpose he had walked back with Alessandro. When he saw the neat whitewashed adobe, with its broad veranda, the sheds and corrals all in good order, he instantly resolved to get possession of them by fair means or foul.

"There will be three hundred dollars' worth of wheat in July, Señor, you can see for yourself; and a house so good as that, you cannot build for less than one hundred dollars. What will you give me for them?"

"I suppose I can have them without paying you for them, if I choose," said the man, insolently.

"No, Señor," replied Alessandro.

"What's to hinder, then, I'd like to know!" in a brutal sneer. "You haven't got any rights here, whatever, according to law."

"I shall hinder, Señor," replied Alessandro. "I shall burn down the sheds and corrals, tear down the house; and before a blade of the wheat is reaped, I will burn that." Still in the same calm tone.

"What'll you take?" said the man, sullenly.

"Two hundred dollars," replied Alessandro.

"Well, leave your plough and wagon, and I'll give it to you," said the man; "and a big fool I am, too. Well laughed at, I'll be, do you know it, for buying out an Indian!"

"The wagon, Señor, cost me one hundred and thirty dollars in San Diego. You cannot buy one so good for less. I will not sell it. I need it to take away my things in. The plough you may have. That is worth twenty."

"I'll do it," said the man; and pulling out a heavy buckskin pouch, he counted out into Alessandro's hand two hundred dollars in gold.

"Is that all right?" he said, as he put down the last piece.

"That is the sum I said, Señor," replied Alessandro. "To-morrow, at noon, you can come into the house."

"Where will you go?" asked the man, again slightly touched by Alessandro's manner. "Why don't you stay round here? I expect you could get work enough; there are a lot of farmers coming in here; they'll want hands."

A fierce torrent of words sprang to Alessandro's lips, but he choked them back. "I do not know where I shall go, but I will not stay here," he said; and that ended the interview.

"I don't know as I blame him a mite for feeling that way," thought the man from the States, as he walked slowly back to his pile of lumber. "I expect I should feel just so myself."

Almost before Alessandro had finished this tale, he began to move about the room, taking down, folding up, opening and shutting lids; his restlessness was terrible to see. "By sunrise, I would like to be off," he said. "It is like death, to be in the house which is no longer ours." Ramona had spoken no word since her first cry on hearing that terrible laugh. She was like one stricken dumb. The shock was greater to her than to Alessandro. He had lived with it ever present in his thoughts for a year. She had always hoped. But far more dreadful than the loss of her home, was the anguish of seeing, hearing, the changed face, changed voice, of Alessandro. Almost this swallowed up the other. She obeyed him mechanically, working faster and faster as he grew more and more feverish in his haste. Before sundown the little house was dismantled; everything, except the bed and the stove, packed in the big wagon.

"Now, we must cook food for the journey," said Alessandro.

"Where are we going?" said the weeping Ramona.

"Where?" ejaculated Alessandro, so scornfully that it sounded like impatience with Ramona, and made her tears flow afresh. "Where? I know not, Majella! Into the mountains, where the white men come not! At sunrise we will start."

DRAMA

ALONG THE RIALTO.

EW LOCATION FOR THE PALACE OF PICTURES.

By Grace Kingsley.

Los Angeles is to have a new film [illegible] de luxe. It is to be called [the] Palace Theater. The building formerly known as the Chocolate Den [on] Seventh street, between Hill and [Bro]adway, is being transformed into [a] first-class picture house. The new [the]ater will have [illegible] seats, a mam[mo]th pipe organ, which won a gold [me]dal at the Panama-Pacific Exposi[tio]n, and will be luxuriously fitted out [fro]m top to bottom.

The Palace Amusement Company, [wh]ich has owned and operated the [Pa]lace of Pictures, will control the [ne]w playhouse. Dr. H. B. Breckwedel [is] secretary and treasurer of the cor[por]ation and C. W. Noule president. [Th]e former will act as general man[age]r of the theater.

First-run features will be shown. [Th]e opening will probably take place [the] 19th inst. The first film to be [sho]wn will in all probability be "The [Isl]and of Surprise," filmed from the [Cyr]us Townsend Brady story.

The present Palace of Pictures will [cea]se to exist at the end of this week.

[Go]od-by, William.

With the completion of the Univers-

...

over in a photoplay that was any better than a couple of his actor friends got away with the other night, on the occasion of Charlie's leaving for Chicago.

Following the sad rites at Levy's, Freddie Goodwins and Billie Armstrong of Chaplin's company started for home. It was 2 a.m. and by that time the two didn't know whether it was a celebration or a wake they had attended. They knew only that they were consumed with a great thirst. So, halting a milkman, they bought a whole can of milk and Freddie, being the steadiest on his legs, hoisted it to his shoulder to take it home. Out in front of The Times Building a policeman halted them. He was assured that the milk was paid for all safe, but nevertheless insisted on walking Freddie and Billie back four blocks in pursuit of the milkman, Freddie still bearing the can. Then he gave the two a certificate to the following effect to show to any other inquiring limb of the law: "These men bought this can of milk and are taking it home with them."

"Did he think we were going to stop and do a Keystone with it right on Broadway?" demands Freddie.

Douglas Gets New One.

Douglas Fairbanks is appearing in a new photoplay for the Triangle, en-

Romance and comedy.

[A]da Gleason (above,) as Ramona Phail in the big Clune production of California's famous romance "Ramona," which had its premiere yesterday at the Auditorium, and Mabel Normand, ever popular comedy queen, who is being seen this week at the Majestic in "He Did and He Didn't."

serial, "The Journal of Lord ... Herbert Rawlinson without any

from the Los Angeles Times, Circa 1916.

Ramona wished to say good-by to their friends. There were women in the village that she tenderly loved. But Alessandro was unwilling. "There will be weeping and crying, Majella; I pray you do not speak to one. Why should we have more tears? Let us disappear. I will say all to Ysidro. He will tell them."

This was a sore grief to Ramona. In her heart she rebelled against it, as she had never yet rebelled against an act of Alessandro's; but she could not distress him. Was not his burden heavy enough now?

Without a word of farewell to any one, they set off in the gray dawn, before a creature was stirring in the village, — the wagon piled high; Ramona, her baby in her arms, in front; Alessandro walking. The load was heavy. Benito and Baba walked slowly. Capitan, unhappy, looking first at Ramona's face, then at Alessandro's, walked dispiritedly by their side. He knew all was wrong.

As Alessandro turned the horses into a faintly marked road leading in a northeasterly direction, Ramona said with a sob, "Where does this road lead, Alessandro?"

"To San Jacinto," he said. "San Jacinto Mountain. Do not look back, Majella! Do not look back!" he cried, as he saw Ramona, with streaming eyes, gazing back towards San Pasquale. "Do not look back! It is gone! Pray to the saints now, Majella! Pray! Pray!"

Chapter XXI

THE Señora Moreno was dying. It had been a sad two years in the Moreno house. After the first excitement following Ramona's departure had died away, things had settled down in a surface similitude of their old routine. But nothing was really the same. No one was so happy as before. Juan Canito was heart-broken. There had been set over him the very Mexican whose coming to the place he had dreaded. The sheep had not done well; there had been a drought; many had died of hunger, — a thing for which the new Mexican overseer was not to blame, though it pleased Juan to hold him so, and to say from morning till night that if his leg had not been broken, or if the lad Alessandro had been there, the wool-crop would have been as big as ever. Not one of the servants liked this Mexican; he had a sorry time of it, poor fellow; each man and woman on the place had or fancied some reason for being set against him; some from sympathy with Juan Can, some from idleness and general impatience; Margarita, most of all, because he was not Alessandro. Margarita, between remorse about her young mistress and pique and disappointment about Alessandro, had become a very unhappy girl; and her mother, instead of comforting or soothing her, added to her misery by continually bemoaning Ramona's fate. The void that Ramona had left in the whole household seemed an irreparable one; nothing came to fill it; there was no forgetting; every day her name was mentioned by some one; mentioned with bated breath, fearful conjecture, compassion, and regret. Where had she vanished? Had she indeed gone to the convent, as she said, or had she fled with Alessandro?

Margarita would have given her right hand to know. Only Juan Can felt sure. Very well Juan Can knew that nobody but Alessandro had the wit and the power over Baba to lure him out of that corral, " and never a rail out of its place." And the saddle, too! Ay, the smart lad! He had done the best he could for the Señorita; but, Holy Virgin! what had got into the Señorita to run off like that, with an Indian, — even Alessandro! The fiends had

The Chapel bells at Camulos. — Photograph by V.C. Vroman. Circa 1913

Juan Can. —Illustration by Henry Sandham. Circa 1883.

bewitched her. Tirelessly Juan Can questioned every traveller, every wandering herder he saw. No one knew anything of Alessandro, beyond the fact that all the Temecula Indians had been driven out of their village, and that there was now not an Indian in the valley. There was a rumor that Alessandro and his father had both died; but no one knew anything certainly. The Temecula Indians had disappeared, that was all there was of it, — disappeared, like any wild creatures, foxes or coyotes; hunted down, driven out; the valley was rid of them. But the Señorita! She was not with these fugitives. That could not be! Heaven forbid!

"If I'd my legs, I'd go and see for myself!" said Juan Can. "It would be some comfort to know even the worst. Perdition take the Señora, who drove her to it! Ay, drove her to it! That's what I say, Luigo." In some of his most venturesome wrathy moments he would say: "There's none of you know the truth about the Señorita but me! It's a hard hand the Señora's reared her with, from the first. She's a wonderful woman, our Señora! She gets power over one."

But the Señora's power was shaken now. More changed than all else in the changed Moreno household, was the relation between the Señora Moreno and her son Felipe. On the morning after Ramona's disappearance, words had been spoken by each which neither would ever forget. In fact, the Señora believed that it was of them she was dying, and perhaps that was not far from the truth; the reason that forces could no longer rally in her to repel disease, lying no doubt largely in the fact that to live seemed no longer to her desirable.

Felipe had found the note Ramona had laid on his bed. Before it was yet dawn he had waked, and tossing uneasily under the light covering had heard the rustle of the paper, and knowing instinctively that it was from Ramona, had risen instantly to make sure of it. Before his mother opened her window, he had read it. He felt like one bereft of his senses as he read. Gone! Gone with Alessandro! Stolen away like a thief in the night, his dear, sweet little sister! Ah, what a cruel shame! Scales seemed to drop from Felipe's eyes as he lay motionless, thinking of it. A shame! a cruel shame! And he and his mother were the ones who had brought it on Ramona's head, and on the house of Moreno. Felipe felt as if he had been under a spell all along, not to have realized this. "That's what I told my mother!" he groaned, — "that it drove her to running away! Oh, my sweet Ramona! what will become of her? I will go after them, and bring them back;" and Felipe rose, and hastily dressing himself, ran down the veranda steps, to gain a little more time to think. He returned shortly, to meet his mother standing in the doorway, with pale, affrighted face.

"Felipe!" she cried, "Ramona is not here."

"I know it," he replied in an angry tone. "That is what I told you we should do, — drive her to running away with Alessandro!"

"With Alessandro!" interrupted the Señora.

"Yes," continued Felipe, — "with Alessandro, the Indian! Perhaps you think it is less disgrace to the names of Ortegna and Moreno to have her run away with him, than to be married to him here under our roof! I do not! Curse the day, I say, when I ever lent myself to breaking the girl's heart! I am going after them, to fetch them back!"

If the skies had opened and rained fire, the Señora had hardly less quailed and wondered than she did at these words; but even for fire from the skies she would not surrender till she must.

"How know you that it is with Alessandro?" she said.

"Because she has written it here!" cried Felipe, defiantly holding up his little note. "She left this, her good-by to me. Bless her! She writes like a saint, to thank me for all my goodness to her, — I, who drove her to steal out of my house like a thief!"

The phrase, "my house," smote the Señora's ear like a note from some other sphere, which indeed it was, — from the new world into which Felipe had been in an hour born. Her cheeks flushed, and she opened her lips to reply; but before she had uttered a word, Luigo came running round the corner, Juan Can hobbling after him at a miraculous pace on his crutches. "Señor Felipe! Señor Felipe! Oh, Señora!" they cried. "Thieves have been here in the night! Baba is gone, — Baba, and the Señorita's saddle."

A malicious smile broke over the Señora's countenance, and turning to Felipe, she said in a tone — what a tone it was! Felipe felt as if he must put his hands to his ears to shut it out; Felipe would never forget, — "As you were saying, like a thief in the night!"

With a swifter and more energetic movement than any had ever before seen Señor Felipe make, he stepped forward, saying in an undertone to his mother, "For God's sake, mother, not a word before the men! — What is that you say, Luigo? Baba gone? We must see to our corral. I will come down, after breakfast, and look at it;" and turning his back on them, he drew his mother by a firm grasp, she could not resist, into the house.

She gazed at him in sheer, dumb wonder.

"Ay, mother," he said, "you may well look thus in wonder; I have been no man, to let my foster-sister, I care not what blood were in her veins, be driven to this pass! I will set out this day, and bring her back."

"The day you do that, then, I lie in this house dead!" retorted the Señora, at white heat. "You may rear as many Indian families as you please under the Moreno roof, I will at least have my grave!" In spite of her anger, grief convulsed her; and in another second she had burst into tears, and sunk helpless and trembling into a chair. No counterfeiting now. No pretences. The Señora Moreno's heart broke within her, when those words passed her lips to her adored Felipe. At the sight, Felipe flung himself on his knees before her; he kissed the aged hands as they lay trembling in her lap. "Mother mia," he cried, "you will break my heart if you speak like that! Oh, why, why do you command me to do what a man may not? I would die for you, my mother; but how can I see my sister a homeless wanderer in the wilderness?"

"I suppose the man Alessandro has something he calls a home," said the Señora, regaining herself a little. "Had they no plans? Spoke she not in her letter of what they would do?"

"Only that they would go to Father Salvierderra first," he replied.

"Ah!" The Señora reflected. At first startled, her second thought was that this would be the best possible thing which could happen.

"Father Salvierderra will counsel them what to do," she said. "He could no doubt establish them in Santa Barbara in some way. My son, when you reflect, you will see the impossibility of bringing them here. Help them in any way you like, but do not bring them here." She paused. "Not until I am dead, Felipe! It will not be long."

Felipe bowed his head in his mother's lap. She laid her hands on his hair, and stroked it with passionate tenderness. "My Felipe!" she said. "It was a cruel fate to rob me of you at the last!"

"Mother! mother!" he cried in anguish. "I am yours, — wholly, devotedly yours! Why do you torture me thus?"

"I will not torture you more," she said wearily, in a feeble tone. "I ask only one thing of you; let me never hear again the name of that wretched girl, who has brought all this woe on our house; let her name never be spoken on this place by man, woman, or child. Like a thief in the night! Ay, a horse-thief!"

Felipe sprang to his feet.

"Mother!" he said, "Baba was Ramona's own; I myself gave him to her as soon as he was born!"

The Señora made no reply. She had fainted. Calling the maids, in terror and sorrow Felipe bore her to her bed, and she did not leave it for many days. She seemed hovering between life and death. Felipe watched over her as a lover might; her great mournful eyes followed his every motion. She spoke little, partly because of physical weakness, partly from despair. The Señora had got her death-blow. She would die hard. It would take long. Yet she was dying, and she knew it.

Felipe did not know it. When he saw her going about again, with a step only a little slower than before, and with a countenance not so much changed as he had feared, he thought she would be well again, after a time. And now he would go in search of Ramona. How he hoped he should find them in Santa Barbara! He must leave them there, or wher-

Sharon Taber appeared as the Señora and Crist Thomas as Felipe in the 1987 Hemet productiuon. —Courtesy of the Ramona Pageant Assoc., Inc.

ever he should find them; never again would he for a moment contemplate the possibility of bringing them home with him. But he would see them; help them, if need be. Ramona should not feel herself an outcast, so long as he lived.

When he said, agitatedly, to his mother, one night, "You are so strong now, mother, I think I will take a journey; I will not be away long, — not over a week," she understood, and with a deep sigh replied: "I am not strong; but I am as strong as I shall ever be. If the journey must be taken, it is as well done now."

How was the Señora changed!

"It must be, mother," said Felipe, "or I would not leave you. I will set off before sunrise, so I will say farewell to-night."

But in the morning, at his first step, his mother's window opened, and there she stood, wan, speechless, looking at him. "You must go, my son?" she asked at last.

"I must, mother!" and Felipe threw his arms around her, and kissed her again and again. "Dearest mother! Do smile! Can you not?"

"No, my son, I cannot. Farewell. The saints keep you. Farewell." And she turned, that she might not see him go.

Felipe rode away with a sad heart, but his purpose did not falter. Following straight down the river road to the sea, he then kept up along the coast, asking here and there, cautiously, if persons answering to the description of Alessandro and Ramona had been seen. No one had seen any such persons.

When, on the night of the second day, he rode up to the Santa Barbara Mission, the first figure he saw was the venerable Father Salvierderra sitting in the corridor. As Felipe approached, the old man's face beamed with pleasure, and he came forward totteringly, leaning on a staff in each hand. "Welcome, my son!" he said. "Are all well? You find me very feeble just now; my legs are failing me sorely this autumn."

Dismay seized on Felipe at the Father's first words. He would not have spoken thus, had he seen Ramona. Barely replying to the greeting, Felipe exclaimed: "Father, I come seeking Ramona. Has she not been with you?"

Father Salvierderra's face was reply to the question. "Ramona!" he cried. "Seeking Ramona! What has befallen the blessed child?"

It was a bitter story for Felipe to tell; but he told it, sparing himself no shame. He would have suffered less in the telling, had he known how well Father Salvierderra understood his mother's character, and her almost unlimited power over all persons around her. Father Salvierderra was not shocked at the news of Ramona's attachment for Alessandro. He regretted it, but he did not think it shame, as the Señora had done. As Felipe talked with him, he perceived even more clearly how bitter and unjust his mother had been to Alessandro.

"He is a noble young man," said Father Salvierderra. "His father was one of the most trusted of Father Peyri's assistants. You must find them, Felipe. I wonder much they did not come to me. Perhaps they may yet come. When you find them, bear them my blessing, and say that I wish they would come hither. I would like to give them my blessing before I die. Felipe, I shall never leave Santa Barbara again. My time draws near."

Felipe was so full of impatience to continue his search, that he hardly listened to the Father's words. "I will not tarry," he said. "I cannot rest till I find her. I will ride back as far as Ventura to-night."

"You will send me word by a messenger, when you find them," said the Father. "God grant no harm has befallen them. I will pray for them, Felipe;" and he tottered into the church.

Felipe's thoughts, as he retraced his road, were full of bewilderment and pain. He was wholly at loss to conjecture what course Alessandro and Ramona had taken, or what could have led them to abandon their intention of going to Father Salvierderra. Temecula seemed the only place, now, to look for them; and yet from Temecula Felipe had heard, only a few days before leaving home, that there was not an Indian left in the valley. But he could at least learn there where the Indians had gone. Poor as the clew seemed, it was all he had. Cruelly Felipe urged his horse on his return journey. He grudged an hour's rest to himself or to the beast; and before he reached the head of the Temecula cañon the creature was near spent. At the steepest part he jumped off and walked, to save her strength. As he was toiling slowly up a narrow, rocky pass, he suddenly saw an Indian's head peering over the ledge. He made signs to him to come down. The Indian turned his head, and spoke to some one behind; one after another a score of figures rose. They made signs to Felipe to come up. "Poor things!" he thought; "they are afraid." He shouted to them that his horse was too tired to climb that wall; but if they would come down, he would give them money, holding up a gold-piece. They consulted among themselves; presently they began slowly descending, still halting at intervals, and looking suspiciously at him. He held up the gold again, and beckoned. As soon as they could see his face distinctly, they broke into a run. That was no enemy's face.

Only one of the number could speak Spanish. On hearing this man's reply to Felipe's first question, a woman, who had listened sharply and caught the word Alessandro, came forward, and spoke rapidly in the Indian tongue.

"This woman has seen Alessandro," said the man.

"Where?" said Felipe, breathlessly.

"In Temecula, two weeks ago," he said.

"Ask her if he had any one with him," said Felipe.

"No," said the woman. "He was alone."

A convulsion passed over Felipe's face. "Alone!" What did this mean? He reflected. The woman watched him. "Is she sure he was alone; there was no one with him?"

"Yes."

"Was he riding a big black horse?"

"No, a white horse," answered the woman, promptly. "A small white horse."

It was Carmena, every nerve of her loyal nature on the alert to baffle this pursuer of Alessandro and Ramona. Again Felipe reflected "Ask her if she saw him for any length of time; how long she saw him."

"All night," he answered. "He spent the night where she did."

Felipe despaired. "Does she know where he is now?" he asked.

"He was going to San Luis Obispo, to go in a ship to Monterey."

"What to do?"

"She does not know."

"Did he say when he would come back?"

"Yes."

"When?"

"Never! He said he would never set foot in Temecula again."

"Does she know him well?"

"As well as her own brother."

What more could Felipe ask? With a groan, wrung from the very depths of his heart, he tossed the man a gold-piece; another to the woman. "I am sorry," he said. "Alessandro was my friend I wanted to see him;" and he rode away, Carmena's eyes following him with a covert gleam of triumph.

When these last words of his were interpreted to her, she started, made as if she would run after him, but checked herself. "No," she thought. "It may be a lie. He may be an enemy, for all that. I will not tell. Alessandro wished not to be found. I will not tell."

And thus vanished the last chance of succor for Ramona; vanished in a moment; blown like a thistle-down on a chance breath, — the breath of a loyal, loving friend, speaking a lie to save her.

Distraught with grief, Felipe returned home. Ramona had been very ill when she left home. Had she died, and been buried by the lonely, sorrowing Alessandro? And was that the reason Alessandro was going away to the North, never to return? Fool that he was, to have shrunk from speaking Ramona's name to the Indians! He would return, and ask again. As soon as he had seen his mother, he would set off again, and never cease searching till he had found either Ramona or her grave. But when Felipe entered his mother's presence, his first look in her face told him that he would not leave her side again until he had laid her at rest in the tomb.

"Thank God! you have come, Felipe," she said in a feeble voice. "I had begun to fear you would not come in time to say farewell to me. I am going to

—Illustration by Henry Sandham. Circa 1900.

Inner court, Santa Barbara. —Illustration by Henry Sandham. Circa 1913.

—Illustration by Henry Sandham. Circa 1883.

leave you, my son;" and the tears rolled down her cheeks.

Though she no longer wished to live, neither did she wish to die, — this poor, proud, passionate, defeated, bereft Señora. All the consolations of her religion seemed to fail her. She had prayed incessantly, but got no peace. She fixed her imploring eyes on the Virgin's face and on the saints; but all seemed to her to wear a forbidding look. "If Father Salvierderra would only come!" she groaned. "He could give me peace. If only I can live till he comes again!"

When Felipe told her of the old man's feeble state, and that he would never again make the journey, she turned her face to the wall and wept. Not only for her own soul's help did she wish to see him: she wished to put into his hands the Ortegna jewels. What would become of them? To whom should she transfer the charge? Was there a secular priest within reach that she could trust? When her sister had said, in her instructions, "the Church," she meant, as the Señora Moreno well knew, the Franciscans. The Señora dared not consult Felipe; yet she must. Day by day these fretting anxieties and perplexities wasted her strength, and her fever grew higher and higher. She asked no questions as to the result of Felipe's journey, and he dared not mention Ramona's name. At last he could bear it no longer, and one day said, "Mother, I found no trace of Ramona. I have not the least idea where she is. The Father had not seen her or heard of her. I fear she is dead."

"Better so," was the Señora's sole reply; and she fell again into still deeper, more perplexed thought about the hidden treasure. Each day she resolved, "To-morrow I will tell Felipe;" and when to-morrow came, she put it off again. Finally she decided not to do it till she found herself dying. Father Salvierderra might yet come once more, and then all would be well. With trembling hands she wrote him a letter, imploring him to be brought to her, and sent it by messenger, who was empowered to hire a litter and four men to bring the Father gently and carefully all the way. But when the messenger reached Santa Barbara, Father Salvierderra was too feeble to be moved; too feeble even to write. He could write only by amanuensis, and wrote, therefore, guardedly, sending her his blessing, and saying that he hoped her foster-child might yet be restored to the keeping of her friends. The Father had been in sore straits of mind, as month after month had passed without tidings of his "blessed child."

Soon after this came the news that the Father was dead. This dealt the Señora a terrible blow. She never left her bed after it. And so the year had worn on; and Felipe, mourning over his sinking and failing mother, and haunted by terrible fears about the lost Ramona, had been tortured indeed.

But the end drew near, now. The Señora was plainly dying. The Ventura doctor had left off coming, saying that he could do no more; nothing remained but to give her what ease was possible; in a day or two more all would be over. Felipe hardly left her bedside. Rarely was mother so loved and nursed by son. No daughter could have shown more tenderness and devotion. In the close relation and affection of these last days, the sense of alienation and antagonism faded from both their hearts.

"My adorable Felipe!" she would murmur. "What a son hast thou been!" And, "My beloved mother! How shall I give you up?" Felipe would reply, bowing his head on her hands, — so wasted now, so white, so weak; those hands which had been cruel and strong little more than one short year ago. Ah, no one could refuse to forgive the Señora now! The gentle Ramona, had she seen her, had wept tears of pity. Her eyes wore at times a look almost of terror. It was the secret. How should she speak it? What would Felipe say? At last the moment came. She had been with difficulty roused from a long fainting; one more such would be the last, she knew, — knew even better than those around her. As she regained consciousness, she gasped, "Felipe! Alone!"

He understood, and waved the rest away.

"Alone!" she said again, turning her eyes to the door.

"Leave the room," said Felipe; "all — wait outside;" and he closed the door on them. Even then the Señora hesitated. Almost was she ready to go out of life leaving the hidden treasure to its chance of discovery, rather than with her own lips reveal to Felipe what she saw now, saw with the terrible, relentless clear-sightedness of death, would make him, even after she was in her grave, reproach her in his thoughts.

But she dared not withhold it. It must be said. Pointing to the statue of Saint Catharine, whose face seemed, she thought, to frown unforgiving upon her, she said, "Felipe — behind that statue — look!"

Felipe thought her delirious, and said tenderly, "Nothing is there, dearest mother. Be calm. I am here."

New terror seized the dying woman. Was she to be forced to carry the secret to the grave? to be denied this late avowal? "No! no! Felipe — there is a door there — secret door. Look! Open! I must tell you!"

Hastily Felipe moved the statue. There was indeed the door, as she had said.

"Do not tell me now, mother dear. Wait till you are stronger," he said. As he spoke, he turned, and saw, with alarm, his mother sitting upright in the bed, her right arm outstretched, her hand pointing to the door, her eyes in a glassy stare, her face convulsed. Before a cry could pass his lips, she had fallen back. The Señora Moreno was dead.

At Felipe's cry, the women waiting in the hall hurried in, wailing aloud as their first glance showed them all was over. In the confusion, Felipe, with a pale, set face, pushed the statue back into its place. Even then a premonition of horror swept over him. What was he, the son, to find behind that secret door, at sight of which his mother had died with that look of anguished terror in her eyes? All through the sad duties of the next four days Felipe was conscious of the undercurrent of this premonition. The funeral ceremonies were impressive. The little chapel could not hold the quarter part of those who came, from far and near. Everybody wished to do honor to the Señora Moreno. A priest from Ventura and one from San Luis Obispo were there. When all was done, they bore the Señora to the little graveyard on the hillside, and laid her by the side of her husband and her children; silent and still at last, the restless, passionate, proud, sad heart! When, the night after the funeral, the servants saw Señor Felipe going into his mother's room, they shuddered, and whispered, "Oh, he must not! He will break his heart, Señor Felipe! How he loved her!"

Old Marda ventured to follow him, and at the threshold said: "Dear Señor Felipe, do not! It is not good to go there! Come away!"

But he put her gently by, saying, "I would rather be here, good Marda;" and went in and locked the door.

It was past midnight when he came out. His face was stern. He had buried his mother again. Well might the Señora have dreaded to tell to Felipe the tale of the Ortegna treasure. Until he reached the bottom of the jewel-box, and found the Señora Ortegna's letter to his mother, he was in entire bewilderment at all he saw. After he had read this letter, he sat motionless for a long time, his head buried in his hands. His soul was wrung.

"And she thought that shame, and not this!" he said bitterly.

But one thing remained for Felipe now. If Ramona lived, he would find her, and restore to her this her rightful property. If she were dead, it must go to the Santa Barbara College.

"Surely my mother must have intended to give it to the Church," he said. "But why keep it all this time? It is this that has killed her. Oh, shame! oh, disgrace!" From the grave in which Felipe had buried his mother now, was no resurrection.

Replacing everything as before in the safe hiding-place, he sat down and wrote a letter to the Superior of the Santa Barbara College, telling him of the existence of these valuables, which in certain contingencies would belong to the College. Early in the morning he gave this letter to Juan Canito, saying: "I am going away, Juan, on a journey. If anything happens to me, and I do not return, send this letter by trusty messenger to Santa Barbara."

"Will you be long away, Señor Felipe?" asked the old man, piteously.

"I cannot tell, Juan," replied Felipe. "It may be only a short time; it may be long. I leave everything in your care. You will do all according to

A monk's bedroom at Santa Barbara. —Photograph by George Wharton James. Circa 1911.

The chapel bells at Camulos, "the Moreno House." —Illustration by Henry Sandham. Circa 1913.

your best judgment, I know. I will say to all that I have left you in charge."

"Thanks, Señor Felipe! Thanks!" exclaimed Juan, happier than he had been for two years. "Indeed, you may trust me! From the time you were a boy till now, I have had no thought except for your house."

Even in heaven the Señora Moreno had felt woe as if in hell, had she known the thoughts with which her Felipe galloped this morning out of the gateway through which, only the day before, he had walked weeping behind her body borne to burial.

"And she thought this no shame to the house of Moreno!" he said. "My God!"

Chapter XXII

DURING the first day of Ramona's and Alessandro's sad journey they scarcely spoke. Alessandro walked at the horses' heads, his face sunk on his breast, his eyes fixed on the ground. Ramona watched him in anxious fear. Even the baby's voice and cooing laugh won from him no response. After they were camped for the night, she said, "Dear Alessandro, will you not tell me where we are going?"

In spite of her gentleness, there was a shade of wounded feeling in her tone. Alessandro flung himself on his knees before her, and cried: "My Majella! my Majella! it seems to me I am going mad! I cannot tell what to do. I do not know what I think; all my thoughts seem whirling round as leaves do in brooks in the time of the spring rains. Do you think I can be going mad? It was enough to make me!"

Ramona, her own heart wrung with fear, soothed him as best she could. "Dear Alessandro," she said, "let us go to Los Angeles, and not live with the Indians any more. You could get work there. You could play at dances sometimes; there must be plenty of work. I could get more sewing to do, too. It would be better, I think."

He looked horror-stricken at the thought. "Go live among the white people!" he cried. "What does Majella think would become of one Indian, or two, alone among whites? If they will come to our villages and drive us out a hundred at a time, what would they do to one man alone? Oh, Majella is foolish!"

"But there are many of your people at work for whites at San Bernardino and other places," she persisted. "Why could not we do as they do?"

"Yes," he said bitterly, "at work for whites; so they are! Majella has not seen. No man will pay an Indian but half wages; even long ago, when the Fathers were not all gone, and tried to help the Indians, my father has told me that it was the way only to pay an Indian one-half that a white man or a Mexican had. It was the Mexicans, too, did that, Majella. And now they pay the Indians in money sometimes, half wages; sometimes in bad flour, or things he does not want; sometimes in whiskey; and if he will not take it, and asks for his money, they laugh, and tell him to go, then. One man in San Bernardino last year, when an Indian would not take a bottle of sour wine for pay for a day's work, shot him in the cheek with his pistol, and told him to mind how he was insolent any more! Oh, Majella, do not ask me to go work in the towns! I should kill some man, Majella, if I saw things like that."

Ramona shuddered, and was silent. Alessandro continued: "If Majella would not be afraid, I know a place, high up on the mountain, where no white man has ever been, or ever will be. I found it when I was following a bear. The beast led me up. It was his home; and I said then, it was a fit hiding-place for a man. There is water, and a little green valley. We could live there; but it would be no more than to live; it is very small, the valley. Majella would be afraid?"

"Yes, Alessandro, I would be afraid, all alone on a high mountain. Oh, do not let us go there! Try something else first, Alessandro. Is there no other Indian village you know?"

"There is Saboba," he said, "at foot of the San Jacinto Mountain; I had thought of that. Some of my people went there from Temecula; but it is a poor little village, Majella. Majella would not like to live in it. Neither do I believe it will long be any safer than San Pasquale. There was a kind, good old man who owned all that valley,—Señor Ravallo; he found the village of Saboba there when he came to the country. It is one of the very oldest of all; he was good to all Indians, and he said they should never be disturbed, never. He is dead; but his three sons have the estate yet, and I think they would keep their father's promise to the Indians. But you see, to-morrow, Majella, they may die, or go back to Mexico, as Señor Valdez did, and then the Americans will get it, as they did Temecula. And there are already white men living in the valley. We will go that way, Majella. Majella shall see. If she says stay, we will stay."

It was in the early afternoon that they entered the broad valley of San Jacinto. They entered it from the west. As they came in, though the sky over their heads was overcast and gray, the eastern and northeastern part of the valley was flooded with a strange light, at once ruddy and golden. It was a glorious sight. The jagged tops and spurs of San Jacinto Mountain shone like the turrets and posterns of a citadel built of rubies. The glow seemed preternatural.

"Behold San Jacinto!" cried Alessandro.

Ramona exclaimed in delight. "It is an omen!" she said. "We are going into the sunlight, out of the shadow;" and she glanced back at the west, which was of a slaty blackness.

"I like it not!" said Alessandro. "The shadow follows too fast!"

San Jacinto Mountain. —Illustration by Henry Sandham. Circa 1900.

While serving as Special Commissioner of Indian Affairs in Southern California, Jackson and her party were admiring the spring sunshine as they climbed the mountains near Julian when suddenly a freak snowstorm occurred. The party took shelter in an abandoned shack where they were imprisoned for three days while the storm beat down on them, penetrating the cracks in the wall. 1

When the storm showed no sign of abating and they could stand the cold and hunger no longer, their driver proposed a daring plan. He would drive into the very teeth of the storm. Staggering out into the blizzard, he somehow managed to harness the horses. Jackson, her assistant, Abbot Kinney, and artist, Henry Sandham, floundered their way to the wagon and climbed in. Cracking his whip, praying and cursing, the driver guided.

Although that was the most harrowing experience, none of the trip was easy. Jackson's self imposed assignments took them to seemingly endless deserts and bleak mountain passes, areas so hazardous that they had to abandon their wagon for burros, the only creatures sure footed enough to negotiate the precipitous mountain trails.

Often Sandham remonstrated with Jackson—it was too difficult, too dangerous for a woman, particularly at her age. Possibly he hoped that if she gave up, he could as well; if so, the strategy failed. Helen was openly scornful; it was usually Henry who tired the fastest and complained the most. "I'll go if it kills me," she frequently challenged him.

Artist Henry Sandham's sketch of the rude hut where the Jackson party had taken shelter. Circa 1900.

The always-stylish Jackson adapted remarkably well to her environment and circum-stances. A friend meeting her at this time remarked on the

Indeed it did. Even as he spoke, a fierce wind blew from the north, and tearing off fleeces from the black cloud, sent them in scurrying masses across the sky. In a moment more, snow-flakes began to fall.

"Holy Virgin!" cried Alessandro. Too well he knew what it meant. He urged the horses, running fast beside them. It was of no use. Too much even for Baba and Benito to make any haste, with the heavily loaded wagon.

"There is an old sheep-corral and a hut not over a mile farther, if we could but reach it!" groaned Alessandro. "Majella, you and the child will freeze."

"She is warm on my breast," said Ramona; "but, Alessandro, what ice in this wind! It is like a knife at my back!"

Alessandro uttered another ejaculation of dismay. The snow was fast thickening; already the track was covered. The wind lessened.

"Thank God, that wind no longer cuts as it did," said Ramona, her teeth chattering, clasping the baby closer and closer.

"I would rather it blew than not," said Alessandro; "it will carry the snow before it. A little more of this, and we cannot see, any more than in the night."

1 Still thicker and faster fell the snow; the air was dense; it was, as Alessandro had said, worse than the darkness of night, — this strange opaque whiteness, thick, choking, freezing one's breath. Presently the rough jolting of the wagon showed that they were off the road. The horses stopped; refused to go on.

"We are lost, if we stay here!" cried Alessandro. "Come, my Benito, come!" and he took him by the head, and pulled him by main force back into the road, and led him along. It was terrible. Ramona's heart sank within her. She felt her arms growing numb; how much longer could she hold the baby safe? She called to Alessandro. He did not hear her; the wind had risen again; the snow was being blown in masses; it was like making headway among whirling snow-drifts.

"We will die," thought Ramona. "Perhaps it is as well!" And that was the last she knew, till she heard a shouting, and found herself being shaken and beaten, and heard a strange voice saying, "Sorry ter handle yer so rough, ma'am, but we've got ter git yer out ter the fire!"

"Fire!" Were there such things as fire and warmth? Mechanically she put the baby into the unknown arms that were reaching up to her, and tried to rise from her seat; but she could not move.

"Set still! set still!" said the strange voice. "I'll jest carry the baby ter my wife, an' come back fur you. I allowed yer could n't git up on yer feet;" and the tall form disappeared. The baby, thus vigorously disturbed from her warm sleep, began to cry.

"Thank God!" said Alessandro, at the plunging horses' heads. "The child is alive! Majella!" he called.

"Yes, Alessandro," she answered faintly, the gusts sweeping her voice like a distant echo past him.

It was a marvellous rescue. They had been nearer the old sheep-corral than Alessandro had thought; but except that other storm-beaten travellers had reached it before them, Alessandro had never found it. Just as he felt his strength failing him, and had thought to himself, in almost the same despairing words as Ramona, "This will end all our troubles," he saw a faint light to the left. Instantly he had turned the horses' heads towards it. The ground was rough and broken, and more than once he had been in danger of overturning the wagon; but he had pressed on, shouting at intervals for help. At last his call was answered, and another light appeared; this time a swinging one, coming slowly towards him, — a lantern, in the hand of a man, whose first words, "Wall, stranger, I allow yer inter trouble," were as intelligible to Alessandro as if they had been spoken in the purest San Luiseno dialect.

Not so, to the stranger, Alessandro's grateful reply in Spanish.

"Another o' these no-'count Mexicans, by thunder!" thought Jeff Hyer to himself. "Blamed ef I'd lived in a country all my life, ef I would n't know better'n to git caught out in such weather's this!" And as he put the crying babe into his wife's arms, he said half impatiently, "Ef I'd knowed 'twuz Mexicans, Ri, I would n't ev' gone out ter 'um. They're more ter hum 'n I am, 'n these yer tropicks."

"Naow, Jeff, yer know yer would n't let ennythin' in shape ev a human creetur go perishin' past aour fire sech weather's this," replied the woman, as she took the baby, which recognized the motherly hand at its first touch, and ceased crying.

"Why, yer pooty, blue-eyed little thing!" she exclaimed, as she looked into the baby's face. "I declar, Jos, think o' sech a mite's this bein' aout 'n this weather. I'll jest warm up some milk for it this minnit." 2

"Better see t' th' mother fust, Ri," said Jeff, leading, half carrying, Ramona into the hut. "She's nigh abaout froze stiff!"

But the sight of her baby safe and smiling was a better restorative for Ramona than anything else, and in a few moments she had fully recovered. It was in a strange group she found herself. On a mattress, in the corner of the hut, lay a young man apparently about twenty-five, whose bright eyes and flushed cheeks told but too plainly the story of his disease. The woman, tall, ungainly, her face gaunt, her hands hardened and wrinkled, gown ragged, shoes ragged, her dry and broken light hair wound in a careless, straggling knot in her neck, wisps of it flying over her forehead, was certainly not a prepossessing figure. Yet spite of her careless, unkempt

author's "dainty neatness and sense of fitness which led her to choose without thinking much about it, what was becoming and best suited her style." One wonders what the author selected for sleeping in haystacks, which she did upon occasion.

2 Mrs. C.C. Jordan, the original Aunt Ri, ran a boarding house in Saboba where Jackson stayed while on her fact finding mission.

Mrs. C.C. Jordan. —Photograph by George Wharton James. Circa 1911.

—Illustration by Henry Sandham. Circa 1900.

condition, there was a certain gentle dignity in her bearing, and a kindliness in her glance, which won trust and warmed hearts at once. Her pale blue eyes were still keen-sighted; and as she fixed them on Ramona, she thought to herself, "This ain't no common Mexican, no how." "Be ye movers?" she said.

Ramona stared. In the little English she knew, that word was not included. "Ah, Señora," she said regretfully, "I cannot talk in the English speech; only in Spanish."

"Spanish, eh? Yer mean Mexican? Jos, hyar, he kin talk thet. He can't talk much, though; 't ain't good fur him; his lungs is out er kilter. Thet's what we're bringin' him hyar fur, — fur warm climate! 'pears like it, don't it?" and she chuckled grimly, but with a side glance of ineffable tenderness at the sick man. "Ask her who they be, Jos," she added.

Jos lifted himself on his elbow, and fixing his shining eyes on Ramona, said in Spanish, "My mother asks if you are travellers?"

"Yes," said Ramona. "We have come all the way from San Diego. We are Indians."

"Injuns!" ejaculated Jos's mother. "Lord save us, Jos! Hev we reelly took in Injuns? What on airth — Well, well, she's fond uv her baby's enny white woman! I kin see thet; an', Injun or no Injun, they've got to stay naow. Yer could n't turn a dog out 'n sech weather's this. I bet thet baby's father wuz white, then. Look at them blue eyes."

Ramona listened and looked intently, but could understand nothing. Almost she doubted if the woman were really speaking English. She had never before heard so many English sentences without being able to understand one word. The Tennessee drawl so altered even the commonest words, that she did not recognize them. Turning to Jos, she said gently, "I know very little English. I am so sorry I cannot understand. Will it tire you to interpret to me what your mother said?"

Jos was as full of humor as his mother. "She wants me to tell her what you wuz sayin'," he said. "I allow, I'll only tell her the part on 't she'll like best. — My mother says you can stay here with us till the storm is over," he said to Ramona.

Swifter than lightning, Ramona had seized the woman's hand and carried it to her heart, with an expressive gesture of gratitude and emotion. "Thanks! thanks! Señora!" she cried.

"What is it she calls me, Jos?" asked his mother.

"Señora," he replied. "It only means the same as lady."

"Shaw, Jos! You tell her I ain't any lady. Tell her everybody round where we live calls me 'Aunt Ri,' or 'Mis Hyer;' she kin call me whichever she's a mind to. She's reel sweet-spoken."

With some difficulty Jos explained his mother's disclaimer of the title of Señora, and the choice of names she offered to Ramona.

Ramona, with smiles which won both mother and son, repeated after him both names, getting neither exactly right at first trial, and finally said, "I like 'Aunt Ri' best; she is so kind, like aunt, to every one."

"Naow, ain't thet queer, Jos," said Aunt Ri, "aout here 'n thes wilderness to ketch sumbody sayin' thet, — jest what they all say ter hum? I donno 's I'm enny kinder 'n ennybody else. I don't want ter see ennybody put upon, nor noways sufferin', ef so be 's I kin help; but thet ain't ennythin' stronary, ez I know. I donno how ennybody could feel enny different."

"There's lots doos, mammy," replied Jos, affectionately. "Yer'd find out fast enuf, ef yer went raound more. There's mighty few's good 's you air ter everybody."

Ramona was crouching in the corner by the fire, her baby held close to her breast. The place which at first had seemed a haven of warmth, she now saw was indeed but a poor shelter against the fearful storm which raged outside. It was only a hut of rough boards, carelessly knocked together for a shepherd's temporary home. It had been long unused, and many of the boards were loose and broken. Through these crevices, at every blast of the wind, the fine snow swirled. On the hearth were burning a few sticks of wood, dead cottonwood branches, which Jeff Hyer had hastily collected before the storm reached its height. A few more sticks lay by the hearth. Aunt Ri glanced at them anxiously. A poor provision for a night in the snow. "Be ye warm, Jos?" she asked.

"Not very, mammy," he said; "but I ain't cold, nuther; an' thet's somethin'."

It was the way in the Hyer family to make the best of things; they had always possessed this virtue to such an extent, that they suffered from it as from a vice. There was hardly to be found in all Southern Tennessee a more contented, shiftless, ill-bestead family than theirs. But there was no grumbling. Whatever went wrong, whatever was lacking, it was "jest like aour luck," they said, and did nothing, or next to nothing, about it. Good-natured, affectionate, humorous people; after all, they got more comfort out of life than many a family whose surface conditions were incomparably better than theirs. When Jos, their oldest child and only son, broke down, **had hemorrhage after hemorrhage,** and the doctor said the only thing that could save him was to go across the plains in a wagon to California, they said, "What good luck 'Lizy was married last year! Now there ain't nuthin' ter hinder sellin' the farm 'n' goin' right off." And they sold their little place for half it was worth, traded cattle for a pair of horses and a covered wagon, and set off, half beggared, with their sick boy on a bed in the bottom of the wagon, as cheery as if they were rich people on a pleasure-trip. A pair of steers "to spell" the horses, and a cow to give milk for Jos, they drove before them; and so they had come by slow stages, sometimes camping for a week at a time, all the way from Tennessee to the San Jacinto Valley. They were rewarded. Jos was getting well. Another six months, they thought, would see him cured; and it would have gone hard with any one who had tried to persuade either Jefferson or Maria Hyer that they were not as lucky a couple as could be found. Had they not saved Joshua, their son?

Nicknames among this class of poor whites in the South seem singularly like those in vogue in New England. From totally opposite motives, the lazy, easy-going Tennesseean and the hurry-driven Vermonter cut down all their family names to the shortest. To speak three syllables where one will answer, seems to the Vermonter a waste of time; to the Tennesseean, quite too much trouble. Mrs. Hyer could hardly recollect ever having heard her name, "Maria," in full; as a child, and until she was married, she was simply "Ri;" and as soon as she had a house of her own, to become a centre of hospitality and help, she was adopted by common consent of the neighborhood, in a sort of titular and universal aunt-hood, which really was a much greater tribute and honor than she dreamed. Not a man, woman, or child, within her reach, that did not call her or know of her as "Aunt Ri."

"I donno whether I 'd best make enny more fire naow or not," she said reflectively; "ef this storm 's goin' to last till mornin', we 'll come short o' wood, thet 's clear." As she spoke, the door of the hut burst open, and her husband staggered in, followed by Alessandro, both covered with snow, their arms full of wood. Alessandro, luckily, knew of a little clump of young cottonwood-trees in a ravine, only a few rods from the house; and the first thing he had thought of, after tethering the horses in shelter between the hut and the wagons, was to get wood. Jeff, seeing him take a hatchet from the wagon, had understood, got his own, and followed; and now there lay on the ground enough to keep them warm for hours. As soon as Alessandro had thrown down his load, he darted to Ramona, and kneeling down, looked anxiously into the baby's face, then into hers; then he said devoutly, "The saints be praised; my Majella! It is a miracle!"

Jos listened in dismay to this ejaculation. "Ef they ain't Catholics!" he thought. "What kind o' Injuns be they, I wonder. I won't tell mammy they 're Catholics; she 'd feel wuss 'n ever. I don't care what they be. Thet gal 's got the sweetest eyes 'n her head ever I saw sence I wuz born."

By help of Jos's interpreting, the two families soon became well acquainted with each other's condition and plans; and a feeling of friendliness, surprising under the circumstances, grew up between them.

"Jeff," said Aunt Ri, — "Jeff, they can't understand a word we say, so 't's no harm done, I s'pose, to speak afore 'em, though 't don't seem hardly fair to take advantage o' their not knowin' any language but their own; but I jest tell you thet I 've got a lesson 'n the subjeck uv Injuns. I 've always hed a reel mean feelin' about 'em; I did n't want ter come nigh 'em, nor ter hev 'em come nigh me. This woman, here, she 's ez sweet a creetur 's ever I see; 'n' ez bound up 'n thet baby 's yer could ask enny woman to be; 'n' 's fur thet man, can't yer see, Jeff, he jest worships the ground she walks on? Thet 's a fact, Jeff. I donno 's ever I see a white man think so much uv a woman; come, naow, Jeff, d' yer think yer ever did yerself?"

Aunt Ri was excited. The experience was, to her, almost incredible. Her ideas of Indians had been drawn from newspapers, and from a book or two of narratives of massacres, and from an occasional sight of vagabond bands or families they had encountered in their journey across the plains. Here she found herself sitting side by side in friendly intercourse with an Indian man and Indian woman, whose appearance and behavior were attractive; towards whom she felt herself singularly drawn.

"I 'm free to confess, Jos," she said, "I would n't ha' bleeved it. I hain't seen nobody, black, white, or gray, sence we left hum, I 've took to like these yere folks. An' they 're real dark; 's dark 's any nigger in Tennessee; 'n' he 's pewer Injun; her father wuz white, she sez, but she don't call herself nothin' but an Injun, the same 's he is. D' yer notice the way she looks at him, Jos? Don't she jest set a store by thet feller? 'N' I don't blame her."

Indeed, Jos had noticed. No man was likely to see Ramona with Alessandro without perceiving the rare quality of her devotion to him. And now there was added to this devotion an element of indefinable anxiety which made its vigilance unceasing. Ramona feared for Alessandro's reason. She had hardly put it into words to herself, but the terrible fear dwelt with her. She felt that another blow would be more than he could bear.

The storm lasted only a few hours. When it cleared, the valley was a solid expanse of white, and the stars shone out as if in an Arctic sky.

"It will be all gone by noon to-morrow," said Alessandro to Jos, who was dreading the next day.

"Not really!" he said.

"You will see," said Alessandro. "I have often known it thus. It is like death while it lasts; but it is never long."

The Hyers were on their way to some hot springs on the north side of the valley. Here they proposed to camp for three months, to try the waters for Jos. They had a tent, and all that was necessary for living in their primitive fashion. Aunt Ri was looking forward to the rest with great anticipation; she was heartily tired of being on the move. Her husband's anticipations were of a more stirring nature. He had heard that there was good hunting on San Jacinto Mountain. When he found that Alessandro knew the region thoroughly, and had been thinking of settling there, he was rejoiced, and proposed to him to become his companion and guide in hunting expe

Jackson made the 75 mile drive to Saboba from San Diego with Father Ubach in the spring of 1882 excited by the prospect of seeing the first Indian school in the state. She found a village of some 150 Indians. Their chief, Jesus Castillo—who in the modern fashion called himself captain—explained that his people had settled themselves there more than one hundred years earlier. Looking about at the attractive, well cared for homes, the lush fields, vineyards, livestock, and orchards, the author thought it too good to be true—and it was. 3

Jane Darwell appeared as Aunt Ri in the 1937 20th Century Fox production of *Ramona.*

While in Saboba, Jackson learned that the Indians were in danger of losing their lands. In 1842 the Mexican government had granted most of the San Jacinto Valley to Jose Antonio Estudillo with the stipulation that he safeguard the security of the Indians living there. The Indians' position had been strengthened once more in 1880 when the United States government confirmed the original Mexican patent. Through the years Estudillo had been faithful to his promise. Indians had thrived unmolested; but now the patriarch was dead and his many heirs were not so conscientious. Parcels of land were sold at random whenever anyone in the family wanted money. One of the new owners, M.R. Byrnes, threatened to evict the Indians unless the United States government agreed to buy his entire 700 acres.

—Illustration by Henry Sandham. Circa 1883.

ditions. Ramona grasped eagerly at the suggestion; companionship, she was sure, would do Alessandro good, — companionship, the outdoor life, and the excitement of hunting, of which he was fond. This hot-spring cañon was only a short distance from the
3 Saboba village, of which they had spoken as a possible home; which she had from the first desired to try. She no longer had repugnance to the thought of an Indian village; she already felt a sense of kinship and shelter with any Indian people. She had become, as Carmena had said, " one of them."

A few days saw the two families settled, — the Hyers in their tent and wagon, at the hot springs, and Alessandro and Ramona, with the baby, in a little adobe house in the Saboba village. The house belonged to an old Indian woman who, her husband having died, had gone to live with a daughter, and was very glad to get a few dollars by renting her own house. It was a wretched place: one small room, walled with poorly made adobe bricks, thatched with tule, no floor, and only one window. When Alessandro heard Ramona say cheerily, " Oh, this will do very well, when it is repaired a little," his face was convulsed, and he turned away; but he said nothing. It was the only house to be had in the village, and there were few better. Two months later, no one would have known it. Alessandro had had good luck in hunting. Two fine deerskins covered the earth floor; a third was spread over the bedstead; and the horns, hung on the walls, served for hooks to hang clothes upon. The scarlet calico canopy was again set up over the bed, and the woven cradle, on its red manzanita frame, stood near. A small window in the door, and one more cut in the walls, let in light and air. On a shelf near one of these windows stood the little Madonna, again wreathed with vines as in San Pasquale.

When Aunt Ri first saw the room, after it was thus arranged, she put both arms akimbo, and stood in the doorway, her mouth wide open, her eyes full of wonder. Finally her wonder framed itself in an ejaculation: " Wall, I allow yer air fixed up ! "

Aunt Ri, at her best estate, had never possessed a room which had the expression of this poor little mud hut of Ramona's. She could not understand it. The more she studied the place, the less she understood it. On returning to the tent, she said to Jos: " It beats all ever I see, the way thet Injun woman 's got fixed up out er nothin'. It ain't no more 'n a hovel, a mud hovel, Jos, not much bigger 'n this yer tent, fur all three on 'em, an' the bed an' the stove an' everythin'; an' I vow, Jos, she 's fixed it so 't looks jest like a parlor! It beats me, it doos. I 'd jest like you to see it."

And when Jos saw it, and Jeff, they were as full of wonder as Aunt Ri had been. Dimly they recognized the existence of a principle here which had never entered into their life. They did not know it by name, and it could not have been either taught, transferred, or explained to the good-hearted wife and mother who had been so many years the affectionate disorderly genius of their home. But they felt its charm; and when, one day, after the return of Alessandro and Jeff from a particularly successful hunt, the two families had sat down together to a supper of Ramona's cooking, — stewed venison and artichokes, and *frijoles* with chili, — their wonder was still greater.

"Ask her if this is Injun style of cooking, Jos," said Aunt Ri. "I never thought nothin' o' beans; but these air good, 'n' no mistake!"

Ramona laughed. "No; it is Mexican," she said. "I learned to cook from an old Mexican woman."

"Wall, I'd like the receipt on 't; but I allow I should n't never git the time to fuss with it," said Aunt Ri; "but I may 's well git the rule, naow I'm here."

Alessandro began to lose some of his gloom. He had earned money. He had been lifted out of himself by kindly companionship; he saw Ramona cheerful, the little one sunny; the sense of home, the strongest passion Alessandro possessed, next to his love for Ramona, began again to awake in him. He began to talk about building a house. He had found things in the village better than he feared. It was but a poverty-stricken little handful, to be sure; still, they were unmolested; the valley was large; their stock ran free; the few white settlers, one at the upper end and two or three on the south side, had manifested no disposition to crowd the Indians; the Ravallo brothers were living on the estate still, and there was protection in that, Alessandro thought. And Majella was content. Majella had found friends. Something, not quite hope, but akin to it, began to stir in Alessandro's heart. He would build a house; Majella should no longer live in this mud hut. But to his surprise, when he spoke of it, Ramona said no; they had all they needed, now. Was not Alessandro comfortable? She was. It would be wise to wait longer before building.

Ramona knew many things that Alessandro did not. While he had been away on his hunts, she had had speech with many a one he never saw. She had gone to the store and post-office several times, to exchange baskets or lace for flour, and she had heard talk there which disquieted her. She did not believe that Saboba was safe. One day she had heard a man say, "If there is a drought we shall have the devil to pay with our stock before winter is over." "Yes," said another; "and look at those damned Indians over there in Saboba, with water running all the time in their village! It's a shame they should have that spring!"

Not for worlds would Ramona have told this to Alessandro. She kept it locked in her own breast, but it rankled there like a ceaseless warning and prophecy. When she reached home that day she went down to the spring in the centre of the village, and stood a long time looking at the bubbling water. It was indeed a priceless treasure; a long irrigating ditch led from it down into the bottom, where lay the cultivated fields, — many acres in wheat, barley, and vegetables. Alessandro himself had fields there from which they would harvest all they needed for the horses and their cow all winter, in case pasturage failed. If the whites took away this water, Saboba would be ruined. However, as the spring began in the very heart of the village, they could not take it without destroying the village. "And the Ravallos would surely never let that be done," thought Ramona. "While they live, it will not happen."

It was a sad day for Ramona and Alessandro when the kindly Hyers pulled up their tent-stakes and left the valley. Their intended three months had stretched into six, they had so enjoyed the climate, and the waters had seemed to do such good to Jos. But, "We ain't rich folks, yer know, not by a long ways, we ain't," said Aunt Ri; "an' we 've got pretty nigh down to where Jeff an' me 's got to begin airnin' suthin'. Ef we kin git settled 'n some o' these towns where there 's carpenterin' to be done. Jeff, he 's a master hand to thet kind o' work, though yer might n't think it; 'n' I kin airn right smart at weavin'; jest give me a good carpet-loom, 'n' I won't be beholden to nobody for vittles. I jest du love weavin'. I donno how I 've contented myself this hull year, or nigh about a year, without a loom. Jeff, he sez to me once, sez he, 'Ri, do yer think yer'd be contented in heaven without yer loom?' an' I was free to say I did n't know 's I should."

"Is it hard?" cried Ramona. "Could I learn to do it?" It was wonderful what progress in understanding and speaking English Ramona had made in these six months. She now understood nearly all that was said directly to her, though she could not follow general and confused conversation.

"Wall, 't is, an' 't ain't," said Aunt Ri. "I don't s'pose I 'm much of a jedge; fur I can't remember when I fust learned it. I know I set in the loom to weave when my feet could n't reach the floor; an' I don't remember nothin' about fust learnin' to spool 'n' warp. I 've tried to teach lots of folks; an' sum learns quick, an' some don't never learn; it 's jest 's 't strikes 'em. I should think, naow, thet you wuz one o' the kind could turn yer hand to anythin'. When we get settled in San Bernardino, if yer 'll come down thar, I 'll teach yer all I know, 'n' be glad ter. I donno 's 't 's goin' to be much uv a place for carpet-weavin' though, anywheres raound 'n this yer country; not but what thar 's plenty o' rags, but folks seems to be wearin' 'em; pooty gen'ral wear, I sh'd say. I 've seen more cloes on folks' backs hyar, thet wan't no more 'n fit for carpet-rags, than any place ever I struck. They 're dreffful sheftless lot, these yere Mexicans; 'n' the Injuns is wuss. Naow when I say Injuns, I don't never mean yeow, yer know thet. Yer ain't ever seemed to me one mite like an Injun."

4 In the concluding chapter of her book, *Century of Dishonor*, Jackson had written: "President after President has appointed commission after commision to inquire into and report upon Indian affairs, and to make suggestions as to the best methods of managing them ... These reports are bound up with the Government's Annual Reports, and that is the end of them ... yet any one of them, circulated throughout the country, read by the right-thinking, right-feeling men and women of this land, would be of itself, a 'campaign document' that would initiate a revoulution which would not subside until the Indians' wrongs were, so far as is now left possible, righted." As an added challenge to the nation's legislators she presented a copy of her book to each.

"Most of our people have n't had any chance," said Ramona. "You would n't believe if I were to tell you what things have been done to them; how they are robbed, and cheated, and turned out of their homes."

Then she told the story of Temecula, and of San Pasquale, in Spanish, to Jos, who translated it with no loss in the telling. Aunt Ri was aghast; she found no words to express her indignation.

"I don't bleeve the Guvvermunt knows anything about it!" she said. "Why, they take folks up, 'n' penetentiarize 'em fur life, back 'n Tennessee, fur things thet ain't so bad 's thet! Somebody ought ter be sent ter tell 'em 't Washington what 's goin' on hyar."

4 "I think it 's the people in Washington that have done it," said Ramona, sadly. "Is it not in Washington all the laws are made?"

"I bleeve so!" said Aunt Ri. "Ain't it, Jos? It 's Congress, ain't 't, makes the laws?"

"I bleeve so!" said Jos. "They make some, at any rate. I donno 's they make 'em all."

"It is all done by the American law," said Ramona, "all these things; nobody can help himself; for if anybody goes against the law he has to be killed or put in prison; that was what the sheriff told Alessandro, at Temecula. He felt very sorry for the Temecula people, the sheriff did; but he had to obey the law himself. Alessandro says there is n't any help."

Aunt Ri shook her head. She was not convinced "I sh'll make a business o' findin' out abaout this thing yit," she said. "I think yer hain't got the rights on 't yit. There 's cheatin' somewhere!"

"It 's all cheating!" said Ramona; "but there is n't any help for it, Aunt Ri. The Americans think it is no shame to cheat for money."

"I 'm an Ummeriken!" cried Aunt Ri; "an' Jeff Hyer, and Jos! We 're Ummerikens! 'n' we would n't cheat nobody, not ef we knowed it, not out er a dollar. We 're pore, an' I allus expect to be, but we 're above cheatin'; an' I tell you, naow, the Ummeriken people don't want any o' this cheatin' done, naow! I 'm going to ask Jeff haow 't is. Why, it 's a burnin' shame to any country! So 't is! I think something oughter be done abaout it! I would n't mind goin' myself, 'ef thar wan't anybody else!"

A seed had been sown in Aunt Ri's mind which was not destined to die for want of soil. She was hot with shame and anger, and full of impulse to do something. "I ain't nobody," she said; "I know thet well enough, — I ain't nobody nor nothin'; but I allow I 've got suthin' to say abaout the country I live in, 'n' the way things hed oughter be; or 't least Jeff hez; 'n' thet 's the same thing. I tell yer, Jos, I ain't goin' to rest, nor ter give yeou 'n' yer father no rest nuther, till yeou find aout what all this yere means she 's been tellin' us."

But sharper and closer anxieties than any connected with rights to lands and homes were pressing upon Alessandro and Ramona. All summer the baby had been slowly drooping; so slowly that it was each day possible for Ramona to deceive herself, thinking that there had been since yesterday no loss, perhaps a little gain; but looking back from the autumn to the spring, and now from the winter to the autumn, there was no doubt that she had been steadily going down. From the day of that terrible chill in the snow-storm, she had never been quite well, Ramona thought. Before that, she was strong, always strong, always beautiful and merry. Now her pinched little face was sad to see, and sometimes for hours she made a feeble wailing cry without any apparent cause. All the simple remedies that Aunt Ri had known, had failed to touch her disease; in fact, Aunt Ri from the first had been baffled in her own mind by the child's symptoms. Day after day Alessandro knelt by the cradle, his hands clasped, his face set. Hour after hour, night and day, indoors and out, he bore her in his arms, trying to give her relief. Prayer after prayer to the Virgin, to the saints, Ramona had said; and candles by the dozen, though money was now scant, she had burned before the Madonna; all in vain. At last she implored Alessandro to go to San Bernardino and see a doctor. "Find Aunt Ri," she said; "she will go with you, with Jos, and talk to him; she can make him understand. Tell Aunt Ri she seems just as she did when they were here, only weaker and thinner."

Alessandro found Aunt Ri in a sort of shanty on the outskirts of San Bernardino. "Not to rights yit," she said, — as if she ever would be. Jeff had found work; and Jos, too, had been able to do a little on pleasant days. He had made a loom and put up a loom-house for his mother, — a floor just large enough to hold the loom; rough walls, and a roof; one small square window, — that was all; but if Aunt Ri had been presented with a palace, she would not have been so well pleased. Already she had woven a rag carpet for herself, was at work on one for a neighbor, and had promised as many more as she could do before spring; the news of the arrival of a rag-carpet weaver having gone with despatch all through the lower walks of San Bernardino life. "I would n't hev bleeved they hed so many rags besides what they 're wearin'," said Aunt Ri, as sack after sack appeared at her door. Already, too, Aunt Ri had gathered up the threads of the village life; in her friendly, impressionable way she had come into relation with scores of people, and knew who was who, and what was what, and why, among them all, far better than many an old resident of the town.

When she saw Benito galloping up to her door, she sprang down from her high stool at the loom, and ran bareheaded to the gate, and before Alessandro had dismounted, cried: "Ye 're jest the man I wanted; I 've been tryin' to 'range it so 's we could go down 'n' see yer, but Jeff could n't leave the job he 's got; an' I 'm druv nigh abaout off my feet, 'n' I donno when we'd hev fetched it. How's all? Why did n't yer come in ther wagon 'n' fetch 'em 'long? I 've got heaps ter tell yer. I allowed yer had n't got the rights o' all them things. The Guvvermunt ain't on the side o' the thieves, as yer said. I knowed they could n't be; an' they 've jest sent out a man a purpose to look after things fur yer, — to take keer o' the Injuns 'n' nothin' else. Thet 's what he 's here fur. He come last month; he 's a reel nice man. I seen him 'n' talked with him a spell, last week; I 'm gwine to make his wife a rag carpet. 'N' there 's a doctor, too, to 'tend ter yer when ye 're sick, 'n' the Guvvermunt pays him; yer don't hev to pay nothin'; 'n' I tell yeow, thet's a heap o' savin', to git yer docterin' fur nuthin'!"

Aunt Ri was out of breath. Alessandro had not understood half she said. He looked about helplessly for Jos. Jos was away. In his broken English he tried to explain what Ramona had wished her to do.

"Doctor! Thet's jest what I 'm tellin' yer! There 's one here 's paid by the Guvvermunt to 'tend to all Injuns thet 's sick. I 'll go 'n' show yer ter his house. I kin tell him jest how the baby is. P'r'aps he 'll drive down 'n' see her!"

Ah! if he would! What would Majella say, should she see him enter the door bringing a doctor!

Luckily Jos returned in time to go with them to the doctor's house as interpreter. Alessandro was bewildered. He could not understand this new phase of affairs. Could it be true? As they walked along, he listened with trembling, half-incredulous hope to Jos's interpretation of Aunt Ri's voluble narrative.

The doctor was in his office. To Aunt Ri's statement of Alessandro's errand he listened indifferently, and then said, "Is he an Agency Indian?"

"A what?" exclaimed Aunt Ri.

"Does he belong to the Agency? Is his name on the Agency books?"

"No," said she; "he never heern uv any Agency till I wuz tellin' him, jest naow. We knoo him, him 'n' her, over 'n San Jacinto. He lives in Saboba. He 's never been to San Bernardino sence the Agent come aout."

"Well, is he going to put his name down on the books?" said the doctor, impatiently. "You ought to have taken him to the Agent first."

"Ain't you the Guvvermunt doctor for all Injuns?" asked Aunt Ri, wrathfully. "Thet 's what I heerd."

"Well, my good woman, you hear a great deal, I expect, that is n't true;" and the doctor laughed coarsely but not ill-naturedly, Alessandro all the time studying his face with the scrutiny of one awaiting life and death; "I am the Agency physician, and I suppose all the Indians will sooner or later come in and report themselves to the Agent; you 'd better take this man over there. What does he want now?"

Home of the agency doctor. —Illustration by Henry Sandham. Circa 1913

5 Writing on February 5, 1880, an editorial writer on the *New York Daily Tribune* commented: "Our people could travel from the Mississippi river to the Pacific without fear of molestation. But one day we created a new department — that of the Interior — and the Indian Bureau was placed in that department. Then came the Indian ring. There was 'millions in it.' The Indian Bureau became a great political machine, wielding an immense patronage and expending large amounts of public money, now no political party would wish to give it up. The Secretary of the Interior recently said: 'I will not consider the Indian policy in any other way than that of *expediency.*'"

Aunt Ri began to explain the baby's case. Cutting her short, the doctor said, "Yes, yes, I understand. I 'll give him something that will help her;" and going into an inner room, he brought out a bottle of dark-colored liquid, wrote a few lines of prescription, and handed it to Alessandro, saying, "That will do her good, I guess."

"Thanks, Señor, thanks," said Alessandro.

The doctor stared. "That 's the first Indian 's said 'Thank you' in this office," he said. "You tell the Agent you 've brought him a *rara avis.*"

"What 's that, Jos?" said Aunt Ri, as they went out.

"Donno!" said Jos. "I don't like thet man, anyhow, mammy. He 's no good."

Alessandro looked at the bottle of medicine like one in a dream. Would it make the baby well? Had it indeed been given to him by that great Government in Washington? Was he to be protected now? Could this man, who had been sent out to take care of Indians, get back his San Pasquale farm for him? Alessandro's brain was in a whirl.

From the doctor's office they went to the Agent's house. Here, Aunt Ri felt herself more at home.

"I 've brought ye thet Injun I wuz tellin' ye uv," she said, with a wave of her hand towards Alessandro. "We 've ben ter ther doctor's to git some meteen fur his baby. She 's reel sick, I 'm afeerd."

The Agent sat down at his desk, opened a large ledger, saying as he did so, "The man 's never been here before, has he?"

"No," said Aunt Ri.

"What is his name?"

Jos gave it, and the Agent began to write it in the book. "Stop him!" cried Alessandro, agitatedly, to Jos. "Don't let him write, till I know what he puts my name in his book for!"

"Wait," said Jos. "He does n't want you to write his name in that book. He wants to know what it 's put there for."

Wheeling his chair with a look of suppressed impatience, yet trying to speak kindly, the Agent said: "There 's no making these Indians understand anything. They seem to think if I have their names in my book, it gives me some power over them."

"Wall, don't it?" said the direct-minded Aunt Ri. "Hain't yer got any power over 'em? If yer hain't got it over them, who have yer got it over? What yer goin' to do for 'em?"

The Agent laughed in spite of himself. "Well, Aunt Ri," — she was already "Aunt Ri" to the Agent's boys, — "that 's just the trouble with this Agency. It is very different from what it would be if I had all my Indians on a reservation."

Alessandro understood the words "my Indians."
5 He had heard them before.

"What does he mean by his Indians, Jos?" he asked fiercely. "I will not have my name in his book if it makes me his."

When Jos reluctantly interpreted this, the Agent lost his temper. "That 's all the use there is trying to do anything with them! Let him go, then, if he does n't want any help from the Government!"

"Oh, no, no!" cried Aunt Ri. "Yeow jest explain it to Jos, an' he 'll make him understand."

Alessandro's face had darkened. All this seemed to him exceedingly suspicious. Could it be possible that Aunt Ri and Jos, the first whites except Mr. Hartsel he had ever trusted, were deceiving him? No; that was impossible. But they themselves might be deceived. That they were simple and ignorant, Alessandro well knew. "Let us go!" he said. "I do not wish to sign any paper."

"Naow don't be a fool, will yeow? Yeow ain't signin' a thing!" said Aunt Ri. "Jos, yeow tell him I say there ain't anythin' a bindin' him,, hevin' his name 'n thet book. It's only so the Agent kin know what Injuns wants help, 'n' where they air. Ain't thet so?" she added, turning to the Agent. "Tell him he can't hev the Agency doctor, ef he ain't on the Agency books."

Not have the doctor? Give up this precious medicine which might save his baby's life? No! he could not do that. Majella would say, let the name be written, rather than that.

"Let him write the name, then," said Alessandro, doggedly; but he went out of the room feeling as if he had put a chain around his neck.

Chapter XXIII

THE medicine did the baby no good. In fact, it did her harm. She was too feeble for violent remedies. In a week, Alessandro appeared again at the Agency doctor's door. This time he had come with a request which to his mind seemed not unreasonable. He had brought Baba for the doctor to ride. Could the doctor then refuse to go to Saboba? Baba would carry him there in three hours, and it would be like a cradle all the way. Alessandro's name was in the Agency books. It was for this he had written it, — for this and nothing else, — to save the baby's life. Having thus enrolled himself as one of the Agency Indians, he had a claim on this the Agency doctor. And that his application might be all in due form, he took with him the Agency interpreter. He had had a misgiving, before, that Aunt Ri's kindly volubility had not been well timed. Not one unnecessary word, was Alessandro's motto.

To say that the Agency doctor was astonished at being requested to ride thirty miles to prescribe for an ailing Indian baby, would be a mild statement of the doctor's emotion. He could hardly keep from laughing, when it was made clear to him that this was what the Indian father expected.

"Good Lord!" he said, turning to a crony who chanced to be lounging in the office. "Listen to that beggar, will you? I wonder what he thinks the Government pays me a year for doctoring Indians!"

Alessandro listened so closely it attracted the doctor's attention. "Do you understand English?" he asked sharply.

"A very little, Señor," replied Alessandro.

The doctor would be more careful in his speech, then. But he made it most emphatically clear that the thing Alessandro had asked was not only out of the question, but preposterous. Alessandro pleaded. For the child's sake he could do it. The horse was at the door; there was no such horse in San Bernardino County; he went like the wind, and one would not know he was in motion, it was so easy. Would not the doctor come down and look at the horse? Then he would see what it would be like to ride him.

1 While visiting Saboba, Jackson expressed a desire to see an Indian home. Mary Sheriff, a school teacher who became the author's friend and confidant, later recalled the visit. "A young and rather pretty Indian woman invited us to enter. Her baby was ill and she had it in just such a cradle as Mrs. Jackson afterwards described in *Ramona.* The mother said she feared the baby would die. Then with quivering lips, she said, 'We sent to San Bernardino for a doctor to come to the village to see if he could not cure my little one, but he refused. He told my husband to give the medicine he gave him and if she did not get better to bring her to San Bernardino but she is too ill to bear the journey.' Mrs. Jackson's eyes flashed fire as she questioned the woman to make sure the doctor understood how sick the child was when he refused to come."

That night Sheriff, who was sharing her room, realized that her guest was wide awake. "I grew uneasy," she recalled, and asked Mrs. Jackson if she was ill. 'No,' she said, 'but when I close my eyes, I see that poor suffering baby that might get well if the doctor had a heart.'"

The burial scene in the 1910 Biograph production of *Ramona* which starred Mary Pickford and H.B. Walthall.

"Oh, I've seen plenty of your Indian ponies," said the doctor. "I know they can run."

Alessandro lingered. He could not give up this last hope. The tears came into his eyes. "It is our only child, Señor," he said. "It will take you but six hours in all. My wife counts the moments till you come! If the child dies, she will die."

"No! no!" The doctor was weary of being importuned. "Tell the man it is impossible! I'd soon have my hands full, if I began to go about the country this way. They'd be sending for me down to Agua Caliente next, and bringing up their ponies to carry me."

"He will not go?" asked Alessandro.

The interpreter shook his head. "He cannot," he said.

Without a word Alessandro left the room. Presently he returned. "Ask him if he will come for money?" he said. "I have gold at home. I will pay him, what the white men pay him."

"Tell him no man of any color could pay me for going sixty miles!" said the doctor.

And Alessandro departed again, walking so slowly, however, that he heard the coarse laugh, and the words, "Gold! Looked like it, didn't he?" which followed his departure from the room.

When Ramona saw him returning alone, she wrung her hands. Her heart seemed breaking. The baby had lain in a sort of stupor since noon; she was
1 plainly worse, and Ramona had been going from the door to the cradle, from the cradle to the door, for an hour, looking each moment for the hoped-for aid. It had not once crossed her mind that the doctor would not come. She had accepted in much fuller faith than Alessandro the account of the appointment by the Government of these two men to look after the Indians' interests. What else could their coming mean, except that, at last, the Indians were to have justice? She thought, in her simplicity, that the doctor must have died, since Alessandro was riding home alone.

"He would not come!" said Alessandro, as he threw himself off his horse, wearily.

"Would not!" cried Ramona. "Would not! Did you not say the Government had sent him to be the doctor for Indians?"

"That was what they said," he replied. "You see it is a lie, like the rest! But I offered him gold, and he would not come then. The child must die, Majella!"

"She shall not die!" cried Ramona. "We will carry her to him!" The thought struck them both as an inspiration. Why had they not thought of it before? "You can fasten the cradle on Baba's back, and he will go so gently, she will think it is but play; and I will walk by her side, or you, all the way!" she continued. "And we can sleep at Aunt Ri's house. Oh, why, why did we not do it before? Early in the morning we will start."

All through the night they sat watching the little

creature. If they had ever seen death, they would have known that there was no hope for the child. But how should Ramona and Alessandro know?

The sun rose bright and warm. Before it was up, the cradle was ready, ingeniously strapped on Baba's back. When the baby was placed in it, she smiled. "The first smile she has given for days," cried Ramona. "Oh, the air itself will do good to her! Let me walk by her first! Come, Baba! Dear Baba!" and Ramona stepped almost joyfully by the horse's side, Alessandro riding Benito. As they paced along, their eyes never leaving the baby's face, Ramona said, in a low tone, "Alessandro, I am almost afraid to tell you what I have done. I took the little Jesus out of the Madonna's arms and hid it! Did you never hear, that if you do that, the Madonna will grant you anything, to get him back again in her arms? Did you ever hear of it?"

"Never!" exclaimed Alessandro, with horror in his tone. "Never, Majella! How dared you?"

"I dare anything now!" said Ramona. "I have been thinking to do it for some days, and to tell her she could not have him any more till she gave me back the baby well and strong; but I knew I could not have courage to sit and look at her all lonely without him in her arms, so I did not do it. But now we are to be away, I thought, that is the time; and I told her, 'When we come back with our baby well, you shall have your little Jesus again, too; now, Holy Mother, you go with us, and make the doctor cure our baby!' Oh, I have heard, many times, women tell the Señora they had done this, and always they got what they wanted. Never will she let the Jesus be out of her arms more than three weeks before she will grant any prayer one can make. It was that way she brought you to me, Alessandro. I never before told you. I was afraid. I think she had brought you sooner, but I could keep the little Jesus hid from her only at night. In the day I could not, because the Señora would see. So she did not miss him so much; else she had brought you quicker."

"But, Majella," said the logical Alessandro, "it was because I could not leave my father that I did not come. As soon as he was buried, I came."

"If it had not been for the Virgin, you would never have come at all," said Ramona, confidently.

For the first hour of this sad journey it seemed as if the child were really rallying; the air, the sunlight, the novel motion, the smiling mother by her side, the big black horses she had already learned to love, all roused her to an animation she had not shown for days. But it was only the last flicker of the expiring flame. The eyes drooped, closed; a strange pallor came over the face. Alessandro saw it first. He was now walking, Ramona riding Benito. "Majella!" he cried, in a tone which told her all.

In a second she was at the baby's side, with a cry which smote the dying child's consciousness. Once more the eyelids lifted; she knew her mother; a swift spasm shook the little frame; a convulsion as of agony swept over the face, then it was at peace. Majella's shrieks were heart-rending. Fiercely she put Alessandro away from her, as he strove to caress her. She stretched her arms up towards the sky. "I have killed her! I have killed her!" she cried. "Oh, let me die!"

Slowly Alessandro turned Baba's head homeward again.

"Oh, give her to me! Let her lie on my breast! I will hold her warm!" gasped Ramona.

Silently Alessandro laid the body in her arms. He had not spoken since his first cry of alarm. If Ramona had looked at him, she would have forgotten her grief for her dead child. Alessandro's face seemed turned to stone.

When they reached the house, Ramona, laying the child on the bed, ran hastily to a corner of the room, and lifting the deerskin, drew from its hiding-place the little wooden Jesus. With tears streaming, she laid it again in the Madonna's arms, and flinging herself on her knees, sobbed out prayers for forgiveness. Alessandro stood at the foot of the bed, his arms folded, his eyes riveted on the child. Soon he went out, still without speaking. Presently Ramona heard the sound of a saw. She groaned aloud, and her tears flowed faster: Alessandro was making the baby's coffin. Mechanically she rose, and, moving like one half paralyzed, she dressed the little one in fresh white clothes for the burial; then laying her in the cradle, she spread over it the beautiful lace-wrought altar-cloth. As she adjusted its folds, her mind was carried back to the time when she embroidered it, sitting on the Señora's veranda; the song of the finches, the linnets; the voice and smile of Felipe; Alessandro sitting on the steps, drawing divine music from his violin. Was that she, — that girl who sat there weaving the fine threads in the beautiful altar-cloth? Was it a hundred years ago? Was it another world? Was it Alessandro yonder, driving those nails into a coffin? How the blows rang, louder and louder! The air seemed deafening full of sound. With her hands pressed to her temples, Ramona sank to the floor. A merciful unconsciousness set her free, for an interval, from her anguish.

When she opened her eyes, she was lying on the bed. Alessandro had lifted her and laid her there, making no effort to rouse her. He thought she would die too; and even that thought did not stir him from his lethargy. When she opened her eyes, and looked at him, he did not speak. She closed them. He did not move. Presently she opened them again. "I heard you out there," she said.

"Yes," he replied. "It is done." And he pointed to a little box of rough boards by the side of the cradle.

"Is Majella ready to go to the mountain now?" he asked.

"Yes, Alessandro, I am ready," she said.

"We will hide forever," he said.

"It makes no difference," she replied.

The Saboba women did not know what to think of Ramona now. She had never come into sympathetic relation with them, as she had with the women of San Pasquale. Her intimacy with the Hyers had been a barrier the Saboba people could not surmount. No one could be on such terms with whites, and be at heart an Indian, they thought; so they held aloof from Ramona. But now in her bereavement they gathered round her. They wept at sight of the dead baby's face, lying in its tiny white coffin. Ramona had covered the box with white cloth, and the lace altar-cloth thrown over it fell in folds to the floor. "Why does not this mother weep? Is she like the whites, who have no heart?" said the Saboba mothers among themselves; and they were embarrassed before her, and knew not what to say. Ramona perceived it, but had no life in her to speak to them. Benumbing terrors, which were worse than her grief, were crowding Ramona's heart now. She had offended the Virgin; she had committed a blasphemy: in one short hour the Virgin had punished her, had smitten her child dead before her eyes. And now Alessandro was going mad; hour by hour Ramona fancied she saw changes in him. What form would the Virgin's vengeance take next? Would she let Alessandro become a raging madman, and finally kill both himself and her? That seemed to Ramona the most probable fate in store for them. When the funeral was over, and they returned to their desolate home, at the sight of the empty cradle Ramona broke down.

"Oh, take me away, Alessandro! Anywhere! I don't care where! anywhere, so it is not here!" she cried.

"Would Majella be afraid, now, on the high mountain, the place I told her of?" he said.

"No!" she replied earnestly. "No! I am afraid of nothing! Only take me away!"

A gleam of wild delight flitted across Alessandro's face. "It is well," he said. "My Majella, we will go to the mountain; we will be safe there."

The same fierce restlessness which took possession of him at San Pasquale again showed itself in his every act. His mind was unceasingly at work, planning the details of their move and of the new life. He mentioned them one after another to Ramona. They could not take both horses; feed would be scanty there, and there would be no need of two horses. The cow also they must give up. Alessandro would kill her, and the meat, dried, would last them for a long time. The wagon he hoped he could sell; and he would buy a few sheep; sheep and goats could live well in these heights to which they were going. Safe at last! Oh, yes, very safe; not only against whites, who, because the little valley was so small and bare, would not desire it, but against Indians also. For the Indians, silly things, had a terror of the upper heights of San Jacinto; they believed the Devil lived there, and money would not hire one of the Saboba Indians to go so high as this valley which Alessandro had discovered. Fiercely he gloated over each one of these features of safety in their hiding-place. "The first time I saw it, Majella,—I believe the saints led me there,—I said, it is a hiding-place. And then I never thought I would be in want of such,—of a place to keep my Majella safe! safe! Oh, my Majel!" And he clasped her to his breast with a terrifying passion.

For an Indian to sell a horse and wagon in the San Jacinto valley was not an easy thing, unless he would give them away. Alessandro had hard work to give civil answers to the men who wished to buy Benito and the wagon for quarter of their value. He knew they would not have dared to so much as name such prices to a white man. Finally Ramona, who had felt unconquerable misgivings as to the wisdom of thus irrevocably parting from their most valuable possessions, persuaded him to take both horses and wagon to San Bernardino, and offer them to the Hyers to use for the winter.

It would be just the work for Jos, to keep him in the open air, if he could get teaming to do; she was sure he would be thankful for the chance. "He is as fond of the horses as we are ourselves, Alessandro," she said. "They would be well cared for; and then, if we did not like living on the mountain, we could have the horses and wagon again when we came down, or Jos could sell them for us in San Bernardino. Nobody could see Benito and Baba working together, and not want them."

"Majella is wiser than the dove!" cried Alessandro. "She has seen what is the best thing to do. I will take them."

When he was ready to set off, he implored Ramona to go with him; but with a look of horror she refused. "Never," she cried, "one step on that accursed road! I will never go on that road again unless it is to be carried, as we brought her, dead."

Neither did Ramona wish to see Aunt Ri. Her sympathy would be intolerable, spite of all its affectionate kindliness. "Tell her I love her," she said, "but I do not want to see a human being yet; next year perhaps we will go down,—if there is any other way besides that road."

Aunt Ri was deeply grieved. She could not understand Ramona's feeling. It rankled deep. "I allow I'd never hev bleeved it uv her, never," she said. "I shan't never think she wuz quite right 'n her head, to do 't! I allow we shan't never set eyes on ter her, Jos. I've got jest thet feelin' abaout it. 'Pears like she'd gone klar out 'er this yer world inter anuther."

The majestic bulwark of San Jacinto Mountain looms in the southern horizon of the San Bernardino valley. It was in full sight from the door of the little shanty in which Aunt Ri's carpet-loom stood.

As she sat there hour after hour, sometimes seven hours to the day, working the heavy treadle, and slipping the shuttle back and forth, she gazed with tender yearnings at the solemn, shining summit. When sunset colors smote it, it glowed like fire; on cloudy days, it was lost in the clouds.

"'Pears like 't was next door to heaven, up there, Jos," Aunt Ri would say. "I can't tell yer the feelin' 't comes over me, to look up t' it, ever sence I knowed she wuz there. 'T shines enuf to put yer eyes aout, sometimes; I allow 't ain't so light 's thet when you air into 't; 't can't be; ther could n't nobody stan' it, ef 't wuz. I allow 't must be like bein' dead, Jos, don't yer think so, to be livin' thar? He sed ther could n't nobody git to 'em. Nobody ever seed the place but hisself. He found it a huntin'. Thar 's water thar, 'n' thet 's abaout all that is, 's fur 's I cud make aout; I allow we shan't never see her agin."

The horses and the wagon were indeed a godsend to Jos. It was the very thing he had been longing for; the only sort of work he was as yet strong enough to do, and there was plenty of it to be had in San Bernardino. But the purchase of a wagon suitable for the purpose was at present out of their power; the utmost Aunt Ri had hoped to accomplish was to have, at the end of a year, a sufficient sum laid up to buy one. They had tried in vain to exchange their heavy emigrant-wagon for one suitable for light work "'Pears like I 'd die o' shame," said Aunt Ri, "sometimes when I ketch myself er thinkin' what luck et 's ben to Jos, er gettin' thet Injun's hosses an' waggin. But ef Jos keeps on, airnin' ez much ez he hez so fur, he 's goin' ter pay the Injun part on 't, when he cums. I allow ter Jos 't ain't no more 'n fair. Why, them hosses, they 'll dew good tew days' work 'n one. I never see sech hosses; 'n' they 're jest like kittens; they 've ben drefful pets, I allow. I know she set all the world, 'n' more tew, by thet nigh one. He wuz hern, ever sence she wuz a child. Pore thing,— 'pears like she hed n't hed no chance!"

Alessandro had put off, from day to day, the killing of the cow. It went hard with him to slaughter the faithful creature, who knew him, and came towards him at the first sound of his voice. He had pastured her, since the baby died, in a cañon about three miles northeast of the village,—a lovely green cañon with oak-trees and a running brook. It was here that he had thought of building his house if
they had stayed in Saboba. But Alessandro laughed 2
bitterly to himself now, as he recalled that dream. Already the news had come to Saboba that a company had been formed for the settling up of the San Jacinto valley; the Ravallo brothers had sold to this company a large grant of land. The white ranchmen in the valley were all fencing in their lands; no more free running of stock. The Saboba people were too poor to build miles of fencing; they must soon give up keeping stock; and the next

2 At Jackson's insistence, the twenty-year-old grandson of the Saboba captain, stated the case of his people to the Secretary of the Interior:

> San Jacinto, Cal., May 29, 1882
> Dear Mr. Teller:
>
> Dear Sir:
>
> At the request of my friends, I write you in regard to the land of my people.
>
> More than one hundred years ago, my great grandfather who was chief of his tribe, settled with his people in the San Jacinto Valley. The people have always been peaceful, never caring for war, and have welcomed Americans into the valley.
>
> Some years ago a land grant was given to the Estudillos by the Mexican Government. The first survey did not take any of the land claimed by the Indians; but four years ago a new survey was made taking in all the little farms, the stream of water and the village. Upon this survey the U.S. Government gave a patent. It seems very hard for us to be driven from our homes that we love as much as other people do theirs, and this danger is at our doors now, for the grant is being divided and the village and land will be assigned to some of the present owners of the grant.
>
> And now, dear sir, after this statement of facts, I for my people (I ask nothing for myself), appeal to you for help.
>
> Cannot you find some way to right this wrong done to a quiet and industrious people?
>
> Hoping that we may have justice done us, I am
>
> Respectfully yours,
> José Jesus Castillo

Henry Teller promised to "take the matter under advisement," which meant that nothing happened. Jackson then approached S.S. Lawson, the local Indian agent. Lawson resented her interference and made it eminently clear that he had no intention of locking horns with local dignitaries.

thing would be that they would be driven out, like the people of Temecula. It was none too soon that he had persuaded Majella to flee to the mountain. There, at least, they could live and die in peace, — a poverty-stricken life, and the loneliest of deaths; but they would have each other. It was well the baby had died; she was saved all this misery. By the time she had grown to be a woman, if she had lived, there would be no place in all the country where an Indian could find refuge. Brooding over such thoughts as these, Alessandro went up into the cañon one morning. It must be done. Everything was ready for their move; it would take many days to carry even their few possessions up the steep mountain trail to their new home; the pony which had replaced Benito and Baba could not carry a heavy load. While this was being done, Ramona would dry the beef which would be their supply of meat for many months. Then they would go.

At noon he came down with the first load of the meat, and Ramona began cutting it into long strips, as is the Mexican fashion of drying. Alessandro returned for the remainder. Early in the afternoon, as Ramona went to and fro about her work, she saw a group of horsemen riding from house to house, in the upper part of the village; women came running out excitedly from each house as the horsemen left it; finally one of them darted swiftly up the hill to Ramona. "Hide it! hide it!" she cried, breathless; "hide the meat! It is Merrill's men, from the end of the valley. They have lost a steer, and they say we stole it. They found the place, with blood on it, where it was killed; and they say we did it. Oh, hide the meat! They took all that Fernando had; and it was his own, that he bought; he did not know anything about their steer!"

"I shall not hide it!" cried Ramona, indignantly. "It is our own cow. Alessandro killed it to-day."

"They won't believe you!" said the woman, in distress. "They'll take it all away. Oh, hide some of it!" And she dragged a part of it across the floor, and threw it under the bed, Ramona standing by, stupefied.

Before she had spoken again, the forms of the galloping riders darkened the doorway; the foremost of them, leaping off his horse, exclaimed: "By God! here's the rest of it. If they ain't the damnedest impudent thieves! Look at this woman, cutting it up! Put that down, will you? We'll save you the trouble of dryin' our meat for us, besides killin' it! Fork over, now, every bit you've got, you ——." And he called Ramona by a vile epithet.

Every drop of blood left Ramona's face. Her eyes blazed, and she came forward with the knife uplifted in her hand. "Out of my house, you dogs of the white color!" she said. "This meat is our own; my husband killed the creature but this morning."

Her tone and bearing surprised them. There were six of the men, and they had all swarmed into the little room.

"I say, Merrill," said one of them, "hold on; the squaw says her husband only jest killed it to-day. It might be theirs."

Ramona turned on him like lightning. "Are you liars, you all," she cried, "that you think I lie? I tell you the meat is ours; and there is not an Indian in this village would steal cattle!"

A derisive shout of laughter from all the men greeted this speech; and at that second, the leader, seeing the mark of blood where the Indian woman had dragged the meat across the ground, sprang to the bed, and lifting the deerskin, pointed with a sneer to the beef hidden there. "Perhaps, when you know Injuns 's well 's I do," he said, "you won't be for believin' all they say! What's she got it hid under the bed for, if it was their own cow?" and he stooped to drag the meat out. "Give us a hand here, Jake!"

"If you touch it, I will kill you!" cried Ramona, beside herself with rage; and she sprang between the men, her uplifted knife gleaming.

"Hoity-toity!" cried Jake, stepping back; "that's a handsome squaw when she's mad! Say, boys, let's leave her some of the meat. She was n't to blame; of course, she believes what her husband told her."

"You go to grass for a soft-head, you Jake!" muttered Merrill, as he dragged the meat out from beneath the bed.

"What is all this?" said a deep voice in the door; and Ramona, turning, with a glad cry, saw Alessandro standing there, looking on, with an expression which, even in her own terror and indignation, gave her a sense of dread, it was so icily defiant. He had his hand on his gun. "What is all this?" he repeated. He knew very well.

"It's that Temecula man," said one of the men, in a low tone, to Merrill. "If I'd known 't was his house, I would n't have let you come here. You're up the wrong tree, sure!"

Merrill dropped the meat he was dragging over the floor, and turned to confront Alessandro's eyes. His countenance fell. Even he saw that he had made a mistake. He began to speak. Alessandro interrupted him. Alessandro could speak forcibly in Spanish. Pointing to his pony, which stood at the door with a package on its back, the remainder of the meat rolled in the hide, he said: "There is the remainder of the beef. I killed the creature this morning, in the cañon. I will take Señor Merrill to the place, if he wishes it. Señor Merrill's steer was killed down in the willows yonder, yesterday."

"That's so!" cried the men, gathering around him. "How did you know? Who did it?"

Alessandro made no reply. He was looking at Ramona. She had flung her shawl over her head, as the other woman had done, and the two were cowering in the corner, their faces turned away. Ramona dared not look on; she felt sure Alessandro would kill some one. But this was not the type of outrage that roused Alessandro to dangerous wrath. He even felt a certain enjoyment in the discomfiture of the self-constituted *posse* of searchers for stolen goods. To all their questions in regard to the stolen steer, he maintained silence. He would not open his lips. At last, angry, ashamed, with a volley of coarse oaths at him for his obstinacy, they rode away. Alessandro went to Ramona's side. She was trembling. Her hands were like ice. 3

"Let us go to the mountain to-night!" she gasped. "Take me where I need never see a white face again!"

A melancholy joy gleamed in Alessandro's eyes. Ramona, at last, felt as he did.

"I would not dare to leave Majella there alone, while there is no house," he said; "and I must go and come many times, before all the things can be carried."

"It will be less danger there than here, Alessandro," said Ramona, bursting into violent weeping as she recalled the insolent leer with which the man Jake had looked at her. "Oh! I cannot stay here!"

"It will not be many days, my Majel. I will borrow Fernando's pony, to take double at once; then we can go sooner."

"Who was it stole that man's steer?" said Ramona. "Why did you not tell them? They looked as if they would kill you."

"It was that Mexican that lives in the bottom, José Castro. I myself came on him, cutting the steer up. He said it was his; but I knew very well by the way he spoke, he was lying. But why should I tell? They think only Indians will steal cattle. I can tell them, the Mexicans steal more."

"I told them there was not an Indian in this village would steal cattle," said Ramona, indignantly.

"That was not true, Majella," replied Alessandro, sadly. "When they are very hungry, they will steal a heifer or steer. They lose many themselves, and they say it is not so much harm to take one when they can get it. This man Merrill, they say, branded twenty steers for his own, last spring, when he knew they were Saboba cattle!"

"Why did they not make him give them up?" cried Ramona.

"Did not Majella see to-day why they can do nothing? There is no help for us, Majella, only to hide; that is all we can do!"

A new terror had entered into Ramona's life; she dared not tell it to Alessandro; she hardly put it into words in her thoughts. But she was haunted by the face of the man Jake, as by a vision of evil, and on one pretext and another she contrived to secure the presence of some one of the Indian women in her house whenever Alessandro was away. Every day she saw the man riding past. Once he had galloped up to the open door, looked in, spoken in a friendly way to her, and ridden on. Ramona's instinct was right. Jake was merely biding his time. He had made up his mind to settle in the San Jacinto

Loretta Young and Don Ameche, as Ramona and Alessandro, confront the bad guys in the 1936 20th Century-Fox production.

3 Acts of violence against Indians took many forms in Southern California but one of the most common was the rape of Indian girls and women. Contemporary documents such as newspapers and diaries indicate that this was a frequent occurrence.

Karen Grant Thomas portrayed Ramona and Tom Marian was Farrar in the 1986 Hemet Pageant.
—Courtesy of the Ramona Pageant Asso., Inc.

4 Less violent than rape, but nonetheless a form of sexual as well as emotional abuse, was the practice of Anglo males taking Indian women as temporary wives. Southern California had its share of "squaw men"— the popular frontier term applied to those who took an Indian mistress until a suitable white wife could be found or until it was time to move on. Frequent rapes as well as these transitory relationships caused a crisis within the Indian communities. One Indian agent wrote, "It is almost impossible for an Indian to get a wife unless he takes one second hand."

4 valley, at least for a few years, and he wished to have an Indian woman come to live with him and keep his house. Over in Santa Ysabel, his brother had lived in that way with an Indian mistress for three years; and when he sold out, and left Santa Ysabel, he had given the woman a hundred dollars and a little house for herself and her child. And she was not only satisfied, but held herself, in consequence of this temporary connection with a white man, much above her Indian relatives and friends. When an Indian man had wished to marry her, she had replied scornfully that she would never marry an Indian; she might marry another white man, but an Indian,—never. Nobody had held his brother in any less esteem for this connection; it was quite the way in the country. And if Jake could induce this handsomest squaw he had ever seen, to come and live with him in a similar fashion, he would consider himself a lucky man, and also think he was doing a good thing for the squaw. It was all very clear and simple in his mind; and when, seeing Ramona walking alone in the village one morning, he overtook her, and walking by her side began to sound her on the subject, he had small misgivings as to the result. Ramona trembled as he approached her. She walked faster, and would not look at him; but he, in his ignorance, misinterpreted these signs egregiously.

"Are you married to your husband?" he finally said. "It is but a poor place he gives you to live in. If you will come and live with me, you shall have the best house in the valley, as good as the Ravallos'; and—" Jake did not finish his sentence. With a cry which haunted his memory for years, Ramona sprang from his side as if to run; then, halting suddenly, she faced him, her eyes like javelins, her breath coming fast. "Beast!" she said, and spat towards him; then turned and fled to the nearest house, where she sank on the floor and burst into tears, saying that the man below there in the road had been rude to her. Yes, the women said, he was a bad man; they all knew it. Of this Ramona said no word to Alessandro. She dared not; she believed he would kill Jake.

When the furious Jake confided to his friend Merrill his repulse, and the indignity accompanying it, Merrill only laughed at him, and said: "I could have told you better than to try that woman. She 's married, fast enough. There 's plenty you can get, though, if you want 'em. They 're first-rate about a house, and jest 's faithful 's dogs. You can trust 'em with every dollar you 've got."

From this day, Ramona never knew an instant's peace or rest till she stood on the rim of the refuge valley, high on San Jacinto. Then, gazing around, looking up at the lofty pinnacles above, which seemed to pierce the sky, looking down upon the world,—it seemed the whole world, so limitless it stretched away at her feet,—feeling that infinite unspeakable sense of nearness to Heaven, remoteness from earth which comes only on mountain heights, she drew in a long breath of delight, and cried: "At last! at last, Alessandro! Here we are safe! This is freedom! This is joy!"

"Can Majella be content?" he asked.

"I can almost be glad, Alessandro!" she cried, inspired by the glorious scene. "I dreamed not it was like this!"

It was a wondrous valley. The mountain seemed to have been cleft to make it. It lay near midway to the top, and ran transversely on the mountain's side, its western or southwestern end being many feet lower than the eastern. Both the upper and lower ends were closed by piles of rocks and tangled fallen trees; the rocky summit of the mountain itself made the southern wall; the northern was a spur, or ridge, nearly vertical, and covered thick with pine-trees. A man might roam years on the mountain and not find this cleft. At the upper end gushed out a crystal spring, which trickled rather than ran, in a bed of marshy green, the entire length of the valley, disappeared in the rocks at the lower end, and came out no more; many times Alessandro had searched for it lower down, but could find no trace of it. During the summer, when he was hunting with Jeff, he had several times climbed the wall and descended it on the inner side, to see if the rivulet still ran; and, to his joy, had found it the same in July as in January. Drought could not harm it, then. What salvation in such a spring! And the water was pure and sweet as if it came from the skies.

A short distance off was another ridge or spur of the mountain, widening out into almost a plateau. This was covered with acorn-bearing oaks; and under them were flat stones worn into hollows, where bygone generations of Indians had ground the nuts into meal. Generations long bygone indeed, for it was not in the memory of the oldest now living, that Indians had ventured so high up as this on San Jacinto. It was held to be certain death to climb to its summit, and foolhardy in the extreme to go far up its sides.

There was exhilaration in the place. It brought healing to both Alessandro and Ramona. Even the bitter grief for the baby's death was soothed. She did not seem so far off, since they had come so much nearer to the sky. They lived at first in a tent; no time to build a house, till the wheat and vegetables were planted. Alessandro was surprised, when he came to the ploughing, to see how much good land he had. The valley thrust itself, in inlets and coves, into the very rocks of its southern wall; lovely sheltered nooks these were, where he hated to wound the soft, flower-filled sward with his plough. As soon as the planting was done, he began to fell trees for the house. No mournful gray adobe this time, but walls of hewn pine, with half the bark left on; alternate yellow and brown, as gay as if glad hearts had devised it. The roof, of thatch, tule, and yucca-stalks, double laid and thick, was carried out several feet in front of the house, making a sort of bower-like veranda, supported

—Illustration by Henry Sandham. Circa 1883.

A Saboba Indian woman. —Photograph by George Wharton James. Circa 1911.

by young fir-tree stems, left rough. Once more Ramona would sit under a thatch with birds'-nests in it. A little corral for the sheep, and a rough shed for the pony, and the home was complete: far the prettiest home they had ever had. And here, in the sunny veranda, when autumn came, sat Ramona, plaiting out of fragrant willow twigs a cradle. The one over which she had wept such bitter tears in the valley, they had burned the night before they left their Saboba home. It was in early autumn she sat plaiting this cradle. The ground around was strewn with wild grapes drying; the bees were feasting on them in such clouds that Ramona rose frequently from her work to drive them away, saying, as she did so, "Good bees, make our honey from something else; we gain nothing if you drain our grapes for it; we want these grapes for the winter;" and as she spoke, her imagination sped fleetly forward to the winter. The Virgin must have forgiven her, to give her again the joy of a child in her arms. Ay, a joy! Spite of poverty, spite of danger, spite of all that cruelty and oppression could do, it would still be a joy to hold her child in her arms.

The baby was born before winter came. An old Indian woman, the same whose house they had hired in Saboba, had come up to live with Ramona. She was friendless now, her daughter having died, and she thankfully came to be as a mother to Ramona. She was ignorant and feeble; but Ramona saw in her always the picture of what her own mother might perchance be, wandering, suffering, she knew not what or where; and her yearning, filial instinct found sad pleasure in caring for this lonely, childless, aged one.

Ramona was alone with her on the mountain at the time of the baby's birth. Alessandro had gone to the valley, to be gone two days; but Ramona felt no fear. When Alessandro returned, and she laid the child in his arms, she said with a smile, radiant once more, like the old smiles, "See, beloved! The Virgin has forgiven me; she has given us a daughter again!"

But Alessandro did not smile. Looking scrutinizingly into the baby's face, he sighed, and said, "Alas, Majella, her eyes are like mine, not yours!"

"I am glad of it," cried Ramona. "I was glad the first minute I saw it."

He shook his head. "It is an ill fate to have the eyes of Alessandro," he said. "They look ever on woe;" and he laid the baby back on Ramona's breast, and stood gazing sadly at her.

"Dear Alessandro," said Ramona, "it is a sin to always mourn. Father Salvierderra said if we repined under our crosses, then a heavier cross would be laid on us. Worse things would come."

"Yes," he said. "That is true. Worse things will come." And he walked away, with his head sunk deep on his breast.

Chapter XXIV

THERE was no real healing for Alessandro. His hurts had gone too deep. His passionate heart, ever secretly brooding on the wrongs he had borne, the hopeless outlook for his people in the future, and most of all on the probable destitution and suffering in store for Ramona, consumed itself as by hidden fires. Speech, complaint, active antagonism, might have saved him; but all these were foreign to his self-contained, reticent, repressed nature. Slowly, so slowly that Ramona could not tell on what hour or what day her terrible fears first changed to an even more terrible certainty, his brain gave way, and the thing, in dread of which he had cried out the morning they left San Pasquale, came upon him. Strangely enough, and mercifully, now that it had really come, he did not know it. He knew that he suddenly came to his consciousness sometimes, and
1 discovered himself in strange and unexplained situations; had no recollection of what had happened for an interval of time, longer or shorter. But he thought it was only a sort of sickness; he did not know that during those intervals his acts were the acts of a madman; never violent, aggressive, or harmful to any one; never destructive. It was piteous to see how in these intervals his delusions were always shaped by the bitterest experiences of his life. Sometimes he fancied that the Americans were pursuing him, or that they were carrying off Ramona, and he was pursuing them. At such times he would run with maniac swiftness for hours, till he fell exhausted on the ground, and slowly regained true consciousness by exhaustion. At other times he believed he owned vast flocks and herds; would enter any enclosure he saw, where there were sheep or cattle, go about among them, speak of them to passers-by as his own. Sometimes he would try to drive them away; but on being remonstrated with, would bewilderedly give up the attempt. Once he suddenly found himself in the road driving a small flock of goats, whose he knew not, nor whence he got them. Sitting down by the roadside, he buried his head in his hands. "What has happened to my memory?" he said. "I must be ill of a fever!" As he sat there,

1 This is an accurate description of a real Indian whose tragic story was related to Jackson in 1881. Juan Diego, a Cahuilla Indian, had built himself a home and cultivated a small patch of ground on a high mountain ledge. There he lived with his wife and baby. Diego was known by all to be "loco" (an expression derived from the effect a weed of that name has upon horses, making them wild and unmanageable.) Since he was never in any manner threatening, his temporary confusion was recognized and accepted by residents who knew him as a good and honest worker.

the goats, of their own accord, turned and trotted back into a corral near by, the owner of which stood, laughing, on his door-sill; and when Alessandro came up, said good-naturedly, "All right, Alessandro! I saw you driving off my goats, but I thought you 'd bring 'em back."

Everybody in the valley knew him, and knew his condition. It did not interfere with his capacity as a worker, for the greater part of the time. He was one of the best shearers in the region, the best horse-breaker; and his services were always in demand, spite of the risk there was of his having at any time one of these attacks of wandering. His absences were a great grief to Ramona, not only from the loneliness in which it left her, but from the anxiety she felt lest his mental disorder might at any time take a more violent and dangerous shape. This anxiety was all the more harrowing because she must keep it locked in her own breast, her wise and loving instinct telling her that nothing could be more fatal to him than the knowledge of his real condition. More than once he reached home, breathless, panting, the sweat rolling off his face, crying aloud, "The Americans have found us out, Majella! They were on the trail! I baffled them. I came up another way." At such times she would soothe him like a child; persuade him to lie down and rest; and when he waked and wondered why he was so tired, she would say, "You were all out of breath when you came in dear. You must not climb so fast; it is foolish to tire one's self so."

In these days Ramona began to think earnestly of Felipe. She believed Alessandro might be cured. A wise doctor could surely do something for him. If Felipe knew what sore straits she was in, Felipe would help her. But how could she reach Felipe without the Señora's knowing it? And, still more, how could she send a letter to Felipe without Alessandro's knowing what she had written? Ramona was as helpless in her freedom on this mountain eyrie as if she had been chained hand and foot.

And so the winter wore away, and the spring. What wheat grew in their fields in this upper air! Wild oats, too, in every nook and corner. The goats frisked and fattened, and their hair grew long and silky; the sheep were already heavy again with wool, and it was not yet midsummer. The spring rains had been good; the stream was full, and flowers grew along its edges thick as in beds.

The baby had thrived; as placid, laughing a little thing as if its mother had never known sorrow. "One would think she had suckled pain," thought Ramona, "so constantly have I grieved this year; but the Virgin has kept her well."

If prayers could compass it, that would surely have been so; for night and day the devout, trusting, and contrite Ramona had knelt before the Madonna and told her golden beads, till they were wellnigh worn smooth of all their delicate chasing.

At midsummer was to be a fête in the Saboba village, and the San Bernardino priest would come there. This would be the time to take the baby down to be christened; this also would be the time to send the letter to Felipe, enclosed in one to Aunt Ri, who would send it for her from San Bernardino. Ramona felt half guilty as she sat plotting what she should say and how she should send it,—she, who had never had in her loyal, transparent breast one thought secret from Alessandro since they were wedded. But it was all for his sake. When he was well, he would thank her.

She wrote the letter with much study and deliberation; her dread of its being read by the Señora was so great, that it almost paralyzed her pen as she wrote. More than once she destroyed pages, as being too sacred a confidence for unloving eyes to read. At last, the day before the fête, it was done, and safely hidden away. The baby's white robe, finely wrought in open-work, was also done, and freshly washed and ironed. No baby would there be at the fête so daintily wrapped as hers; and Alessandro had at last given his consent that the name should be Majella. It was a reluctant consent, yielded finally only to please Ramona; and, contrary to her wont, she had been willing in this instance to have her own wish fulfilled rather than his. Her heart was set upon having the seal of baptism added to the name she so loved; and, "If I were to die," she thought, "how glad Alessandro would be, to have still a Majella!"

All her preparations were completed, and it was yet not noon. She seated herself on the veranda to watch for Alessandro, who had been two days away, and was to have returned the previous evening, to make ready for the trip to Saboba. She was disquieted at his failure to return at the appointed time. As the hours crept on and he did not come, her anxiety increased. The sun had gone more than an hour past the mid-heavens before he came. He had ridden fast; she had heard the quick strokes of the horse's hoofs on the ground before she saw him. "Why comes he riding like that?" she thought, and ran to meet him. As he drew near, she saw to her surprise that he was riding a new horse. "Why, Alessandro!" she cried. "What horse is this?"

He looked at her bewilderedly, then at the horse. True; it was not his own horse! He struck his hand on his forehead, endeavoring to collect his thoughts. "Where is my horse, then?" he said.

"My God! Alessandro," cried Ramona. "Take the horse back instantly. They will say you stole it."

"But I left my pony there in the corral," he said. "They will know I did not mean to steal it. How could I ever have made the mistake? I recollect nothing, Majella. I must have had one of the sicknesses."

Ramona's heart was cold with fear. Only too well

she knew what summary punishment was dealt in that region to horse-thieves. "Oh, let me take it back, dear!" she cried. "Let me go down with it. They will believe me."

"Majella!" he exclaimed, "think you I would send you into the fold of the wolf? My wood-dove! It is in Jim Farrar's corral I left my pony. I was there last night, to see about his sheep-shearing in the autumn. And that is the last I know. I will ride back as soon as I have rested. I am heavy with sleep."

Thinking it safer to let him sleep for an hour, as his brain was evidently still confused, Ramona assented to this, though a sense of danger oppressed her. Getting fresh hay from the corral, she with her own hands rubbed the horse down. It was a fine, powerful black horse; Alessandro had evidently urged him cruelly up the steep trail, for his sides were steaming, his nostrils white with foam. Tears stood in Ramona's eyes as she did what she could for him. He recognized her good-will, and put his nose to her face. "It must be because he was black like Benito, that Alessandro took him," she thought. "Oh, Mary Mother, help us to get the creature safe back!" she said.

When she went into the house, Alessandro was asleep. Ramona glanced at the sun. It was already in the western sky. By no possibility could Alessandro go to Farrar's and back before dark. She was on the point of waking him, when a furious barking from Capitan and the other dogs roused him instantly from his sleep, and springing to his feet, he ran out to see what it meant. In a moment more Ramona followed,—only a moment, hardly a moment; but when she reached the threshold, it was to hear a gun-shot, to see Alessandro fall to the ground, to see, in the same second, a ruffianly man leap from his horse, and standing over Alessandro's body, fire his pistol again, once, twice, into the forehead, cheek. Then with a volley of oaths, each word of which seemed to Ramona's reeling senses 2
to fill the air with a sound like thunder, he untied the black horse from the post where Ramona had fastened him, and leaping into his saddle again, galloped away, leading the horse. As he rode away, he shook his fist at Ramona, who was kneeling on the ground, striving to lift Alessandro's head, and to stanch the blood flowing from the ghastly wounds. "That'll teach you damned Indians to leave off stealing our horses!" he cried, and with another volley of terrible oaths was out of sight.

With a calmness which was more dreadful than any wild outcry of grief, Ramona sat on the ground by Alessandro's body, and held his hands in hers. There was nothing to be done for him. The first shot had been fatal, close to his heart,—the murderer aimed well; the after-shots, with the pistol, were from mere wanton brutality. After a few seconds Ramona rose, went into the house, brought out the white altar-cloth, and laid it over the mutilated face.

2 The brutal incident actually occurred exactly as related. The Indian was the aforementioned Juan Diego, the white man Sam Temple. The murder was witnessed by Diego's wife, whose name was actually Ramona.

Jackson later wrote, "Every incident in Ramona. . .is true. A Cahuilla Indian was shot two years ago exactly as Alessandro is — and his wife's name was Ramona and I never knew this last fact until Ramona was half written!" Perhaps it was this coincidence that caused her to change the proposed title from "In the Name of the Law" to Ramona.

Sam Temple, the Jim Farrar of *Ramona*, achieved local renown by touting himself as "the man who shot Alessandro." Far from being ashamed of the act, he boasted of it and even attempted to find donors to bankroll his appearances at the World's Fairs in St. Louis and Chicago. Some disapproved, but Temple had sympathizers as well. As late as 1900, a writer for the *San Diego Union* described him as a "good fellow in his way." The killing of an Indian for an alleged horse stealing was still considered by many as justifiable homicide. "Once an Indian, always an Indian" was not an uncommon sentiment. Temple died peacefully in his sleep in 1909.

Sam Temple, the Jim Farrar of *Ramona*.
—Photograph by George Wharton James. Circa 1911.

—Illustration by Henry Sandham. Circa 1900.

3

Juan Diego's wife, Ramona.
—Photograph by George Wharton James.
Circa 1911.

4

The path up which Ramona fled to Cahuilla.
—Photograpph by George Wharton James.
Circa 1911.

Historian George Wharton James, author of *Through Ramona's Country,* visiting the area in 1910, found that the Cahuilla Indians still avoided this area after nearly forty years. It was to them a place of violent death, a place where evil spirits still held sway.

As she did this, she recalled words she had heard Father Salvierderra quote as having been said by Father Junipero, when one of the Franciscan Fathers had been massacred by the Indians, at San Diego. "Thank God!" he said, "the ground is now watered by the blood of a martyr!"

"The blood of a martyr!" The words seemed to float in the air; to cleanse it from the foul blasphemies the murderer had spoken. "My Alessandro!" she said. "Gone to be with the saints;
3 one of the blessed martyrs; they will listen to what
a martyr says." His hands were warm. She laid them in her bosom, kissed them again and again. Stretching herself on the ground by his side, she threw one arm over him, and whispered in his ear, "My love, my Alessandro! Oh, speak once to Majella! Why do I not grieve more? My Alessandro! Is he not blest already? And soon we will be with him! The burdens were too great. He could not bear them!" Then waves of grief broke over her, and she sobbed convulsively; but still she shed no tears. Suddenly she sprang to her feet, and looked wildly around. The sun was not many hours high. Whither should she go for help? The old Indian woman had gone away with the sheep, and would not be back till dark. Alessandro must not lie there on the ground. To whom should she go? To walk to Saboba was out of the question. There was another Indian village nearer, — the village of the Cahuillas, on one of the high plateaus of San Jacinto. She had once been there. Could she find that trail now? She must try. There was no human help nearer.

Taking the baby in her arms, she knelt by Alessandro, and kissing him, whispered, "Farewell, my beloved. I will not be long gone. I go to bring friends." As she set off, swiftly running, Capitan, who had been lying by Alessandro's side, uttering heart-rending howls, bounded to his feet to follow her. "No, Capitan," she said; and leading him back to the body, she took his head in her hands, looked into his eyes, and said, "Capitan, watch here." With a whimpering cry, he licked her hands, and stretched himself on the ground. He understood, and would obey; but his eyes followed her wistfully till she disappeared from sight.

The trail was rough, and hard to find. More than
4 once Ramona stopped, baffled, among the rocky ridges
and precipices. Her clothes were torn, her face bleeding, from the thorny shrubs; her feet seemed leaden, she made her way so slowly. It was dark in the ravines; as she climbed spur after spur, and still saw nothing but pine forests or bleak opens, her heart sank within her. The way had not seemed so long before. Alessandro had been with her; it was a joyous, bright day, and they had lingered wherever they liked, and yet the way had seemed short. Fear seized her that she was lost. If that were so, before morning she would be with Alessandro; for fierce beasts roamed San Jacinto by night. But for the

baby's sake, she must not die. Feverishly she pressed on. At last, just as it had grown so dark she could see only a few hand-breadths before her, and was panting more from terror than from running, lights suddenly gleamed out, only a few rods ahead. It was the Cahuilla village. In a few moments she was there.

It is a poverty-stricken little place, the Cahuilla
village, — a cluster of tule and adobe huts, on a nar- 5
row bit of bleak and broken ground, on San Jacinto Mountain; the people are very poor, but are proud and high-spirited, — veritable mountaineers in nature, fierce and independent.

Alessandro had warm friends among them, and the news that he had been murdered, and that his wife had run all the way down the mountain, with her baby in her arms, for help, went like wild-fire through the place. The people gathered in an excited group around the house where Ramona had taken refuge. She was lying, half unconscious, on a bed. As soon as she had gasped out her terrible story, she had fallen forward on the floor, fainting, and the baby had been snatched from her arms just in time to save it. She did not seem to miss the child; had not asked for it, or noticed it when it was brought to the bed. A merciful oblivion seemed to be fast stealing over her senses. But she had spoken words enough to set the village in a blaze of excitement. It ran higher and higher. Men were everywhere mounting their horses, — some to go up and bring Alessandro's body down; some organizing a party to
go at once to Jim Farrar's house and shoot him:
these were the younger men, friends of Alessandro. 6
Earnestly the aged Capitan of the village implored them to refrain from such violence.

"Why should ten be dead instead of one, my sons?" he said. "Will you leave your wives and your children like his? The whites will kill us all if you lay hands on the man. Perhaps they themselves will punish him."

A derisive laugh rose from the group. Never yet within their experience had a white man been punished for shooting an Indian. The Capitan knew that as well as they did. Why did he command them to sit still like women, and do nothing, when a friend was murdered?

"Because I am old, and you are young. I have seen that we fight in vain," said the wise old man. "It is not sweet to me, any more than to you. It is a fire in my veins; but I am old. I have seen. I forbid you to go."

The women added their entreaties to his, and the young men abandoned their project. But it was with sullen reluctance; and mutterings were to be heard, on all sides, that the time would come yet. There was more than one way of killing a man. Farrar would not be long seen in the valley. Alessandro should be avenged.

As Farrar rode slowly down the mountain, leading his recovered horse, he revolved in his thoughts what

5 The Cahuillas (pronounced ka-wee-yahs) had been among the fiercest and most powerful of the California Indian tribes, their name signifying "master" or "powerful nation." At the time of Jackson's visit in the early 1880s, she found them very poor, but industrious and enterprising.

6 Chief Cabazon of the Cahuillas

—Photograpph by George Wharton James. Circa 1911. 7

Judge Tripp (Wells) and Sam Temple (Jim Farrar) at the home where the mock trial took place. As late as December 4, 1938, the judge's granddaughter, Vollie Tripp, wrote an article defending her ancestor which appeared in the *San Diego Union.*

E STORY OF FAMOUS 'RAMONA' REVI

ooting Scrape Was Basis for Helen Hunt Jackson's Novel; Started by Horse T

Reproduction of *San Diego Union.* December 4, 1938.

Helen Hunt Jackson assembling her facts for the writing of 8
Ramona, wrote from New York requesting information from her school teacher friend, Mary Sheriff. "How—if at all—" she asked, " does justice work in San Diego County? How do they impanel a jury, and how many jurors are there? Where did they meet? What did the judge say? What did Sam Temple say? Was he sworn in? Was he ever detained at all? Any and every detail you can get will be of value."

course to pursue. A few years before, he would have gone home, no more disquieted at having killed an Indian than if he had killed a fox or a wolf. But things were different now. This Agent, that the Government had taken it into its head to send out to look after the Indians, had made it hot, the other day, for some fellows in San Bernardino who had maltreated an Indian; he had even gone so far as to arrest several liquor-dealers for simply selling whiskey to Indians. If he were to take this case of Alessandro's in hand, it might be troublesome. Farrar concluded that his wisest course would be to make a show of good conscience and fair-dealing by delivering himself up at once to the nearest justice of the peace, as having killed a man in self-defence. Accordingly he rode straight to the house of a Judge
7 Wells, a few miles below Saboba, and said that he wished to surrender himself as having committed "justifiable homicide" on an Indian, or Mexican, he did not know which, who had stolen his horse. He told a plausible story. He professed not to know the man, or the place; but did not explain how it was, that, knowing neither, he had gone so direct to the spot.

He said: "I followed the trail for some time, but when I reached a turn, I came into a sort of blind trail, where I lost the track. I think the horse had been led up on hard sod, to mislead any one on the track. I pushed on, crossed the creek, and soon found the tracks again in soft ground. This part of the mountain was perfectly unknown to me, and very wild. Finally I came to a ridge, from which I looked down on a little ranch. As I came near the house, the dogs began to bark, just as I discovered my horse tied to a tree. Hearing the dogs, an Indian, or Mexican, I could not tell which, came out of the house, flourishing a large knife. I called out to him, 'Whose horse is that?' He answered in Spanish, 'It is mine.' 'Where did you get it?' I asked. 'In San Jacinto,' was his reply. As he still came towards me, brandishing the knife, I drew my gun, and said, 'Stop, or I'll shoot!' He did not stop, and I fired; still he did not stop, so I fired again; and as he did not fall, I knocked him down with the butt of my gun. After he was down, I shot him twice with my pistol."

The duty of a justice in such a case as this was
8 clear. Taking the prisoner into custody, he sent out messengers to summon a jury of six men to hold inquest on the body of said Indian, or Mexican; and early the next morning, led by Farrar, they set out for the mountain. When they reached the ranch, the body had been removed; the house was locked; no signs left of the tragedy of the day before, except a few blood-stains on the ground, where Alessandro had fallen. Farrar seemed greatly relieved at this unexpected phase of affairs. However, when he found that Judge Wells, instead of attempting to return to the valley that night, proposed to pass the night at a ranch only a few miles from the Cahuilla

village, he became almost hysterical with fright. He declared that the Cahuillas would surely come and murder him in the night, and begged piteously that the men would all stay with him to guard him.

At midnight Judge Wells was roused by the arrival of the, Capitan and head men of the Cahuilla village. They had heard of his arrival with his jury, and they had come to lead them to their village, where the body of the murdered man lay. They were greatly distressed on learning that they ought not to have removed the body from the spot where the death had taken place, and that now no inquest could be held.

Judge Wells himself, however, went back with them, saw the body, and heard the full account of the murder as given by Ramona on her first arrival. Nothing more could now be learned from her, as she was in high fever and delirium; knew no one, not even her baby when they laid it on her breast. She lay restlessly tossing from side to side, talking incessantly, clasping her rosary in her hands, and constantly mingling snatches of prayers with cries for Alessandro and Felipe; the only token of consciousness she gave was to clutch the rosary wildly, and sometimes hide it in her bosom, if they attempted to take it from her.

Judge Wells was a frontiersman, and by no means sentimentally inclined; but the tears stood in his eyes as he looked at the unconscious Ramona.

Farrar had pleaded that the preliminary hearing might take place immediately; but after this visit to the village, the judge refused his request, and appointed the trial a week from that day, to give time for Ramona to recover, and appear as a witness. He impressed upon the Indians as strongly as he could the importance of having her appear. It was evident that Farrar's account of the affair was false from first to last. Alessandro had no knife. He had not had time to go many steps from the door; the volley of oaths, and the two shots almost simultaneously, were what Ramona heard as she ran to the door. Alessandro could not have spoken many words.

The day for the hearing came. Farrar had been, during the interval, in a merely nominal custody; having been allowed to go about his business, on his own personal guarantee of appearing in time for the trial. It was with a strange mixture of regret and relief that Judge Wells saw the hour of the trial arrive, and not a witness on the ground except Farrar himself. That Farrar was a brutal ruffian, the whole country knew. This last outrage was only one of a long series; the judge would have been glad to have committed him for trial, and have seen him get his deserts. But San Jacinto Valley, wild, sparsely settled as it was, had yet as fixed standards and criterions of popularity as the most civilized of communities could show; and to betray sympathy with Indians was more than any man's political head was worth. The word "justice" had

A photograph taken in 1899 by George Wharton James shows Ramona Diego crying at the grave of her husband, Juan.

lost its meaning, if indeed it ever had any, so far as they were concerned. The valley was a unit on that question, however divided it might be upon others. On the whole, the judge was relieved, though it was not without a bitter twinge, as of one accessory after the deed, and unfaithful to a friend; for he had known Alessandro well. Yet, on the whole, he was relieved when he was forced to accede to the motion made by Farrar's counsel, that "the prisoner be discharged on ground of justifiable homicide, no witnesses having appeared against him."

He comforted himself by thinking — what was no doubt true — that even if the case had been brought to a jury trial, the result would have been the same; for there would never have been found a San Diego County jury that would convict a white man of murder for killing an Indian, if there were no witnesses to the occurrence except the Indian wife. But he derived small comfort from this. Alessandro's face haunted him, and also the memory of Ramona's, as she lay tossing and moaning in the wretched Cahuilla hovel. He knew that only her continued illness, or her death, could explain her not having come to the trial. The Indians would have brought her in their arms all the way, if she had been alive and in possession of her senses.

During the summer that she and Alessandro had lived in Saboba he had seen her many times, and had been impressed by her rare quality. His children knew her and loved her; had often been in her house; his wife had bought her embroidery. Alessandro also had worked for him; and no one knew better than Judge Wells that Alessandro in his senses was as incapable of stealing a horse as any white man in the valley. Farrar knew it; everybody knew it. Everybody knew, also, about his strange fits of wandering mind; and that when these half-crazed fits came on him, he was wholly irresponsible. Farrar knew this. The only explanation of Farrar's deed was, that on seeing his horse spent and exhausted from having been forced up that terrible trail, he was seized by ungovernable rage, and fired on the second, without knowing what he did. "But he would n't have done it, if it had n't been an Indian!" mused the judge. "He'd ha' thought twice before he shot any white man down, that way."

Day after day such thoughts as these pursued the judge, and he could not shake them off. An uneasy sense that he owed something to Ramona, or, if Ramona were dead, to the little child she had left, haunted him. There might in some such way be a sort of atonement made to the murdered, unavenged Alessandro. He might even take the child, and bring it up in his own house. That was by no means an uncommon thing in the valley. The longer he thought, the more he felt himself eased in his mind by this purpose; and he decided that as soon as he could find leisure he would go to the Cahuilla village and see what could be done.

But it was not destined that stranger hands should bring succor to Ramona. Felipe had at last found trace of her. Felipe was on the way.

Chapter XXV

San Carlos Mission. — Painting by Henry Sandham. Circa 1883.

EFFECTUALLY misled by the faithful Carmena, Felipe had begun his search for Alessandro by going direct to Monterey. He found few Indians in the place, and not one had ever heard Alessandro's name. Six miles from the town was a little settlement of them, in hiding, in the bottoms of the San Carlos River, near the old Mission. The Catholic priest advised him to search there; sometimes, he said, fugitives of one sort and another took refuge in this settlement, lived there for a few months, then disappeared as noiselessly as they had come. Felipe searched there also; equally in vain.

He questioned all the sailors in port; all the shippers. No one had heard of an Indian shipping on board any vessel; in fact, a captain would have to be in straits before he would take an Indian in his crew.

"But this was an exceptionally good worker, this Indian; he could turn his hand to anything; he might have gone as ship's carpenter."

"That might be," they said; "nobody had ever heard of any such thing, however;" and very much they all wondered what it was that made the handsome, sad Mexican gentleman so anxious to find this Indian.

Felipe wasted weeks in Monterey. Long after he had ceased to hope, he lingered. He felt as if he would like to stay till every ship that had sailed out of Monterey in the last three years had returned. Whenever he heard of one coming into harbor, he hastened to the shore, and closely watched the disembarking. His melancholy countenance, with its eager, searching look, became a familiar sight to every one; even the children knew that the pale gentleman was looking for some one he could not find. Women pitied him, and gazed at him tenderly, wondering if a man could look like that for anything save the loss of a sweetheart. Felipe made no confidences. He simply asked, day after day, of every one he met, for an Indian named Alessandro Assis.

Finally he shook himself free from the dreamy spell of the place, and turned his face southward

The Monterey coast. — Painting by Henry Sandham. Circa 1883.

San Antonio Mission. — Painting by Henry Sandham. Circa 1883.

Interior of the San Carlos Mission
— Painting by Henry Sandham. Circa 1883.

— Painting by Henry Sandham. Circa 1883.

again. He went by the route which the Franciscan Fathers used to take, when the only road on the California coast was the one leading from Mission to Mission. Felipe had heard Father Salvierderra say that there were in the neighborhood of each of the old Missions Indian villages, or families still living. He thought it not improbable that, from Alessandro's father's long connection with the San Luis Rey Mission, Alessandro might be known to some of these Indians. He would leave no stone unturned; no Indian village unsearched; no Indian unquestioned.

San Juan Bautista came first; then Soledad, San Antonio, San Miguel, San Luis Obispo, Santa Inez; and that brought him to Santa Barbara. He had spent two months on the journey. At each of these places he found Indians; miserable, half-starved creatures, most of them. Felipe's heart ached, and he was hot with shame, at their condition. The ruins of the old Mission buildings were sad to see, but the human ruins were sadder. Now Felipe understood why Father Salvierderra's heart had broken, and why his mother had been full of such fierce indignation against the heretic usurpers and despoilers of the estates which the Franciscans once held. He could not understand why the Church had submitted, without fighting, to such indignities and robberies. At every one of the Missions he heard harrowing tales of the sufferings of those Fathers who had clung to their congregations to the last, and died at their posts. At Soledad an old Indian, weeping, showed him the grave of Father Sarria, who had died there of starvation. "He gave us all he had, to the last," said the old man. "He lay on a raw-hide on the ground, as we did; and one morning, before he had finished the mass, he fell forward at the altar and was dead. And when we put him in the grave, his body was only bones, and no flesh; he had gone so long without food, to give it to us."

At all these Missions Felipe asked in vain for Alessandro. They knew very little, these northern Indians, about those in the south, they said. It was seldom one from the southern tribes came northward. They did not understand each other's speech. The more Felipe inquired, and the longer he reflected, the more he doubted Alessandro's having ever gone to Monterey. At Santa Barbara he made a long stay. The Brothers at the College welcomed him hospitably. They had heard from Father Salvierderra the sad story of Ramona, and were distressed, with Felipe, that no traces had been found of her. It grieved Father Salvierderra to the last, they said; he prayed for her daily, but said he could not get any certainty in his spirit of his prayers being heard. Only the day before he died, he had said this to Father Francis, a young Brazilian monk, to whom he was greatly attached.

In Felipe's overwrought frame of mind this seemed to him a terrible omen; and he set out on his journey with a still heavier heart than before. He believed Ramona was dead, buried in some unknown, unconsecrated spot, never to be found; yet he would not give up the search. As he journeyed southward, he began to find persons who had known of Alessandro; and still more, those who had known his father, old Pablo. But no one had heard anything of Alessandro's whereabouts since the driving out of his people from Temecula; there was no knowing where any of those Temecula people were now. They had scattered "like a flock of ducks," one Indian said, — "like a flock of ducks after they are fired into. You'd never see all those ducks in any one place again. The Temecula people were here, there, and everywhere, all through San Diego County. There was one Temecula man at San Juan Capistrano, however. The Señor would better see him. He no doubt knew about Alessandro. He was living in a room in the old Mission building. The priest had given it to him for taking care of the chapel and the priest's room, and a little rent besides. He was a hard man, the San Juan Capistrano priest; he would take the last dollar from a poor man."

It was late at night when Felipe reached San Juan Capistrano; but he could not sleep till he had seen this man. Here was the first clew he had gained. He found the man, with his wife and children, in a large corner room opening on the inner court of the Mission quadrangle. The room was dark and damp as a cellar; a fire smouldered in the enormous fireplace; a few skins and rags were piled near the hearth, and on these lay the woman, evidently ill. The sunken tile floor was icy cold to the feet; the wind swept in at a dozen broken places in the corridor side of the wall; there was not an article of furniture. "Heavens!" thought Felipe, as he entered, "a priest of our Church take rent for such a hole as this!"

There was no light in the place, except the little which came from the fire. "I am sorry I have no candle, Señor," said the man, as he came forward. "My wife is sick, and we are very poor."

"No matter," said Felipe, his hand already at his purse. "I only want to ask you a few questions. You are from Temecula, they tell me."

"Yes, Señor," the man replied in a dogged tone,— no man of Temecula could yet hear the word without a pang, — "I was of Temecula."

"I want to find one Alessandro Assis who lived there. You knew him, I suppose," said Felipe, eagerly.

At this moment a brand broke in the smouldering fire, and for one second a bright blaze shot up; only for a second, then all was dark again. But the swift blaze had fallen on Felipe's face, and with a start which he could not control, but which Felipe did not see, the Indian had recognized him. "Ha, ha!" he thought to himself. "Señor Felipe Moreno, you come to the wrong house asking for news of Alessandro Assis!"

It was Antonio, — Antonio, who had been at the Moreno sheep-shearing; Antonio, who knew even

San Juan Capistrano Mission, showing door to room where Felipe found Antonio.
— Illustration by Henry Sandham. Circa 1913.

Painting by Henry Sandham. Circa 1883.

more than Carmena had known, for he knew what a marvel and miracle it seemed that the beautiful Señorita from the Moreno house should have loved Alessandro, and wedded him; and he knew that on the night she went away with him, Alessandro had lured out of the corral a beautiful horse for her to ride. Alessandro had told him all about it, — Baba, fiery, splendid Baba, black as night, with a white star in his forehead. Saints! but it was a bold thing to do, to steal such a horse as that, with a star for a mark; and no wonder that even now, though near three years afterwards, Señor Felipe was in search of him. Of course it could be only the horse he wanted. Ha! much help might he get from Antonio!

"Yes, Señor, I knew him," he replied.

"Do you know where he is now?"

"No, Señor."

"Do you know where he went, from Temecula?"

"No, Señor."

"A woman told me he went to Monterey. I have been there looking for him."

"I heard, too, he had gone to Monterey."

"Where did you see him last?"

"In Temecula."

"Was he alone?"

"Yes, Señor."

"Did you ever hear of his being married?"

"No, Señor."

"Where are the greater part of the Temecula people now?"

"Like this, Señor," with a bitter gesture, pointing to his wife. "Most of us are beggars. A few here, a few there. Some have gone to Capitan Grande, some way down into Lower California."

Wearily Felipe continued his bootless questioning. No suspicion that the man was deceiving him crossed his mind. At last, with a sigh, he said, "I hoped to have found Alessandro by your means. I am greatly disappointed."

"I doubt not that, Señor Felipe Moreno," thought Antonio. "I am sorry, Señor," he said.

It smote his conscience when Felipe laid in his hand a generous gold-piece, and said, "Here is a bit of money for you. I am sorry to see you so poorly off."

The thanks which he spoke sounded hesitating and gruff, so remorseful did he feel. Señor Felipe had always been kind to them. How well they had fared always in his house! It was a shame to lie to him; yet the first duty was to Alessandro. It could not be avoided. And thus a second time help drifted away from Ramona.

At Temecula, from Mrs. Hartsel, Felipe got the first true intelligence of Alessandro's movements; but at first it only confirmed his worst forebodings. Alessandro had been at Mrs. Hartsel's house; he had been alone, and on foot; he was going to walk all the way to San Pasquale, where he had the promise of work.

How sure the kindly woman was that she was telling the exact truth. After long ransacking of her memory and comparing of events, she fixed the time so nearly to the true date, that it was to Felipe's mind a terrible corroboration of his fears. It was, he thought, about a week after Ramona's flight from home that Alessandro had appeared thus, alone, on foot, at Mrs. Hartsel's. In great destitution, she said; and she had lent him money on the expectation of selling his violin; but they had never sold it; there it was yet. And that Alessandro was dead, she had no more doubt than that she herself was alive; for else, he would have come back to pay her what he owed. The honestest fellow that ever lived, was Alessandro. Did not the Señor Moreno think so? Had he not found him so always? There were not many such Indians as Alessandro and his father. If there had been, it would have been better for their people. "If they 'd all been like Alessandro, I tell you," she said, "it would have taken more than any San Diego sheriff to have put them out of their homes here."

"But what could they do to help themselves, Mrs. Hartsel?" asked Felipe. "The law was against them. We can't any of us go against that. I myself have lost half my estate in the same way."

"Well, at any rate they would n't have gone without fighting!" she said. "'If Alessandro had been here!' they all said."

Felipe asked to see the violin. "But that is not Alessandro's," he exclaimed. "I have seen his."

"No!" she said. "Did I say it was his? It was his father's. One of the Indians brought it in here to hide it with us at the time they were driven out. It is very old, they say, and worth a great deal of money, if you could find the right man to buy it. But he has not come along yet. He will, though. I am not a bit afraid but that we 'll get our money back on it. If Alessandro was alive, he 'd have been here long before this."

Finding Mrs. Hartsel thus friendly, Felipe suddenly decided to tell her the whole story. Surprise and incredulity almost overpowered her at first. She sat buried in thought for some minutes; then she sprang to her feet, and cried: "If he's got that girl with him, he 's hiding somewhere. There 's nothing like an Indian to hide; and if he is hiding, every other Indian knows it, and you just waste your breath asking any questions of any of them. They will die before they will tell you one thing. They are as secret as the grave. And they, every one of them, worshipped Alessandro. You see they thought he would be over them, after Pablo, and they were all proud of him because he could read and write, and knew more than most of them. If I were in your place," she continued, "I would not give it up yet. I should go to San Pasquale. Now it might just be that she was along with him that night he stopped here, hid somewhere, while he came in to get the money. I know I urged him to stay all night, and he said he could not do it. I don't know, though, where he could possibly have left her while he came here."

Never in all her life had Mrs. Hartsel been so puzzled and so astonished as now. But her sympathy, and her confident belief that Alessandro might yet be found, gave unspeakable cheer to Felipe.

"If I find them, I shall take them home with me, Mrs. Hartsel," he said as he rode away; "and we will come by this road and stop to see you." And the very speaking of the words cheered him all the way to San Pasquale.

But before he had been in San Pasquale an hour, he was plunged into a perplexity and disappointment deeper than he had yet felt. He found the village in disorder, the fields neglected, many houses deserted, the remainder of the people preparing to move away. In the house of Ysidro, Alessandro's kinsman, was living a white family, — the family of a man who had pre-empted the greater part of the land on which the village stood. Ysidro, profiting by Alessandro's example, when he found that there was no help, that the American had his papers from the land-office, in all due form, certifying that the land was his, had given the man his option of paying for the house or having it burned down. The man had bought the house; and it was only the week before Felipe arrived, that Ysidro had set off, with all his goods and chattels, for Mesa Grande. He might possibly have told the Señor more, the people said, than any one now in the village could; but even Ysidro did not know where Alessandro intended to settle. He told no one. He went to the north. That was all they knew.

To the north! That north which Felipe thought he had thoroughly searched. He sighed at the word. The Señor could, if he liked, see the house in which Alessandro had lived. There it was, on the south side of the valley, just in the edge of the foot-hills; some Americans lived in it now. Such a good ranch Alessandro had; the best wheat in the valley. The American had paid Alessandro something for it, — they did not know how much; but Alessandro was very lucky to get anything. If only they had listened to him. He was always telling them this would come. Now it was too late for most of them to get anything for their farms. One man had taken the whole of the village lands, and he had bought Ysidro's house because it was the best; and so they would not get anything. They were utterly disheartened, broken-spirited.

In his sympathy for them, Felipe almost forgot his own distresses. "Where are you going?" he asked of several.

"Who knows, Señor?" was their reply. "Where can we go? There is no place."

When, in reply to his questions in regard to Alessandro's wife, Felipe heard her spoken of as "Majella," his perplexity deepened. Finally he asked if no one had ever heard the name Ramona.

"Never."

What could it mean? Could it be possible that this was another Alessandro than the one of whom he was in search? Felipe bethought himself of a possible marriage-record. Did they know where Alessandro had married this wife of his, of whom every word they spoke seemed both like and unlike Ramona?

Yes. It was in San Diego they had been married, by Father Gaspara.

Hoping against hope, the baffled Felipe rode on to San Diego; and here, as ill-luck would have it, he found, not Father Gaspara, who would at his first word have understood all, but a young Irish priest, who had only just come to be Father Gaspara's assistant. Father Gaspara was away in the mountains, at Santa Ysabel. But the young assistant would do equally well, to examine the records. He was courteous and kind; brought out the tattered old book, and, looking over his shoulder, his breath coming fast with excitement and fear, there Felipe read, in Father Gaspara's hasty and blotted characters, the fatal entry of the names, "Alessandro Assis and Majella Fa —"

Heart-sick, Felipe went away. Most certainly Ramona would never have been married under any but her own name. Who, then, was this woman whom Alessandro Assis had married in less than ten days from the night on which Ramona had left her home? Some Indian woman for whom he felt compassion, or to whom he was bound by previous ties? And where, in what lonely, forever hidden spot, was the grave of Ramona?

Now at last Felipe felt sure that she was dead. It was useless searching farther. Yet, after he reached home, his restless conjectures took one more turn, and he sat down and wrote a letter to every priest between San Diego and Monterey, asking if there were on his books a record of the marriage of one Alessandro Assis and Ramona Ortegna.

It was not impossible that there might be, after all, another Alessandro Assis. The old Fathers, in baptizing their tens of thousands of Indian converts, were sore put to it to make out names enough. There might have been another Assis besides old Pablo, and of Alessandros there were dozens everywhere.

This last faint hope also failed. No record anywhere of an Alessandro Assis, except in Father Gaspara's book.

As Felipe was riding out of San Pasquale, he had seen an Indian man and woman walking by the side of mules heavily laden. Two little children, too young or too feeble to walk, were so packed in among the bundles that their faces were the only part of them in sight. The woman was crying bitterly. "More of these exiles. God help the poor creatures!" thought Felipe; and he pulled out his purse, and gave the woman a piece of gold. She looked up in as great astonishment as if the money had fallen from the skies. "Thanks! Thanks, Señor!" she exclaimed; and the man coming up to Felipe said also, "God reward you, Señor! That is more money than I

A scene from the 20th Century-Fox production of *Ramona*.

"She is there!" —Illustration by Henry Sandham. Circa 1913.

had in the world! Does the Señor know of any place where I could get work?"

Felipe longed to say, "Yes, come to my estate; there you shall have work!" In the olden time he would have done it without a second thought, for both the man and the woman had good faces, — were young and strong. But the pay-roll of the Moreno estate was even now too long for its dwindled fortunes. "No, my man, I am sorry to say I do not," he answered. "I live a long way from here. Where were you thinking of going?"

"Somewhere in San Jacinto," said the man. "They say the Americans have not come in there much yet. I have a brother living there. Thanks, Señor; may the saints reward you!"

"San Jacinto!" After Felipe returned home, the name haunted his thoughts. The grand mountain-top bearing that name he had known well in many a distant horizon. "Juan Can," he said one day, "are there many Indians in San Jacinto?"

"The mountain?" said Juan Can.

"Ay, I suppose, the mountain," said Felipe. "What else is there?"

"The valley, too," replied Juan. "The San Jacinto Valley is a fine, broad valley, though the river is not much to be counted on. It is mostly dry sand a good part of the year. But there is good grazing. There is one village of Indians I know in the valley; some of the San Luis Rey Indians came from there; and up on the mountain is a big village; the wildest Indians in all the country live there. Oh, they are fierce, Señor!"

The next morning Felipe set out for San Jacinto. Why had no one mentioned, why had he not himself known, of these villages? Perhaps there were yet others he had not heard of. Hope sprang in Felipe's impressionable nature as easily as it died. An hour, a moment, might see him both lifted up and cast down. When he rode into the sleepy little village street of San Bernardino, and saw, in the near horizon, against the southern sky, a superb mountain-peak, changing in the sunset lights from turquoise to ruby, and from ruby to turquoise again, he said to himself, "She is there! I have found her!"

The sight of the mountain affected him, as it had always affected Aunt Ri, with an indefinable, solemn sense of something revealed, yet hidden. "San Jacinto?" he said to a bystander, pointing to it with his whip.

"Yes, Señor," replied the man. As he spoke, a pair of black horses came whirling round the corner, and he sprang to one side, narrowly escaping being knocked down. "That Tennessee fellow 'll run over somebody yet, with those black devils of his, if he don't look out," he muttered, as he recovered his balance.

Felipe glanced at the horses, then driving his spurs deep into his horse's sides, galloped after them. "Baba! by God!" he cried aloud in his excitement; and forgetful of everything, he urged his horse faster, shouting as he rode, "Stop that man! Stop that man with the black horses!"

Jos, hearing his name called on all sides, reined in Benito and Baba as soon as he could, and looked around in bewilderment to see what had happened. Before he had time to ask any questions, Felipe had overtaken him, and riding straight to Baba's head, had flung himself from his own horse and taken Baba by the rein, crying, "Baba! Baba!" Baba knew his voice, and began to whinny and plunge. Felipe was nearly unmanned. For the second, he forgot everything. A crowd was gathering around them. It had never been quite clear to the San Bernardino mind that Jos's title to Benito and Baba would bear looking into; and it was no surprise, therefore, to some of the on-lookers, to hear Felipe cry in a loud voice, looking suspiciously at Jos, "How did you get him?"

Jos was a wag, and Jos was never hurried. The man did not live, nor could the occasion arrive, which would quicken his constitutional drawl. Before even beginning his answer he crossed one leg over the other and took a long, observant look at Felipe; then in a pleasant voice he said: "Wall, Señor,— I allow yer air a Señor by yer color,—it would take right smart uv time tew tell yeow haow I cum by thet hoss, 'n' by the other one tew. They ain't mine, neither one on 'em."

Jos's speech was as unintelligible to Felipe as it had been to Ramona. Jos saw it, and chuckled.

"Mebbe 't would holp yer tew understand me ef I wuz tew talk Mexican," he said, and proceeded to repeat in tolerably good Spanish the sum and substance of what he had just said, adding: "They belong to an Indian over on San Jacinto; at least, the off one does; the nigh one's his wife's; he would n't ever call thet one anything but hers. It had been hers ever sence she was a girl, they said. I never saw people think so much of horses as they did."

Before Jos had finished speaking, Felipe had bounded into the wagon, throwing his horse's reins to a boy in the crowd, and crying, "Follow along with my horse, will you? I must speak to this man."

Found! Found, — the saints be praised, — at last! How should he tell this man fast enough? How should he thank him enough?

Laying his hand on Jos's knee, he cried: "I can't explain to you; I can't tell you. Bless you forever, — forever! It must be the saints led you here!"

"Oh, Lawd!" thought Jos; "another o' them 'saint' fellers! I allow not, Señor," he said, relapsing into Tennesseean. "It wur Tom Wurmsee led me; I wuz gwine ter move his truck fur him this arternoon."

"Take me home with you to your house," said Felipe, still trembling with excitement; "we cannot talk here in the street. I want to hear all you can tell me about them. I have been searching for them all over California."

Jos's face lighted up. This meant good fortune for that gentle, sweet Ramona, he was sure. "I'll take you straight there," he said; "but first I must stop at Tom's. He will be waiting for me."

The crowd dispersed, disappointed; cheated out of their anticipated scene of an arrest for horse-stealing. "Good for you, Tennessee!" and, "Fork over that black horse, Jos!" echoed from the departing groups. Sensations were not so common in San Bernardino that they could afford to slight so notable an occasion as this.

As Jos turned the corner into the street where he lived, he saw his mother coming at a rapid run towards them, her sun-bonnet half off her head, her spectacles pushed up in her hair.

"Why, thar 's mammy!" he exclaimed. "What ever hez gone wrong naow?"

Before he finished speaking, she saw the black horses, and snatching her bonnet from her head waved it wildly, crying, "Yeow Jos! Jos, hyar! Stop! I wuz er comin' ter hunt yer!"

Breathlessly she continued talking, her words half lost in the sound of the wheels. Apparently she did not see the stranger sitting by Jos's side. "Oh, Jos, thar 's the terriblest news come! Thet Injun Alessandro 's got killed; murdered; jest murdered, I say; 't ain't no less. Thar wuz an Injun come down from ther mounting with a letter to the Agent."

"Good God! Alessandro killed!" burst from Felipe's lips in a heart-rending voice.

Jos looked bewilderedly from his mother to Felipe; the complication was almost beyond him. "Oh, Lawd!" he gasped. Turning to Felipe, "Thet's mammy," he said. "She wuz real fond o' both on 'em." Turning to his mother, "This hyar 's her brother," he said. "He jest knowed me by Baba, hyar on ther street. He 's been huntin' 'em everywhar."

Aunt Ri grasped the situation instantly. Wiping her streaming eyes, she sobbed out: "Wall, I'll allow, arter this, thar is sech a thing ez a Providence, ez they call it. 'Pears like ther could n't ennythin' less brung yer hyar jest naow. I know who yer be; ye 're her brother Feeleepy, ain't yer? Menny 's ther time she 's tolt me about yer! Oh, Lawd! How air we ever goin' to git ter her? I allow she 's dead! I allow she 'd never live arter seein' him shot down dead! He tolt me thar could n't nobody git up thar whar they 'd gone; no white folks, I mean. Oh, Lawd, Lawd!"

Felipe stood paralyzed, horror-stricken. He turned in despair to Jos. "Tell me in Spanish," he said. "I cannot understand."

As Jos gradually drew out the whole story from his mother's excited and incoherent speech, and translated it, Felipe groaned aloud, "Too late! Too late!" He too felt, as Aunt Ri had, that Ramona never could have survived the shock of seeing her husband murdered. "Too late! Too late!" he cried, as he staggered into the house. "She has surely died of the sight."

"I allow she did n't die, nuther," said Jos; "not ser long ez she hed thet young un to look arter!"

"Yer air right, Jos!" said Aunt Ri. "I allow yer air right. Thar could n't nothin' kill her, short er wild beasts, ef she hed ther baby 'n her arms! She ain't dead, not ef the baby ez erlive, I allow. Thet 's some comfort."

Felipe sat with his face buried in his hands. Suddenly looking up, he said, "How far is it?"

"Thirty miles 'n' more inter the valley, where we wuz," said Jos, "'n' the Lawd knows how fur 't is up on ter the mounting, where they wuz livin'. It 's like goin' up the wall uv a house, goin' up San Jacinto Mounting, daddy sez. He wuz thar huntin' all summer with Alessandro."

How strange, how incredible it seemed, to hear Alessandro's name thus familiarly spoken, — spoken by persons who had known him so recently, and who were grieving, grieving as friends, to hear of his terrible death! Felipe felt as if he were in a trance. Rousing himself, he said, "We must go. We must start at once. You will let me have the horses?"

"Wall, I allow yer 've got more right ter 'em 'n —" began Jos, energetically, forgetting himself; then, dropping Tennesseean, he completed in Spanish his cordial assurances that the horses were at Felipe's command.

"Jos! He 's got ter take me!" cried Aunt Ri. "I allow I ain't never gwine ter set still hyar, 'n' thet girl inter sech trouble; 'n' if so be ez she is reely dead, thar 's the baby. He hed n't orter go alone by hisself."

Felipe was thankful, indeed, for Aunt Ri's companionship, and expressed himself in phrases so warm, that she was embarrassed.

"Yeow tell him, Jos," she said, "I can't never git used ter bein' called Señory. Yeow tell him his sister allers called me Aunt Ri, 'n' I jest wish he would. I allow me 'n' him 'll git along all right. 'Pears like I 'd known him all my days, jest ez 't did with her, arter the fust. I 'm free to confess I take more ter these Mexicans than I do ter these low-down, driven Yankees, ennyhow, — a heap more; but I can't stand bein' Señory'd! Yeow tell him, Jos. I s'pose thar 's a word for 'aunt' in Mexican, ain't there? 'Pears like thar could n't be no langwedge 'thout sech a word! He 'll know what it means! I 'd go off with him a heap easier ef he 'd call me jest plain Aunt Ri, ez I 'm used ter, or Mis Hyer, either un on 'em; but Aunt Ri 's the nateralest."

Jos had some anxiety about his mother's memory of the way to San Jacinto. She laughed.

"Don't yeow be a mite oneasy," she said. "I bet yeow I 'd go clean back ter the States ther way we cum. I allow I 've got every mile on 't 'n my hed plain 's a turnpike. Yeow nor yer dad, neiry one on yer, could n't begin to do 't. But what we air gwine ter do, fur gittin' up the mounting, thet 's another thing. Thet 's more 'n I dew know. But thar 'll be a way pervided, Jos, sure 's yeow 're bawn. The Lawd ain't gwine to git hisself hindered er holpin' Ramony this time; I ain't a mite afeerd."

Felipe could not have found a better ally. The comparative silence enforced between them by reason of lack of a common vehicle for their thoughts was on the whole less of a disadvantage than would have at first appeared. They understood each other well enough for practical purposes, and their unity in aim, and in affection for Ramona, made a bond so strong, it could not have been enhanced by words.

It was past sundown when they left San Bernardino, but a full moon made the night as good as day for their journey. When it first shone out, Aunt Ri, pointing to it, said curtly, "Thet 's lucky."

"Yes," replied Felipe, who did not know either of the words she had spoken, "it is good. It shows to us the way."

"Thar, naow, say he can't understand English!" thought Aunt Ri.

Benito and Baba travelled as if they knew the errand on which they were hurrying. Good forty miles they had gone without flagging once, when Aunt Ri, pointing to a house on the right hand of the road, the only one they had seen for many miles, said: "We 'll hev to sleep hyar. I donno the road beyant this. I allow they 're gone ter bed; but they 'll hev to git up 'n' take us in. They 're used ter doin' it. They dew consid'able business keepin' movers. I know 'em. They 're reel friendly fur the kind o' people they air. They 're druv to death. It can't be far frum their time to git up, ennyhow. They 're up every mornin' uv thar lives long afore daylight, a feedin' their stock, an' gittin' ready fur the day's work. I used ter hear 'em 'n' see 'em, when we wuz campin' here. The fust I saw uv it, I thought somebody wuz sick in the house, to git 'em up thet time o' night; but arterwards we found out 't wan't nothin' but thar reggerlar way. When I told dad, sez I, 'Dad, did ever yer hear sech a thing uz gittin' up afore light to feed stock?' 'n' ter feed theirselves tew. They 'd their own breakfast all clared away, 'n' dishes washed, too, afore light; 'n' prayers said beside; they 're Methodys, terrible pious. I used ter tell dad they talked a heap about believin' in God; I don't allow but what they dew believe in God, tew, but they don't worship Him so much 's they worship work; not nigh so much. Believin' 'n' worshippin' 's tew things. Yeow would n't see no sech doin's in Tennessee. I allow the Lawd meant some time fur sleepin'; 'n' I 'm satisfied with his times o' lightin' up. But these Merrills air reel nice folks, fur all this I 've ben tellin' yer! — Lawd! I don't believe he 's understood a word I 've said, naow!" thought Aunt Ri to herself, suddenly becoming aware of the hopeless bewilderment on Felipe's face. "'T ain't much use sayin' anything more 'n plain yes 'n' no, between folks thet can't understand each other's langwedge; 'n' 's fur 's thet goes, I allow thar ain't any gret use 'n the biggest part o' what 's sed between folks thet doos!"

When the Merrill family learned Felipe's purpose of going up the mountain to the Cahuilla village, they attempted to dissuade him from taking his own horses. He would kill them both, high-spirited horses like those, they said, if he took them over that road. It was a cruel road. They pointed out to him the line where it wound, doubling and tacking on the sides of precipices, like a path for a goat or chamois. Aunt Ri shuddered at the sight, but said nothing.

"I 'm gwine whar he goes," she said grimly to herself. "I ain't a gwine ter back daown naow; but I dew jest wish Jeff Hyer wuz along."

Felipe himself disliked what he saw and heard of the grade. The road had been built for bringing down lumber, and for six miles it was at perilous angles. After this it wound along on ridges and in ravines till it reached the heart of a great pine forest, where stood a saw-mill. Passing this, it plunged into still darker, denser woods, some fifteen miles farther on, and then came out among vast opens, meadows, and grassy foot-hills, still on the majestic mountain's northern or eastern slopes. From these, another steep road, little more than a trail, led south, and up to the Cahuilla village. A day and a half's hard journey, at the shortest, it was from Merrill's; and no one unfamiliar with the country could find the last part of the way without a guide. Finally it was arranged that one of the younger Merrills should go in this capacity, and should also take two of his strongest horses, accustomed to the road. By the help of these the terrible ascent was made without difficulty, though Baba at first snorted, plunged, and resented the humiliation of being harnessed with his head at another horse's tail.

Except for their sad errand, both Felipe and Aunt Ri would have experienced a keen delight in this ascent. With each fresh lift on the precipitous terraces, the view off to the south and west broadened, until the whole San Jacinto Valley lay unrolled at their feet. The pines were grand; standing, they seemed shapely columns; fallen, the upper curve of their huge yellow disks came above a man's head, so massive was their size. On many of them the bark had been riddled from root to top, as by myriads of bullet-holes. In each hole had been cunningly stored away an acorn,—the woodpeckers' granaries.

"Look at thet, naow!" exclaimed the observant Aunt Ri; "an' thar 's folks thet sez dumb critters ain't got brains. They ain't noways dumb to each other, I notice; an' we air dumb aourselves when we air ketched with furriners. I allow I 'm next door to dumb myself with this hyar Mexican I 'm er travellin' with."

Sam Temple hauling lumber down the San Jacinto Mountains.
—Photograph by George Wharton James. Circa 1911.

"That 's so!" replied Sam Merrill. "When we fust got here, I thought I 'd ha' gone clean out o' my head tryin' to make these Mexicans sense my meanin'; my tongue was plaguy little use to me. But now I can talk their lingo fust-rate; but pa, he can't talk to 'em nohow; he hain't learned the fust word; 'n' he 's ben here goin' on two years longer 'n we have."

The miles seemed leagues to Felipe. Aunt Ri's drawling tones, as she chatted volubly with young Merrill, chafed him. How could she chatter! But when he thought this, it would chance that in a few moments more he would see her clandestinely wiping away tears, and his heart would warm to her again.

They slept at a miserable cabin in one of the clearings, and at early dawn pushed on, reaching the Cahuilla village before noon. As their carriage came in sight, a great running to and fro of people was to be seen. Such an event as the arrival of a comfortable carriage drawn by four horses had never before taken place in the village. The agitation into which the people had been thrown by the murder of Alessandro had by no means subsided; they were all on the alert, suspicious of each new occurrence. The news had only just reached the village that Farrar had been set at liberty, and would not be punished for his crime, and the flames of indignation and desire for vengeance, which the aged Capitan had so much difficulty in allaying in the outset, were bursting forth again this morning. It was therefore a crowd of hostile and lowering faces which gathered around the carriage as it stopped in front of the Capitan's house.

Aunt Ri's face was a ludicrous study of mingled terror, defiance, and contempt. "Uv all ther low-down, no-'count, beggarly trash ever I laid eyes on," she said in a low tone to Merrill, "I allow these yere air the wust! But I allow they 'd flatten us all aout in jest abaout a minnit, ef they wuz to set aout tew! Ef she ain't hyar, we air in a scrape, I allow."

"Oh, they 're friendly enough," laughed Merrill. "They 're all stirred up, now, about the killin' o' that Injun; that 's what makes 'em look so fierce. I don't wonder! 'T was a derned mean thing Jim Farrar did, a firin' into the man after he was dead. I don't blame him for killin' the cuss, not a bit; I 'd have shot any man livin' that 'ad taken a good horse o' mine up that trail. That 's the only law we stock
1 men 've got out in this country. We 've got to protect ourselves. But it was a mean, low-lived trick to blow the feller's face to pieces after he was dead; but Jim 's a rough feller, 'n' I expect he was so mad, when he see his horse, that he did n't know what he did."

Aunt Ri was half paralyzed with astonishment at this speech. Felipe had leaped out of the carriage, and after a few words with the old Capitan, had hurried with him into his house. Felipe had evidently forgotten that she was still in the carriage. His going into the house looked as if Ramona were there. Aunt Ri, in all her indignation and astonishment

1 The opinion that Temple's true sin was bad form rather than murder continued into the early decades of this century. Jackson had written her novel as a means of inciting righteous indignation, but when angry protests did occur, they generally came from San Diego and were leveled at *her*. It was the settlers and not the Indians that were championed by a vehement segment of society that bitterly resented her portrayal of Alessandro as saintly.

was conscious of this train of thought running through her mind; but not even the near prospect of seeing Ramona could bridle her tongue now, or make her defer replying to the extraordinary statements she had just heard. The words seemed to choke her as she began. "Young man," she said, "I donno much abaout yeour raisin'. I've heered yeour folks wuz great on religion. Naow, we ain't, Jeff 'n' me; we war n't raised thet way; but I allow ef I wuz ter hear my boy, Jos, — he 's jest abaout yeour age, 'n' make tew, though he 's narrerer chested, — ef I should hear him say what yeou 've jest said, I allow I sh'd expect to see him struck by lightnin'; 'n' I sh'd n't think he hed got more 'n his deserts, I allow I sh'd n't!"

What more Aunt Ri would have said to the astounded Merrill was never known, for at that instant the old Capitan, returning to the door, beckoned to her; and springing from her seat to the ground, sternly rejecting Sam's offered hand, she hastily entered the house. As she crossed the threshold, Felipe turned an anguished face towards her, and said, "Come, speak to her." He was on his knees by a wretched pallet on the floor. Was that Ramona, — that prostrate form; hair dishevelled, eyes glittering, cheeks scarlet, hands playing meaninglessly, like the hands of one crazed, with a rosary of gold beads? Yes, it was Ramona; and it was like this she had lain there now ten days; and the people had exhausted all their simple skill for her in vain.

Aunt Ri burst into tears. "Oh, Lawd!" she said. "Ef I had some 'old man' hyar, I'd bring her aout er thet fever! I dew bleeve I seed some on 't growin' not more 'n er mile back." And without a second look, or another word, she ran out of the door, and springing into the carriage, said, speaking faster than she had been heard to speak for thirty years: "Yeow jest turn raound 'n' drive me back a piece, the way we come. I allow I 'll git a weed thet 'll break thet fever. Faster, faster! Run yer hosses. 'T ain't above er mile back, whar I seed it," she cried, leaning out, eagerly scrutinizing each inch of the barren ground. "Stop! Here 't is!" she cried. "I knowed I smelt the bitter on 't somewhars along hyar;" and in a few minutes more she had a mass of the soft, shining, gray, feathery leaves in her hands, and was urging the horses fiercely on their way back. "This 'll cure her, ef ennything will," she said, as she entered the room again; but her heart sank as she saw Ramona's eyes roving restlessly over Felipe's face, no sign of recognition in them. "She 's bad;" she said, her lips trembling; "but, 'Never say die!' ez allers our motto; 't ain't never tew late fur ennything but oncet, 'n' yer can't tell when thet time 's come till it 's past 'n' gone."

Steaming bowls of the bitterly odorous infusion she held at Ramona's nostrils; with infinite patience she forced drop after drop of it between the unconscious lips; she bathed the hands and head, her own hands blistered by the heat. It was a fight with death; but love and life won. Before night Ramona was asleep.

Felipe and Aunt Ri sat by her, strange but not uncongenial watchers, each taking heart from the other's devotion. All night long Ramona slept. As Felipe watched her, he remembered his own fever, and how she had knelt by his bed and prayed there. He glanced around the room. In a niche in the mud wall was a cheap print of the Madonna, one candle just smouldering out before it. The village people had drawn heavily on their poverty-stricken stores, keeping candles burning for Alessandro and Ramona during the past ten days. The rosary had slipped from Ramona's hold; taking it cautiously in his hand, Felipe went to the Madonna's picture, and falling on his knees, began to pray as simply as if he were alone. The Indians, standing on the doorway, also fell on their knees, and a low-whispered murmur was heard.

For a moment Aunt Ri looked at the kneeling figures with contempt. "Oh, Lawd!" she thought, "the pore heathen, prayin' ter a picter!" Then a sudden revulsion seized her. "I allow I ain't gwine ter be the unly one out er the hull number thet don't seem to hev nothin' ter pray ter; I allow I 'll jine in prayer, tew, but I shan't say mine ter no picter!" And Aunt Ri fell on her knees; and when a young Indian woman by her side slipped a rosary into her hand, Aunt Ri did not repulse it, but hid it in the folds of her gown till the prayers were done. It was a moment and a lesson Aunt Ri never forgot.

Chapter XXVI

THE Capitan's house faced the east. Just as day broke, and the light streamed in at the open door, Ramona's eyes unclosed. Felipe and Aunt Ri were both by her side. With a look of bewildered terror, she gazed at them.

"Thar, thar, naow! Yer jest shet yer eyes 'n' go right off ter sleep agin, honey," said Aunt Ri, composedly, laying her hand on Ramona's eyelids, and compelling them down. "We air hyar, Feeleepy 'n' me, 'n' we air goin' ter stay. I allow yer need n't be afeerd o' nothin'. Go ter sleep, honey."

The eyelids quivered beneath Aunt Ri's fingers. Tears forced their way, and rolled slowly down the cheeks. The lips trembled; the voice strove to speak, but it was only like the ghost of a whisper, the faint question that came, — "Felipe?"

"Yes, dear! I am here, too," breathed Felipe; "go to sleep. We will not leave you!"

And again Ramona sank away into the merciful sleep which was saving her life.

"Ther longer she kin sleep, ther better," said Aunt Ri, with a sigh, deep-drawn like a groan. "I allow I dread ter see her reely come to. 'T 'll be wus 'n the fust; she 'll hev ter live it all over agin!"

But Aunt Ri did not know what forces of fortitude had been gathering in Ramona's soul during these last bitter years. Out of her gentle constancy had been woven the heroic fibre of which martyrs are made; this, and her inextinguishable faith, had made her strong, as were those of old, who "had trial of cruel mocking, wandered about, being destitute, afflicted, tormented, wandered in deserts and in mountains, and in dens and caves of the earth."

When she waked the second time, it was with a calm, almost beatific smile that she gazed on Felipe, and whispered, "How did you find me, dear Felipe?" It was rather by the motions of her lips than by any sound that he knew the words. She had not yet strength enough to make an audible sound. When they laid her baby on her breast, she smiled again, and tried to embrace her, but was too weak. Pointing to the baby's eyes, she whispered, gazing earnestly at Felipe, "Alessandro." A convulsion passed over her face as she spoke the word, and the tears flowed.

Felipe could not speak. He glanced helplessly at Aunt Ri, who promptly responded: "Naow, honey, don't yeow talk. 'T ain't good fur ye; 'n' Feeleepy 'n' me, we air in a powerful hurry ter git yer strong 'n' well, 'n' tote ye out er this — " Aunt Ri stopped. No substantive in her vocabulary answered her need at that moment. "I allow ye kin go 'n a week, ef nothin' don't go agin ye more 'n I see naow; but ef yer git ter talkin', thar 's no tellin' when yer 'll git up. Yeow jest shet up, honey. We 'll look arter everythin'."

Feebly Ramona turned her grateful, inquiring eyes on Felipe. Her lips framed the words, "With you?"

"Yes, dear, home with me," said Felipe, clasping her hand in his. "I have been searching for you all this time."

An anxious look came into the sweet face. Felipe knew what it meant. How often he had seen it in the olden time. He feared to shock her by the sudden mention of the Señora's death; yet that would harm her less than continued anxiety. "I am alone, dear Ramona," he whispered. "There is no one now but you, my sister, to take care of me. My mother has been dead a year."

The eyes dilated, then filled with sympathetic tears. "Dear Felipe!" she sighed; but her heart took courage. Felipe's phrase was like one inspired; another duty, another work, another loyalty, waiting for Ramona. Not only her child to live for, but to "take care of Felipe"! Ramona would not die! Youth, a mother's love, a sister's affection and duty, on the side of life, — the battle was won, and won quickly, too.

To the simple Cahuillas it seemed like a miracle; and they looked on Aunt Ri's weather-beaten face with something akin to a superstitious reverence. They themselves were not ignorant of the value of the herb by means of which she had wrought the marvellous cure; but they had made repeated experiments with it upon Ramona, without success. It must be that there had been some potent spell in Aunt Ri's handling. They would hardly believe her when, in answer to their persistent questioning, she reiterated the assertion that she had used nothing except the hot water and "old man," which was her name for the wild wormwood; and which, when explained to them, impressed them greatly, as having no doubt some significance in connection with the results of her preparation of the leaves.

Rumors about Felipe ran swiftly throughout the region. The presence in the Cahuilla village of a rich Mexican gentleman who spent gold like water, and kept mounted men riding day and night, after everything, anything, he wanted for his sick sister, was an event which in the atmosphere of that lonely country loomed into colossal proportions. He had travelled all over California, with four horses, in search of her. He was only waiting till she was well, to take her to his home in the south; and then he was going to arrest the man who had murdered her husband, and have him hanged, — yes, hanged! Small doubt about that; or, if the law cleared him, there was still the bullet. This rich Señor would see him shot, if rope were not to be had. Jim Farrar heard these tales, and quaked in his guilty soul. The rope he had small fear of, for well he knew the temper of San Diego County juries and judges; but the bullet, that was another thing: and these Mexicans were like Indians in their vengeance. Time did not tire them, and their memories were long. Farrar cursed the day he had let his temper get the better of him on that lonely mountain-side; how much the better, nobody but he himself knew, — nobody but he and Ramona: and even Ramona did not know the bitter whole. She knew that Alessandro had no knife, and had gone forward with no hostile intent; but she knew nothing beyond that. Only the murderer himself knew that the dialogue which he had reported to the judge and jury, to justify his act, was an entire fabrication of his own, and that, instead of it, had been spoken but four words by Alessandro, and those were, "Señor, I will explain;" and that even after the first shot had pierced his lungs, and the blood was choking in his throat, he had still run a step or two farther, with his hand uplifted deprecatingly, and made one more effort to speak before he fell to the ground dead. Callous as Farrar was, and clear as it was in his mind that killing an Indian was no harm, he had not liked to recall the pleading anguish in Alessandro's tone and in his face as he fell. He had not liked to recall this, even before he heard of this rich Mexican brother-in-law who had appeared on the scene; and now, he found the memories still more unpleasant. Fear is a wonderful goad to remorse. There was another thing, too, which to his great wonder had been apparently overlooked by everybody; at least, nothing had been said about it; but the bearing of it on his case, if the case were brought up a second time and minutely investigated, would be most unfortunate. And this was, that the only clew he had to the fact of Alessandro's having taken his horse, was that the poor, half-crazed fellow had left his own well-known gray pony in the corral in place of the horse he took. A strange thing, surely, for a horse-thief to do! Cold sweat burst out on Farrar's forehead, more than once, as he realized how this, coupled with the well-known fact of Alessandro's liability to attacks of insanity, might be made to tell against him, if he should be brought to trial for the murder. He was as cowardly as he was cruel: never yet were the two traits separate in human nature; and after a few days of this torturing suspense and apprehension, he suddenly resolved to leave the country, if not forever, at least for a few years, till this brother-in-law should be out of the way. He lost no time in carrying out his resolution; and it was well he did not, for it was only three days after he had disappeared, that Felipe walked into Judge Wells's office, one morning, to make inquiries relative to the preliminary hearing which had been held there in the matter of the murder of the Indian, Alessandro Assis, by James Farrar. And when the judge, taking down his books, read to Felipe his notes of the case, and went on to say, "If Farrar's testimony is true, Ramona's, the wife's, must be false," and "at any rate, her testimony would not be worth a straw with any jury," Felipe sprang to his feet, and cried, "She of whom you speak is my foster-sister; and, by God, Señor, if I can find that man, I will shoot him as I would a dog! And I'll see, then, if a San Diego County jury will hang me for ridding the country of such a brute!" and Felipe would have been as good as his word. It was a wise thing Farrar had done in making his escape.

When Aunt Ri heard that Farrar had fled the country, she pushed up her spectacles and looked reflectively at her informant. It was young Merrill. "Fled ther country, hez he?" she said. "Wall, he kin flee ez many countries ez he likes, an' 't won't dew him no good. I know yeow folks hyar don't seem ter think killin' an Injun's enny murder, but I say 't is; an' yeow'll all git it brung home ter yer afore yer die: ef 't ain't brung one way, 't 'll be anuther; yeow jest mind what I say, 'n' don't yeow furgit it. Naow this miser'ble murderer, this Farrar, thet's lighted out er hyar, he's nothin' more 'n a skunk, but he's got the Lawd arter him, naow. It's jest 's well he's gawn; I never did b'leeve in hangin'. I never could. It's jest tew men dead 'stead o' one. I don't want to see no man hung, no marter what he's done, 'n' I don't want to see no man shot down, nuther, no marter what he's done; 'n' this hyar Feeleepy, he's thet high-strung, he'd ha' shot thet Farrar, any minnit, quicker 'n lightnin', ef he'd ketched him; so it's better all raound he's lit aout. But I tell yeow, naow, he hain't made much by goin'! Thet Injun he murdered 'll foller him night 'n' day, till he dies, 'n' long arter; he'll wish he wuz dead afore he doos die, I allow he will, naow. He'll be jest like a man I knowed back in Tennessee. I wa'n't but a mite then, but I never forgot it. 'T's a great country fur gourds, East Tennessee is, whar I wuz raised; 'n' thar wuz two houses, 'n' a fence between 'em, 'n' these gourds a runnin' all over the fence; 'n' one o' ther childun picked one o' them gourds, an' they fit abaout it; 'n' then the women took it up, — ther childun's mothers, yer know, — 'n' they got fightin' abaout it; 'n' then 't the last the men took it up, 'n' they fit; 'n' Rowell he got his butcher-knife, 'n' he ground it up, 'n' he picked a querril with Claiborne, 'n' he cut him inter pieces. They hed him up for 't, 'n' somehow they clared him. I don't see how they ever did, but they put 't off, 'n' put 't off, 'n' 't last they got him free; 'n' he lived on thar a spell, but he could n't stan' it; 'peared like he never hed no peace; 'n' he come over ter our 'us, 'n' sed he, 'Jake,' — they allers called daddy 'Jake,' or 'Uncle

Jackson was something of a frontier renegade herself. 1
One of her *Century* articles had begun, "There are in Colorado Springs seven places of worship, the Episcopal, Methodist, Baptist, Presbyterian, Congregational and Unitarian churches, and Cheyenne Canyon." Many residents were furious. "She might just as well have said there were fifty places of worship, and enumerated all the places of resort and mountain tops that she was in the habit of visiting on the Lord's day," one neighbor indignantly complained to a local newspaper.

Helen Hunt Jackson's house.
— Reproduced with permission of the California State Library, California Section.

The writer, still fuming—though Jackson had by this time been dead for nearly a year— continued, "Her residence was directly across the street from the side front of the Presbyterian church, and more than once on summer days, the church services were disturbed by the loud talking and laughing of picnickers coming or going from the front door. In pleasant weather she could be seen most every Sabbath going on an excursion or picnic. We had a right to have expected better things from the daughter of an orthodox clergyman."

Jake,' — 'Jake,' sed he, 'I can't stan' it, livin' hyar.' 'Why,' sez daddy, 'the law o' the country 's clar'd ye.' 'Yes,' sez he, 'but the law o' God hain't; 'n' I've got Claiborne allers with me. Thar ain't any path so narrer, but he 's a walkin' in it, by my side, all day; 'n' come night, I sleep with him ter one side, 'n' my wife t' other; 'n' I can't stan' it!' Them 's ther very words I heered him say, 'n' I wuz n't ennythin' but a mite, but I did n't furgit it. Wall, sir, he went West, way aout hyar to Californy, 'n' he could n't stay thar nuther, 'n' he come back hum agin; 'n' I wuz bigger then, a gal grown, 'n' daddy sez to him, — I heern him, — 'Wal,' sez he, 'did Claiborne foller yer?' 'Yes,' sez he, 'he follered me. I 'll never git shet o' him in this world. He 's allers clost to me everywhar.' Yer see, 't was jest his conscience er whippin' him. Thet 's all 't wuz. 'T least, thet's all I think 't wuz; though thar wuz those thet said 't wuz Claiborne's ghost. 'N' thet 'll be the way 't 'll be with this miser'ble Farrar. He 'll live ter wish he 'd let hisself be hanged er shot, er erry which way, ter git out er his misery."

Young Merrill listened with unwonted gravity to Aunt Ri's earnest words. They reached a depth in his nature which had been long untouched; a stratum, so to speak, which lay far beneath the surface. The character of the Western frontiersman is
1 often a singular accumulation of such strata, — the training and beliefs of his earliest days overlain by successions of unrelated and violent experiences, like geological deposits. Underneath the exterior crust of the most hardened and ruffianly nature often remains — its forms not yet quite fossilized — a realm full of the devout customs, doctrines, religious influences, which the boy knew, and the man remembers. By sudden upheaval, in some great catastrophe or struggle in his mature life, these all come again into the light. Assembly Catechism definitions, which he learned in his childhood, and has not thought of since, ring in his ears, and he is thrown into all manner of confusions and inconsistencies of feeling and speech by this clashing of the old and new man within him. It was much in this way that Aunt Ri's words smote upon young Merrill. He was not many years removed from the sound of a preaching of the straitest New England Calvinism. The wild frontier life had drawn him in and under, as in a whirlpool; but he was New Englander yet at heart.

"That 's so, Aunt Ri!" he exclaimed. "That 's so! I don't s'pose a man that 's committed murder 'll ever have any peace in this world, nor in the next, nuther, without he repents; but ye see this horse-stealin' business is different. 'T ain't murder to kill a hoss-thief, any way you can fix it; everybody admits that. A feller that 's caught horse-stealin' had ought to be shot; and he will be, too, I tell you, in this country!"

A look of impatient despair spread over Aunt Ri's

face. "I hain't no patience left with yer," she said, "er talkin' abaout stealin' hosses ez ef hosses wuz more 'n human bein's! But lettin' thet all go, this Injun, he wuz crazy. Yer all knowed it. Thet Farrar knowed it. D' yer think ef he 'd ben stealin' the hoss, he 'd er left his own hoss in the corral, same ez, yer might say, leavin' his kyerd to say 't wuz he done it; 'n' the hoss er tied in plain sight 'n front uv his house fur ennybody ter see?"

"Left his own horse, so he did!" retorted Merrill. "A poor, miserable, knock-kneed old pony, that wa'n't worth twenty dollars; 'n' Jim's horse was worth two hundred, 'n' cheap at that."

"Thet ain't nuther here nor thar in what we air sayin'," persisted Aunt Ri. "I ain't a speakin' on 't ez a swap er hosses. What I say is, he wa'n't tryin' to cover 't up thet he 'd tuk the hoss. We air sum used ter hoss-thieves in Tennessee; but I never heered o' one yit thet left his name fur a refference berhind him, ter show which road he tuk, 'n' fastened ther stolen critter ter his front gate when he got hum! I allow me 'n' yeow hed n't better say anythin' much more on ther subjeck, fur I allow we air bound to querril ef we dew;" and nothing that Merrill said could draw another word out of Aunt Ri in regard to Alessandro's death. But there was another subject on which she was tireless, and her speech eloquent. It was the kindness and goodness of the Cahuilla people. The last vestige of her prejudice against Indians had melted and gone, in the presence of their simple-hearted friendliness. "I 'll never hear a word said agin 'em, never, ter my longest day," she said. "The way the pore things hed jest stripped theirselves, to git things fur Ramony, beat all ever I see among white folks, 'n' I 've ben raound more 'n most. 'N' they wa'n't lookin' fur no pay, nuther; fur they did n't know, till Feeleepy 'n' me cum, thet she hed any folks ennywhar, 'n' they 'd ha' taken care on her till she died, jest the same. The sick allers ez took care on among them, they sed, 's long uz enny on 'em hez got a thing left. Thet 's ther way they air raised; I allow white folks might take a lesson on 'em, in thet; 'n' in heaps uv other things tew. Oh, I 'm done talkin' agin Injuns, naow, don't yeow furgit it! But I know, fur all thet, 't won't make any difference; 'pears like there cudd n't nobody b'leeve ennythin' 'n this world 'thout seein' 't theirselves. I wuz thet way tew; I allow I hain't got no call ter talk; but I jest wish the hull world could see what I 've seen! Thet 's all!"

It was a sad day in the village when Ramona and her friends departed. Heartily as the kindly people rejoiced in her having found such a protector for herself and her child, and deeply as they felt Felipe's and Aunt Ri's good-will and gratitude towards them, they were yet conscious of a loss, — of a void. The gulf between them and the rest of the world seemed defined anew, their sense of isolation deepened, their hopeless poverty emphasized. Ramona, wife of Alessandro, had been as their sister, — one of them; as such, she would have had share in all their life had to offer. But its utmost was nothing, was but hardship and deprivation; and she was being borne away from it, like one rescued, not so much from death, as from a life worse than death.

The tears streamed down Ramona's face as she bade them farewell. She embraced again and again the young mother who had for so many days suckled her child, even, it was said, depriving her own hardier babe that Ramona's should not suffer. "Sister, you have given me my child," she cried; "I can never thank you; I will pray for you all my life."

She made no inquiries as to Felipe's plans. Unquestioningly, like a little child, she resigned herself into his hands. A power greater than hers was ordering her way; Felipe was its instrument. No other voice spoke to guide her. The same old simplicity of acceptance which had characterized her daily life in her girlhood, and kept her serene and sunny then, — serene under trials, sunny in her routine of little duties, — had kept her serene through all the afflictions, and calm, if not sunny, under all the burdens of her later life; and it did not desert her even now.

Aunt Ri gazed at her with a sentiment as near to veneration as her dry, humorous, practical nature was capable of feeling. "I allow I donno but I sh'd cum ter believin' in saints tew," she said, "ef I wuz ter live 'long side er thet gal. 'Pears like she wuz suthin' more 'n human. 'T beats me plum out, ther way she takes her troubles. Thar 's sum would say she hed n't no feelin'; but I allow she hez more 'n most folks. I kin see, 't ain't thet. I allow I did n't never expect ter think 's well uv prayin' to picters, 'n' strings er beads, 'n' sech; but ef 't 's thet keeps her up ther way she 's kept up, I allow thar 's more in it 'n it 's hed credit fur. I ain't gwine ter say enny more agin it, nor agin Injuns. 'Pears like I 'm gittin' heaps er new idears inter my head, these days. I 'll turn Injun, mebbe, afore I git through!"

The farewell to Aunt Ri was hardest of all. Ramona clung to her as to a mother. At times she felt that she would rather stay by her side than go home with Felipe; then she reproached herself for the thought, as for a treason and ingratitude. Felipe saw the feeling, and did not wonder at it. "Dear girl," he thought; "it is the nearest she has ever come to knowing what a mother's love is like!" And he lingered in San Bernardino week after week, on the pretence that Ramona was not yet strong enough to bear the journey home, when in reality his sole motive for staying was his reluctance to deprive her of Aunt Ri's wholesome and cheering companionship.

Aunt Ri was busily at work on a rag carpet for the Indian Agent's wife. She had just begun it, had woven only a few inches, on that dreadful morning when the news of Alessandro's death reached her. It was of her favorite pattern, the "hit-er-miss" pattern, as she called it: no set stripes or regular alternation of colors, but ball after ball of the indiscriminately mixed tints, woven back and forth; on a warp of a single color. The constant variety in it, the unexpectedly harmonious blending of the colors, gave her delight, and afforded her a subject, too, of not unphilosophical reflection.

"Wall," she said, "it 's called ther 'hit-er-miss' pattren; but it 's 'hit' oftener 'n 't is 'miss.' Thar ain't enny accountin' fur ther way ther breadths 'll come, sometimes; 'pears like 't wuz kind er magic, when they air sewed tergether; 'n' I allow thet 's ther way it 's gwine ter be with heaps er things in this life. It 's jest a kind er 'hit-er-miss' pattren we air all on us livin' on; 't ain't much use tryin' ter reckon how 't 'll come aout; but the breadths doos fit heaps better 'n yer 'd think; come ter sew 'em, 't ain 't never no sech colors ez yer thought 't wuz gwine ter be, but it 's allers pooty, allers; never see a 'hit-er-miss' pattren 'n my life yit, thet wa'n't pooty. 'N' ther wa'n't never nobody fetched me rags, 'n' hed 'em all planned aout, 'n' jest ther way they wanted ther warp, 'n' jest haow ther stripes wuz ter come, 'n' all, thet they wa'n't orful diserpynted when they cum ter see 't done. It don't never look 's they thought 't would, never! I larned thet lesson airly; 'n' I allers make 'em write 't aout on a paper, jest ther wedth er every stripe, 'n' each er ther colors, so 's they kin see it 's what they ordered; 'r else they 'd allers say I hed n't wove 't 's I wuz told ter. I got ketched thet way oncet! I allow ennybody 's a bawn fool gits ketched twice runnin' ther same way. But fur me, I 'll take ther 'hit-er-miss' pattren, every time, sir, straight along."

When the carpet was done, Aunt Ri took the roll in her own independent arms, and strode with it to the Agent's house. She had been biding the time when she should have this excuse for going there. Her mind was burdened with questions she wished to ask, information she wished to give, and she chose an hour when she knew she would find the Agent himself at home.

"I allow yer heered why I wuz behind time with this yere carpet," she said; "I wuz up ter San Jacinto Mounting, where thet Injun wuz murdered. We brung his widder 'n' ther baby daown with us, me 'n' her brother. He 's tuk her home ter his house ter live. He 's reel well off."

Yes, the Agent had heard this; he had wondered why the widow did not come to see him; he had expected to hear from her.

"Wall, I did hent ter her thet p'raps yer could dew something, ef she wuz ter tell yer all abaout it; but she allowed thar wa'n't enny use in talkin'. Ther jedge, he sed her witnessin' would n't be wuth nuthin' to no jury; 'n' thet wuz what I wuz a wantin' to ask yeow, ef thet wuz so."

"Yes, that is what the lawyers here told me," said the Agent. "I was going to have the man arrested, but they said it would be folly to bring the case to trial. The woman's testimony would not be believed."

"Yeow 've got power ter git a man punished fur sellin' whiskey to Injuns, I notice," broke in Aunt Ri; "hain't yer? I see yeour man 'n' the marshal here arrestin' 'em pooty lively last month; they sed 't was yeour doin'; yeow was a gwine ter prossacute every livin' son o' hell — them wuz thar words — thet sold whiskey ter Injuns."

"That 's so!" said the Agent. "So I am; I am determined to break up this vile business of selling whiskey to Indians. It is no use trying to do anything for them while they are made drunk in this way; it 's a sin and a shame."

"Thet 's so, I allow ter yeow," said Aunt Ri. "Thar ain't any gainsayin' thet. But ef yeow 've got power ter git a man put in jail fur sellin' whiskey t' 'n Injun, 'n' hain't got power to git him punished ef he goes 'n' kills thet Injun, 't sems ter me thar 's suthin' cur'us abaout thet."

"That is just the trouble in my position here, Aunt Ri," he said. "I have no real power over my Indians, as I ought to have."

"What makes yer call 'em yeour Injuns?" broke in Aunt Ri.

The Agent colored. Aunt Ri was a privileged character, but her logical method of questioning was inconvenient.

"I only mean that they are under my charge," he said. "I don't mean that they belong to me in any way."

"Wall, I allow not," retorted Aunt Ri, "enny more 'n I dew. They air airnin' their livin', sech 's 't is, ef yer kin call it a livin'. I 've ben 'mongst 'em, naow, this hyar last tew weeks, 'n' I allow I 've hed my eyes opened ter some things. What 's thet docter er yourn, him thet they call the Agency docter, — what 's he got ter do?"

"To attend to the Indians of this Agency when they are sick," replied the Agent, promptly.

"Wall, thet 's what I heern; thet 's what yeow sed afore, 'n' thet 's why Alessandro, the Injun thet wuz murdered, — thet 's why he put his name down 'n yeour books, though 't went agin him orful ter do it. He wuz high-spereted, 'n' 'd allers took keer er hisself; but he 'd ben druv out er fust one place 'n' then another, tell he 'd got clar down, 'n' pore; 'n' he jest begged thet docter er yourn to go to see his little gal, 'n' the docter would n't; 'n' more 'n thet, he laughed at him fur askin'. 'N' they set the little thing on the hoss ter bring her here, 'n' she died afore they 'd come a mile with her; 'n' 't wuz thet, on top er all the rest, druv Alessandro crazy. He never hed none er them wandrin' spells till arter thet. Naow I allow thet wa'n't right er thet docter. I would n't hev no sech docter 's thet raound my Agency, ef I wuz yeow. Pr'aps yer never heered uv thet. I told Ramony I did n't bleeve yer knowed it, or ye 'd hev made him go."

"No, Aunt Ri," said the Agent; "I could not have done that; he is only required to doctor such Indians as come here."

"I allow, then, thar ain't any gret use en hevin' him at all," said Aunt Ri; "'pears like thar ain't more 'n a harndful uv Injuns raound here. I expect he gits well paid?" and she paused for an answer. None came. The Agent did not feel himself obliged to reveal to Aunt Ri what salary the Government paid the San Bernardino doctor for sending hap-hazard prescriptions to Indians he never saw.

After a pause Aunt Ri resumed: "Ef it ain't enny offence ter yeow, I allow I 'd like ter know jest what 't is yeow air here ter dew fur these Injuns. I 've got 2
my feelin's considdable stirred up, bein' among 'em 'n' knowing this hyar one, thet's ben murdered. Hev ye got enny power to giv' 'em ennything, — food or sech? They air powerful pore, most on 'em."

"I have had a little fund for buying supplies for them in times of special suffering," replied the Agent, "a very little; and the Department has appropriated some money for wagons and ploughs; not enough, however, to supply every village; you see these Indians are in the main self-supporting."

"Thet's jest it," persisted Aunt Ri. "Thet's what I 've ben seein'; 'n' thet's why I want so bad ter git at what 't is the Guvvermunt means ter hev yeow dew fur 'em. I allow ef yeow ain't ter feed 'em, an' ef yer can't put folks inter jail fur robbin' 'n' cheatin' 'em, not ter say killin' 'em, — ef yer can't dew ennythin' more 'n keep 'em from gettin' whiskey, wall, I 'm free ter say — " Aunt Ri paused; she did not wish to seem to reflect on the Agent's usefulness, and so concluded her sentence very differently from her first impulse, — "I 'm free ter say I should n't like ter stan' in yer shoes."

"You may very well say that, Aunt Ri," laughed the Agent, complacently. "It is the most troublesome Agency in the whole list, and the least satisfactory."

"Wall, I allow it mought be the least satisfyin'," rejoined the indefatigable Aunt Ri; "but I donno whar the trouble comes in, ef so be 's thar 's no more kin be done than yer wuz er tellin'." And she looked honestly puzzled.

"Look there, Aunt Ri!" said he, triumphantly, pointing to a pile of books and papers. "All those to be gone through with, and a report to be made out every month, and a voucher to be sent for every lead-pencil I buy. I tell you I work harder than I ever did in my life before, and for less pay."

"I allow yer hev hed easy times afore, then," retorted Aunt Ri, good-naturedly satirical, "ef yeow air plum tired doin' thet!" And she took her leave, not a whit clearer in her mind as to the real nature and function of the Indian Agency than she was in the beginning.

Through all of Ramona's journey home she seemed to herself to be in a dream. Her baby in her arms; the faithful creatures, Baba and Benito, gayly trotting along at a pace so swift that the carriage seemed gliding; Felipe by her side, — the dear Felipe, — his

2 Jackson hoped through *Ramona* to "open the eyes" of an entire nation. Using the simple, homespun character of Aunt Ri to speak for her, she outlined her case, pointing up the inequities and idiosyncrasies of the Indian Agency.

eyes wearing the same bright and loving look as of old, — what strange thing was it which had happened to her to make it all seem unreal? Even the little one in her arms, — she, too, seemed unreal! Ramona did not know it, but her nerves were still partially paralyzed. Nature sends merciful anæsthetics in the shocks which almost kill us. In the very sharpness of the blow sometimes lies its own first healing. It would be long before Ramona would fully realize that Alessandro was dead. Her worst anguish was yet to come.

Felipe did not know and could not have understood this; and it was with a marvelling gratitude that he saw Ramona, day after day, placid, always ready with a smile when he spoke to her. Her gratitude for each thoughtfulness of his smote him like a reproach; all the more that he knew her gentle heart had never held a thought of reproach in it towards him. "Grateful to me!" he thought. "To me, who might have spared her all this woe if I had been strong!"

Never would Felipe forgive himself, — no, not to the day of his death. His whole life should be devoted to her and her child; but what a pitiful thing was that to render!

As they drew near home, he saw Ramona often try to conceal from him that she had shed tears. At last he said to her: "Dearest Ramona, do not fear to weep before me. I would not be any constraint on you. It is better for you to let the tears come freely, my sister. They are healing to wounds."

"I do not think so, Felipe," replied Ramona. "Tears are only selfish and weak. They are like a cry because we are hurt. It is not possible always to keep them back; but I am ashamed when I have wept, and think also that I have sinned, because I have given a sad sight to others. Father Salvierderra always said that it was a duty to look happy, no matter how much we might be suffering."

"That is more than human power can do!" said Felipe.

"I think not," replied Ramona. "If it were, Father Salvierderra would not have commanded it. And do you not recollect, Felipe, what a smile his face always wore? and his heart had been broken for many, many years before he died. Alone, in the night, when he prayed, he used to weep, from the great wrestling he had with God, he told me; but we never saw him except with a smile. When one thinks in the wilderness, alone, Felipe, many things become clear. I have been learning, all these years in the wilderness, as if I had had a teacher. Sometimes I almost thought that the spirit of Father Salvierderra was by my side putting thoughts into my mind. I hope I can tell them to my child when she is old enough. She will understand them quicker than I did, for she has Alessandro's soul; you can see that by her eyes. And all these things of which I speak were in his heart from his childhood. They belong to the air and the sky and the sun, and all trees know them."

When Ramona spoke thus of Alessandro, Felipe marvelled in silence. He himself had been afraid to mention Alessandro's name; but Ramona spoke it as if he were yet by her side. Felipe could not fathom this. There were to be many things yet which Felipe could not fathom in this lovely, sorrowing, sunny sister of his.

When they reached the house, the servants, who had been on the watch for days, were all gathered in the court-yard, old Marda and Juan Can heading the group; only two absent, — Margarita and Luigo. They had been married some months before, and were living at the Ortega's ranch, where Luigo, to Juan Can's scornful amusement, had been made head shepherd.

On all sides were beaming faces, smiles, and glad cries of greeting. Underneath these were affectionate hearts quaking with fear lest the home-coming be but a sad one after all. Vaguely they knew a little of what their dear Señorita had been through since she left them; it seemed that she must be sadly altered by so much sorrow, and that it would be terrible to her to come back to the place so full of painful associations. "And the Señora gone, too," said one of the outdoor hands, as they were talking it over; "it's not the same place at all that it was when the Señora was here."

"Humph!" muttered Juan Can, more consequential and overbearing than ever, for this year of absolute control of the estate. "Humph! that's all you know. A good thing the Señora died when she did, I can tell you! We'd never have seen the Señorita back here else; I can tell you that, my man! And for my part, I'd much rather be under Señor Felipe and the Señorita than under the Señora, peace to her ashes! She had her day. They can have theirs now."

When these loving and excited retainers saw Ramona — pale, but with her own old smile on her face — coming towards them with her babe in her arms, they broke into wild cheering, and there was not a dry eye in the group.

Singling out old Marda by a glance, Ramona held out the baby towards her, and said in her old gentle, affectionate voice, "I am sure you will love my baby, Marda!"

"Señorita! Señorita! God bless you, Señorita!" they cried; and closed up their ranks around the baby, touching her, praising her, handing her from one to another.

Ramona stood for a few seconds watching them; then she said, "Give her to me, Marda. I will myself carry her into the house;" and she moved towards the inner door.

"This way, dear; this way," cried Felipe. "It is Father Salvierderra's room I ordered to be prepared for you, because it is so sunny for the baby!"

"Thanks, kind Felipe!" cried Ramona, and her

eyes said more than her words. She knew he had divined the one thing she had most dreaded in returning,— the crossing again the threshold of her own room. It would be long now before she would enter that room. Perhaps she would never enter it. How tender and wise of Felipe!

Yes; Felipe was both tender and wise, now. How long would the wisdom hold the tenderness in leash, as he day after day looked upon the face of this beautiful woman,— so much more beautiful now than she had been before her marriage, that Felipe sometimes, as he gazed at her, thought her changed even in feature? But in this very change lay a spell which would for a long time surround her, and set her as apart from lover's thoughts as if she were guarded by a cordon of viewless spirits. There was a rapt look of holy communion on her face, which made itself felt by the dullest perception, and sometimes overawed even where it attracted. It was the same thing which Aunt Ri had felt, and formulated in her own humorous fashion. But old Marda put it better, when, one day, in reply to a half-terrified, low-whispered suggestion of Juan Can, to the effect that it was "a great pity the Señor Felipe had n't married the Señorita years ago,— what if he were to do it yet?" she said, also under her breath, "It is my opinion he'd as soon think of Saint Catharine herself! Not but that it would be a great thing if it could be!"

And now the thing that the Señora had imaged to herself so often had come about,— the presence of a little child in her house, on the veranda, in the garden, everywhere; the sunny, joyous, blest presence. But how differently had it come! Not Felipe's child, as she proudly had pictured, but the child of Ramona: the friendless, banished Ramona returned now into full honor and peace as the daughter of the house,— Ramona, widow of Alessandro. If the child had been Felipe's own, he could not have felt for it a greater love. From the first, the little thing had clung to him as only second to her mother. She slept hours in his arms, one little hand hid in his dark beard, close to his lips, and kissed again and again when no one saw. Next to Ramona herself in Felipe's heart came Ramona's child; and on the child he could lavish the fondness he felt that he could never dare to show to the mother. Month by month it grew clearer to Felipe that the mainsprings of Ramona's life were no longer of this earth; that she walked as one in constant fellowship with one unseen. Her frequent and calm mention of Alessandro did not deceive him. It did not mean a lessening grief: it meant an unchanged relation.

One thing weighed heavily on Felipe's mind,— the concealed treasure. A sense of humiliation withheld him, day after day, from speaking of it. But he could have no peace until Ramona knew it. Each hour that he delayed the revelation he felt himself almost as guilty as he had held his mother to be. At last he spoke. He had not said many words, before Ramona interrupted him. "Oh, yes!" she said. "I knew about those things; your mother told me. When we were in such trouble, I used to wish sometimes we could have had a few of the jewels. But they were all given to the Church. That was what the Señora Ortegna said must be done with them if I married against your mother's wishes."

It was with a shame-stricken voice that Felipe replied: "Dear Ramona, they were not given to the Church. You know Father Salvierderra died; and I suppose my mother did not know what to do with them. She told me about them just as she was dying."

"But why did you not give them to the Church, dear?" asked Ramona, simply.

"Why?" cried Felipe. "Because I hold them to be yours, and yours only. I would never have given them to the Church, until I had sure proof that you were dead and had left no children."

Ramona's eyes were fixed earnestly on Felipe's face. "You have not read the Señora Ortegna's letter?" she said.

"Yes, I have," he replied, "every word of it."

"But that said I was not to have any of the things if I married against the Señora Moreno's will."

Felipe groaned. Had his mother lied? "No, dear," he said, "that was not the word. It was, if you married unworthily."

Ramona reflected. "I never recollected the words," she said. "I was too frightened; but I thought that was what it meant. I did not marry unworthily. Do you feel sure, Felipe, that it would be honest for me to take them for my child?"

"Perfectly," said Felipe.

"Do you think Father Salvierderra would say I ought to keep them?"

"I am sure of it, dear."

"I will think about it, Felipe. I cannot decide hastily. Your mother did not think I had any right to them, if I married Alessandro. That was why she showed them to me. I never knew of them till then. I took one thing,— a handkerchief of my father's. I was very glad to have it; but it got lost when we went from San Pasquale. Alessandro rode back a half-day's journey to find it for me; but it had blown away. I grieved sorely for it."

The next day Ramona said to Felipe: "Dear Felipe, I have thought it all over about those jewels. I believe it will be right for my daughter to have them. Can there be some kind of a paper written for me to sign, to say that if she dies they are all to be given to the Church,— to Father Salvierderra's College, in Santa Barbara? That is where I would rather have them go."

"Yes, dear," said Felipe; "and then we will put them in some safer place. I will take them to Los Angeles when I go. It is wonderful no one has stolen them all these years!"

And so a second time the Ortegna jewels were passed on, by a written bequest, into the keeping of that mysterious, certain, uncertain thing we call the future, and delude ourselves with the fancy that we can have much to do with its shaping.

Life ran smoothly in the Moreno household, — smoothly to the eye. Nothing could be more peaceful, fairer to see, than the routine of its days, with the simple pleasures, light tasks, and easy diligence of all. Summer and winter were alike sunny, and had each its own joys. There was not an antagonistic or jarring element; and, flitting back and forth, from veranda to veranda, garden to garden, room to room, equally at home and equally welcome everywhere, there went perpetually, running, frisking, laughing, rejoicing, the little child that had so strangely drifted into this happy shelter, — the little Ramona. As unconscious of aught sad or fateful in her destiny as the blossoms with which it was her delight to play, she sometimes seemed to her mother to have been from the first in some mysterious way disconnected from it, removed, set free from all that could ever by any possibility link her to sorrow.

Ramona herself bore no impress of sorrow; rather her face had now an added radiance. There had been a period, soon after her return, when she felt that she for the first time waked to the realization of her bereavement; when every sight, sound, and place seemed to cry out, mocking her with the name and the memory of Alessandro. But she wrestled with this absorbing grief as with a sin; setting her will steadfastly to the purposes of each day's duty, and, most of all, to the duty of joyfulness. She repeated to herself Father Salvierderra's sayings, till she more than knew them by heart; and she spent long hours of the night in prayer, as it had been his wont to do.

No one but Felipe dreamed of these vigils and wrestlings. He knew them; and he knew, too, when they ceased, and the new light of a new victory diffused itself over Ramona's face: but neither did the first dishearten, nor the latter encourage him. Felipe was a clearer-sighted lover now than he had been in his earlier youth. He knew that into the world where Ramona really lived he did not so much as enter; yet her every act, word, look, was full of loving thoughtfulness of and for him, loving happiness in his companionship. And while this was so, all Felipe's unrest could not make him unhappy.

There were other causes entering into this unrest besides his yearning desire to win Ramona for his wife. Year by year the conditions of life in California were growing more distasteful to him. The methods, aims, standards of the fast incoming Americans were to him odious. Their boasted successes, the crowding of colonies, schemes of settlement and development, — all were disagreeable and irritating. The passion for money and reckless spending of it, the great fortunes made in one hour, thrown away in another, savored to Felipe's mind more of brigandage and gambling than of the occupations of gentlemen. He loathed them. Life under the new government grew more and more intolerable to him; both his hereditary instincts and prejudices, and his temperament, revolted. He found himself more and more alone in the country. Even the Spanish tongue was less and less spoken. He was beginning to yearn for Mexico, — for Mexico, which he had never seen, yet yearned for like an exile. There he might yet live among men of his own race and degree, and of congenial beliefs and occupations. Whenever he thought of this change, always came the quick memory of Ramona. Would she be willing to go? Could it be that she felt a bond to this land, in which she had known nothing but suffering?

At last he asked her. To his unutterable surprise, Ramona cried: "Felipe! The saints be praised! I should never have told you. I did not think that you could wish to leave this estate. But my most beautiful dream for Ramona would be, that she should grow up in Mexico."

And as she spoke, Felipe understood by a lightning intuition, and wondered that he had not foreknown it, that she would spare her daughter the burden she had gladly, heroically borne herself, in the bond of race.

The question was settled. With gladness of heart almost more than he could have believed possible, Felipe at once communicated with some rich American proprietors who had desired to buy the Moreno estate. Land in the valley had so greatly advanced in value, that the sum he received for it was larger than he had dared to hope; was ample for the realization of all his plans for the new life in Mexico. From the hour that this was determined, and the time for their sailing fixed, a new expression came into Ramona's face. Her imagination was kindled. An untried future beckoned, — a future which she would embrace and conquer for her daughter. Felipe saw the look, felt the change, and for the first time hoped. It would be a new world, a new life; why not a new love? She could not always be blind to his devotion; and when she saw it, could she refuse to reward it? He would be very patient, and wait long, he thought. Surely, since he had been patient so long without hope, he could be still more patient now that hope had dawned! But patience is not hope's province in breasts of lovers. From the day when Felipe first thought to himself, "She will yet be mine," it grew harder, and not easier, for him to refrain from pouring out his love in words. Her tender sisterliness, which had been such balm and comfort to him, grew at times intolerable; and again and again her gentle spirit was deeply disquieted with the fear that she had displeased him, so strangely did he conduct himself.

He had resolved that nothing should tempt him to disclose to her his passion and its dreams, until they had reached their new home. But there came a moment which mastered him, and he spoke.

It was in Monterey. They were to sail on the morrow, and had been on board the ship to complete the last arrangements. They were rowed back to shore in a little boat. A full moon shone. Ramona sat bareheaded in the end of the boat, and the silver radiance from the water seemed to float up around her, and invest her as with a myriad halos. Felipe gazed at her till his senses swam; and when, on stepping from the boat, she put her hand in his, and said, as she had said hundreds of times before, "Dear Felipe, how good you are!" he clasped her hands wildly, and cried, "Ramona, my love! Oh, can you not love me?"

The moonlight was bright as day. They were alone on the shore. Ramona gazed at him for one second, in surprise. Only for a second; then she knew all. "Felipe! My brother!" she cried, and stretched out her hands as if in warning.

"No! I am not your brother!" he cried. "I will not be your brother! I would rather die!"

"Felipe!" cried Ramona again. This time her voice recalled him to himself. It was a voice of terror and of pain.

"Forgive me, my sweet one!" he exclaimed. "I will never say it again. But I have loved you so long — so long!"

Ramona's head had fallen forward on her breast, her eyes fixed on the shining sands; the waves rose and fell, rose and fell, at her feet gently as sighs. A great revelation had come to Ramona. In this supreme moment of Felipe's abandonment of all disguises, she saw his whole past life in a new light. Remorse smote her. "Dear Felipe," she said, clasping her hands, "I have been very selfish. I did not know — "

"Of course you did not, love," said Felipe. "How could you? But I have never loved any one else. I have always loved you. Can you not learn to love me? I did not mean to tell you for a long time yet. But now I have spoken; I cannot hide it any more."

Ramona drew nearer to him, still with her hands clasped. "I have always loved you," she said. "I love no other living man; but, Felipe," — her voice sank to a solemn whisper, — "do you not know, Felipe, that part of me is dead, — dead? can never live again? You could not want me for your wife, Felipe, when part of me is dead!"

Felipe threw his arms around her. He was beside himself with joy. "You would not say that if you did not think you could be my wife," he cried. "Only give yourself to me, my love, I care not whether you call yourself dead or alive!"

Ramona stood quietly in his arms. Ah, well for Felipe that he did not know, never could know, the Ramona that Alessandro had known. This gentle, faithful, grateful Ramona, asking herself fervently now if she would do her brother a wrong, yielding up to him what seemed to her only the broken fragment of a life; weighing his words, not in the light of passion, but of calmest, most unselfish affection, — ah, how unlike was she to that Ramona who flung herself on Alessandro's breast, crying, "Take me

Monterey — Illustration by Henry Sandham. Circa 1913.

—Painting by Henry Sandham. Circa 1900.

Cover of the 1940 Hemet program. Jean Inness and Onslow Stevens.
— Courtesy of the Ramona Pageant Assoc., Inc.

with you! I would rather die than have you leave me!"

Ramona had spoken truth. Part of her was dead. But Ramona saw now, with infallible intuition, that even as she had loved Alessandro, so Felipe loved her. Could she refuse to give Felipe happiness, when he had saved her, saved her child? What else now remained for them, these words having been spoken? "I will be your wife, dear Felipe," she said, speaking solemnly, slowly, "if you are sure it will make you happy, and if you think it is right."

"Right!" ejaculated Felipe, mad with the joy unlooked for so soon. "Nothing else would be right! My Ramona, I will love you so, you will forget you ever said that part of you was dead!"

A strange look which startled Felipe swept across Ramona's face; it might have been a moonbeam. It passed. Felipe never saw it again.

General Moreno's name was still held in warm remembrance in the city of Mexico, and Felipe found himself at once among friends. On the day after their arrival he and Ramona were married in the cathedral, old Marda and Juan Can, with his crutches, kneeling in proud joy behind them. The story of the romance of their lives, being widely rumored, greatly enhanced the interest with which they were welcomed. The beautiful young Señora Moreno was the theme of the city; and Felipe's bosom thrilled with pride to see the gentle dignity of demeanor by which she was distinguished in all assemblages. It was indeed a new world, a new life. Ramona might well doubt her own identity. But undying memories stood like sentinels in her breast. When the notes of doves, calling to each other, fell on her ear, her eyes sought the sky, and she heard a voice saying, "Majella!" This was the only secret her loyal, loving heart had kept from Felipe. A loyal, loving heart indeed it was, — loyal, loving, serene. Few husbands so blest as the Señor Felipe Moreno.

Sons and daughters came to bear his name. The daughters were all beautiful; but the most beautiful of them all, and, it was said, the most beloved by both father and mother, was the eldest one: the one who bore the mother's name, and was only step-daughter to the Señor, — Ramona, — Ramona, daughter of Alessandro the Indian.

THE END

Epilogue

The Cahuilla Ramona told her story to historian, George Wharton James, who later urged her to repeat it into a gramophone. Though terrified of this new fangled contraption, the woman finally agreed, "I can see that wicked man riding up the top of the hill and looking down on my little home, and I hear him cry 'Juan Diego! Juan Diego!' I see my poor husband tired and sleepy almost to death, stagger to a doorway, and that wicked man shouting foul oaths, put his gun to his shoulder and fired, bang! bang!—two shots—right into the heart of my poor husband."

—Photograph by George Wharton James. Circa 1911.

From this tragic incident and the genius of the woman who transformed it into what was considered for years to be the great American novel, a far reaching mystique was born. Much of it was commercial. Cities, songs, products — sprang into being—all bearing the name, Ramona.

On her deathbed Jackson had said: I didn't write *Ramona;* it was written through me. My lifeblood went into all I thought, felt and suffered for five years on the Indian question. Never in her wildest dreams would she have imagined the furor and controversy that her novel would create or the tide of tourism that it would unleash. In 1916 — thirty-two years after publication of the novel — it was deemed a conservative estimate that *Ramona* had been worth $50,000,000 in tourist revenue to Southern California.

Born in 1856, Cave Couts Jr., — a partial inspiration for the character, Felipe — was to live all his life on Rancho Guajome. His marriage in 1887 to Elizabeth Clemens, niece of Mark Twain, was the social event of the season. The couple had one child, Cave Couts III. The last days of Doña Ysidora, who continued to live with them on the ranch, must have been as miserable as Señora Moreno's. The marriage was a blatant failure and ended a few months before Ysidora's death in a scandalous divorce. The union had lasted ten years.

Elizabeth, known to her friends as Lily Bell, stated frankly in her suit that Cave had bestowed "the attention and kindness due me upon others of his female acquaintance." She departed the area with Cave III and much of the Couts fortune.

Cave J. Couts Jr. July, 10, 1942. —Courtesy of the San Diego Historical Society – Ticor Collection

The years that followed were dismal for Rancho Guajome. Refuse littered the floors, the fountain was dry and shattered. Couts lived on in virtual poverty. Then in the 1920s, his Aunt Arcadia died. Having no children, Arcadia's vast fortune was divided among her many nieces and nephews.

Couts's share enabled him to purchase his grandparents former home, the Casa Bandini in Old Town, and turn it into a hotel. The rest was devoted to the restoration of Rancho Guajome. He rebuilt the chapel—once used as a roller skating rink by his son—and dedicated it to memory of his mother, but was not able to recoup the family relics which she had willed to nearby Mission San Luis Rey.

Couts relished his refurbished reputation as "the last of the Dons." He entertained lavishly and enjoyed giving newspaper interviews. A colorful piece of California history died with him on July 15, 1943. He was 87.

Ida Richardson, his companion-housekeeper, was the beneficiary of the estate which she held in trust for their two children. In 1973, Rancho Guajome was purchased by the County of San Diego for more than a million dollars for preservation as a state treasure.

* * *

Helen Hunt Jackson's *Ramona* is credited with the enactment of the Dawes Act in 1887. This was a trust patent enabling those Indians who were willing to relinquish any rights to reservation land—those who had it—and to eliminate the tribal elements of their culture to receive 100 acres of land a piece. Outright ownership would not be granted for 25 years. There was much fanfare and for some it seemed that the "Indian problem" had been solved. Unfortunately this was not the case. The Dawes Act aided some, but for most was merely one more broken promise.

Some recognition of the Indians' service in the armed forces during World I came in 1924 when Congress gave them the rights to citizenship in the United States. The particular injustice done the California Indians by failure to ratify reservation treaties of the 1850s promising them more than seven million acres of land was noted at this time.

In 1928 Congress authorized the attorney general of California to bring suit against the United States in favor of the California Indians to determine what financial compensation was owed them. The case dragged on until 1944 when an award of $5 million — about $200 a person—was made.

The result of another case, this one involving the Cahuilla tribe—also known as the Palm Springs Indians — was strikingly different. In the 1870s the federal government had granted the odd numbered sections of desert land in the Palm Springs area to the Southern Pacific Railroad and the even-numbered sections, checkerboard-fashion, to the Cahuilla Indians. When Palm Springs boomed as a resort town in the 1920s, the 100 surviving Cahuillas, asked the federal government's permission to the lease some of their lands to hotel promoters.

When the government refused, the Indians persuaded a former justice of the California Supreme Court to take the case to the Supreme Court of the United States. In 1944 the Court ruled that each of the Cahuillas should receive the rental from $365,000 worth of individually allotted tribal land, as well as a share of the income from 30,000 acres of communal tribal land.

The contrast between the two rulings within the same year was so great that it embarrassed Congress into passing the Indian Claims Commission Act of 1946. This law entitled Indians to payments from the federal government equivalent to the original value of the lands their ancestors had once occupied. In 1965 after many years of hearings, the descendants of the California Indians finally received and voted to accept an award of a little more than $29 million. This represented about 45 cents an acre for 64 million acres of land—nearly two-thirds of the total area of California.

About The Author

Antoinette May grew up in Ramona country. Among her earliest memories are visits to San Diego's colorful Old Town where vestiges of Californio days may still be found. As a biographer and an historian, she has long been fascinated by the Ramona legend and its profound effect upon California history. Inevitably she was drawn to explore the life of its controversial creator. The writing of the critically acclaimed, *Helen Hunt Jackson—A Lonely Voyage of Conscience,* was the result.

May is the founder and publisher of a women's magazine and former newspaper editor. She writes a weekly column for the San Francisco Chronicle, and lectures on biography writing at universities and colleges.

Other books by May include
Witness to War
Different Drummers
Psychic Women
Haunted Houses and Wandering Ghosts of California
The Yucatan—A Guide to the Land of Maya Mysteries.